For Rose Mary Derry

Contents

Acknowledgments

My primary debts are to Stuart Kaminsky, who is directly responsible for my own interest in film's popular forms, and to John Russell Taylor, who indirectly suggested the course of this present work: I thank them for their intelligence, the integrity and perception of their own work, and, I hope, their influence. I am also grateful to those who have provided intellectual assistance: Russell Campbell, for his discovery in 1975 of Altan Löker; Jack Ellis; the late, gracious Paddy Whannel; the Maple Heights Public Library; Films Incorporated in Wilmette, Illinois; and the Swank organization in Glen Ellyn, Illinois. I am grateful as well to Wright State University for providing the sabbatical leave which enabled this manuscript to be completed, particularly to Dr. Abe Bassett of the Department of Theatre Arts, and to Dean Perry Moore of the College of Liberal Arts. I especially want to acknowledge my friend Patti Russo for her invaluable assistance in proofreading my manuscript. Thanks too go to those moral supporters Tom and Kathy Patz Zamostny, Merle Kaminsky, Sharon Kern, Florence Iacano, Jim Klein, Julia Reichert, and all those who so stoically put up with years of the suspense thriller without themselves resorting to violence. And finally, a special acknowledgment must be made to Tom Kohn, whose encouragement and contributions illuminate both my life and my work, and without whom, going to the movies would seem empty indeed.

Part I

Toward a Definition of the Suspense Thriller

1
Perceptions and Dilemmas

At the climax of *North by Northwest,* a dapper Cary Grant and glamorous Eva Marie Saint climb frantically across the impassive stone faces of Mount Rushmore, their pursuers close behind them. The dialogue is almost surreal in its silliness. "What happened to your first two marriages?" asks Saint. "My wives divorced me," answers Grant, "I think they said I led too dull a life. . . ." Suddenly the villain catches up with Saint. There is a scuffle, and she falls off the embankment, managing to regain her foothold only in the final instant. Grant reaches down to help her. One of his hands holds tightly onto the ledge, the other slowly extends down to her hand. Just as Saint grabs his hand, the rocks under her feet give way, her legs dangle, and both she and Grant now find themselves precariously suspended over the yawning chasm. Grant looks up at the villain: "Help me," he says. There is a long pause, and then the villain comes forward, puts his heavy foot on Grant's grasping hand, and begins slowly and steadily grinding it into the rock.

In the central scene of Z, a pacifist deputy has just given a speech in which he has spoken out strongly against the militaristic and repressive policies of his government. As he emerges from the hall, he discovers the streets are filled with supporters and detractors, chanting and counter-chanting in certain pre-riot conditions. As he tries to make his peaceful departure, two thugs emerge from the crowd and approach him, as if to attack. Exhibiting tremendous dignity and presence, the deputy quietly stares them down, and they run off. Suddenly, as if out of nowhere, a delivery truck speeds past the deputy, and a vicious militarist beats him the ground with a club.

At the climax of *Wait Until Dark,* the blind Audrey Hepburn knows that her sadistic tormentor will stop at nothing until he gets what he wants. In the moments before he returns, she races around her apartment, systematically breaking every lightbulb and light source so that she and her tormentor will be on equal terms. When her tormentor returns, he slyly opens the refrigerator door and illumines the room with the light from the refrigerator bulb. Although Hepburn manages to stab him in the chest, it is not enough to prevent him from suddenly jumping across the room after her. He himself removes the bloody knife from his chest and uses it to drag himself across the floor toward Hepburn, who frenziedly tries to pull the plug of the refrigerator in order to plunge the room once again into darkness.

In the central sequence of *La Femme Infidèle*, the forty-year-old insurance broker Michel Bouquet visits his wife's young and handsome lover. When he discovers that his wife has given her lover the cigarette lighter he had himself presented to her on their anniversary, Bouquet becomes so upset that he bludgeons the lover to death with a statuette. He then loads the corpse into the trunk of his car and drives away anxiously: will he be caught? When, after much trouble, he dumps the corpse into a pond, it most uncooperatively refuses to sink.

What, if anything, do these four films have in common? Writing in *TV Movies*, Leonard Maltin calls *North by Northwest* a "lively Hitchcock thriller." Writing in the *Saturday Review*, Roland Gelatt calls Z a "superb suspense thriller directed against political repression." Writing in the *New York Times*, Bosley Crowther calls *Wait Until Dark* "the suspense thriller with Audrey Hepburn." Writing in the *New Yorker*, Pauline Kael calls *La Femme Infidèle* a "suspense story" and a "thriller." Might there exist some film genre which we might call the "suspense thriller?"

Although there does seem to be some kind of critical consensus that a genre of sorts exists, exactly what kinds of films this genre includes is by no means clear. *North by Northwest* is a kind of picaresque adventure, moving rapidly from place to place, its thrills and suspense constantly juxtaposed with humor. Z is a thoughtful, although fast-paced film about political assassination and repression, occasionally almost documentary in its qualities. *Wait Until Dark* is a continuously sober entertainment, although certainly fictitious, confined almost completely to the one location of the blind heroine's apartment. And *La Femme Infidèle* is a very slow-moving "art-house" film in which the sympathetic protagonist is a murderer. If, indeed, a film genre exists which can be called the "suspense thriller," what kind of genre must it be that can contain such disparate films?

Although there exists no real critical vocabulary to deal with these films because they have generally been ignored by theorists, cursorily pigeon-holed, or discussed only in terms of their creators, these films can nevertheless be studied as a group. Perhaps the most important contributing factor to this critical lack is that Alfred Hitchcock's reputation as a suspense thriller director has been so great, that any genre concerns have unfortunately been regarded as irrelevant. My aim is to develop in this book a useful generic classification and vocabulary with which these films can be analyzed. In one sense, this endeavor, like the suspense thriller itself, seems suspended over the yawning chasm in the shadow of Alfred Hitchcock. But Hitchcock no more owns the suspense thriller than John Ford, the western or Douglas Sirk, the melodrama—even if each may have been the most outstanding practitioner of his chosen form. In the pages that follow, I enthusiastically uphold genre criticism as relevant to these exceedingly interesting films, relevant even to those films of Hitchcock, which I greatly admire.

The concept of genre is, at least abstractly, not a complex one. It is a way of relating works of art to other similar works of art and finding significance in the similarities. The similarities become significant not because they derive from facts relating to the works' geneses, but because they arise from details of the works' contents.

For John Cawelti, the concept of genre is best described as "an archetypal story pattern embodied in the images, symbols, themes, and myths of a particular culture."[1] Thus, for instance, the archetypal story pattern of the quest—present in the Bible as well as in King Arthur legends—can also be recognized in the particular genre of the western, where the quest archetype is translated into the specific images, symbols, themes, and myths of the western: the cowboy vs. the outlaw and the Indian; the image of the Conestoga wagon crossing the great plain toward the promised land; the symbols of the gun and the log cabin; the thematic antitheses of civilization/wilderness, wilderness/garden, good/evil, law/transgression, and so forth.

A generic way of looking at the western would be on one level to relate westerns to each other—clarifying their iconographical consistencies and meanings, elaborating their historical development, and examining the relationship between their evolution and the particular society and culture which produced them; and on another level, to relate the whole of the western genre to other genres or works which take advantage of the same archetypal story patterns—such as the Bible, the King Arthur legends, the Japanese samurai films, specific Greek myths, etc. Although of these two approaches, this book will emphasize the former, both derive from a basic concept of genre which inherently diminishes the artist's traditional role as demigod. No longer the individual genius who creates from nothing a totally unique work, the artist is rather a catalyst who translates archetypal material into the images, symbols, themes and myths of a particular culture.

This book on the suspense thriller does not attempt to break radical new ground in the understanding of the theoretical concept of genre, nor to forage murkily through the supposedly stormy straits between genre and auteur methodologies which so many theorists have found troubling, difficult, and so crucial to navigate. Certainly, I do not believe that genre and authorship criticism need be mutually exclusive. If we have, in the past, overpraised Hitchcock as a genius without understanding the extent to which the structures of the suspense thriller genre transcended their use in Hitchcock's own films, it is nevertheless true that within the structures of the thriller, respective characteristics in films by artists such as Hitchcock,

Claude Chabrol, John Frankenheimer, and Costa-Gavras can be quite easily discerned as distinctive and consistent.

By and large, however, this book will not so much attempt to deal with these filmmakers as artists per se as it will attempt to understand their work through sustained comparison and description of others' similar work. In short, I hope to define and analyze—primarily through content analysis—a genre which has never been satisfactorily defined or understood. Not to be forgotten at any point, however, is that I write about these films primarily because I like them and find them interesting and personally enriching. Why, when the balloons are released at the end of Claude Chabrol's *La Rupture,* do I feel such rapturous psychological release? Why am I so moved at the end of *Shadow of a Doubt* when Teresa Wright finds herself so suddenly a melancholy adult whose naïveté is but a distant memory? In one sense, this book represents my own journey toward understanding my own responses; as such, I see its theory not as an end in itself, but as an attempt to reveal these films and to facilitate an appreciation of their significance and value. Perhaps the most important step in understanding these films is in the not inconsiderable task of recognizing exactly what we mean when we refer to the "suspense thriller" genre.

Some film genres are, on at least the most superficial level, easier to recognize than other genres because the names we give them refer specifically to some aspect of their content; the presence therefore of the "name" element works as a kind of instant sign of a particular work's inclusion in the genre. A western film, for instance, takes place in the old American West. A musical is a film which highlights singing and or dancing. A gangster film is invariably about a gangster, as is a detective film about a detective.

Other generic titles are, on this most superficial level, more difficult. Horror and comedy, for instance, both seem to refer more to a particular audience response than a particular content. In popular conception, a horror film is that which provokes screams or fear and a comedy is that which provokes laughter, yet what people find horrifying or comic varies tremendously from person to person. A genre, by the definition provided by Cawelti, cannot essentially be described in terms of its effect on its audience, but requires analysis of its content. Therefore, it may be more useful to think of horror films as monster movies, which can be recognized by the presence of some kind of mystical or nonhuman monster; similarly, comedy can be recognized by the overwhelming presence of physical or metaphorical pratfalls or jokes. Certain other genres define themselves by even more tentative terms. The *film noir,* for instance, identifies itself nominally at least, by a stylistic feature: the presence of low lighting levels and dark shadows.

How, then, should we consider the suspense thriller? Like the terms "horror" and "comedy," the term "suspense thriller" does not overtly reflect content, but implies a certain response; certainly what is thrilling to one spectator is not necessarily so to another. Perhaps the suspense thriller can be perceived not so much as a group of films which thrill their audiences (although this may often be the case), but as a group of films whose content consists essentially of thrills. Indeed, Chapter 2 of this book will use Michael Balint's psychoanalytic definition of the concept "thrill" in order to develop an argument along exactly such lines.

Instead of proceeding from the term "thrill," one might instead try to develop a definition from the term "suspense." What is suspense? On first glance, it would appear to be a strictly structural device — specifically, a narrative construction whereby the spectator is apprised of certain facts of the plot before the work's protagonists are, thus allowing the spectator to anticipate plot developments (especially of the threatening variety) before the protagonists themselves. In this sense, the concept of suspense is related, say, to a concept such as "the flashback" — it is merely a means toward any of a variety of ends. It seems unlikely to me, however, that a stylistic device so pervasive to a group of films would not also have a relationship to or effect on content.

Although the *film noir* is, in an important sense, a stylistic genre, its visual darkness relates to specific, recurring content, including a doomed protagonist, a *femme fatale*, locations such as diners and nightclubs, and a cynical, existential *Weltanschauung*. Similarly, it seems that any definition of the suspense thriller according to strictly stylistic means is doomed to failure, because style and content are inevitably linked. And indeed, the extended study of the concept of suspense in Chapter 3, based largely on the work of Altan Löker, verifies this claim. For Löker, the structural concept of suspense is immediately transformed into a psychological concept; and both concepts are more easily embodied through certain specific types of content.

One can find the terms "suspense thriller," "thriller," and "suspense film" used again and again in the popular press, in the writings of the academic community, and even within the film industry itself. However, there is no clear consensus as to what these terms mean, only the paradoxical agreement that these terms do have some meaning. Before I propose my own triptychal definition, I shall examine the various existing and contradictory conceptions of the suspense thriller as well as the inherent perceptions, dilemmas, and limitations associated with each one. This process is valuable in that it allows us to come to an understanding, however unscientific and primitive, of the problems and principles associated with this heretofore undefined genre.

Not surprisingly, many of the references to the suspense thriller clearly provide evidence to the genre's problematic nature. One interesting reference is that provided by Gary Gerani's historical account of the television program *Thriller*, which ran on the NBC network from 1960 to 1962 (and which is still seen in syndication). The program was sold to the network by producer Hubbel Robinson, veteran of other television series such as *Studio One*, *Climax!* and *Playhouse 90*, on the basis of his description that *Thriller* was to be the "*Studio One* of mystery, a quality anthology drawing on the whole rich field of suspense literature. . . ."[2] Consequently, a crisis of definition developed among Robinson, producer Fletcher Markle, and associate producer–story editor James P. Cavanagh over exactly what constituted a thriller. Now that they had the forum for their show, they could not themselves decide what kinds of shows to put on.

Did a thriller require violence? Could a thriller be humorous? Was the thriller related more to the horror film or more to the detective film? Under the threat of imminent cancellation, and under the direction of the parent studio, Revue, they finally decided to limit their concept to two different kinds of films: "the bone-chilling horror story with supernatural overtones" and "the violent, fast-paced crime melodrama."[3] Robinson freely admitted that this choice eliminated a vast amount of material which could also be considered in the range of the thriller. Ultimately, however, even this limiting definition could not save *Thriller* from cancellation. According to Gerani, it was the very problematic concept of the anthology that doomed the series. "A realistic heist could not chill the blood of a horror fan and crime lovers simply did not find fantastic horror tales credible. Consequently, the show failed to project a consistent image and could not keep its audience from week to week."[4] In 1962, *Thriller* was cancelled.

Among directors, only Alfred Hitchcock seems to have a firm (and uncomplicated) understanding of the suspense thriller. For Hitchcock, the suspense thriller is associated unquestionably and completely with the concept of suspense. (Indeed, the relationship between Hitchcock's work and the concept of the suspense thriller is so complete that for many critics as well as much of the public, the suspense thriller is defined almost exclusively in terms of Hitchcock's own work. Thus, a movie is judged to be a suspense thriller only if it can be related to specific works of Hitchcock or general qualities present in his films.)

According to Hitchcock, "the whodunit generates the kind of curiosity that is void of emotion, and emotion is an essential ingredient of suspense,"[5] which is why, for Hitchcock, mystery is seldom suspenseful. And since suspense entails the necessity that "the public be made perfectly aware of all the facts involved"[6] so that they can most strongly empathize, the genre excludes supernatural superpositions which the public would know absolutely to be outright fantasy. For Hitchcock, the suspense thriller becomes a kind of "subtractive" genre: a film of suspense which nevertheless excludes horror films, traditional whodunnits, and detective films.

William Castle, director of such films as *Homicidal* and *House on Haunted Hill*, also finds a distinction between the horror film and the suspense thriller, although, significantly, he too pays tribute at the temple of Hitchcock. "Of course," says Castle, "I have my own definition of the thriller. Hitchcock makes thrillers . . . I make both [thrillers and horror pictures]. A horror picture is taking a monster and having the audience scream or be frightened by this monster. . . . A thriller or a shocker involves an identifiable person that you might be—a girl in jeopardy, or somebody in trouble—that the audience roots for or identifies with."[7] And although Claude Chabrol's films are consistently termed suspense thrillers, he himself, in an essay on the evolution of the detective film, claims that, "It is difficult to clearly trace the borderline between the suspense film and the thriller,"[8] and therefore uses the names interchangeably.

There are several books, some more scholarly than others, that attempt to come to some kind of understanding of the suspense thriller. Brian Davis, in his book *The Thriller: The Suspense Film from 1946*, suggests that a genre exists which can be called either the "thriller" or the "suspense film," and that this genre evolved naturally from the gangster films like *Little Caesar* and *White Heat* through the documentary crime films like *The House on 92nd Street*. As Davis describes the process, "Directors seeking a new realism, a new way of keeping the audiences on the edge of their seats, began to make suspense thrillers—and inadvertently discovered the formula that was to keep box office takings healthy for over thirty years."[9]

One weakness of this argument is in its implication that there could exist no suspense thrillers prior to the forties (and Hitchcock's own career dates back to the twenties.) Like Hitchcock, Davis subscribes to a "subtractive" theory of the suspense thriller and specifically excludes from the genre what he calls conventional gangster thrillers and hardline horror films. "Most of the thrillers discussed in this survey," claims Davis, "fall easily into familiar categories, obeying rules which have been fixed by repetition."[10] Davis does not attempt to explore exactly what those rules are, nor does he try to rationalize why he includes the traditional hard-boiled detective film (such as *The Big Sleep*) as a variety of suspense thriller, but ignores the classical detective film (such as those in the Sherlock Holmes series).

Davis's organization appears to be structurally deficient: some chapters, such as "the private eye" and "the spy," clearly deal with a particular (sub-)genre of suspense thriller, while other chapters, such as "the chase" or "thrillers with a message," deal with, in the first case, a theme common to all suspense thrillers, and in the second case, the presence of certain pretensions. Typical of Davis's approach (as well as of many of the other books dealing with the suspense thriller) is a very subtle kind of condescension which undercuts and underestimates the concept of genre: "Whenever thriller scriptwriters run out of fresh ideas or novel twists, they can, and usually do, fall back on the genre's most popular stock device, the chase."[11]

Statements like this miss, I think, the point: if the suspense thriller is in part defined by the presence of the chase, the chase can never be an element to be dragged in for box-office reasons, because it is a generic center of meaning and an essential part of the genre's metaphysical structure, much the same way "the gunfight" is to the western. In the same way, Davis can consider certain suspense thrillers like *The Manchurian Candidate* to be more important than others, because they are using "the thriller format to examine themes which the front office would otherwise regard as unacceptable."[12] While I especially admire *The Manchurian Candidate* and may agree with Davis's *taste*, Davis expresses himself in a way which is also subtly antigenre in that it suggests that valuable ideas and themes make their way into films only as a result of a conscious decision on the part of filmmakers to aggrandize their forms. Thus, this kind of thinking implicitly denies that popular forms (with their symbols and structures) can express themes naturally and inherently.

Gordon Gow's book *Suspense in the Cinema* describes itself as an "in-depth study of the components of suspense and the motivations of the audience [in which] the characteristics of isolation, irony, phobia, accident, and other elements of 'thrillers' are examined themselves and in relation to films as entities."[13] Unfortunately, Gow does not achieve all this; his work is primarily composed of often persuasive readings of individual films, with some theoretical overlay. In one passage, Gow overtly rejects the possibility that a suspense genre can exist, when he says that "the word 'suspense' does not imply a distinct genre, because suspense is as appropriate in a profound film as it is in the lightest of parody-thrillers," but that, most commonly, "suspense is associated with thrillers."[14]

Gow does not, however, define what he means by the term "thriller"; he assumes we inherently understand the term much as we would understand terms such as "the western" or "the gangster film." And yet, despite his caveat against the existence of a suspense genre, he says at one point that "the key figure in a suspense film is very often isolated and vulnerable,"[15] which suggests that "the suspense film" exists as a generic concept. Does this reflect sloppy terminology or rather the standard dilemma that has confronted virtually every writer attempting to discuss the intertwined concepts of "suspense," "thrills," and "suspense thrillers" without the benefit of clear cultural or theoretical definitions?

Like Davis, Gow structures his book eclectically in that many of the chapters seem to deal with generic principles, whereas others seem to deal with various (sub-)genres of film. The chapters on isolation, irony and phobia, for instance, are applicable in principle to most suspense thrillers, whereas a chapter called "Among Thieves" seems to be a straightforward look at the gangster and caper films, and a chapter on "The Occult" includes some material on horror and science-fiction. Although Gow's book is plentiful with insights, it does not offer a clear structural understanding of the suspense thriller as a generic concept.

Perhaps the most interesting sections in Gow are nevertheless those on isolation, irony and phobia, which, although not extensively developed, are examined through studies of particular films. It is clear, for instance, that in a film like *Wait Until Dark*, a central structural element is the increasing isolation of Audrey Hepburn from the outside world, particularly from the forces of law and order which might theoretically rescue her. I would suggest that in *Wait Until Dark*, and certain other films I would like to call suspense thrillers, isolation is necessary for the setting of the antagonisms and the resolution of the moral conflict (in *Wait Until Dark*, the primary antagonisms being good vs. evil, innocence vs. knowledge, and passivity vs. action). Only by isolating the protagonist can the moral and thematic conflicts emerge clearly and meaningfully. The concept of isolation is not, however, present to the same degree in all the films considered consensually to be suspense thrillers. Although Hepburn is isolated in *Wait Until Dark*, the deputy in Z has a whole platoon of pacifist followers; and in *North by Northwest*, Cary Grant quickly latches onto Eva Marie Saint as a partner-in-adventure.

Gow's section on irony primarily discusses "that ironic notion of the pleasant place imbued with unexpected menace"[16] by specifically citing various suspenseful uses of trains, yachts and islands. This seems as well a useful idea, because it accounts for the suspense thriller's fascination with specific locations. One thinks, for instance, of Mount Rushmore or the bare field in *North by Northwest*. Even in *Wait Until Dark*, although the action is limited to one location, the importance of that location is paramount, and we become aware of its various lighting sources, the position of the refrigerator, the usefulness of the kitchen window, the possibilities offered by the apartment in terms of hiding places, and so on.

Finally, Gow's section on phobia suggests the relevance to the suspense thriller of concepts such as claustrophobia and agoraphobia, although (rather mysteriously) most of this chapter deals with *The Phantom of the Opera* and the use of color and tinting. What is discussed directly, albeit cursorily, about the two phobias is primarily their physical aspect—the recurrence in these films of actual spaces which are claustrophobic or agoraphobic. Claustrophobia can be related to the central scene in Z already described, as well as to the whole gradual movement of *Wait Until Dark*. The famous crop-dusting sequence in *North by Northwest*, in which the tranquility of the completely open, deserted area is disturbed, seems to suggest agoraphobia.

Interestingly, these two concepts, modified and put in different terms, are used by Michael Balint in his psychoanalytic *Thrills and Regressions* which provides the basis for my discussion of the concept "thrill" in Chapter 2. Although Gow doesn't extend or develop his analysis, it certainly would be interesting to expand the concepts of agoraphobia and claustrophobia to either psychological or structural-narrative terms. In *Shadow of a Doubt*, for instance, Teresa Wright (as Charlie) experiences a kind of psychological claustrophobia as she eventually realizes that she must do something about Joseph Cotten (her evil Uncle Charlie), even if it means killing him herself.

The opposite of this can be seen in the openness of choice at the end of *Knife in the Water*, in which the protagonist is allowed to choose what to believe and is so paralyzed by the choice that he is physically unable to move. In narrative terms, one might analyze *La Rupture* as a film in which the claustrophobic inexorability of the structure reaches a climax as the antagonism between the heroine and her maligner, as well as the subplots dealing with the retarded girl, the landlady, and the balloon man, finally converge and then give way to the openness and agoraphobic structure of the climactic LSD trip.

Lawrence Hammond's *Thriller Movies: Classic Films of Suspense and Mystery* is particularly interesting in the way its author confronts an inability to define what he is doing. The title is confusing, in that it seems to suggest that thrillers can be subdivided into two kinds: films of suspense and films of mystery. In conflict with the title, the text deals primarily (if not exclusively) with what Hammond calls "the suspense film." Anticipating the reader's desire for a definition, Hammond claims that the suspense film "is not the horror film; it is not (necessarily) the film of violence. Anyone who has ever edged towards the front of that upholstered seat, who has unconsciously reached out a hand to seek a consoling grip on the hand of a companion when the tension flitting across the screen became unbearable—that cinemagoer knows what a suspense film is. It is not true to say that when you have seen one you have seen them all. But it is true that when you have seen one you want to see a thousand more, and you do not need any definition."[17]

Like Hitchcock and others, Hammond subscribes to what might be called the subtractive theory of the suspense thriller—that is, whatever the genre is, it is not, for instance, the horror film. Hammond is useful as a consensual barometer; his inclination, like that of most of the newspaper and magazine reviewers, is to define the suspense thriller through its relationship to the audience, emphasizing its ability to provoke in the spectator certain anxious responses. Hammond is opposed to the idea of definition and claims that, "In fact, a thesis could be written (and doubtless has been) to define its irrelevance."[18]Yet somehow, the anti-intellectualism of Hammond remains likeable, for he cheerfully admits that his book is not an academic book, a catalogue, nor an encyclopedia; it is, rather, a "personal book about the suspense movies that haunt him, written by a man who has never been able to resist them."[19]

By writing about his own psyche and its response to these films, Hammond often comes up with very perceptive understandings of these films' appeal and, occasionally, their structures. His list of the images that particularly haunt him—the crossed hairlines of a telescopic sight, a shadow across a hallway, a closed door, a bunch of chatelaine keys—suggests the importance of objects in suspense thrillers, as well as their dual nature (that is, each object generally implying the eventual presence of something else and therefore setting up suspense—for example, the gun's implication that someone will be shot, the door's implication that someone will walk through it). Hammond's negative evaluation of *Lifeboat* is useful in that the basis of his judgment—that the film's characters are primarily one-dimensional people who might as well be wearing labels such as Communist Stoker, Fascist Businessman, Selfish Woman Journalist, Pretty Young Nurse, and Nice Negro—is perceptive, and sheds light on the kinds of characterization prevalent in many of the films that critics tend to call suspense thrillers.

Like Gow and Davis, Hammond organizes his book in eclectic and nonparallel fashion. Some of the chapters are organized according to principles, such as "Trapped," "The Helpless Ones," or "It's All in the Mind"; some chapters are organized around specific auteur-directors such as Hitchcock, Orson Welles, and Stanley Kubrick; other chapters are organized by overt genre considerations such as "The Day of the Private Eye." Hammond's organization thus belies his idea that the thriller exists as a clear, if undefinable, genre. Yet still, of Gow, Davis, and Hammond, Hammond is the only one who discusses *Spellbound, Marnie,* and *Vertigo* side by side, as will this book later in more detail.

Of all the scholarly books, Ralph Harper's *The World of the Thriller* is by far the most problematic. Containing hundreds of footnotes and seeming to be the most scholarly of all these accounts, Harper's book is consistently nonlinear and impressionistic. His arguments fail to build point by point and are filled with generalizations constantly requiring qualifications that are not forthcoming. One is early forewarned of rough going when, in his preface, Harper says that his interest in the thriller is primarily in its existential themes and in the psychology of the reader's involvement: "It is natural," he continues, "that one should want to make one's point as simply as possible, and for this reason alone it seems to be proper to illustrate my discussion almost exclusively from spy novels. In them all the salient features of the Western and detective story can be found. . . ."[20]

Thus, for Harper, the thriller is defined as some gigantic amalgam which includes the detective film, the spy film, and the western—three genres one might consider unusually diverse. Now certainly it is possible that all three of these varieties of film may very well reflect a particular archetypal story pattern, such as the quest (to use Cawelti's terms), but that is a very different proposition; and in my case, any reasoned examination of these three genres would have to take into account the vast differences with which each translates the archetypal story into specific images and themes.

This faulty premise—the amalgam of three genres—upon which Harper's book is based leads him time and again to generalizations which any astute reader must of necessity reject. For instance, in discussing the thriller's protagonist, Harper states that "setting out to arrest evil, he will find in the course of his efforts that he himself is on trial."[21] Although this may sometimes be true in certain spy films or in Harper's own detective example, *Oedipus,* this situation is by no means generalizable. In many of the super-spy films of the sixties (James Bond, for instance), the spy's authority or ability is never questioned. And although *Oedipus* can be perceptively read in the context of detective fiction, it is by no means a typical example; in the literature of Arthur Conan Doyle and Agatha Christie, for example, the classical detective is never truly on trial—his abilities are omnipresent and virtually incapable of failure.

Whether the detective is on trial even in the works of Hammett and Chandler, the writers of hard-boiled fiction, is not as clear as Harper would have us believe either. Although the hard-boiled detective may be beaten up, bamboozled, and challenged to perform, his position as a moral crusader in a world which is corrupt and guilty is never really questioned. Thus, to consider the hard-boiled detective on trial in the same way as the spy who questions the morality of his job seems to me quite misleading.

For Harper, the purpose of the thriller is transfiguration. "For the brief time of reading a novel, we ourselves are sometimes transfigured; through the joint imaginative effort of writer and reader, we are placed in a world where we become what we really wish we were."[22] The various popular forms are thus reduced to the simplistic level of wish-fulfillment. Harper seems unaware of the implied condescension of this view or of its implication that works of art can be divided into those which are "escapist" and those which are not. Harper's implicit elitist position makes his subsequent "serious" discussion of "escapist" works all the more puzzling.

Occasionally, he does come up with a useful concept: his contention that successful thrillers often begin with evil or the threat of evil undermining our confidence in the social order can be seen reflected, for example, in Cary Grant's inability to survive placidly in his Madison Avenue world or in the questioning of government agencies in *North by Northwest,* in the assassination of the deputy and the questioning of the entire militaristic government in *Z,* in the discovery of the nude corpse in Audrey Hepburn's closet in *Wait Until Dark,* and even in the inherent criticism of the bourgeoisie in *La Femme Infidèle.* Perceptive too is Hammond's view of the thriller's representation of the soul's struggle between dichotomous elements such as good/evil, desire/satisfaction, and gentleness/violence.

Perhaps more interesting than scholarly accounts of the suspense thriller are accounts by those who either write suspense thrillers themselves or try to give advice to those who would write them. Ayn Rand, for instance, has described her own novels (particularly what is regarded as her greatest work, *Atlas Shrugged)* as philosophical novels with fundamentally thriller constructions. For Rand, "'thrillers' are detective, spy, or adventure stories. Their basic characteristic is conflict, which means: a clash of goals, which means: purposeful action in pursuit of values."[23] Rand sees thrillers as the popular offshoot of the Romantic school of art, which regards man as maker of his own destiny and which attempts to present to us an idealized and courageous *Weltanschauung.* For Rand, thrillers "are not concerned with a delineation of values, but, taking certain fundamental values for granted, they are concerned with only one aspect of a moral being's existence: the battle of good against evil in terms of purposeful action—a dramatized abstraction of the basic pattern of: choice, goal, conflict, danger, struggle, victory."[24]

Again, although Rand's point of view is simplistic and certainly most useful in the study of her own work, her association of popular genres with notions of morality is nevertheless perceptive. Both the classical detective and the hard-boiled detective work as moral forces, even though the world in which each resides is at times antithetical: the classical detective's world civilized, structured, and only temporarily in disarray; the hard-boiled detective's world cynical, disintegrating, and often beyond repair. Yet even in the more suspense-oriented films such as *Wait Until Dark* or *Z,* the concepts of good and evil are constantly operative. The struggle of Audrey Hepburn to vanquish her tormentor and rise above her blindness is metaphysical, and the spectator is meant to celebrate her victory and find in it value; the position of the assassinated deputy and his pacifists is not merely ideological, and the spectator is meant to uphold it as a moral position as well.

It becomes clear that the struggle between good and evil is a major thematic concern of many of the works we tend to call suspense thrillers. This idea is echoed in a different way by C.A. Lejeune, who, writing in 1946, claimed that "It is a very healthy and natural thing to enjoy a thriller . . . in a certain sense, the thriller is the most moral of all stories, because it seeks to discover what has thrown a single mind out of gear"[25]; this idea describes *La Femme Infidèle,* although director Chabrol relates that single mind to the society which produced it. Rand proceeds to elaborate a complex proscriptive philosophy of literature in which thrillers become not only reflectors of moral thought, but highly moral works themselves representing the last vestige of romanticism; this moralistic position leads Rand to compare, for instance, Mickey Spillane favorably to Thomas Wolfe and Thomas Mann, and to condemn humor in thrillers, especially that which is commonly called tongue-in-cheek.

In *Bloody Murder: From the Detective Story to the Crime Novel,* mystery writer Julian Symons admits that generic definitions are often troublesome "The first problem facing anybody writing about crime fiction," he writes, "is to stake out the limits of his theme. Historians of the detective story have been insistent that it is a unique literary form, distinct from the crime or mystery story, not to be confused with the police novel, and even more clearly separate from the many varieties of thriller."[26] Symons never really defines what the thriller is, although this is not surprising, since his main interest lies elsewhere.

Symons' main thesis is that there exists what he calls a general crime literature; more specifically, one can isolate a particular form called the detective story, which includes a puzzle, clues, and a detective. This specific classical form (as practiced by Conan Doyle and Agatha Christie) was undermined by writers like Chandler and Hammett; what resulted was a more general crime novel of multiple varieties, which may or may not have had a detective and which dealt primarily with characters, psychological considerations, and social issues. Contradictorily, although Symons constantly uses terms such as "thriller," "mystery," "crime story," and "police procedural," he decries such classifications as "more confusing than helpful. . . ."[27] For Symons, the thriller "is so loose a word that it should really be abandoned as a form of description. Some spy stories may be called thrillers, some adventure stories may be called thrillers. The label is very much a matter of taste."[28]

Bill Hogarth, in his 1936 book *Writing Thrillers for Profit*, is one of the few writers who is not hesitant to clarify his own usage of the term thriller, which he defines as "any type of fiction, irrespective of length, in which the sensational element preponderates." Thus, Hogarth's book becomes a "practical study of the conventions and techniques of the detective story, the spy story, the story of escape, all stories of crime and intrigue, the underworld, and stories of thrilling adventure."[29] Like other writers, Hogarth finds himself in part reduced to saying that some thrillers are defined by their being thrilling.

Hogarth's extremely broad definition of the thriller is certainly to be expected in 1936, for then the concept of a general and popular crime literature was itself a newer concept. For many critics of the era, "the thriller" was a catch-all term applicable to any of the popular works dealing with crime, murder, and adventure. Hogarth also offers other points encountered previously: he believes, for instance, that in a thriller, plot and incident are foremost, while character analysis and description are subsidiary. He also claims that "the primary business of the thriller is to puzzle and mystify, and to hold the reader breathless with suspense. . ."[30] (although of course Hogarth's juxtaposition of mystification with suspense would appear to contradict the more sophisticated Hitchcockian distinctions between surprise and suspense, between "whodunits" and "suspense thrillers"). Particularly perceptive (if suffused with a racism not uncommon to the thrillers of the era) is Hogarth's analysis of what he calls the "thriller of sensation," which works very well as a description of many Hitchcock films:

> It is necessary to put the heroine and hero in great danger at regular intervals, just snatching them from the jaws of horrid death in the nick of time. Climax must be piled on climax, and the whole thing must move swiftly. There is no time for thought. . . .[31] Force and threats play an important part in the plot. The abduction of the heroine or hero, his or her enforced captivity and in

> hourly danger, a plot to kill them both, and a final fight brought to a successful issue, these are the strands that weave the web of intrigue and action, plot, counterplot, coincidence, and terror of the thriller. The more violent the action, the better. Large man-eating apes, poisonous snakes, murderous negroes and bloodthirsty Chinese, surly Mexicans and plotting anarchists may run riot.[32]

Certainly one recognizes many of these elements in *North by Northwest:* the abduction of Cary Grant early in the film; his enforced captivity; the constant plots to kill him as well as the eventual plot to kill Eva Marie Saint, his heroine; and of course, the final confrontation between the hero, the heroine and those villains that would destroy them. "In order to keep up the illusion of movement," continues Hogarth, "yachts, ships, fast-moving limousines, and airplanes are called in; likewise all the scientific apparatus of wireless, television, etc. Parallel plots and double intrigues can be used to spread out the plot."[33] These statements reiterate the concept that the suspense thriller is filled with transportation devices, as well as peculiar objects. And, of course, the general thrust of Hogarth's analysis is the idea that the suspense thriller contains "thrills"—episodes in which the hero and heroine are placed in physical danger.

Although Patricia Highsmith, noted writer of works often called suspense thrillers by her critics, does not use the term in her book *Plotting and Writing Suspense Fiction,* she does define the concept of "suspense stories" as "stories with a threat of violent physical action and danger, or the danger and action itself."[34] Like Hitchcock, Highsmith draws a distinction between suspense and mystery, claiming further that the suspense writer often deals much more closely with the criminal mind. Because the criminal's mind is generally revealed to the reader, the suspense writer foregoes the traditional classical detective ploy of keeping the identity of the criminal or his motives secret until the work's denouement. Highsmith points out that if the traditional mystery emphasizes the detective, the "suspense genre" inverts the formula and almost immediately emphasizes the murderer, attenuating if not completely displacing the detective. It is noteworthy that one of Hitchcock's most celebrated films, *Strangers on a Train,* is based on a novel by Highsmith that studiously adheres to her own principles.

The French mystery writers Pierre Boileau and Thomas Narcejac, in their book *Le Roman Policier,* try to unravel many of these complex issues as well. According to Boileau-Narcejac, the crime genre, as originally created by Edgar Allan Poe, has never ceased to continuously renew itself in a variety of different forms such as the *roman problème,* the *roman à suspense,* and the *roman noir.* They admit the need for a definition of the term "thriller" and conclude that the thriller is composed of works which create fear. They then dichotomize this theoretical genre into works of horror such as *Frankenstein* and certain primarily American works which try to upset the reader with shock and violence. Boileau-Narcejac seem more interested in the suspense genre, which they define as *"le roman de la victime"* (the novel of the victim). They believe that suspense is created when an innocent victim is attacked or besieged by a horrific assassin. However, the balance between the good and the evil is a delicate and crucial one: the contrast between the innocent protagonist and the guilty antagonist must be great enough that we are able to be moved by the moral struggle which is presented to us, yet not so great—such as *"une petite fille infirme et le criminel une brute sadique"*[35]—that the work risks transformation into *grand guignol*. This emphasis on the victim seems a particularly useful concept: Cary Grant, for instance, is certainly an initial victim in *North by Northwest;* Yves Montand is a victim in *Z;* and Audrey Hepburn is a victim in *Wait Until Dark*—although Hepburn is virtually the disabled young girl fighting the brutal, sadistic criminal—the example Boileau-Narcejac warn against as being too extreme to be believed. Yet even the concept of the victim is not completely universal, for some suspense thrillers, like *La Femme Infidèle* or *Strangers on a Train*, emphasize the murderous criminal—although even in these films, the criminals are often in more subtle terms *psychological* victims who lack the kind of power and assurance we expect of many fictional criminals.

Let me end this survey with three brief definitions which provide some very important, if intuitive, ideas. *A Handbook of Literary Terms* defines the thriller as "a story or play of action which aims at holding the reader or audience spellbound as the plot unfolds. The story rises to a gripping climax in an atmosphere of fear, excitement or suspense. Characterization is subordinated to the plot, which in a good thriller is all important."[36] *Webster's Dictionary* defines the thriller as "a sensational story or play, the perusal or hearing of which sends a thrill of pleasure, pity, or excitement through one." What is significant about both these definitions is that they each define the thriller primarily in terms of the thriller's relationship to its audience. The final defining perception is one provided by Stuart Kaminsky in the film catalogue *Rediscovering the American Cinema*. Kaminsky suggests that films frequently called "thrillers" tend to involve the flight of the possible victim from both the cops and the criminals, and that identification is not with the man in control, but with the pursued.[34] Indeed, Kaminsky, who has written a distinguished series of Hollywood-set hard-boiled detective novels using the private eye Toby Peters, abandoned the use of a detective as a central character in his two all-out thrillers, *When the Dark Man Calls* and *Exercise in Terror*, in order to emphasize the pursuits of protagonists and antagonists who compete to gain control over each other. This concept of the pursued is in part a critically useful extension of Boileau-Narcejac's concept of the victim—significant because, although victims are invariably pursued, so too are the murderous criminals in films such as *La Femme Infidèle* and *Strangers on a Train*. The concept of a protagonist who is not in control thus seems virtually universal to the genre and important in understanding not only how these works are structured, but also why these works tend to invite such identification in the spectator.

What does this preceding survey of critical writings prove? A variety of things: certainly, that there is tremendous confusion and disagreement as to what exactly the term "suspense thriller" refers to; but as well, that the term is used even by those writers who reject the possibility or value of defining it. Perhaps one can begin to salvage the term for respectable critical use by enumerating potential characteristics gleaned from a consensus of these varied usages:

1) The suspense thriller has a relationship to a variety of other works—particularly to works of horror, espionage, and the varieties of crime.

2) The suspense thriller may not be a single, unified genre like the western, but an amalgam of several distinct sub-genres which have, nevertheless, significant relationships to each other.

3) The suspense thriller, although a popular genre, deals inherently with "important themes." According to Graham Greene: "If you can excite your audience first, you can put over what you will of horror, suffering, truth."[38] According to Claude Chabrol: "No matter how much a scenarist or director may seek to distract, a thriller must be profound, because it speaks of life and death."[39] According to Patricia Highsmith: "If a suspense writer is going to write about murders and victims . . . he should be interested in justice or the absence of it in the world we live in; he should be interested in the morality, good and bad, that exists today; he should be interested in human cowardice or courage, and not merely as forces to push his plot this way and that."[40]

4) The suspense thriller is a genre which uses thrills—which are on one level a simple depiction of danger and violence, and on a second level a vicarious psychological experience which provides the spectator with a particular kind of catharsis. And finally,

5) The suspense thriller is a genre which uses suspense—which is on one level a simple structural device, and on a second level a psychological device which directly engages the spectator by causing anxiety and setting off complex subconscious mechanisms.

These last two points particularly are crucial to any understanding of how these films work. What do we really mean when we talk about the thrills, fear, and danger that so many of these films tend to evoke? We note that suspense films frequently provoke emotional and anxious responses in the spectator. Since the screen cannot cause physical harm, what exactly is it that makes the spectator take in a breath?

Attempting to describe these films, critics writing about the thriller have instead again and again fallen back upon rather nonintellectual descriptions of the effects of these films, the sensations created by their structures rather than the structures themselves. Although my own interests are more precisely located with the structures of the films (descriptions of which, indeed, make up the largest component by far of this book in Part II), it is necessary, I think, to explore the particular relationship that these films have with their audiences, to understand the potential reasons these films provoke such strong physiological and psychological responses. The next two chapters, tentative, if tantalizing, provide some theoretical musings—intuitive and not proven—on the concepts of "the thrill" and "suspense" as elaborated by psychoanalytic thinkers. Chapter Two examines the concept of the thrill as it relates to the content of the suspense thriller (particularly its use of objects, locations, and empty spaces) and the psychological implications of this content, using Michael Balint as its primary source. Chapter Three examines the concept of suspense as it relates to the narrative structure of the suspense thriller and the psychological mechanism this structure incites in the spectator, using Altan Löker as its primary source. Only then can we tentatively attempt to arrive at any coherent definitions, at any fuller understanding of these films which time and again propel the spectators to the edges of their seats.

2
Thrills; or, How Objects and Empty Spaces Compete to Threaten Us

In his book *The American Cinema,* the always perceptive Andrew Sarris discusses memorable objects that appear as visual correlatives in the work of Alfred Hitchcock: the cymbals in *The Man Who Knew Too Much,* the windmill in *Foreign Correspondent,* the glass of milk in *Suspicion,* the blood-stained doll in *Stage Fright.* One reason these objects are so memorable is because in each case the object stands not only for itself, but for something else: the cymbals for the assassination and of the whole movement of the narrative, the windmill for the arrival of an airplane to take away the villains, the glass of milk for the imminent poisoning of Joan Fontaine, the bloodstained doll for an accusation of murder.

The use of objects as visual correlatives is not limited, however, to the works of Hitchcock; objects appear constantly in all suspense thrillers. One thinks, for example, of the painting of the Madonna in *Obsession,* which works as a symbol of the protagonist's dilemma and the narrative; the escaping balloons in *La Rupture,* which work as a complex symbol of escape and freedom; Faye Dunaway's photographs in *Three Days of the Condor,* which work as a symbol of trust in a morally bankrupt world; the mirrors in *Lady from Shanghai,* which work in part as a symbol of the destructive nature of the American woman.

One might also comment on the all-important sense of place in the suspense thriller: one thinks, for example, of the empty field in *North by Northwest,* the parking garage in *All the President's Men,* the deck of the boat in *Knife in the Water,* the deserted highway in *Duel.* Physical environments seem constantly to either threaten the protagonist or comment obliquely on the action in which he or she is involved.

This kind of oblique comment is typified by the often commented-upon final scene in *North by Northwest* in which the chaotic chase is juxtaposed with the implacable authority figures of the United States presidents in stone on Mount Rushmore. Another example is the newspaper-wallpapered inquisition room in *State of Siege,*[46] which calls into question the whole concept of "objective history"—reminding us and the protagonist that those who wield power can, through the media, define the issues and orchestrate the "truth."

One way of understanding the all-important significance of both objects and places in the suspense thriller is through an understanding of the concept of the "thrill." In his book *Thrills and Regressions,* Michael Balint develops a comprehensive theory of thrills for use in psychoanalysis which has, nevertheless, much relevance to this study of the suspense thriller.

Balint begins by asking a seemingly simple question which turns out to be rather profound: Why do some people enjoy amusement park rides whereas other people don't? Balint observes three characteristic attitudes associated with people who enjoy these rides: first, some amount of conscious fear, or at least an awareness that a real external danger does exist (even if only in a marginal, controlled form), second, a voluntary exposure to this danger and to the fear aroused by it, and third, a confident hope that the fear will be tolerated or mastered, the danger will end, and a return to safety will follow. "This mixture of fear, pleasure, and confident hope in the face of an external danger is what constitutes the fundamental elements of all thrills."[1] In classical times, real thrills were continuously experienced: people were killed by wild animals, in fights with others, and so on.

As civilization progressed, thrills were experienced increasingly in controlled or vicarious forms. Vicarious thrills were provided, for instance, by the circus, the theatre, and the other arts.[2] Thrills could also be provided in displaced or symbolic forms, such as in children's games like tag, hide-and-go-seek, or musical chairs. As Balint points out, all these games basically consist of (1) a safe zone and an external danger represented by the catcher or seeker, (2) the other players' being forced to leave the zone of security, which is often called home, and to accept exposure to the danger, in (3) the hope that they will reach security again.[3]

Although obviously, the movies cannot provide actual thrills nor controlled thrills like those provided by amusement park rides (with the advent of devices like Sensurround, 3-D, and holographic representations, however, the movies may eventually reach that point), they certainly can provide vicarious thrills. And indeed, most suspense thriller plots are constructed precisely around this kind of three-part progression. Thus, I believe it is possible to use Balint as a model for understanding the suspense thriller, which can be seen, then, as the genre that most consistently presents to its audience a series of vicarious thrills.

Other kinds of thrills (not necessarily of the dangerous life-and-death variety) include those associated with *high speed,* such as racing, horse-riding, skiing, sailing, and flying; those associated with *exposed situations,* such as jumping, diving, rock climbing, taming wild animals, and traveling into foreign lands; and those associated with *unfamiliar forms of satisfaction,* such as new foods, new customs, and new sexual experience.[4] From each of these varieties of thrills can be elaborated particular elements associated with the suspense thriller.

Related to the thrill of high speed is the generic chase. Suspense thriller protagonists are constantly running: Cary Grant runs from a plane in *North by Northwest,* Warren Beatty runs from the onrushing water in *The Parallax View,* Stéphane Audran runs from her tormentor in *La Rupture,* the Tupamaros run from the police in *State of Siege,* and Marilyn Monroe runs from her husband in *Niagara.* The chase includes among its apparatus various conveyances, including boats, cars, planes, trains, blimps, helicopters, garbage trucks, buses, and bicycles.

The thrill of the exposed situation is related to the suspense thriller quite congruently: Cary Grant actually climbs against the Mount Rushmore rocks at the climax of *North by Northwest,* Paul Newman jumps off a bridge into the water in *The Prize,* and President Kennedy rides in an open limousine in real life and in *Executive Action.* Related to the thrill of the unfamiliar satisfaction is the protagonist's sexual adventures, as well as his or her newfound moral values. Thus, Stéphane Audran engages in adultery in *Wedding in Blood* before she decides to kill her husband; Dustin Hoffman as Carl Bernstein writes more objectively than he is used to as he explores the dangerous area of President Nixon's involvement in a nationwide conspiracy in *All the President's Men;* Gene Wilder learns to relax and take advantage of sexual pleasures and irresponsibility under the tutelage of Jill Clayburgh in *Silver Streak;* and Rock Hudson comes to an appreciation of the gifts of life and identity in *Seconds,* only to have both of these gifts taken away from him.

Expanding his model, Balint proposes two fundamental terms which can be used to describe our orientation toward the world of thrills: *philobatism* and *ocnophilia.* A philobat (derived from the Greek verb for "to walk on tiptoes") is one who enjoys such thrills; an ocnophil (derived from the Greek verb for "to shrink, to hesitate, to cling") is one who doesn't. Obviously, most people reside in a state somewhere between either extreme; mental health is probably best achieved by a balance between these two tendencies. Generally, most suspense thrillers can be seen as representing in symbolic terms a protagonist's evolution from an ocnophilic position in which he or she is isolated from the world of thrills and afraid, toward a more integrated balance in which the expression of his or her philobatic tendencies allows a more successful and meaningful functioning of personality.

Although the protagonist often does not want to leave the ocnophilic state, psychological change is generally achieved as a result of his or her ultimate acceptance of the thrills thrust upon him or her by the suspense thriller's narrative. Thus, the suspense thriller, presenting vicarious thrills, becomes what Balint would call a three-act philobatic drama. In *Wait Until Dark,* for instance, the ocnophilic and clinging Audrey Hepburn loses the secure protection of her husband and home base, faces a series of terrifying

In the denouement of *All the President's Men*, the reactionary "ocnophilia" of Richard Nixon is juxtaposed with the progressive "philobatism" of reporter Bob Woodward (played by Robert Redford).

thrills through which she conquers her fears, emerges victorious, and returns unharmed to the security of her husband, although now in touch with her own philobatic abilities and no longer in need of his protection. In *All the President's Men*, the ocnophilic world is equated with the status quo of Nixon and is pitted against the philobatic world of the investigative reporters who try to rid the government of its ocnophilic psychoses and return it to a security which is more meaningful and in balance. In *Portrait in Black*, although the lovers experience sexual and criminal thrills which fulfill their philobatic urges, they ultimately do not want to give up their security (often associated with respectability or money) and thus try to reinvent their new lives partially in terms of the old.

As these examples suggest, it would be possible to describe virtually every suspense thriller using Balint's vocabulary. In the second half of this book, I do not do so—not because the ideas are not perceptive or useful in understanding generic consistencies in the thriller, but because the exercise would be rather formulaic and repetitive, since so many of the thrillers function—in Balint's terms—in almost exactly the same way.

Philobatism in general, continues Balint, is the tendency of the adventurer. Although the ocnophil clings to possessions and those many secure

Yves Montand in *The Confession:* handcuffs as the symbol of ocnophilic repression.

surrounding objects; the philobat often clings to at least one special object, which Balint terms the ocnophilic object. Thus, the lion-tamer holds onto the whip, the tight-rope walker a pole, the skier a pair of ski-poles, the conductor a baton, the soldier a rifle, the artist a paint brush, and the pilot a joy-stick.

The philobat perceives the world much differently than the ocnophil. For the philobat, often with the solitary ocnophilic object in hand, the world is a vast space to be explored; unnecessary attachment to objects prevents exploration. Indeed, it is the objects that he or she considers dangerous and unpredictable. Significantly, one of the objects that recurs in the suspense thriller, particularly in the work of Hitchcock, is the pair of handcuffs. An object like this is perhaps the antithesis of the safe "ocnophilic object" embraced by the philobat and represents the most overwhelming symbol of the philobat's inability to get away from objects that are unconquerable and oppressive.

Of course, the objects that the philobat encounters need not be instantly harmful. Often the philobat is given an opportunity to try to turn the encountered object into an ocnophilic one. Balint notes that often in fairy tales (and by extension, in other works), the philobat "watches for objects which present a psychological problem to the hero who has, so to speak, to conquer them by solving the problem or puzzle presented. This kind of conquest—changing an indifferent or hostile object into a co-operative partner—is achieved, as are all such conquests, by showing consideration, regard, or concern about them."[5]

This idea particularly relates to certain scenes of escape which recur in suspense thrillers time and again. In *North by Northwest,* for instance, Cary Grant turns the objects at the auction into his cooperative partners and is able thus to escape the villains. A similar escape takes place in *Torn Curtain* when Paul Newman allows the paper flames in the ballet set to provide him the inspiration to escape from the theatre.

Related too, are the many instances in films such as *Three Days of the Condor, The 39 Steps,* or *The Prize,* in which a protagonist enlists or kidnaps a generally unwilling heroine, ultimately turning her into a cooperative partner as well. (Although female protagonists in thrillers enlist male partners, they rarely, if ever, kidnap them—the typicality of the reverse situation an indication of the devalued position of women which underlies virtually all popular film, including the thriller.) Balint claims that often these enlisted objects are similar to the secondary characters in fairy tales, who may often transform themselves from ocnophilic associates into adversaries. One thinks of the secondary characters in so many suspense thrillers who, although initially helpful to the protagonist, generally turn out to be villains who would destroy him or her. Related too is that object in certain thrillers, such as the ladder in *The Postman Always Rings Twice,* which initially helps the protagonist philobatically commit a murder, but which later turns on the protagonist when found or noted by the police and becomes an incriminating object that leads to the character's incarceration: a certainly ocnophilic punishment.

For the ocnophil, on the other hand, the world consists of objects which are separated by terrifying empty spaces. "The ocnophil lives from object to object, cutting his sojourns in the empty spaces as short as possible. Fear is provoked by leaving the objects, and allayed by rejoining them."[6] In *Wait Until Dark,* for instance, it is precisely the empty spaces that are terrifying to the blind heroine; the empty spaces are blank, and she is unable to maneuver herself from place to place without the help of the anchored objects which make up her world. When her apartment is finally a complete shambles and her objects are destroyed, she attempts to turn the refrigerator into her single ocnophilic object by pulling the plug and severing it from its traditional, secure purpose.

A similar ocnophilic fear of empty spaces is reflected in the two central scenes of *North by Northwest:* first, when Cary Grant is attacked in the empty spaces of the open field; second, when he clings to the ocnophilic rock as he and Eva Marie Saint hang over the yawning abyss. The ocnophil inhabits such an anxious existence because his or her relationship to objects is inevitably tenuous. "The object, however kindly attuned to the subject, has nevertheless its own life, and must occasionally go its own way, which

Audrey Hepburn as the blind ocnophil in *Wait Until Dark:* a world of terrifying empty space anchored by her familiar objects.

conversely means that there is a constant danger of the individual being dropped by his object, which danger periodically becomes a bitter fact."[7] Thus, the protagonist in *Ministry of Fear* is separated from his cake; both Farley Granger and Robert Walker in *Strangers on a Train* become separated from the crucial lighter; and in film after film, characters are separated from the weapons that would protect them.

An object which remains nonthreatening is a source of much security, and the philobat certainly doesn't want this object taken away. Balint suggests that this principle may also be operative in regard to aesthetic experience: "Modern art, which tends to dissolve the objects and threatens to merge them once again back into their environment, undermines this reassuring experience. The diminishing importance or even complete

disappearance of objects must give rise to ocnophilic fears which may explain why certain people have such an inexplicable resistance to, and even disgust for, modern art, while others, more philobatically attuned, welcome it with open arms, occasionally without any criticism."[8] This concept relates most perceptively to a suspense thriller like *Blowup* which can be read as a philobatic fantasy because all the threatening objects in the film are eventually destroyed. The photograph of the dead body is blown up larger and larger until it disappears in empty grey spaces; the corpse disappears from the park; the mime players play tennis with a ball that is "invisible"; and the protagonist literally disappears from the last shot as he stands in the midst of an empty field. Thus, *Blowup* upholds an absolute philobatic world: all empty spaces. All that retains significance is nothingness and movement through space.

Certainly the major problem with Balint, as he develops his ideas, is his entrapment in the sexism of pre-Lacanian Freudian psychoanalytic theory. Inevitably, for Balint, the adventurer is male; Balint's theories are written in sexist language and use a vocabulary which excludes women. Not content to stop with his persuasive and fascinating theories of ocnophilia and philobatism, Balint insists on describing these theories in part through sexual imagery which exalts men, penises, and male potency. Balint thus relates philobatism to erection and insists on seeing the ocnophilic object as phallic. "Seen from this angle," says Balint, "we may say that the philobatic thrills represent in a way the primal scene in symbolic form. A powerful and highly skilled man produces on his own a powerful erection, lifting him far away from security, performing in his lofty state incredible feats of valour and daring, after which, in spite of untold dangers, he returns unhurt to the safe mother earth."[9]

Can then a woman be powerful, skilled or an adventurer? For psychoanalysts like Balint, it would appear not, unless they can produce their own erections and transform their sex. One could, perhaps, argue that the thriller—in general written and produced by men (at least in film)—is informed by precisely this kind of phallic egocentrism, but I think this kind of argument would miss the point. There are many notable female protagonists in thrillers (as for example, in *Shadow of a Doubt, Le Boucher*, or *The China Syndrome)* who become adventurers whose psychological journeys can be illuminated by Balint's theories; and there are so many female spectators who have been moved by the thriller that it would be wrong to argue that these works are—more than any other popular genre—unusually reflective of sexist male fantasy. Certainly, the sexist

Antonioni's *Blowup* is an explicit examination of ocnophilia and philobatism. In the first frame enlargement (top), David Hemmings finds himself in a world devoid of empty spaces. In the second and third frame enlargements the empty spaces so predominate one notices the human being in each only after a search.

dimension of Balint's kind of typical Freudian analysis must be categorically rejected, although I would argue that we be careful to retain that which, uncontaminated by sexism, can provide very useful insight—insight into human interaction with objects and empty spaces and into our relationship with that category of experience we may call "the thrill."

Philobatism and ocnophilia exist theoretically in a dichotomous relationship. While the philobatic world is structured by safe distance and sight, the ocnophilic world is structured by physical proximity and touch.[10] While the philobatic world leads to ultimate detachment and to claustrophobia, the ocnophilic world leads to self-effacement and to agoraphobia. These two tendencies are reflected in the suspense thriller in the way the genre's basic structure corresponds to the three-act philobatic drama, and the genre's objects and empty spaces can be perceived as either hostile or comforting. Obviously, however, the ideal relationship between these two tendencies is one of eventual successful integration, catalyzed in part by the three-act drama. According to Balint, we are constantly striving for a complete harmony between ourselves and our environment, and this balance is approximately achieved in only two specific instances—during orgasm, and in all forms of ecstasy. Again and again, suspense thrillers end with either literal or symbolic representations of one of these two states: Audrey Hepburn embracing her husband happily at the very end of *Wait Until Dark;* the train carrying Cary Grant and Eva Marie Saint through the tunnel in the last shot of *North by Northwest;* or most strikingly, the tremendously expressive release provided by the LSD trip at the climax of *La Rupture.*

Significantly, some political thrillers like Z succeed their orgasmic climaxes—comprised of repressive obstacles being broken down—by showing more ocnophilic repressions, thus emphasizing that the philobatic drama (potentially in political terms as well) is a never-ending process and that absolute integration of the two tendencies may be, although important as a goal, ultimately unattainable. Basically, the obstacle to our integration is our ocnophilic tendency to be too cautious in our approach to life and to fear the thrills that we need and desire; it is in our works of art—particularly in the genre of the suspense thriller—that we can see reflected our search for our proper relationship to objects and spaces and our quest for the optimum balance between our philobatic and ocnophilic tendencies.

3
Suspense That Makes the Spectator Take in a Breath

In his justly famous *Aspects of the Novel*, E.M. Forster discusses the concept of story, which he defines as a simple narrative of events arranged in their time sequence.[1] Forster believes that, like Scheherazade's husband, we continuously want to know what will happen next. Many critics equate the concept of suspense directly with the kind of curiosity associated with Forster's idea of story, but this seems to me a false association. There is a difference between curiosity, which is ultimately satisfied, and suspense, which is ultimately relieved. Although in whodunits such as *Murder on the Orient Express* we certainly want to discover the identity of the murderer, we hardly wait with the kind of anxiety associated with the concepts of relief or suspense. Nor is suspense necessarily created when a story is interrupted. Television soap operas, for instance, interrupt their stories daily. Although their audiences in general want to know what will happen, it is usually a simpler curiosity along the lines of "What will Erica do next?" Furthermore, movies that are considered suspenseful seem to retain this quality for us on repeated viewings. The suspense of the celebrated shower sequence in *Psycho*, for instance, seems largely undiminished by the knowledge many spectators have of the horrific sequence's outcome. Although we may enjoy repeated viewings of *Murder on the Orient Express*, we can never be curious as to the identity of the murderer. Thus, suspense seems significantly different from curiosity.

Indeed, suspense relates not to the vague question of *what* will happen next, but to the expectation that a certain specific action might take place. In the famous story "The Lady or the Tiger" by Frank Richard Stockton, the ending is suspenseful precisely because we know that behind that door waits either a lady or a tiger—one will marry the protagonist, the other will kill him. Suspense does not require a resolution, and in this instance no resolution is offered. If the creation of curiosity demands that information be withheld from the spectator, the creation of suspense demands that enough information be revealed to the spectator so he or she can anticipate what might happen; suspense then remains operative until the spectator's expectations are foiled, fulfilled, or the narrative is frozen without any resolution at all (as in "The Lady or the Tiger" or in Alfred Hitchcock's *The Birds,* in which the battle between birds and people has no clear victor).

This distinction is borne out as well by Hitchcock's famous example—repeated in virtually every interview he has given—which illustrates a difference between surprise and suspense; the example begins by considering two men coming into a room, sitting at a table, and carrying on a long conversation. At the end of the conversation, a bomb suddenly explodes and kills both of them. Certainly this course of events would provide a surprise; and while the conversation was going on, the spectator may also have responded with curiosity as to where the sequence was heading. Imagine, on the other hand, that this sequence is preceded by a scene in which a third man comes into the room, unseen by the first two men, and hides the bomb underneath the table. Because extra information has been provided to the spectator, but not provided to the first two men, the long conversation scene would be virtually transformed. Instead of asking the general question "What will happen next?" the spectator would now ask questions such as "When will the bomb go off?" and "Will the two men get out of the room in time?" Every time one of the men ended a sentence, the spectator would anticipate a termination of the conversation; indeed, the conversation would take on a new meaning because it ironically would become significantly irrelevant.

For Hitchcock, a brief surprise should always be sacrificed to a more protracted suspense. When asked by interviewers about his mystery films, Hitchcock constantly denied that he made them. Although mysteries and suspense thrillers may share certain kinds of content, the mystery construction can be seen as opposite to the suspense construction—the former based on initial concealment, the latter on initial revelation.

The French crime writers Boileau-Narcejac, in their book *Le Roman Policier,* ask the question: if we call this concept "suspense," exactly what is it that is being suspended? Their answer is: time.[2] During those moments that suspense is operative, time seems to extend itself, and each second provides a kind of torture for a spectator who is anxious to have his or her anticipations foiled or fulfilled. It's hard to believe that the shower murder sequence in *Psycho* takes under a minute; and certainly at the climax of *North by Northwest,* Eva Marie Saint seems to be hanging precariously for an awfully long time. The "psychological time" of a suspense sequence can be compared to those crisis moments in our own lives—the highway accident narrowly averted, the real emergency that requires a quick response—which are experienced in similarly extended time and which can afterwards be recalled in precise and extensive detail.

Eva Marie Saint and Cary Grant suspended over the yawning chasm in *North by Northwest.*

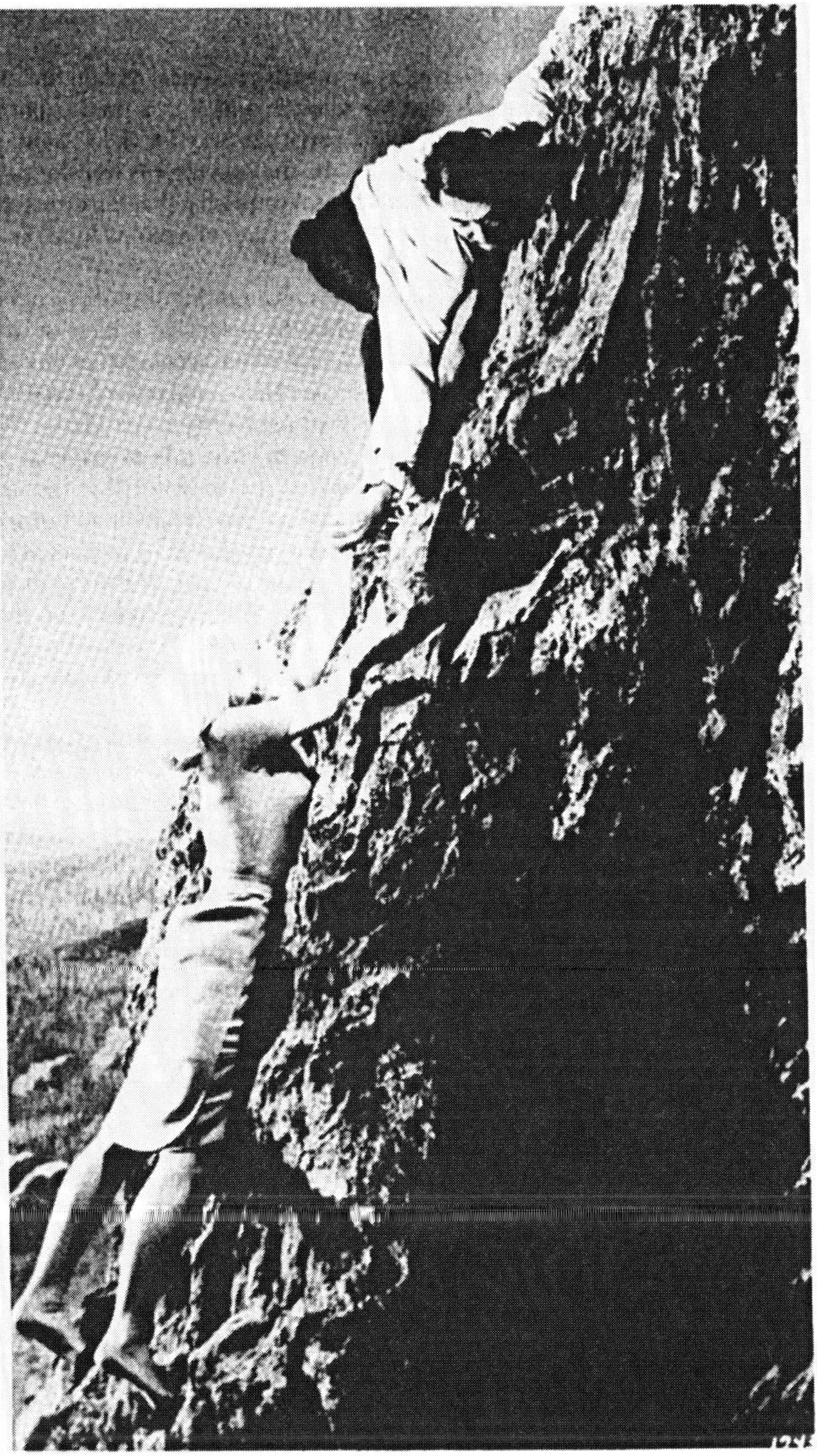

Suspense can also be perceived as an overtly rhetorical tool, in that its revelatory construction reveals that the work in which it is used is but a fictional course of events being told in a particular way for the benefit of the spectator. In Hitchcock's bomb example, the spectator is transformed into a virtual third character. It is not therefore surprising that the directors of suspense thrillers are constantly accused by critics of manipulating their audiences.

Seen as a basically structural device, it is obvious that suspense can be used in any kind of film and is not limited to the suspense thriller—a fact which has added immeasurably to the difficulty which accompanies any attempt to define the suspense thriller. Lawrence Hammond makes a case for Louis Lumière's 1895 one-shot film *L'arroseur arrosé* being considered the first suspense film, because Lumière hit upon the first rule of suspense—"Tell the audience all the facts"[3]—by showing the audience that the *arroseur* was in imminent danger himself of being *arrosé*. Hammond further contends that the expansion of suspense techniques should be attributed to D.W. Griffith, because of Griffith's use of various stylistic devices such as cross-cutting, back-lighting, and long shots. Griffith may indeed be the father of the cinema, but to credit him as the father of suspense as well seems to me much like crediting Technicolor pioneer Herbert Kalmus for the color schemes in recent films of Antonioni.

No matter what films one looks to while playing the game of antecedents and influence, some instances of suspense can be found. A western like *The Searchers*, for instance, takes advantage of a central suspense construction: Ethan (played by John Wayne) and Martin (played by Jeffrey Hunter) spend the whole film looking for Martin's sister, who has been kidnapped by the Indians. When it becomes clear that the sister has been raped by and or married to an Indian, we discover that Ethan intends to kill her when he finds her, out of respect for her lost innocence and womanhood. Martin intends to prevent this. When the two finally meet up with the sister, the suspense is great because the audience has had the opportunity to build up anxiously a variety of expectations.

If all films can take advantage of suspense construction, the suspense thriller seems particularly suited for it—because the genre uses constant thrills and dangers, which allow the spectator to build expectations in simple terms regarding the protagonist's survival, and because works in the genre tend to construct themselves antithetically, constantly following an A with an A′ that the spectator can anticipate. Characters, plot lines, even stylistic devices are often constructed according to an elaborate (and perhaps generally unconscious) duality. Perhaps the most striking example is *Shadow of a Doubt*, which begins with the evil Uncle Charlie juxtaposed with his good niece Charlie and develops dualities increasingly complex; ultimately, we expect everything to be geometrically answered and suspensefully await sequences we know (if perhaps only on a subconscious level) are inevitable. One of the most consistent signs of a suspense thriller is when a film tells us what to expect and then makes us wait.

In her article in the *New York Times* criticizing 1970's thrillers, Nora Sayre precisely misses the point when she says that "Many movies fail to be frightening because the fuses of anticipation have been blown. For example, when a thriller is constructed entirely around one star, you know that he's not going to vanish, that he simply cannot be murdered early in the narrative. Therefore, the threats to his life are no more exciting than watching a shopper being elbowed at a midsummer white sale. Conversely, the mere presence of particular performers reveals the action ahead: an actress like Rhonda Fleming is almost certain to be snuffed."[4] Obviously, one would welcome a Hollywood cinema (beyond Hitchcock's *Psycho*) that could precipitously kill off its stars, but movies' tendencies to keep their stars intact until at least the last reel have never before prevented the successful creation of suspense.

Surprise is not suspense; nevertheless, our expectations for certain performers often help toward the creation of suspense. Mia Farrow, for instance, an archetypal waif/victim in *Rosemary's Baby,* becomes from the first moment of *See No Evil,* the obvious victim. Before Richard Fleischer even begins his conventional suspense constructions, we just know that before the movie is over, Farrow is going to undergo a horrific ordeal that we shall vicariously share. If modern suspense thrillers are not as satisfying as the older ones, it is *not* because they have blown the anticipations, but because these anticipations have not been properly exploited because of some failure of structure, style, or performance. In fact, John Cawelti contends that suspense in general is stronger in generic works than in mimetic works, because mimetic works, in the imitation of the ambiguous, uncertain, and unstructured real world, can create only a kind of uncertainty. "But if we are encouraged to perceive the story world in terms of a well-known formula, the suspense effect will be more emotionally powerful because we are so sure that it must work out."[5]

I think it is also useful to suggest a relationship between suspense in the suspense thriller and suspense in a dream. When one is in a suspenseful situation in a dream (say, being chased by a pack of dogs), often one's semiconscious mind wants the suspense and the dream to end; and yet one's subconscious has nevertheless found it necessary to create and play out that suspenseful dream in the first place. This situation is analogous to film suspense, which we simultaneously dread and enjoy. Because we may enjoy watching the protagonist being dangled out of an open tenth-floor window by the villain doesn't mean we are sadists, rather that our responses are complex: we want the hero rescued, we just don't want him or her rescued too soon. The implication is that the experience of the suspense thriller represents a working out of psychologically contradictory forces — an implication corroborated by the work of Altan Löker.

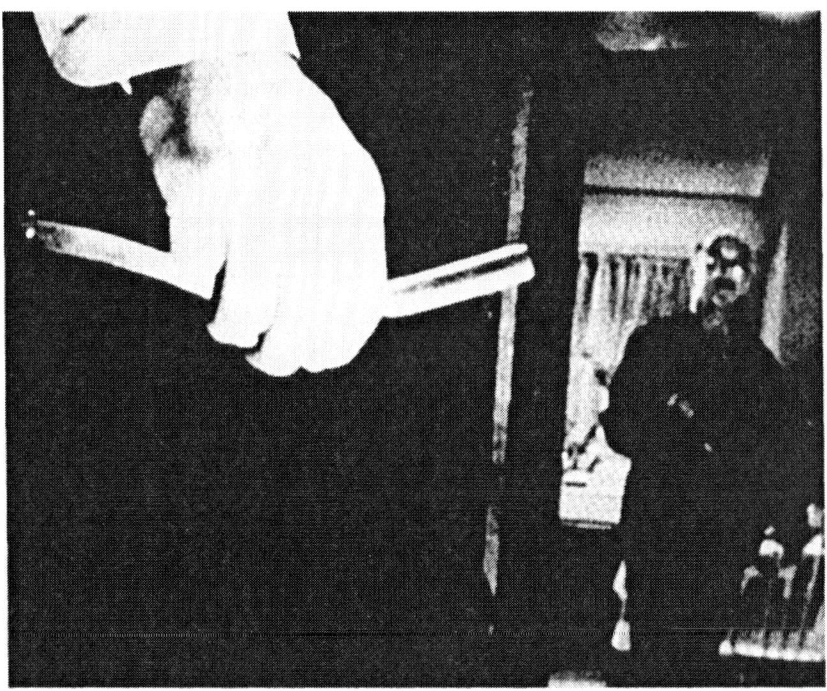

Suspenseful expectations developed in a single frame in Hitchcock's *Spellbound:* will Michael Chekhov (right) be murdered by Gregory Peck?

If suspense can be defined at its simplest as a structure which allows the spectator to develop expectations regarding the fate of the protagonist, the film director must have at his or her disposal means by which this structure may be effected. The specific technique of cross-cutting is one of the many means widely associated with suspense. For instance, a villain is torturing a hero; the spectator is made aware of the imminent arrival of the police (will they arrive in the nick of time?) by a constant cross-cutting between the two events. Examples of suspense techniques can all be taken from Hitchcock's work at various points in his career. In *Strangers on a Train* in 1951, there was a suspenseful scene at the end of the film: will Guy Haines (played by Farley Granger) finish the tennis match before Bruno Anthony (played by Robert Walker) has a chance to plant the damaging evidence at the fairground? When Bruno drops the lighter down a grating, Hitchcock's cutting becomes very frenetic: going from Guy to Bruno to the grate, then back to Guy, and so forth.

By 1962, with *The Birds,* this technique was evolved somewhat. In the now famous scene in which Melanie (played by Tippi Hedren) waits outside the schoolhouse for the children, she looks at the jungle gym and sees a few birds sitting there. She waits, and then a few more birds join them. In a medium shot, Melanie gets out a cigarette and smokes it leisurely. Since this take is long, we want to see if more birds are coming onto the jungle gym; we expect the traditional rhythms of cross-cutting with increasingly shorter shots, which Hitchcock, in his eternal manipulation of the spectator, refuses to provide. After what seems relatively to be a long time, Melanie follows the flight of a crow which flies leisurely to the jungle gym—revealing finally hundreds of birds waiting to attack. In 1964, in one of the most suspenseful scenes from *Marnie*, Marnie (played as well by Tippi Hedren) tries to slowly tiptoe unobserved out of the office she has just robbed; she is situated in the right of the frame in a long shot, while a cleaning lady she cannot see is situated in the left of the frame. In this shot, suspense has been created without the necessity of any cutting, everything taking place within one stationary shot. (This creation of suspense in one shot recalls another bravura shot in Hitchcock's earlier 1937 *Young and Innocent*, in which suspense is created by a leisurely dolly from a long shot of a ballroom filled with people to one eye of a black-faced drummer. As soon as the eye fills the frame, it twitches—thus tipping off the audience that the drummer is the murderer and causing considerable anxiety that the protagonists will never locate him in the midst of such a crowd.)

Hitchcock's sometime eschewal of standard cross-cutting techniques is taken one step further in his 1973 *Frenzy*. In one sequence, Babs and Blaney (played by Anna Massey and Jon Finch) are hiding out in a hotel; Blaney is asleep. The camera pans as the naked Babs goes into the bathroom; and as she disappears, the camera rests on a close shot of the newspaper that has been pushed under the door. The headline reads: Another Necktie Murder. In one shot we have learned that Blaney is still alseep, and that Babs, busy in the bathroom, is unaware that by now the whole city is looking for Blaney. The suspense begins to grow: How long will it take for Babs to come out of the bathroom and notice the paper?

Instead of dwelling on the activities of Babs and Blaney, Hitchcock cuts to the two attendants in the hotel lobby downstairs. There is a series of nine medium shots of the attendants; they realize that Blaney must be the murderer, summon the police, and with the police rush up to Blaney's apartment—which we see is fortunately empty. The sequence is very powerful; all the more so since suspense is achieved not through cross-cutting but through a series of what might individually seem to be rather bland one location medium shots. The lack of cross-cutting increases the tension. Since we would normally expect to see Babs noticing the newspaper, and then later see a fragment of them rushing to get out the window in time, we would think that at least they have a chance to escape. Hitchcock's refusal to cut upstairs so we can follow their progress leaves us anxiously expecting that they will inevitably be caught. Hitchcock achieves something unique: he keeps us in suspense as to whether Babs will see the paper and as to whether they will escape, but *deprives* us of the satisfaction

of viewing their escape firsthand. And finally, in his 1976 *Family Plot,* a very short chase sequence in which one character (played by Bruce Dern) pursues another (played by Katherine Helmond) in a cemetery is photographed in one high-angle long shot so far away that the two figures look like points traveling horizontally and vertically along the paths of one gigantic Mondrian painting; here Hitchcock uses technique which subverts the suspense to serve his minimalist, modern conception.

Why do so many people like suspense and find it relevant to their experience? Gordon Gow suggests that suspense is all around us, that "the big trouble with day-to-day news is that it's a collection of unfinished anecdotes. It leaves questions hovering: will a war be waged? will a murderer be apprehended? will taxes increase?"[6] This idea seems to me less than totally convincing. If there is suspense in our lives, it is usually unclear, so filled are our lives with trivia and constant perceptions. If anything, the daily news provokes in us a kind of lethargy: more problems in the Middle East, more complexities in the never-ending analyses of the American economy, yet another mass murderer on the loose in a major city, and so forth.

Significantly, on those few occasions when the news seems truly suspenseful and provokes in us a strong response, as did the Cuban missile crisis or the Patty Hearst affair, people frequently comment on the fictional nature of the events: "It's exactly like a movie!" Not surprisingly, the Cuban missile crisis turned up before too long in Alfred Hitchcock's *Topaz,* and the Patty Hearst story has been disguised in numerous B films and television episodes. Perhaps the news event which most perfectly crystallized the occasional capacity of news to become suspenseful was the taking of American hostages in Iran. Held for over a year, the hostages and their drama quickly turned into the stuff of thrillers, with the daily installment of dramatic narrative described on a new nightly television program created by ABC. Although ostensibly a news show, ABC introduced its show with a dramatic title and logo—"AMERICA HELD HOSTAGE." With every show, the title served to make the event more fictional, and as the days in captivity increased in the show's title ("AMERICA HELD HOSTAGE: Day 400"), and as each day passed, the suspense grew greater: Would the hostages be killed or released? Would President Carter succeed or fail? Would the Shah of Iran live or die? The climactic moment, one of the great ironic and suspense-filled days in all of American politics, had the national news networks showing Ronald Reagan taking the oath of office—having defeated Carter for the presidency—only minutes before the Iranians released the hostages, their careful timing thus depriving Carter of success or vindication.

Perhaps contradictorily to Gow's claim that suspense is all around us,

The celebrated robbery sequence in *Marnie:* Tippi Hedren on the right side of the frame is balanced by the cleaning woman on the left.

Gow also claims that audiences are attracted to suspense thrillers because they are "drawn there by the boredom of routine lives that are subjected to the pressures that nag at the nerves."[7] This idea, typical of most explanations as to why we enjoy suspense, seems a bit too simple. Surely, one wonders whether Gow (who obviously likes suspense thrillers) has himself a routine life filled with boredom, which must, it appears, be relieved only through the movies. A related view is offered by Ralph Harper, who suggests that "Thriller readers can find their release from the tensions of their own lives by transferring their concern to the tensions of fictional reality,"[8] a condescending notion which implicitly transforms the suspense thriller into an escapist entertainment or emotional crutch. A more dynamic model is needed: one which would allow us to enjoy suspense thrillers whether our lives were boring or exciting, our conflicts hazy or distinct, our perceptions insufficient or overwhelming, our mental healths in crises or at peace.

A more recent theorist, Noël Carroll, has attempted to arrive at his own theory of suspense.[9] Carroll's article is filled with perceptive ideas—not the least of which is a clearly articulated understanding that "suspenseful films" are not always "suspense films." Carroll's basic idea is that suspense is created when the narrative moves spectators to frame narrative questions—questions they may ask either consciously or unconsciously (for instance: Which will emerge, the lady or the tiger? Will the children escape from the basement or will the phony preacher catch them?). Carroll then organizes film narratives into a variety of scenes according to their relationship to concepts of suspense: there are establishing scenes, which introduce information; there are questioning scenes, which introduce a question; there are answering scenes, which answer a question; there are sustaining scenes, which intensify an earlier question without answering it; and so forth. For Carroll, "suspense arises when a well-structured question—with neatly opposed alternatives—emerges from the narrative and calls forth an answering scene. Suspense is a state that accompanies such a scene up to the point when one of the competing alternative outcomes is finalized."[10]

A careful reading of the last statement quoted above reveals the typical, only partially semantic, problem that confronts anyone who tries to discuss suspense: suspense may be a "state," but that word implies an emotional state of being. Since movies are not sentient, they cannot really have states, and it would therefore be more correct to say that the "state" of suspense does not accompany the scene but that the successful scene, throughout its duration, induces the state of suspense in the spectator. According to Carroll's general theory of suspense, typical suspense scenes pose questions which have two logically opposed outcomes, one of which is morally correct but unlikely, the other of which is morally incorrect but likely. In other words, when we see the hero imperiled by the villain with the gun, we wonder if the hero will escape—his escape, though moral, seems unlikely, because the success of the immoral villain seems so likely.

In a significant appendix to his article, Carroll approaches one crucial obstacle to his own theories: in the works of Alfred Hitchcock, we are often invited to empathize with a character who would do "evil" things. Thus, suspense can, it would seem, be created even when the choice is not always between a likely, immoral outcome and an unlikely, moral outcome; it can also be created when an *immoral* action would appear to be improbable. A good example of this is in *Marnie,* for instance, when it seems improbable that the cleaning lady will not hear Marnie robbing the safe. In order to solve this apparent exception to his general theory of suspense, Carroll then creates a "universal theory of suspense," which explains Hitchcock and suggests that perhaps it is best to say instead that thrillers pose questions with two possible outcomes—one improbable but *desired,* the other probable but *not desired.*

In this new formulation, moral correctness is no longer relevant. The problem with this theoretical formulation, aside from offering an important corrective to the main text of Carroll's previously articulated theory, is that when we talk about *what is desired,* we are forced to talk about things outside the content of the film itself and discuss the psyche of the spectator, wherein the desire (again, an emotional state) must reside. Thus, once again, Carroll's arguments bring him, in a roundabout way, back to the spectator. Although Carroll rejects without refuting Altan Löker's theories as "thoroughly unsupported speculations,"[11] his own essay ultimately demonstrates the need for some psychoanalytic theory which will take into account the psyche of the spectator and the spectator's response.

This is precisely what is attempted by Altan Löker in his book *Film and Suspense.* In general, Löker's book is a fascinating conjecture on the psychological underpinnings of suspense. Occasionally the conjunction of its complexities, terminologies, and seemingly endless distinctions, with its conversational, informal English, results in unintentional humor; *Film and Suspense* is an "intellectual" book written in what clearly is not Löker's primary language. It attempts to get at the suspense thriller not through a strict content analysis but through an analysis of the psychological relationship between films and their audiences. Thus, although Löker's argument is elaborated upon a Freudian basis, his argument is basically theoretical, rather than demonstrable. Because this fascinating book is almost impossible to obtain, I will take this opportunity to outline Löker's rather complex position in some detail.

Löker begins, like other theoreticians of suspense, by discussing the verisimilitude of the cinema. The spectator of a stage play, for instance, is constantly aware that he or she is in a theatre perceiving a fictional experience. The spectator at the cinema, on the other hand, has a different kind of experience: he or she is more caught up in the experience, seduced by what Löker calls the medium's many realistic details. Subjects consistently appear on screen as if directly from life. "Camera-work and editing operate as extensions of natural perception and associations of ideas, and they take the spectator from place to place in the middle of the screen action.... Thus the spectator starts living in the screen world."[12] Löker's dominant idea here is that the spectator's increased participation in film derives from film's basic realistic sense; and it is this participation in the fictional experience which promotes suspense. Thus, the cinema can induce suspense much easier than any other medium; and "the ability to change viewpoint quite arbitrarily, with rhythmic or abrupt cutting as the occasion requires, and to restrict or expand the range of vision, gives the film director great control over the spectator's response."[13] (Nora Sayre, incidentally, goes so far as to suggest that the medium's power relates specifically to the actual size of the screen as well as to the sharing of the experience in a dark theatre with other strangers. She contends that when transferred to a format such as the television screen, the verisimilitude of film is seriously reduced; she defies anyone to be frightened by a film on television, because "almost any living room is too familiar, too cozy."[14])

Löker's entire argument is primarily elaborated in response to the basic paradoxical situation: "What happens in a movie house? How can a person, who had a fat dinner, experience an hour later at the theatre the fear of starving to death? Or how can a person sitting in a comfortable armchair experience the fear of falling down from a roof top?"[15] The typical answer to these questions is that the spectator identifies with the protagonist and experiences fear not for him or herself, but for the protagonist. Löker rejects this viewpoint as idealistic and self-ennobling. He suggests that the spectator is not fearful that the protagonist will starve or fall; rather, the spectator responds anxiously as a result of having other fears he or she is not consciously aware of. The spectator fails to understand or be aware of these fears partly out of habit and partly because the fears are buried in the unconscious. To explain away his or her own clenched knuckles, held breath, sympathetic grimace, or other signs of physical and emotional response, the spectator intellectually adopts the self-ennobling explanation, even though it is incorrect.[16]

To understand exactly what these hidden fears are, we must first understand what things we find inherently valuable, and which, if threatened, would therefore cause us anxiety. Löker contends that obviously there is an instinct in us for the propagation of our own pleasures; for films to cause us to experience anxiety, they must first connect with us by depicting our desires. He claims that three desires are particularly cinematic: *sex*, *success*, and *spectacle*. A more satisfactory sex and love life is something

Of all the cinematic desires, sex is one of the most prevalent in the suspense thriller. In *North by Northwest* (top), Cary Grant and Eva Marie Saint make love on a railroad sleeping car. In *Marnie*, Sean Connery tries to arouse the unresponsive Tippi Hedren. In *The Postman Always Rings Twice*, John Garfield and Lana Turner have a steamy encounter on the beach.

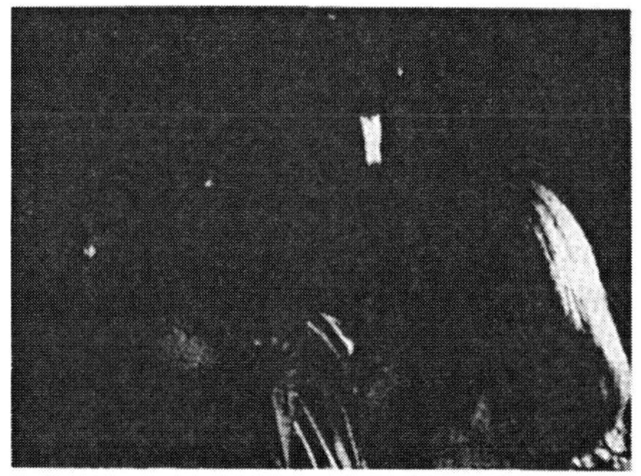

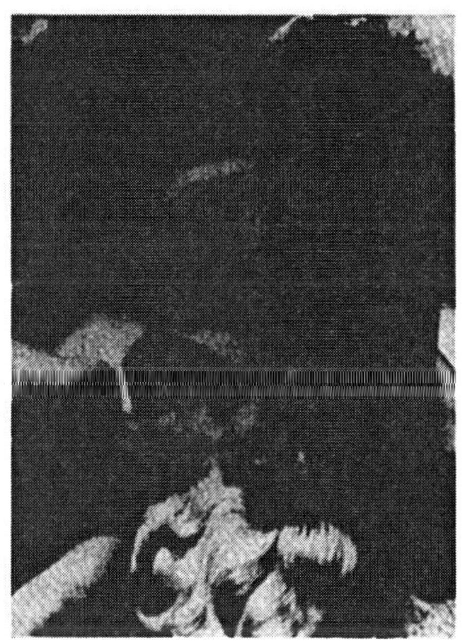

everyone craves. Success corresponds to the universal instinct for self-preservation and can be reflected in concepts of self-realization, superiority, possession, domination, and fighting. Spectacle—meaning "any object or event not usually seen in real life"—is related directly to what could also be called the curiosity instinct. One might generalize these three principles of sex, success, and spectacle into more abstract principles of sex, challenge, and mystery; in any case, they represent the three desires which are the most cinematic.[17]

Why, for instance, is sex any more a cinematic desire than is eating? Löker would claim that desires remain most cinematic when the response provoked in the spectator is congruent with the response provoked in the fictional protagonist. As hungry as a spectator may be, when he or she sees the protagonist indulging in a meal, the spectator becomes absolutely conscious that he or she is not sharing that food; thus, the experience quickly becomes vicarious, and the spectator, aware that his or her desire has not been fulfilled, may even become alienated from the protagonist. On the other hand, a sequence in which the protagonist spends much time ogling or flirting with a potential sexual partner would be highly cinematic (and engage the spectator) because both the spectator and the protagonist would be contemplating sexual experience.

For Löker, a scene in which the hero and the heroine find it impossible to unite (ultimately, in sexual intercourse) is more satisfying for spectators, because once a protagonist is shown achieving orgasm, spectators become aware that their own sexual desires are not being met, and then the film would be strikingly revealed as only fictional. A particularly cinematic story, therefore, would be one in which "The hero rescues the heroine out of flood waters and puts her on a tree trunk. . . . But this is no time for sex because they are carried by the flood and have to fight off countless dangers."[18] One recognizes here a conventional suspense thriller narrative which relates particularly to those films like *North by Northwest* which deal with an innocent on the run.

Löker suggests that there are many ways that the depiction of orgasm can be blocked. A director can, as in the previous example, place the hero and heroine in so much danger that they don't have the chance for a physical union until the fade-out; the union may be blocked by moral considerations as in *Foreign Correspondent* or many other films which deal with a love triangle. That censorship and social pressures also block the union is ultimately beneficial; for Löker, sexual desire is most powerfully exploited by the filmmaker when sex is suggested and then pushed into the bckground and postponed. Indeed, Löker's whole concept of suspense related directly to the systematic blocking of all three of these cinematic desires.

Although what takes place on the screen obviously interests the spectator, Löker contends that "It is the spectator's own experience, or his own story, which really moves him, by making him want certain things to happen for himself, derive satisfaction from them, and become responsible for their consequences."[19]

Löker gives as his example the traditional scene in which the hero takes out his gun, walks toward a door, opens it, and captures a villain. There are, of course, many different ways of filming this scene; ideally, it should be filmed in a way so that it directly engages the spectator. First, the camera could reveal only to the spectator that there is a moving light coming from underneath the door, which suggests that the villain is in the next room.

When the spectator then saw the hero, he or she would say half inwardly, half outwardly to the protagonist: Look at the light underneath the door, the villain is hiding behind it! Perhaps the hero would finally look and notice the light. The spectator would then say: Go to the door. The hero would go to the door. The spectator would then say: Draw your gun. The hero would draw his gun. The spectator would then say: Now open the door. The hero would then open the door. Thus, when the hero had captured the villain, the spectator would have shared in his success. According to Löker, the spectator would have used the hero in much the same way that the hero used the gun.[20]

Thus, if a director wants to take advantage of suspense and draw the spectator into the film, the director must understand how to tell the story so that the spectator's desires will be activated. In one sense, the spectator is transformed into a major character of the film, into "the peculiar character . . . who can see, hear, walk, fly, swim under water, jump from place to place, but, can not touch or move anything except this own body."[21] Löker claims this strange transformation revives in the spectator mental processes which were in favor in childhood: in both instances, the fulfilling of desires is restricted by the limits of one's own mobility and is beyond one's own control. It is significant that children seem to especially like suspense thrillers and have no problem relating to Löker's second and third cinematic desires, if not his first.

Löker claims that since a narrative should not represent before the final fade-out a complete fulfilling of any of the three most cinematic desires (lest the illusion be broken), it needs to be composed of conflicts as well; it is these conflicts which produce fears. "Fear is caused by a danger which is an anticipated happening presenting the possibility of inflicting pain. . . . Since behavior is aimed at procuring pleasure and avoiding pain, fears become the determinants of behavior alongside desires."[22]

If we are able to determine the most cinematic desires, we should also be able to determine the most cinematic fears. Löker claims that the first cinematic fear is the *fear of the unknown*, although this is not particularly strong, because we generally know that the screen cannot really harm us.* The second and most cinematic fear is the *fear of punishment* which arises from the sense of *guilt*. For Löker, "Guilt becomes the key to understanding and making good films. Any film which does not make the audience secretly feel guilty fails to look believable, serious, or satisfying."[23]

The spectator can become guilty as a result of wishing for something to happen which he or she later perceives may be violating a moral rule. Hitchcock constantly takes advantage of this. A good example is *Rear Window*, in which we want the protagonist (played by Jimmy Stewart) to spy on the other tenants because of our cinematic desire for spectacle; however, as the protagonist continues so vicariously and vigorously, we begin to feel like voyeurs, and subconsciously guilty. The guilt, of course, does not prevent our continued voyeurism, because by this time, we are so committed to finding out if the neighbor really did kill and cut up his wife, that we will continue to fulfill our desire no matter what.

Thus, in a film of suspense, "The spectator is pushed to wish and act in order to gratify his selfish instinctual desires. If and when these wishes and acts threaten to hurt, or actually hurt, a person or persons in the story who do not deserve being hurt, at least not as much as they get hurt, the spectator becomes guilty. . . . The film can push the spectator to crime, and thus make him guilty."[24] In a sense, guilt can be perceived as the result of the clash between instincts and ideals. It is guilt, then, and not "starving to death" or "falling from a precipice" that produces the fear we experience while watching a suspense thriller. At first it is the fear of becoming guilty, then the fear of being exposed as guilty, and finally the fear of actually being punished.[25]

Löker goes on to elaborate certain specific rules filmmakers should follow if they want to successfully create guilt. These rules include: (1) "The spectator must be pushed to make wishes." In other words, films should be constructed upon the cinematic desires and fears, with the material structurally presented in a way that the spectator can arrive at wishes before the protagonists themselves attempt to fulfill them. Hitchcock does this, for instance, in *Vertigo*, when he reveals to the spectator the real identity of Madeleine (played by Kim Novak) as Judy. The spectator then wishes for Scotty (played by Jimmy Stewart) to succeed and hopes Scotty's systematic transformation of Judy into Madeleine will unmask the fraud; when the unmasking surprisingly leads to Judy's death as well, the spectator feels responsibility and guilt. (2) "The film-maker must arrange things so that the spectator gets the impression of making the wish all by himself and before

**Or can it? When I saw the Los Angeles premiere of* Earthquake *at what is now Mann's Chinese Theatre, a net had been placed under the high ceiling to catch the sometimes large pieces of plaster the Sensurround sound system was dislodging; on that occasion, there did exist the possibility of some onscreen experience causing real damage to the audience.*

everyone else." Director Sam Peckinpah does this, for instance, in *Straw Dogs*. Until the climax, Dustin Hoffman's David has responded so consistently passively to all his tormentors, that the spectator aggressively wishes David would take more drastic action.

Löker's rules continue: (3) "The spectator attaches himself more or less to any character shown on the screen, but especially to anyone with whom he is left alone for some time. If that character is a thief, he is still a human being and is much more valuable than the inanimate objects around him." Thus, it is not at all difficult to make the spectator empathize with a thief, as Hitchcock does in *Marnie,* or with a murderer, as Chabrol does in almost all of his films.

(Rule 4) "Another source of guilt is sympathy for the villain." Thus, in almost all of Hitchcock's films, the villain is presented as a charming and sympathetic man. In *Foreign Correspondent,* for instance, this situation is particularly disturbing: Stephen Fisher (played by Herbert Marshall) is initially presented to us as a witty and heroic pacifist with whom we sympathize. When, halfway into the film, he is revealed as a villain, he still retains some of our sympathy, even though he arranges to have the protagonist killed. The ultimate guilt is effected when our sympathetic villain participates in the horrific torture of a harmless and kindly old man. Aside from creating guilt, the sympathetic villain also relates, in this film, to Hitchcock's propagandistic purpose of educating Americans to the attractive facade which can mask Nazi evil.

(Rule 5) "The filmmaker can also allow the hero to inadvertently hurt someone while being heroic, allow the hero to be guilty of something himself, or allow the spectator to push the hero to some dangerous action with a bad result."[26] Again, there are many examples from Hitchcock's work: Gregory Peck's amnesiac, from *Spellbound,* for instance, who is guilty of accidentally killing his brother; Tippi Hedren's kleptomaniac, from *Marnie,* who is guilty of killing a sailor.

One of Löker's most important concepts is *"the package deal,"* a concept which is operative when choices are given the spectator that cause a conflict because the spectator is of two minds; his or her subsequent sanctioning of the action causes the spectator then to accept the guilt for the action's bad aspects as well. For instance, as Löker contends, a conflict might arise if the bombing of Hiroshima were presented as a choice. In one sense, we might want it because it would end the war; in another sense, we would not, because it would cause massive killings. Then again, we might want it because of the fame and success that would accrue to us or the spectacle it would provide. Ultimately, we would probably sanction the dropping of the bomb because we would be unable to separate its bad effects from its desired effects and because our desires—being instincts—are invariably stronger than our moral sense; in any case, we would then take responsibility and feel guilty for the bomb's damages as well as for our response to the choice presented to us.

Suspense thrillers tend to construct themselves around these kinds of package deals, which promote guilt in the spectator. In real life, the mind constructs defense mechanisms to disguise or hide these kinds of conflicts. (For instance: "Of course it's all right to keep the hundred-dollar bill I found outside on the street: it probably belonged to someone rich, and the owner was careless and didn't deserve to keep it, and I should have been given a bigger raise this year anyway, and it's not actually against the law to keep it. . .", and so forth.) The suspense filmmaker, according to Löker, must therefore provide the necessary conditions for the formation of defenses as well, because it is only under the protection of defenses that a guilty wish can be made and a guilty action begun. The most common technique in film is that of isolating the positive aspect and revealing its inextricable association with some unpalatable package deal later. (If we were to elaborate a suspense film from the previous example, a good director or writer would have the protagonist later find out that the loss of that hundred-dollar bill caused its owner to commit suicide—thus making the finder suffer tremendous guilt for having kept it.)

The suspense filmmaker becomes a manipulator of the spectator's psychology: creating defenses which enable the spectator to construct certain expectations, then tearing down these defenses so that the spectator feels guilty. If the director is particularly skillful, he or she will be able within one work to consistently stop, start, or protract the action in order to exploit to the fullest the spectator's own contradictory wishes and guilty fear of punishment.

In this psychological context, many traditional concepts must be rethought. A fight between a protagonist and an antagonist, for instance, can no longer be especially considered a conflict, because it does not relate to the spectator. "The only violent conflict possible for the spectator is the guilt-producing type, because this is based on the conflict between the id and the superego which is constantly in operation in real life and has the capacity of becoming violent."[27] *Conflict*, then, can be described as that condition which is caused by "the necessity of making a choice which is found to be impossible to make definitely."[28]

Tension, related to conflict and often accompanied by stasis, becomes "the psychological state of holding energy in a condition ready for action, mental or motor."[29] Tension is created by the anticipation of future action as well as by the contemplation of present unwanted action. Right before the climax of *Wait Until Dark*, for instance, when Audrey Hepburn has realized the enormity of what has been done to her and takes steps, finally, to defend herself in a completely self-reliant way, there are moments of great tension as the camera shows her ultimately waiting quietly for the arrival of the villainous Roat (played by Alan Arkin) and the action that must

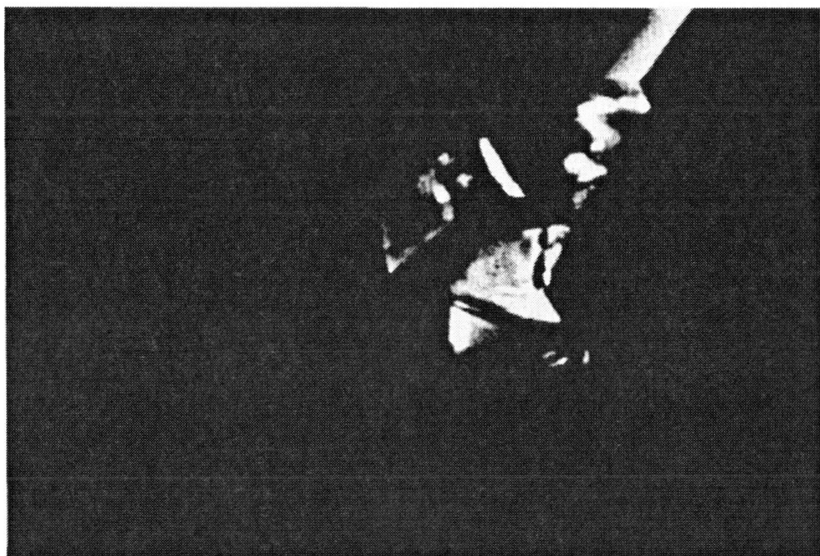

Dynamic tension in *Wait Until Dark:* In an almost completely black frame, Alan Arkin jumps across the room to grab Audrey Hepburn's ankle.

follow. The static tension is related to the conflict provoked by a kind of package deal: we want Hepburn's Suzy to achieve success and vanquish the villain, but we fear that she (and we) may not have anticipated every possibility, and that, by pushing her to such self-reliance, we may bring about her death.

A related concept is *dynamic tension,* which is the variety of tension generated by accelerated action. Static tension generates action, which, if unhindered, accelerates and itself generates dynamic tension. Thus, the stasis of Suzy waiting for Roat in *Wait Until Dark* is balanced by the dynamic tension which erupts when Roat arrives and the film climaxes with violence, screaming, bloodshed, and general hysteria.

The concepts of static and dynamic tension relate to the starts and stops of any particular narrative. In a film like *Psycho,* for instance, the very quiet conversational scene between Marion Crane and Norman Bates (Janet Leigh and Anthony Perkins) in the motel office can be perceived as a scene which generates static tension; conflicts have already been set up, and we sense the narrative may soon either exclude Norman (should Marion return to Phoenix with the stolen money) or change its direction in order to involve him more completely. The narrative, of course, does change its direction, but in a disturbing way which creates much guilt. The scene of static tension is thus balanced by the violent murder of Marion in the shower, which certainly creates dynamic tension. Most suspense thrillers generally end with a brief resolution following a scene of dynamic tension. It is significant that *Psycho* ends with a static shot of the crazy Norman who now refuses to move even to bat a fly; Hitchcock's atypical creation of so much unreleased static tension is most disturbing.

Finally, and only after this long, step-by-step process, does Löker arrive at the concept of suspense. "Suspense is the psychological state of holding energy in a form ready to execute two incompatible, mutually excluding, actions."[30] Suspense is our continued hesitation in choosing between two different actions, both of which create tensions. In a sense, suspense is the complex dialectic of the continuing conflicts engendered by our desires and our fears. Suspense can be illustrated with Löker's example of two men who are sexually interested in a woman they are chasing. Tension is created; although the spectator wants sexual desires gratified, the spectator does not want the woman traumatized or raped, nor presumably the men killed during the pursuit, all possible actions the spectator fears this sexual desire may lead to. Hence, this desire is accompanied by guilt.

If we make the initial situation more complex by transforming the woman into a murderous protagonist who needs psychiatric help and one of her pursuers into a nonviolent policeman who is in actuality trying to help her, the sequence becomes even more complex. Now, tension is also created by the spectator's additional desire that the protagonist woman escape; although the spectator wants her to succeed because she is the protagonist, the spectator doesn't want her to be forever denied the psychiatric treatment she needs, which is what the spectator fears this desire may lead to. Hence, this desire is also accompanied by guilt. This suspense sequence, therefore, would catapult the spectator into a state of constant anxiety, as he or she is forced continuously to make choices between conflicts—each of which simultaneously provides pleasure and provokes guilt.

Theoretically, the director of such a sequence would, after a careful set-up, prolong it so that all the psychological conflicts could be satisfactorily exploited: perhaps, for instance, in the midst of the chase, the pursuers suddenly slip in the mud . . . but then the woman herself slips in the mud . . . after which they finally manage to catch her anyway . . . only to have her pull out a gun . . . which they manage to take away from her . . . and which is ultimately revealed as empty, this discovery enabling her to escape once again . . . although without noticing that one of the men has managed to circle around behind her . . . and so forth.

For Löker, it is extremely important that the suspense thriller organize its actions so that the spectator is forced to consider his or her own expectations and desires and therefore ask, in regard to potential actions of the plot, "Should it happen or not?"—thereby producing as much guilt and conflict in the spectator as possible.

Consider, for instance, certain of the questions provoked by Claude Chabrol's *Le Boucher,* a film in which a beautiful detached schoolteacher (played by Stéphane Audran) finds herself inching towards a possible involvement with a butcher (played by Jean Yanne) who is a homicidal maniac. The questions we ask tend to have contradictory, complex answers. Question: If the butcher is a murderer, should he be found out and punished? Answer: Yes, because our moral instincts tell us murderers should be punished; no, because we want this butcher to succeed in his wooing of the schoolteacher. Question: If the schoolteacher menaces his survival by threatening to reveal his identity, should he kill her? Answer: No, because murder is immoral, and we like the schoolteacher; yes, because the schoolteacher has refused (through her coldness) to sleep with the butcher and allow us any sexual pleasure. Question: Should the schoolteacher take the butcher as her lover? Yes, because we want our sexual desire gratified; no, because he is a dangerous maniac and it may result in her being killed.

What makes *Le Boucher* so fascinating is that even in the resolution of its narrative, it does not really resolve any of the tensions associated with these questions. Nor is the plot resolved with an action we have been particularly guided to consider: instead, the murderous but sympathetic butcher quite suddenly commits suicide—and as a result the schoolteacher feels guilt at not having given herself over to him; we share this guilt and are implicated in his suicide, because Chabrol had ultimately tipped the balance against our wanting the schoolteacher to let the butcher into her house at the crucial moment when he most needed human sustenance.

The last issue to which Löker addresses himself is the distinction between suspense and surprise. Disagreeing with Hitchcock's theory of the opposition of these two concepts, Löker believes that suspense and surprise are complementarily inseparable. He dissects a film surprise into three phases: the preparation of the desired reaction, the diversion, and the surprise proper. If a film is to use surprise widely, it uses it only after a period of suspense and in order either to build a new suspense or to add to the existing suspense.[32]

Perhaps this relationship can be best illustrated with examples from *Psycho*. The brutal murder of Marion in the shower is generally considered the archetypal movie surprise. It seems that not only did Hitchcock want us to be taken aback, but he wanted to induce a feeling of our center being taken away; Hitchcock's desired reaction has been carefully prepared for, especially through techniques promoting absolute identification with Marion. Before the surprise proper, we discover that Marion plans on returning the money she has stolen, which tends to resolve some of our guilt. When Norman Bates spies on the undressing Marion through his keyhole, the scene works as a diversion: we may not know what is going to happen, but by setting up Norman as a voyeur, Hitchcock creates an expectation in us that Norman, though possibly so passive that he is incapable of any action whatsoever, might (though it appears unlikely) attempt to rape Marion. When the surprise proper takes place and Marion is killed, we are unprepared; we might have anticipated a rape, but not a murder. In one sense we wanted to see Marion naked and anticipate sex between her and Norman in order to satisfy our sexual desire; her murder provides the punishment that was inherent in the package deal.

The surprise of the murder works also to transfer our attention from the suspense related to the embezzled money to a new suspense related to Norman and his mother. Will Norman (or his mother) be caught? Again there is a conflict: we want Norman to succeed and cover up the crime, despite our moral sense that the crime should be punished. Yet operating at another level is our own desire for spectacle: we want to know what happened and understand it all. Although these two desires conflict, it is perhaps the latter which turns out to be strongest. We thus compel the detective to investigate the murder, and when he is killed, we feel guilt for that murder as well.

Another surprise takes place when we discover that Norman's mother is dead. Our proper response has been prepared for in that, although we haven't actually seen Mrs. Bates, we feel we do have some knowledge of her. A diversion has even been provided by our glimpse of "the mother" as she was carried out of her room by Norman. The surprise revelation of the mother's death creates other lines of suspense implicating us in Norman's potential madness as well. Löker ends his theoretical work on suspense with detailed analyses of specific Hitchcock films, which certainly seems appropriate considering the universal acknowledgment of Hitchcock as the master of suspense.

As valuable and fascinating as Löker's work is—the only book-length treatise on film suspense and one which recognizes the problems inherent in approaches that fail to acknowledge the psychoanalytic dimension to the phenomenon of suspense—there is, nevertheless, at least one major problem with Altan Löker. Like Michael Balint, Löker comes out of a Freudian tradition of psychoanalysis which is, at times, virulently sexist. Löker's discussion of the spectator always assumes that the spectator is a male. And for a theory that tends to generalize so readily about the psyche and sexual desire of the spectator, this assumption becomes a major shortcoming indeed. Many of the examples Löker tends to provide show sexual desire in the context of male-female relationships in which the female is objectified and in which rape seems a constant possibility. Even if we disregard Löker's fascination with rape, one cannot help but wonder about the extent to which a female spectator will respond positively and with sexual desire to the typical scene in which the female is sexually objectified to a significantly greater degree than her male sexual partner.

I agree with Löker that the spectators' sexual desires are significant in understanding the processes of identification and suspense, but it is dangerous to assume sexual desire is so homogeneous. To what extent do spectators respond differently? And exactly what is required to incite sexual *interest? Is some nudity of a potential sexual partner required? In the Psycho* scene Balint describes, in which Norman Bates, fully clothed, spies on a virtually nude Marion Crane, is the disparity between their depictions and situations so great that only heterosexual males can find the situation at all erotic? Is it possible that there exists a subset of heterosexual males who are themselves so put off by the potential for rape that their sexual instincts cannot be aroused by this scene? As well, Balint's premises exclude from consideration the possibility that any spectators might be gay men or lesbians, who would undoubtedly have a range of sexual responses significantly different from those of heterosexual men and women.

A more sophisticated argument than that which Löker provides might claim that all a spectator needs in order to have his or her own sexual desire aroused is the presence onscreen of another human being in whom the spectator might be sexually interested. In this way, the central heterosexual romance in *Marnie*, for instance, might be just as sexually engaging to the gay man who responds to Sean Connery or to the lesbian who responds to Tippi Hedren. In each instance, the gay spectator might "exclude" the other screen partner by a kind of complex mental process which effectively revises or rewrites the film. Suspense may then be seen as even more complicated, inviting similar mechanisms in radically different ways to various subsets of spectators.

This kind of subconscious rewriting is not at all uncommon or uncommented upon. Many contemporary women, for instance, find in the series of Bette Davis melodramas of the thirties and forties, the liberating role model of a strong woman who refuses to follow men's rules—these contemporary women by and large ignoring or psychologically revising the endings of so many of these films, which often provided Bette Davis a punishment for her attitudes and actions. Although one might argue that gay men and gay women would be most interested and sexually aroused by films which presented gay sexual relationships, it would be hard to deny that sexual interest would not be at least partially incited by heterosexual relationships on screen. As well, the depiction of lesbian sexuality in male heterosexual pornography, and the sexual interest of heterosexual women for the occasional gay protagonist in mainstream media (such as the gay son in the television series *Dynasty* or the men in *Making Love*) suggest that heterosexual spectators can also be aroused by gay characters. Perhaps one "exclusionary" depiction might be gay men from gay women, and vice-versa.[33]

In any case, Löker's theories, at least as he presents them, suffer greatly from his assumption that all spectators are heterosexual men who sexually respond in exactly the same way. It is not my intention here to revise Löker's ideas to make them more universal, which I think may some time be possible; a definitive revision would doubtlessly require a more flexible understanding and probably even a considerable amount of clinical research before one could generalize with any authority. However, I do think that any endeavor which attempts to analyze the spectator's identification and sexual desire, as does Löker's book, is an important accomplishment relevant to our understanding of film suspense. For the moment, though, Löker's theories remain just that: Fascinating theories upon which others will have to build.

4
A Definition

So what, then, is a suspense thriller?

One idea fundamental to my initial thinking was that even though critics disagree, there is a consensus, if imprecise and intuitive, as to what constitutes a suspense thriller. This consensus can guide us. There are reasons why, on a more obvious plane, *North by Northwest* has been called a suspense thriller and *Singin' in the Rain* hasn't; or why, on a more subtle plane, *Silver Streak* has been called a suspense thriller (although a comedic one), while *Murder on the Orient Express* hasn't.

As part of my own research, prior to screening hundreds of films, I systematically went through reviews of a large number of films (concentrating on those made in the late fifties and sixties) and made a cumulative listing including any film consistently described by critics as a "suspense thriller," "thriller," or "suspense film," regardless of the individual critic's (generally unspecified) personal definition of those terms. I used the publication *Film Facts* as my initial research tool: published from 1957 on, with only occasional lapses, *Film Facts* presents a comprehensive and continuing filmography of films released in the United States and lists—for each film—a synopsis, credits, and often extensive excerpts from the film's reviews, primarily from national magazines and New York City newspapers. These reviews proved especially useful, because when, for instance, nine out of ten reviewers call a film a thriller, it becomes easier to generalize the existence of a certain cultural consensus. I then sought out all the films referred to as suspense thrillers and viewed them, working to understand exactly what their similarities were beyond their emotional effects on their audiences (which psychoanalytic theorists like Balint and Löker have helped us to explore).

What are the structural elements in the narratives of these films which prompted critics to identify them as part of a greater genre? As I saw more and more films, I found myself occasionally subtracting a film which seemed strikingly anomalous to the others; or, more often, adding to my initial list other films which were markedly similar. The first group of additional films included those Alfred Hitchcock films made in the thirties and forties, as well as the occasional Fritz Lang or *film noir* which enjoyed obvious parallels to films already on the list. In this way, a core group of suspense thrillers gradually revealed themselves as candidates for analysis. What I was looking for most were similarities in the structures which reflected the very essence of genre: recurring themes, conventions, character types, and iconography—in short, the structural terrains that comprise the genre. Ultimately, this book, in its second part, describes and analyzes the connections and similarities among over two hundred films, based primarily on a kind of content analysis.

Certainly my list is not all-inclusive or exhaustive—and nor did I intend it to be. For instance, the majority of my films come from the American cinema of the fifties to the present or from the most visionary period of the French New Wave, with pre-fifties films rather sparsely represented. I am certain every reader of this book will be able to provide additional titles which could as well have been discussed; I would hope that additional titles be regarded as a measure of the capacity of my observations to spark consideration of similar films. Although I discuss suspense thrillers using a certain amount of chronology as an ordering principle, my impulse is not specifically historical. To do an historical accounting of the thriller would require a much more extensive venture involving access to thousands of films going all the way back to silent cinema, an endeavor not especially relevant to this book's specific goal.

The bias in my book toward films made in the last thirty years is precisely the bias of my own experience, that is: those films that have fascinated me in movie theatres and on television, films made contemporary to my own experience, films toward which I have some firsthand, cultural understanding. Hitchcock's work, much of it pre-fifties, has had an extraordinary impact on the genre and represents the most obvious exception to my typical emphasis on post-fifties films. Although a more comprehensive historical discussion would demonstrate that Hitchcock was by no means the originator of the genre or its formulations, it is clear that his work has been so influential that virtually all directors who work in the genre will remain, to some degree, in Hitchcock's shadow. That alone seemed to me adequate reason to include more of his work in my analysis.

This book of criticism and content analysis, therefore, should be seen as a kind of *anatomy* of the genre, rather than a history. I do not anatomize the representative films in the genre toward the end of providing evaluative judgments or of setting myself up as an arbiter of taste, good or bad—although, of course, as with any work of criticism, the length and rigor of my analysis of certain films give clear testament to my personal evaluation of those films' interest or value.

As I examined my list of films, one consistency immediately became evident: virtually all the films dealt with some crime committed against or by the protagonist; and yet few of the films on the list belonged comfortably in crime genres already articulated by critics or popularly understood by audiences. Most striking in these films called suspense thrillers was the lack of a detective or a gangster as the central protagonist. Where, for instance, are important characters such as Sherlock Holmes, Sam Spade, or Little Caesar in *North by Northwest*, *Z*, *Wait Until Dark*, and *La Femme Infidèle*?

Before defining the suspense thriller, it is necessary to examine the relationship between the suspense thriller and the varieties of crime-related works. The formulations of other critics who have focused on crime literature can prove helpful in this regard. Traditionally, the popular work of art dealing with crime is composed of at least three major characters or elements: the criminal, the victim, and the detective. In most crime works, these three elements coexist in a triangular relationship:

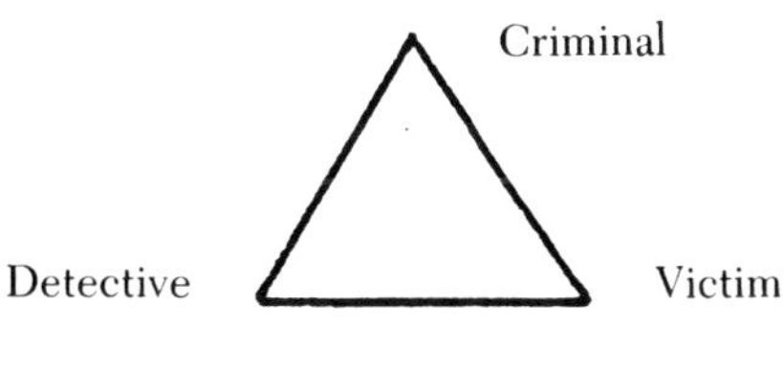

Poe's Triangle

The relationship among the three elements is dynamic. The detective may be a little old lady, a hard-boiled shamus, or Oedipus; the criminal may be Oedipus, a *femme fatale*, or a professional gangster; the victim can be a professional gangster, an innocent bystander, or a little old lady—the possibilities are endless. What is particularly significant is that in most popular works dealing with crime, one of these three elements takes precedence over the others; the works group themselves into specific varieties or (sub-)genres whose popular names often make the dominant element clear. (Although John Cawelti, quoting Poe, suggests that one might transform this triangle into a square by adding a fourth side representing "those threatened by the crime but incapable of solving it,"[1] it is difficult to imagine very many works which could allow this element to dominate.) Onto the following triangle are mapped the general positions of various genres associated with crime. Since each genre generally emphasizes one of the three particular elements, each genre can be placed closest to its appropriate corner of the triangle. For each of these genres, some critical vocabulary has been developed. Brief definitions follow, along with occasional references to especially useful corroborating material.

Crime. This term refers to any work which is structured around the triangular relationship between a detective (or agency of inquiry), a criminal, and a victim. This general category can be subdivided into a variety of genres, including three which emphasize the role of the criminal.

The classical detective. This genre is composed of all those works which emphasize a detective's ratiocination of a crime and (generally) his ultimate

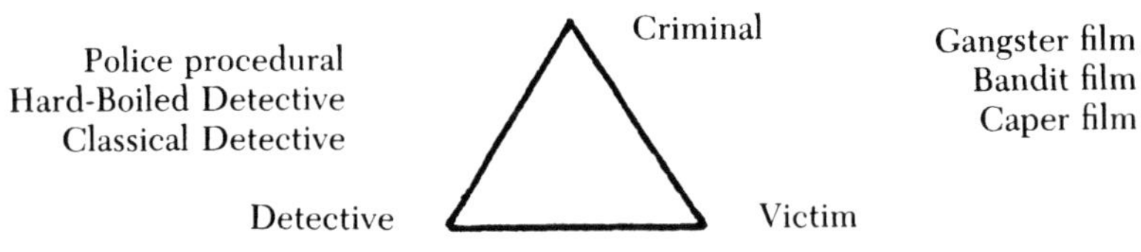

Crime Film—A Preliminary Model

unmasking of the criminal's identity. The victim is usually unimportant and is dispatched early on in the scheme of things. Typical examples of the classical detective include Sherlock Holmes, Hercule Poirot, Lord Peter, Miss Marple, and Charlie Chan; films in this genre include *Murder on the Orient Express, Green for Danger, Mr. Moto Takes a Chance,* and *The Last of Sheila.* A more detailed discussion of the classical detective can be found in John Cawelti's *Adventure, Mystery, and Romance: Formula Stories as Art and Popular Culture,* among other sources.

The hard-boiled detective. This genre is composed of all those works which emphasize a private investigator's adventures in a cynical and corrupt world. The criminal is unmasked not by ratiocination as much as by the detective's dogged persistence. There are often many victims, and most of the characters (except for the detective who, like a medieval knight, has his own code of values) are generally corrupt. Typical examples include Sam Spade, Phillip Marlowe, and Mike Hammer; films in this genre include *The Big Sleep, The Maltese Falcon,* and *Chinatown.* A more detailed discussion of the hard-boiled detective can be found in John Cawelti's *Adventure, Mystery, and Romance,* and Raymond Chandler's nonfiction writing.

The police procedural. This genre is composed of all those works which emphasize a professional policeman's (or police detective's) adventures as a member of society's law-keeping forces. This genre generally emphasizes the protagonist's problems with his superiors, his camaraderie with his peers, and the occasionally unorthodox way in which he goes about his job. The criminals are often gangsters, psychotics, or economically disadvantaged street people. Typical examples include *Dirty Harry, Freebie and the Bean, The New Centurions,* and the many television series of the late sixties and early seventies such as *Toma, Baretta, Starsky and Hutch,* and *Police Story.* Material on the police procedural can be found in Stuart Kaminsky's *American Television Genres.*

The gangster film. This genre is composed of all those works which emphasize the rise and fall of a gangster. The environment is generally urban, and the struggle of the gangster protagonist can be viewed as the malevolent underside of the American Dream whereby anyone can transcend his social class. The tone of the gangster film is decidedly tragic; often a fatal flaw (such as ambition, megalomania, an inferiority complex) leads the gangster to his own destruction—sometimes at the hands of other gangsters, sometimes at the hands of the professional police force. Typical examples include *Little Caeser, White Heat*, and *The Godfather (I* and *II)*. More detailed discussions of the gangster film can be found in Robert Warshow's *The Immediate Experience*, Stuart Kaminsky's *American Film Genres*, as well as in Cawelti.

The bandit film. This genre is often considered a variety of the gangster film and is composed of all those works which are essentially love stories which emphasize the violent adventures of a gangster (generally an ex-convict) and his moll. These two "bandits" are usually pursued in a rural environment by some official detective force such as the police or the FBI; the victims seem rarely to be essential. Typical examples include *You Only Live Twice, Bonnie and Clyde*, and *The Getaway*. More material on the bandit film can be found in Stuart Kaminsky's *American Film Genres.*

The caper (or heist) film. This genre is composed of all those works which emphasize the efforts of a diverse group of criminals to pool their talents, generally under the guidance of a father figure, in order to commit a perfect crime which requires split-second timing. Since the crime is generally a robbery, one might consider the virtual victim the actual location that is to be violated (such as the bank vault, the racetrack receipts truck, the museum display case, etc.), if not the generally nameless businessmen/guards/curators who are supposed to safeguard these locations. The subsidiary detective element is generally provided by a professional police organization. Typical examples include *The Asphalt Jungle, The Killing*, and *Topkapi*. Much material on the caper film can be found in Stuart Kaminsky's *American Film Genres.*

Aside from these seven major genres (the first of which includes the rest), there are a number of other terms associated with the crime film which, although useful, tend to confuse things by providing additional distinctions. These terms include the "detective film," the "whodunit," the "mystery," and the *"film noir."*

The detective film. This term generally refers to any work which emphasizes any kind of detective—but especially of the hard-boiled or classical varieties.

The whodunit. This term generally refers to any of those works which are structured around the eventual answering of the question: "Who comitted the crime?" Classical detective works are most often whodunits, because the detective reveals the identity of the murderer in the work's denouement. Hard-boiled detective works are not generally considered whodunits—not because we don't know the identity of the murderer (usually we don't), but because the detective's adventures and the revelation of the corrupt society around him seem more important to us than the ultimate identity of the "official" murderer. The interesting and often repeated story about the film *The Big Sleep* is that neither Raymond Chandler nor director Howard Hawks could themselves figure out who exactly was responsible for the killing of each of the many victims in the film.

The whodunit, with its emphasis on revealing the identity of the criminal, generally engages in surprising plot twists: the most common is the ultimate revelation that "the least likely" candidate is actually the murderer. Agatha Christie has always been fond of the reverse of this gambit: the ultimate revelation that "the most likely" candidate is in actuality the murderer—a gambit which, in the expected generic context of the "least likely" candidate, becomes even more surprising. (See, for instance, her novel *The Hollow*.) It is also possible in a whodunit for the apparent detective figure to turn out to be the criminal, in which case he or she must often then be unmasked by a secondary detective figure. (Note how this takes place in a film such as *The Last of Sheila*.) A play like *Oedipus* could also be considered a whodunit, in which the detective discovers that he is also the criminal (and in an important sense because of this discovery, is transformed by the end of the play into the tragic victim also).

As well, a whodunit may lack a detective figure altogether. In Agatha Christie's novel *Ten Little Indians*, the narrative presents us with ten victims, one of whom is also the criminal. Since there is no successful detective figure (Poirot and Miss Marple not in service), the crime is not actually solved. The reader finds out ultimately who done it only because the criminal was nice enough to write a first-person confession/explanation, which Christie most thoughtfully provides us with after the conclusion of the book's third-person narrative. A film like André Cayatte's *Two Are Guilty* can be perceived as a kind of unconsummated whodunit. As soon as the crime is committed, we know that two of the three protagonists are guilty, but we don't know which two. By the end of the film, after at least three different kinds of investigations, we still don't know. The considerable power with which this film frustrates its audience derives in large part from our expectation that whodunits provide answers.[2]

The mystery. This term refers to a structural device relating primarily to the difference between plot and narrative—plot relating to the history of events that transpire in a certain work, narrative referring to the way and the order in which those events are revealed to the work's reader or spectator. In a mystery, important events in the plot are purposely withheld in the narrative in order to be revealed out of their chronological sequence. Thus, a whodunit is always a mystery, because we don't know who the murderer is. And although hard-boiled detective films are not whodunits, they are mysteries, because motivations of important characters are frequently initially withheld and often revealed in a continuous series of bursts and surprises.

Gangster films and bandit films tend not to be mysteries. Caper films can sometimes be considered mysteries when they initially omit the explanation as to how the various skills are going to come together and construct a kind of mystery of methodology. (The television series *Mission: Impossible,* for instance, used this device every week: the eventual revelation of how, say, Martin Landau's piece of string or Barbara Bain's hypodermic were to be used, proved amazingly satisfying.) Even films which are not crime films may be considered mysteries because of their structures; a film like *Citizen Kane,* for instance, is a mystery in the way it withholds the identity of Rosebud and then constructs its narrative around the subsequent investigation which takes the revelation of Rosebud as its object.

Film noir. This term, often considered a genre, particularly by the French, can actually cut across many of the generic categories already described. It refers specifically to a group of films produced in America especially after World War II, which are photographed in a dark black-and-white with many shadows. The protagonist may be a hard-boiled detective, a cop, an insurance investigator, an ex-con, or a petty criminal. In any case, he generally meets his downfall through his association with a *femme fatale.* In the *film noir* almost everyone is corrupt, and the cynicism and violence—reflected in the content as well as the style—are unmitigated. Typical examples include *Double Indemnity, Criss Cross, The Killers* (the Robert Siodmak version), and *The Postman Always Rings Twice.* The last several years have seen an extraordinary burst of critical writing on the *film noir,* and there now exist numerous full-length volumes of analysis.

It should be clear that the popular work of art dealing with crime is complex indeed and composed of a variety of genres. So far, the six primary crime genres (the classical detective, the hard-boiled detective, the police procedural, the gangster film, the bandit film, the caper film) all line up on the left of the crime diagram along the detective/criminal side of the triangle. Although each of these genres is distinct, all six of them have similarities, perhaps the most important of which is that they all exhibit a constant moral ethic.

The classical detective exhibits a superiority and a moral understanding of *justice* which allows him to work as the force which ultimately reveals the criminal and re-establishes order to the society. Although the hard-boiled detective works in a more corrupt society in which crime is not so much a transgression as a symptom, he nevertheless exhibits an *integrity* unto himself and becomes a lonely moralist whose ethics are not questioned. The policeman in the police procedural constantly upholds one value: the *professionalism* with which he restores law and order. Although often his methods are questioned by his superiors or by the society, the film context upholds the policeman or police detective as answering to a higher value: an allegiance to his own abilities. Although the participants in a caper film are clearly breaking the law (and hence are sometimes punished), the ethic that drives them is one of *communion and organization.* Even when they fail to escape from the police, the heist is metaphysically considered a worthwhile task, if only because it allowed them to work together and participate in a valuable social process.

As we reach the top of the triangular structure and analyze the bandit and gangster films, the moral ethic, though constant, is not at all clearly upheld. Gangster (and bandit) films certainly reflect the very American concept of *self-interest*, the concepts of capitalism and belief in the American dream; the problem is that although the gangster believes in following his own self-interest, so do those who would destroy him; thus, the gangster film, while reflecting the moral ethic of capitalism, implicitly questions this ethic as interests invariably conflict and the gangster is destroyed. It is significant that gangsters seem often to be portrayed like American businessmen. Their fall is inevitable; even the rise of Michael Corleone in *The Godfather* was eventually balanced by his fall in *The Godfather, Part II.*

The suspense thriller, although a generic subset itself of the popular work of art dealing with crime, stands in opposition to these genres. Films like *North by Northwest, Wait Until Dark, Z,* and *La Femme Infidèle* certainly do not emphasize the detective; their emphasis on the innocent victim or pursued criminal seems to chart the suspense thriller along the victim/criminal side of the crime triangle. Even further, suspense thrillers like these seem not to exhibit anything like the constant moral ethic upheld by the other crime genres. Rather, these films seem more consistently to be searching for or examining various values and ethics—especially in their use of explicit or implicit political content or narratives constructed around an allegorical ordeal which propels the protagonist to a new moral position. Indeed, the values which are upheld at the respective endings of *North by Northwest, Wait Until Dark, Z,* and *La Femme Infidèle,* are quite different from those values which are presented as the status quo at these films' beginnings.

Finally, we have arrived at a plateau of understanding which allows a definition of the suspense thriller to be formulated. My definition has three major points:

(1) *The suspense thriller can be defined as a crime work which presents a violent and generally murderous antagonism in which the protagonist becomes either an innocent victim or a nonprofessional criminal within a narrative structure that is significantly unmediated by a traditional figure of detection in a central position.* Perhaps just as importantly,

(2)*The suspense thriller can be recognized by the multiple presence of various elements* such as murderous passions, conspiracies, assassinations; an innocent protagonist on the run; overt confrontations between good and evil; secret, exchanged, or acquired identities; past psychotraumatic experiences which influence the present; the juxtaposition of fictional adventures with overtly "real" locations; murder, contemporary settings, a dangerous process, a constant emphasis on time; a structural and symbolic doubling which can include parallel narrative; the chase, rescue, and escape; dreaded expectations which are multiply reversed and extended before they are fulfilled; a pervasive suspense construction, thrills and physical dangers, an examination of morality and ethics, a general disavowal of absolute mystery construction; an emphasis on people's relationships to objects and empty spaces; an overt or latent political content; a generally faster pace or else a sense that the narrative is gradually and inexorably tightening; and narrative structures which elaborate themselves in terms of antinomies such as life/death, good/evil, innocence/guilt, trust/suspicion, commitment/detachment, passion/lethargy, honesty/deceit, truth/falsehood, revealing/concealing, openness/secretiveness, sadism/masochism, integration/disintegration, order/chaos, and redemption/damnation. And finally,

(3)*The suspense thriller is actually an "umbrella" genre comprised of an evolving complex of (sub-)genres.*[3] Although all suspense thrillers contain many or most of the elements in the second part of this definition, it is nevertheless fruitful to divide the suspense thriller into a series of more discrete categories or genres; the works in each of these genres tend to elaborate their basic structures around one particular element and to exhibit the remaining elements in typical and isomorphic relationships.

I have therefore divided the umbrella genre of the suspense thriller into six of its most predominant genres and organized most of the films in my basic core group into one of these six categories as well. I have given each of these genres a simple name deriving from the primary suspense thriller element it uses to construct itself. Some of the most pervasive genres which comprise the suspense thriller include *(1) the thriller of murderous passions, (2) the political thriller, (3) the thriller of acquired identity, (4) the psychotraumatic thriller, (5) the thriller of moral confrontation,* and *(6) the innocent-on-the-run thriller.*

Although there are many films which encompass more than one of these categories, a surprisingly large number of suspense thrillers fit into one of these relatively prescribed, if hitherto uncommented-upon formulations. The general position of each of these genres in relation to other crime works can be seen on the chart on page 64; and brief descriptions of each suspense thriller genre appearing on the chart begin below.

The thriller of murderous passions, the first of these genres, is composed of those films which are organized around the triangular grouping of husband/wife/lover. The central scene is generally the murder of one member of the triangle by one or both of the other members. The emphasis is clearly on the criminal protagonist who is implicitly presented as an almost predestined representative of his or her social class (whether high or low) and who therefore provokes our sympathy, if not our empathy. The criminal motive is generally passion or greed; when the murderer is brought to justice, it is usually as a result of his or her own guilt, error, or a betrayal, rather than as a result of the sleuthing of a detective figure, who, if

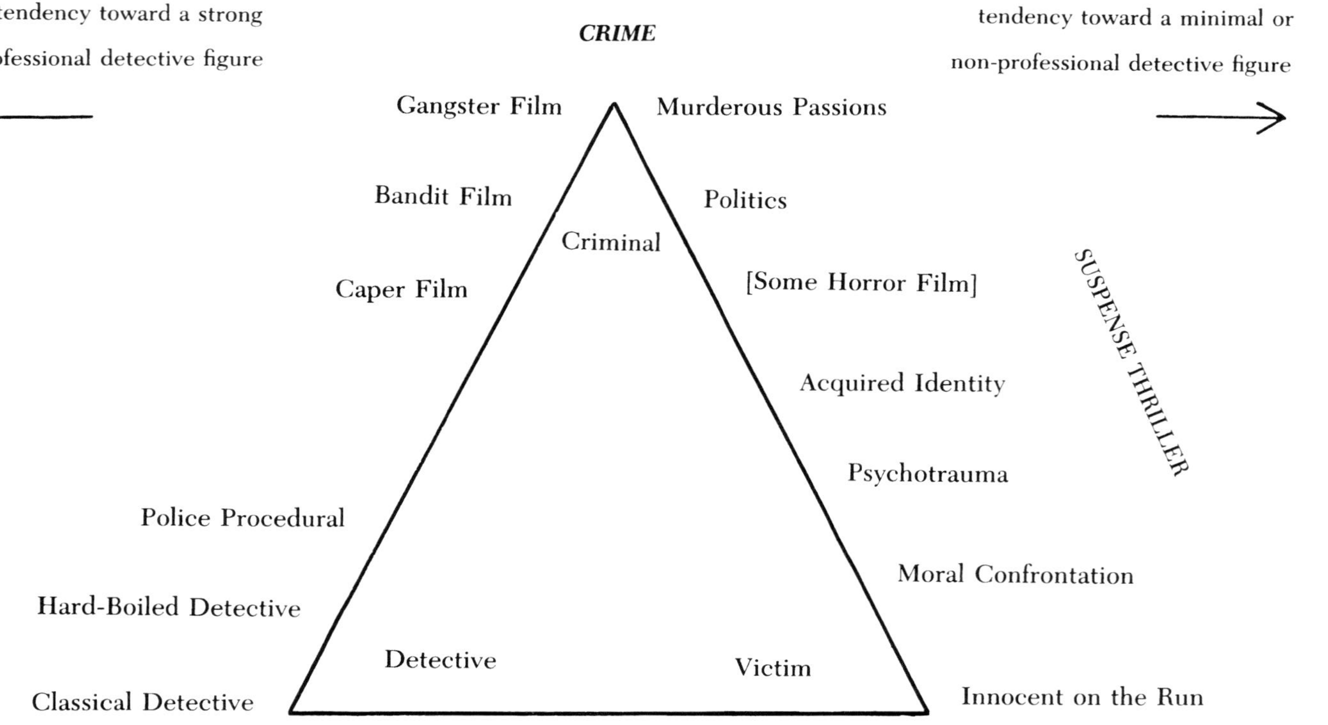
tendency toward a strong
professional detective figure
CRIME
tendency toward a minimal or
non-professional detective figure
Gangster Film
Murderous Passions
Bandit Film
Politics
Criminal
Caper Film
[Some Horror Film]
SUSPENSE THRILLER
Acquired Identity
Psychotrauma
Police Procedural
Moral Confrontation
Hard-Boiled Detective
Detective
Victim
Classical Detective
Innocent on the Run

The Crime Film—A Comprehensive Model

appearing at all, is generally relegated to a clearly subsidiary role. Examples of this kind of film include *Portrait in Black, Crack in the Mirror, The Postman Always Rings Twice,* and *La Femme Infidèle.*

The political thriller, the second of these genres, is composed of those films which are organized around a plot to assassinate a political figure or a revelation of the essential conspiratorial nature of governments and their crimes against their people. These films generally document and dramatize the acts of assassins, conspirators, or criminal governments, as well as the oppositional acts of victim-societies, countercultures, or martyrs. These films may be completely fictional or based on fact; they may also include an actual investigatory force (often represented by a reporter) which works virtually to narrate the revelations. Examples of this kind of film include *The Manchurian Candidate, The Domino Principle,* and *Z.*

The thriller of acquired identity, the third of these genres, is composed of films organized around a protagonist's acquisition of an unaccustomed identity, his or her behavior in coming to terms with the metaphysical and physical consequences of this identity, and the relationship of this acquisition to a murderous plot. The protagonist is often a villain wanting a better life, many times a murderer; and the new identity is that of someone who is dead or nonexistent. Generally the protagonist is killed or punished, although often not as a result of his or her real identity or crimes, but as a result of a murderous plot against the acquired identity or crimes attributed to it. Thus, these films, which are constructed along explicitly ironic lines, consistently raise questions as to what in our lives is meaningful and what in our personalities has value. Examples of this kind of film include *Purple Noon, Dead Ringer,* and *The Passenger.*

The psychotraumatic thriller, the fourth of these genres, is composed of films organized around the psychotic effects of a past trauma on a protagonist's current involvement in a love affair and a crime or intrigue. The protagonist is always a victim—generally of some past trauma and often of real villains who take advantage of his or her masochistic guilt. The protagonist may occasionally be a criminal as well. There is rarely a detective; where there is a force of inquiry, it is generally undertaken by the narrative itself or by the romantic interest of the protagonist, who applies a Freudian psychoanalytic method. This genre of film takes considerable advantage of mystery structures as well as of suspense structures, in that the source of the past trauma or the truth behind the present crime is not revealed until well into the narrative. Examples of this kind of film include *Spellbound, The Locket,* and *Obsession.*

The thriller of moral confrontation, the fifth of these genres, is composed of films organized around an overt antithetical confrontation between a character representing good or innocence and a character representing evil. These films are often constructed in terms of elaborate dualities which emphasize the parallels between the victim and the criminal. The detective force, if present, is inevitably subsidiary. Examples of this kind of film include *Shadow of a Doubt*, *La Rupture*, and *Wait Until Dark*.

The innocent-on-the-run thriller, the sixth of these genres, is composed of those films which are organized around an innocent victim's coincidental entry into the midst of global intrigue; the victim often finds him or herself running from the villains as well as from the police. The protagonist proceeds to have an extensive series of adventures, meeting in the process a romantic interest whom he or she must learn to trust and who ultimately helps to provide a change in his or her moral outlook. In the course of the adventures, the innocent victim becomes, of necessity, the detective force. The antagonist or criminal element is generally divided into three (if not more) related adversaries. Examples of this kind of film include *Silver Streak*, *Three Days of the Condor*, and *North by Northwest*.

Although each of these genres is organized around one particular element from the second part of my definition, the element particular to each can certainly be found in the other genres as well. The element of "assassination," for instance, a primary element in the political thriller (for example, *Z*'s central scene is an assassination attempt, and *The Parallax View* is a fictional exposé of the sixties assassinations in American politics), recurs as a subsidiary element in the other suspense thrillers (for example, the assassination of the United Nations official in *North by Northwest*, the assassination of "Van Meer" in *Foreign Correspondent*, and the assassinations of numerous low-level C.I.A. officials in *Three Days of the Condor*). Similarly, the element of an acquired or exchanged identity, upon which films like *Purple Noon*, *Someone Behind the Door*, and *The Passenger* are organized, recurs in a subsidiary role in other films (for example, Cary Grant's Roger Thornhill being mistaken for George Kaplan in *North by Northwest*, Alan Arkin's Roat taking on multiple identities in *Wait Until Dark*, and Tippi Hedren's kleptomaniac taking on new identities constantly in *Marnie*).

The diagram on page 64 should make clear that the genres comprising the suspense thriller line up opposite those crime genres for which a critical vocabulary has already been developed. Although all the crime genres generally contain all three of Poe's central elements (detective/criminal/victim) in some form or another, a tendency toward a strong professional detective figure can be observed in those genres on the left of the triangle's apex, while a tendency toward a minimal or nonprofessional detective figure can be observed in those genres on the right.

Tzvetan Todorov, in a short essay entitled "The Typology of Detective Fiction," comments in a slightly different way on this same phenomenon. Todorov notes that the classical detective novel tended to have two stories—the story of the crime and the story of the investigation. In the classical form, there was little overlap between these stories: the crime was committed early in the narrative, sometimes at the very beginning; and we find out about the crime (the past story) through the investigation (the present story). According to Todorov, as detective literature evolved, hard-boiled detective novels began emphasizing the crime as much as the investigation. Other evolving categories of detective fiction—to different degrees and in different configurations—fused the two stories to the point where the story of the crime became the central story and took place in the present, rather than the past.

The emphasis on sensation was accompanied by the increased suppression of the story of the investigation, often with the detective replaced completely by the suspect-victim who was forced to take on the detective function.[4] Noted director of suspense thrillers Claude Chabrol notes much the same thing when he asks rather guiltily: "Is it then not a little dishonest to only see the future of the detective film in the diminishing of the detective element in the films, because, in pushing this to its paradox, one may easily conceive an ideal future in the pure and simple suppression of this element?"[5]

Indeed, it is possible to relate the ascendancy of the suspense thriller to the waning of the detective film. The milieu of the classical detective was a pseudo-Victorian or civilized society; the hard-boiled detective was—even in the forties—a purposive anachronism to the corrupt society about him. By the seventies, detective works in the cinema were often done as period pieces (such as *Murder on the Orient Express* or *Farewell, My Lovely*); if a work did have a contemporary setting, the work often seemed particularly fictional or nostalgic (such as the television series *Moonlighting* or the film *The Mirror Crack'd*). Occasionally, if a work took advantage of a contemporary setting, its appeal derived from the self-conscious anachronistic relationship between the genre and the culture: the sturdy private investigator played by Humphrey Bogart in *The Big Sleep* was replaced by the old and ill gumshoe played by Art Carney in *The Late Show*. Even a pseudo-classical detective television series like *Columbo* eschewed the traditional whodunit/mystery structure and placed an almost equal emphasis on the murderer, who is immediately revealed near the beginning of each episode.[6]

Perhaps only in the seventies and eighties on American television has a truly contemporary film detective evolved, climaxing in the Reagan years with a variety of good-natured private investigators like *Magnum, P.I.* and *Simon and Simon*, detectives who, unlike their traditional hard-boiled antecedents, spend as much time devoting themselves to leisure activities—that is, participating in athletics, taking vacations, enjoying friendships, and pursuing a funky, laid-back lifestyle—as actually investigating.[7]

Another difference between those genres on the left of the triangle's apex and those on the right relates to the concept of *process*. In a detective film, the narrative follows the process of the detective's job, which is his or her investigation. In the caper film, the narrative follows the process of the members of the gang doing their communal jobs. Even in the gangster film, the narrative, in its presentation of the gangster's rise and fall, follows the process of the gangster's work: that is, his racketeering and professional crime.

These genres on the left of the triangle should not be called thrillers, but if critics insist on occasionally doing so, they should be aware that these genres are more "process thrillers" than "suspense thrillers." The suspense thrillers on the right of the triangle's apex work very differently: the protagonists in these genres generally find themselves in a new situation and cannot blithely follow the professional processes of their jobs. The concept of process is replaced by that of suspense, because we do not know whether or how a protagonist will rise to accept a challenge; much of a suspense thriller often deals with the indecision and problems facing a protagonist before he or she fully accepts the confrontation (for example, Dustin Hoffman's David in *Straw Dogs*, John Garfield's Frank in *The Postman Always Rings Twice*, or Cary Grant's Roger Thornhill in *North by Northwest*). Fighting evil is *Dirty Harry*'s job; it is not a personal test of courage or rite of passage the way it is for the respective protagonists in *Wait Until Dark*, *North by Northwest*, or *Z*.

Earlier I suggested that a difference between the genres on the left and right sides of the triangle was in their whole orientation to an ethic or a morality—that the "process thrillers" tended to present some distinct moral ethic (such as respect for justice, law and order, professionalism, personal integrity, or social communion) as a consistent value from beginning to end, whereas the suspense thrillers tend to examine and investigate an existing morality or individual commitment to a new code, arriving at some final position by the end.

Because the passions of the murderers are generally seen as deriving from their social situation, the thriller of murderous passions generally ends by implicitly questioning the social order; films such as *La Femme Infidèle* and *Crack in the Mirror* implicate bourgeois society in part by their ambiguous and disturbing endings in which the intervention of the social system does not satisfactorily resolve central issues raised by the films. The political thriller often chronicles the gradual evolution of an uncommitted protagonist toward a radical moral position which places him or her in direct opposition to the dominant moral position of his or her society. The psychotraumatic thriller, in its projection of the protagonist as simultaneously victim and criminal, implies the absolute difficulty with which we distinguish between good and evil. The innocent-on-the-run thriller invariably ends with the protagonist coming around to a new moral position as a result of his or her adventures. The thriller of acquired identity represents the protagonist's search for values—generally beginning with his or her rejection of the values from about and within. The thriller of moral confrontation, particularly interestingly after its initial and overt set-up of two opposite poles of good and evil, proceeds to emphasize the relationship and bondings between these values as the protagonist eventually embraces, out of necessity, some of the antagonist's methods and loses irrevocably (as do the protagonists in *Straw Dogs* and *Shadow of a Doubt)* the innocent self presented at the beginning of the film.

The second part of this book completely embraces the terminology put forward in this chapter and examines, film by film, the works in the various suspense thriller genres which have been articulated. Aside from the initial classification, the films are chronologically ordered so the reader may see—even in this limited historical sampling—some typical progressions and developments. The analysis attempts to detail the themes, narrative structures, conventions, types, and icons typical to each particular genre. I hope the close readings of the major films, based primarily on simple description, will help to demonstrate the films' relationships to the archetype outlined at the beginning of each of the following chapters. Although many of the most notable suspense thrillers have been directed by distinguished artists such as Alfred Hitchcock, Claude Chabrol, Costa-Gavras, and John Frankenheimer, I have tried not to allow the language of authorship to completely supplant that of genre. A final chapter will deal with the potential inclusion of certain horror films, the elaboration of a number of other suspense thriller subgenres, and a suggestion of areas for further research. And now: the films.

Part II

Different Kinds of Thrillers

5
The Thriller of Murderous Passions

William Hurt, as Ned Racine in *Body Heat,* is a somewhat sleazy and second-rate lawyer, but not without a certain charm. As he walks along the beachfront boardwalk, he sees her: a beautiful woman standing languidly and smoking a cigarette as she looks at the ocean, her white dress rustling in the nighttime breeze.

"You can stand there with me if you want," says Ned, "but you'll have to agree not to talk about the heat."

Kathleen Turner, as the woman, gives him a slow once-over.

"I'm a married woman."

"Meaning what?"

"Meaning I'm not looking for company."

"Then maybe you should have said, 'I'm a happily married woman.'"

"That's my business."

"What?"

"How happy I am."

"And how happy is that?"

"You're not too smart, are you?" she says and then pauses briefly; "I like that in a man."

She knows, even in that instant, that although he may not be smart, he will do anything for her. And he knows, at that instant, that he is caught. . . .

The thriller of murderous passions is organized around the triangular grouping of husband/wife/lover. The central scene is generally the murder of one member of the triangle by one or both of the other members. The emphasis is clearly on the criminal protagonist who is implicitly presented as an almost predestined representative of his or her social class (whether high or low) and who therefore provokes our sympathy, if not our empathy. The criminal motive is generally passion or greed; when the murderer is brought to justice, it is usually as a result of his or her own guilt, error, or a betrayal, rather than as a result of the sleuthing of a detective figure, who, if appearing at all, is generally relegated to a clearly subsidiary role.

Certain thematic ideas which are integrated in this generic structure again and again include (1) a view that human relationships are marked by power struggles and fruitless journeys from one unbearable situation to another, (2) the nearness of violence, (3) a view of women as controlling and often sinful, (4) a view of crime as symptomatic of the fissures beneath the surface of bourgeois, capitalist society, (5) human enslavement to sexual needs, (6) the inevitability of the dictum that "each man kills the thing he loves," and (7) an ironic view of fate and retribution.

More specifically, these films tend to proceed along the following lines: the introduction of the three primary characters and their triangular relationship; the contemplation of a murder plot; often, a failed murder attempt; a successful murder of one of the three characters; the arising of complications—such as blackmail or police investigations, which prevent the happiness of the two remaining characters; a subsequent onslaught of guilt, recriminations, or betrayals, occasionally accompanied by further murderous plots, climaxing with the final meting out of an ironic justice in which the surviving characters are always separated by a combination of death or incarceration.

A list of thrillers of murderous passion would include the following:

Double Indemnity (1944)
The Postman Always Rings Twice (1946)
Lady from Shanghai (1948)
Niagara (1953)
What Price Murder (1958)
Frantic (Elevator to the Scaffold) (1959)
Back to the Wall (1959)
Portrait in Black (1960)
L'Avventura (1960)
Crack in the Mirror (1960)
Ophélia (1962)
Knife in the Water (1963)
Les Biches (1968)
La Femme Infidèle (1968)
The Honeymoon Killers (1970)
Just Before Nightfall (1971)
Ten Days' Wonder (1972)
Double Indemnity (1973)
Wedding in Blood (1974)
A Piece of Pleasure (1976)
Body Heat (1981)
The Postman Always Rings Twice (1981)
Blood Simple (1984)
Dance with a Stranger (1984)
Fatal Attraction (1987)

These films can also be recognized by the presence of various other elements: scenes of passion; a beautiful, generally self-possessed woman; characters that may be clever, but not intelligent; a particular home which serves as the principal location; a blackmail letter, often unsigned; a funeral, sometimes attended by police; insurance schemes; dialogue with much subtext; secrets and plotting; a submissive male protagonist; extramarital affairs; automobile accidents; faked murders or suicides; and objects which turn on and incriminate the murderer(s).

In a psychoanalytic perspective using Michael Balint's terminology, the typical thriller of murderous passions presents a passionate couple who are philobatic criminals. Products of a repressive and ocnophilic society, they are unable to fit in; their crimes against society grow until they commit murder with the help of some ocnophilic object. The ocnophilic object turns on the protagonist, reverting its allegiance to the ocnophilic society, which is able to establish revenge by either killing or incarcerating the philobatic criminals. The most ironic and disturbing aspect of this psychoanalytic profile is that the philobatic criminals are never able to articulate their specific and justified hostilities toward the ocnophilic society, and thus, although attempting to overthrow that society with their crime, they nevertheless exhibit no profound understanding of the forces responsible for their own psyches or the social system around them, and often find themselves therefore attempting to replicate, through acquisition, the ocnophilic values around them.

A twentieth-century prototype for the thriller of murderous passions is the actual crime of Ruth Snyder and Judd Gray in 1927. Ruth Snyder had tried unsuccessfully on numerous occasions to murder her husband, partly because she wanted to get out of a marriage she was finding increasingly unbearable, and partly because she wanted to collect his insurance money. Albert Snyder, both dumb and dull, never realized that his wife was actually behind his rather frequent "accidents." After taking the corset salesman Judd Gray as her lover, she convinced Gray to help her in yet another murder attempt. On March 20th, they killed Albert Snyder by bludgeoning him with a weight, covering his mouth and nose with chloroform-soaked cotton, and finally tying and strangling him with picture wire. Although the two tried to make the crime look like a robbery by having Gray tie Ruth up as well, the police quickly saw through their plot. Once in custody, each turned on the other and denied primary responsibility. Both were sentenced to death; and on January 12, 1928, Ruth Snyder became the third woman to be executed in the electric chair.

The Ruth Snyder case must have certainly appealed to James M. Cain; although a writer in the hard-boiled tradition of Dashiell Hammett and Raymond Chandler, Cain seemed more interested in the criminal rather than in the detective. Two Ruth Snyder–influenced thrillers of murderous passions—*Double Indemnity* (1944) and *The Postman Always Rings Twice* (1946)—are based on his novels. *Double Indemnity* was directed by Billy Wilder and starred Barbara Stanwyck as the *femme fatale* who manipulates Fred MacMurray into killing her husband so they can collect on an insurance policy. Much the same plot is used in *The Postman Always Rings Twice*, directed by Tay Garnett, with the respective roles being taken by Lana Turner and John Garfield.

The Postman Always Rings Twice begins with narration by Frank Chambers (played by Garfield), which gives to the film an overwhelming sense of fate; the spectator familiar with *film noir* conventions will expect the protagonist to come to no good end. Frank meets Cora (played by Lana Turner) when he arrives at the café that is run by her and her older,

Sexual passion in *The Postman Always Rings Twice:* Lana Turner is first introduced as a pair of legs, and John Garfield is attracted to her like a moth to a flame. At bottom: Garfield and Turner watch while her murdered husband and his car crash into a ravine.

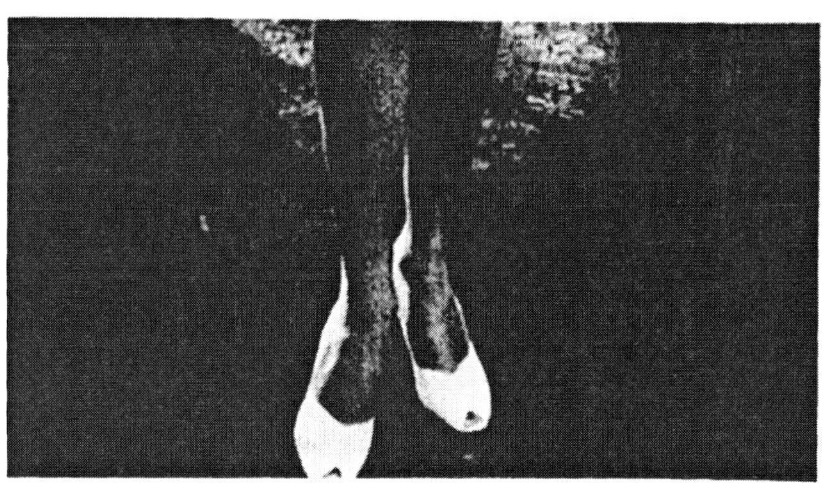

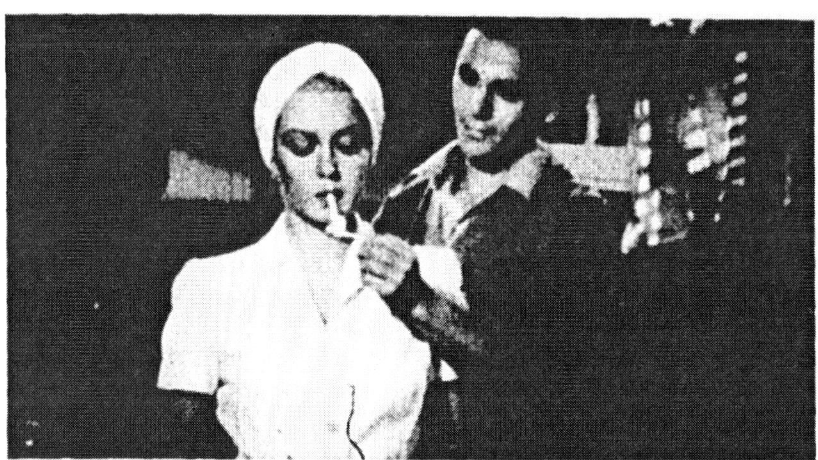

buffoonish husband Nick (played by Cecil Kellaway). Frank is instantly attracted to the sultry Cora; his passion is first juxtaposed with a burning hamburger on the grill, then with the burning "Man Wanted" sign. At one point in the film, Cora runs away with Frank on foot—but when they can't get a ride and she gets dirty, a discouraged Cora returns to the café; although she wants Frank, she also wants the good things in life.

When the two of them see a drunken Nick almost get hit by a truck, Frank has the beginnings of an idea. But it is (of course) the *femme fatale* Cora who explicitly proposes later that they kill him. Their plan is to kill Nick while he is taking a bath; the murder attempt is suspenseful because we know what is supposed to happen. Cora is to go in the bathroom, knock Nick unconscious with a makeshift blackjack made out of a bag of ball bearings, hold him under the water until he drowns, climb out the bathroom window and down a ladder to where Frank is waiting to get rid of the blackjack, and then wait quietly in the kitchen until the bathtub water begins dripping through the ceiling. Just as Cora is about to go in the bathroom, a cop sees the ladder and strikes up a conversation with Frank. Unable to signal to Cora, Frank tries desperately to get the cop to leave before a wet (and potentially bloody) Cora climbs down the ladder.

After the cop finally leaves, a cat climbs to the top of the ladder and steps on the electric wire; Cora screams as all the lights in the house are extinguished. Although she had knocked her husband unconscious, she had not had time to drown him. Frank and Cora quickly abort their plan, afraid that if Nick were to die now, the cop might figure out why the ladder had been leaning against the house. The husband does survive, and like Ruth Snyder's naive husband, believes his wife's nonsensical explanation of his "accident."

Inevitably, Frank and Cora try again, this time successfully. While driving in the car, Frank hits Nick over the head with a bottle; he and Cora then push the car over a cliff. (Perhaps in *hommage,* Chabrol uses a similar scene in his "upperclass" remake, *Wedding in Blood).* The police, however, suspect a murder plot and arrest both of them. Like Ruth Snyder and Judd Gray, Cora and Frank each turn on the other: Frank is manipulated by the D.A. into signing a complaint against Cora, and Cora makes a full confession of their crimes to a man who fortunately turns out to be a colleague of her own defense attorney. Surprisingly, the defense attorney manages to get them both off. Returned to the café, Cora expands it into a beer garden which becomes a huge success because it attracts all the curiosity-seekers anxious to see the cold-blooded murderer.

The emotional climax of the film takes place after Frank and Cora have dealt with various "problems," including the blackmail attempt so typical to the genre. Cora tells Frank that she is pregnant and speculates that it may be a way of atoning for her crime. Despite their hard-boiled context, Frank and Cora are like the characters in later Chabrol and experience persistent

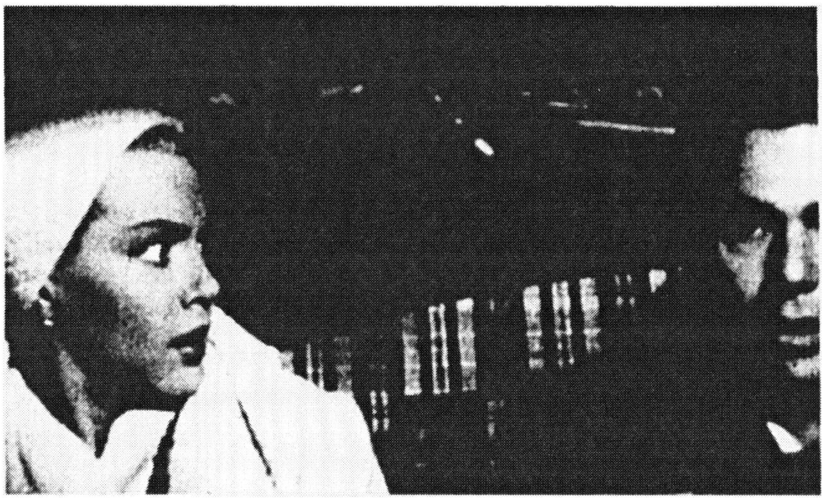

Day and night in *The Postman Always Rings Twice:* In the first still, the archetypal diner where the film is set appears sunny and mundane. In the second still, the roads appear dark and treacherous as intrigue and recrimination envelop the lovers.

guilt. Because Cora is uncertain of Frank's feelings for her, she takes him out to the ocean and has the two of them swim out so far that they can barely make it back. Far out in the water, she tells him that he can leave her to die if he doesn't trust her. Frank refuses to leave her and manages, in a suspenseful scene, to bring her back in to the shore. Their love is now proven, all obstacles have been overcome, and they are deliriously happy—which, of course, means that it is time for the just fate so typical to the genre to intervene.

As a result of a sudden car accident, Cora is killed and Frank is sent to prison for her "murder." The voice-over narration which began the film is now revealed as Frank's confession to a priest as he prepares to go to the gas chamber for the murder of Cora—the whole film having been a flashback. "The postman always rings twice," says Frank. "You may wait by the door, but even if you're in the backyard, you always hear him the second time." The original triangle is now completely destroyed, as its final member prepares for death.

Not surprisingly, the generic concept of duality, emphasized so clearly in the film's title, is manifested throughout the film. Each of the major characters has two primary brushes with death, in each case, the postman returning successfully: Cora first going on trial and almost going to the gas chamber, only to be rightfully punished in the car accident; her husband Nick almost dying in the bathtub and then being killed in the automobile; and of course, Frank, who is spared the gas chamber for the husband's death, only to be given it for Cora's. This duality extends even to seemingly incidental elements of the film, such as the naming of the café "Twin Oaks."

The Lady from Shanghai, directed by Orson Welles in 1948, is a more complicated thriller of murderous passions in that the traditional triangle is amended by the addition of a relatively unimportant fourth character who takes on the untoward fate usually accorded the male protagonist. Michael, the would-be lover in *The Lady from Shanghai*, is played by Orson Welles himself, who falls in love with Elsa Bannister, played by Rita Hayworth, the *femme fatale* who is married to a rich lawyer who no longer makes her happy. From almost the beginning of the film, Michael expresses understanding of the traditional generic outcome of such triangles. "I don't like a girlfriend to have a husband," he says. "If she'll fool him, chances are she'll fool me." And of course, that is precisely what Elsa attempts to do.

Much has been written about Welles' role in turning Hayworth, his wife at the time, into a villainous *femme fatale* with boyishly short hair; yet, this misogyny seems more implicit in the various thriller genres than in the personality of Welles. Indeed, most of the thrillers of murderous passions of the forties and fifties portray the central female of the triangle as duplicitous, if not absolutely evil. If Hayworth as Elsa seems any more evil than the typical genre heroine, it is because in *The Lady from Shanghai* her evil nature is not revealed until the climax of the film, at which point it seems all the more horrifyingly monstrous, and because Michael, the character played by Orson Welles, is, quite uncharacteristically to the genre, given a moral dimension that allows him to be superior to all those around him.

The moral distinction between Michael and Elsa is perhaps best made in the climactic scene in which Michael calls Elsa the murderer, and she is photographed showing absolutely no expression at all: a neutral, beautiful mask. Later, while dying, Elsa repeats the sentiment that "one follows his nature in the end." Filled with revulsion, Michael retorts moralistically, "Haven't you found anything better to follow?" and then walks away—leaving Elsa to die alone. The basic triangular structure of *Lady from Shanghai* is elaborated through at least two famous set-pieces: one, a love scene of sorts between Elsa and Michael in an aquarium amidst images of squid and octopus (a scene which, incidentally, reiterates the prophetic metaphor inherent in Michael's earlier anecdote about sharks eating each other); and the other, the famous climax in which the three protagonists (husband/wife/lover) find themselves in an amusement park funhouse of mirrors, and the husband, played by Everett Sloane, and Elsa destroy each other, shattering all the mirrors and venemous reflections in front of the fundamentally innocent Michael.

A film like *Niagara*, directed by Henry Hathaway in 1953, reveals the decreasing importance of *film noir* sensibilities in the way that the narrative juxtaposes its destructive passionate triangle (of George Loomis, Rose Loomis, and Rose's lover) with the theoretically good marriage (of Ray and Polly Cutler). The Loomises are played by Joseph Cotten and Marilyn Monroe; the Cutlers are played by Jean Peters and Casey Adams. Because Ray Cutler is portrayed so goonishly with a yuk-yuk laugh and insensitive manner, the marriage of Polly Cutler seems not only less interesting than the passionate marriage of Rose Loomis, but not particularly valuable—at least not by today's standards. Part of the de-emphasis of Ray Cutler is, of course, purposive; had the part been played by a Rock Hudson rather than a Casey Adams, the spectator would not sympathize quite so clearly with the murderous Joseph Cotten, who is made attractive in a romantic, self-destructive way.

Perhaps because of *Niagara's* "happy" ending, it becomes one of those Hollywood films which implicitly and unconsciously seems to criticize its own ideology; after all the members of the passionate triangle are destroyed, Polly's reunion with her goonish husband is (at least to this writer) quite disturbing. In any case, Marilyn Monroe is an electrifying *femme fatale* as she walks in a pink dress amidst the Niagara Falls visitors dressed predominately in blues and grays. As usual in a suspense thriller, we are given more information than the characters and quite early find out that Rose and her lover plan on killing George. The attempt backfires, and George kills Rose's lover instead. At this point, an emotionally disturbed George decides to kill Rose as well. There is an extended suspense sequence in which George returns to the cabin and approaches the covered shape in his wife's bed, not realizing it is really Polly Cutler, who has been given the cabin by the management. Will George mistake the shape for his wife?

Later there is another suspenseful sequence in which a fearful Polly in a yellow raincoat runs away from George, who is dressed in black. This sequence has a parallel when Rose as well runs away from George. Like Polly, Rose is shown running up stairs, although this time, the stairs are inside and lead to the bell tower, which suggests that she is surrounded, trapped, doomed. At the moment that George strangles her, there is a montage of the still bells; then an overhead shot of Rose dressed in black, lying motionless against the blue steps. The montage of the still bells is absolutely apposite in that it works to complete a doubling: earlier when Rose's lover was to kill George, a certain song on the bells was to signify his death; thus, the silence now signifies hers. Even though he kills his wife, George's last words to her emphasize his passion: "I loved you, Rose, you know that."

George's attempts to escape the police inadvertently involve Polly. At the film's climax when the boat he is taking goes over the falls (and of course, in a suspense thriller called *Niagara*, we inherently expect this scene from the very beginning), George manages to save Polly in the nick of time, turning himself into a martyr as he plunges to his death. Thus, with the complete destruction of the murderous triangle, Polly can be safely reunited with her secure husband; their rather comic marriage can now continue unsuspensefully, with, most strangely of all, Polly undergoing not the slightest change as a result of her innocent involvement in this murderous intrigue.

The late fifties saw the emergence in France of a number of financially successful thrillers of murderous passions. The French had always been remarkably sensitive to American genre; indeed, they had virtually discovered Edgar Allan Poe, the acknowledged father of the popular work of crime and mystery. The New Wave directors in particular admired the thrillers of murderous passions because of these films' association with *film noir*. And of course a great number of *films noirs* which I do not discuss here—films like *Out of the Past* (1947) and *Criss Cross* (1949), with their protagonists involved in a murder and with a *femme fatale*—are very closely related to these thrillers. The French also worshipped Hitchcock, but it is interesting to note that although Hitchcock worked in a variety of thriller genres, he by and large avoided making thrillers of murderous passions. Was sexual infidelity, for this profoundly Catholic artist, taboo? Or was it, rather, that by the late forties, Hitchcock had developed an antipathy for the lower or working class characters that tended to populate such films?

The closest Hitchcock came to making a thriller of murderous passions was *Notorious*, which he directed in 1946. *Notorious* presents a romantic triangle between Alicia Huberman (played by Ingrid Bergman), her husband Sebastian (played by Claude Rains), and her lover Devlin (played by the dashing and attractive Cary Grant). What makes *Notorious* different from the typical triangular thriller is that Devlin and Alicia fall in love *before* her marriage to Sebastian. In fact, it is the lover who urges the marriage (unlike the typical thriller, in which the lover urges the marriage's dissolution). In *Notorious,* Devlin wants Alicia to pass on to him information about Sebastian, who is a Nazi spy. When Sebastian finds out about Devlin, Sebastian—despite his profound love, almost *amour fou* for his wife—tries to kill her. Although it is Sebastian who is betrayed, Alicia and Devlin garner audience empathy. They succeed in manipulating events so that it will be her husband who will be killed—and not at their hands. Thus, the film has a rather nasty and ambiguous moral dimension and ends with the lovers reunited, not criminals to their society, but heroes in its service.

The confluence of thrillers of murderous passions, *films noirs,* and Hitchcock's *Notorious,* had a great effect on French filmmakers. Doubtless one could profitably trace a history of French suspense thrillers in the late fifties and sixties; they were numerous. This listing is inevitably limited to those representative few which had a significant amount of American distribution, including *What Price Murder (Une Manche et la Belle),* directed by French veteran Henri Verneuil in 1958; *Back to the Wall (Le Dos au Mur),* directed by the New Wave director Edouard Molinaro in 1959; and *Frantic (Ascenseur pour l'Echafaud),* directed by New Wave director Louis Malle in 1958. Each of these films deals with a different variation of the murderous triangle. In *What Price Murder,* a husband and his mistress plot to do away with his wife. After the deed is done, the *femme fatale* mistress (played by Mylène Demongeot) betrays and shoots the husband. When she then returns to the scene of the second crime to retrieve her potentially incriminating purse, the dying husband manages to kill her; thus, the entire triangle is destroyed.

In *Frantic,* a wife (played by Jeanne Moreau) and her lover conspire to kill her husband. Although the murder is successful, fate conspires against them in a series of coincidences; the film ends with the lover in jail and the wife's arrest imminent. In *Back to the Wall,* a husband discovers that his wife (again played by Jeanne Moreau) has taken a lover; he revenges himself by arranging events so that his wife mistakenly believes that her lover is secretly blackmailing her. Increasingly distraught, the wife herself eventually kills her lover. When she finally finds out the truth, she commits suicide, but not before sending word to the police that it was her husband who was responsible for the murder.

American films of the same period include *Portrait in Black,* directed in 1960 by Michael Gordon, and *Crack in the Mirror,* directed that same year by Richard Fleischer. In *Portrait in Black,* as in *The Postman Always Rings Twice,* Lana Turner plays a woman with a lover who wants to get rid of her husband—the husband played by Lloyd Nolan, the lover by Anthony Quinn. Although the wife and lover do successfully kill her husband, complications ensue as the lover experiences guilt, the wife begins receiving blackmail letters, and the wife's daughter discovers the plot. After a climax of recriminations and betrayals, the lover falls to his death while trying to kill the wife's daughter in order to silence her. With both men of the triangle killed, the wife waits quietly for the arrival of the police and her own punishment.

If *Portrait in Black* impresses as a typical studio product, *Crack in the Mirror* impresses as both more sophisticated and compelling—in part because there are two murderous triangles: the characters in one are of the lower class and live in a Parisian slum; the characters in the other are of the upper class and inhabit the highest stratum of Parisian society. In one sense, the combination of both classes within one film makes it possible to view *Crack in the Mirror* as a kind of transition between the forties and fifties *films noirs* and the glossy color melodramas of the sixties and seventies—particularly those of Chabrol. The parallel triangles are emphasized by the fact that the three primary actors all take corresponding double roles; indeed, *Crack in the Mirror* opens with a credit sequence in which spinning mirrors reveal the members of the cast in their dual identities: Orson Welles plays the lowerclass cuckold Emile Hagolin and the upperclass cuckold Lamorciere; Juliette Greco plays the lowerclass murderer Eponine Mercadier and the upperclass, modern *femme fatale* Florence; and Bradford Dillman plays the lowerclass lover Robert Larnier and the upperclass lover Claude Lancastre.

The first major sequences present the passionate eruption that results in the lowerclass triangle when Eponine decides to kill her old and unattractive lover because of her passion for her young lover, Larnier. Violently, Eponine beats her old lover with an iron bar, and then she and Larnier strangle him with a scarf. "Who would have thought the old man was so strong!" says Larnier, in a reference to *Macbeth* which works perhaps to help the spectator impute central culpability. Eponine is a Lady Macbeth, who, if not responsible herself for the actual act that took Hagolin's life, is certainly morally and calculatingly responsible. Indeed, it is Eponine who is able later to cut Hagolin's body into pieces in order to dispose of it.

As the upperclass triangle is elaborated, we discover that the relationships among these characters correspond precisely to those among the lowerclass triangle. Although Florence had been the constant lover of the older, established attorney Lamorciere, she has now taken up with his younger assistant, Claude Lancastre. Lamorciere himself describes his deceased lowerclass alter ego as "the old lover she wanted to replace with a young lover." In the upperclass triangle there is no overt murder plot, although there is the same competition between the men. When the two lowerclass murderers are arrested, they each turn on the other (again, like Ruth Snyder and Judd Gray) and disavow primary responsibility. The ambitious Claude wants to make his reputation and defend Eponine on his own; when he spurns Lamorciere's assistance, Lamorciere signs on to defend Robert Larnier. Thus, Claude finds himself defending Eponine, even though he himself corresponds to her lover, Larnier; and Lamorciere finds himself defending Larnier, even though he is most sympathetic to the victim, Hagolin. The two lawyers now find themselves in a potentially antagonistic legal situation as well.

There is much suspense as to how the parallel plots will resolve themselves. Will both of the murderers go to prison, or will one of them be let off? And if the lowerclass cuckold was killed by the plottings of the woman and her lover, will a similar fate befall the established attorney Lamorciere? The plot parallels in *Crack in the Mirror* are, therefore, consistently compelling; often the transitions between the simultaneous narratives are purposely confounding as if to emphasize the relevance of any action to either triangle.

On the day of the murderers' trial, there is a sequence of the five (surviving) characters all looking in various mirrors to check their appearances before entering the courtroom. The upperclass Florence goes to the trial primarily because she wants to see the woman with whom she finds herself increasingly empathizing. Once in the courtroom, Eponine and Robert Larnier betray each other as they go their separate ways legally, as later, in a less melodramatic way, their upperclass counterparts Florence and Claude will betray each other as they go their separate ways literally. When Lamorciere attacks Eponine for sleeping with both men—one for love, the other for money—the camera dollies in to a close-up of Florence, who is watching intently.

The climax of the upperclass plot takes place during a recess in the trial: in a wide angle shot employing deep focus, Florence and Claude embrace in the foreground, while Lamorciere comes up a stairway in the background and sees them together. The shock of discovering that his mistress Florence, like the woman on trial for murder, has been deceitful and unfaithful, so outrages and inspires Lamorciere that he is able to overwhelm the court with a bravura attack on Eponine that emphasizes the dead man in the lowerclass triangle, with whom he now completely empathizes. Through his attack on Eponine, Lamorciere succeeds also in humiliating his rival Claude. Ultimately, Eponine receives life imprisonment, while Robert Lanier receives only six years in prison.

Incensed at what Claude perceives as Lamorciere's lack of integrity in attacking Claude's own client, Claude loudly berates Lamorciere. We see Lamorciere's reflection in a mirror; the mirror image shakes, and we see Lamorciere falling dead of a heart attack—the upperclass triangle finally being shattered by the death which was inevitable if the dual structures so consistent to the suspense thriller were to be followed. Eponine and Robert Larnier are taken to prison. Their upperclass counterparts, Florence and Claude, sit on a park bench. Florence, feeling guilty over her role in Lamorciere's death, wants to be left alone. Claude goes off in one direction; after a moment, Florence goes off in another. Thus, the formal structure is now

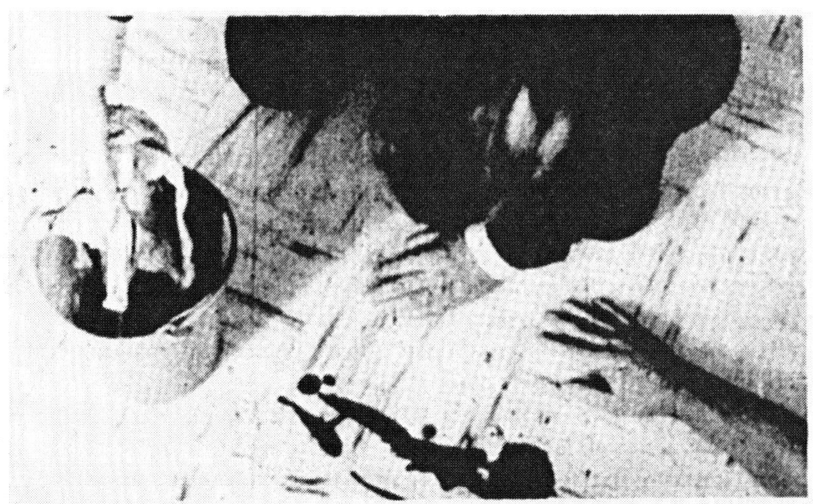

Claude Chabrol's characteristic use of Hitchcockian *hommage* in *La Femme Infidèle:* Michel Bouquet cleans up the blood after having killed his wife's lover—a scene which strongly resembles a parallel Anthony Perkins scene in *Psycho.*

complete: in each triangle, the cuckold has been killed, and the once passionate lovers have become alienated from each other.

Except perhaps for Alfred Hitchcock (about whom much shall be written in subsequent chapters), there may be no director whose work so consistently expresses a commitment to the various genres of the suspense thriller as Claude Chabrol. His films include thrillers of moral confrontation (*Le Boucher* and *La Rupture*), political thrillers (*Nada*), and of course, thrillers of murderous passions. It is clear that Chabrol is consciously aware of the generic ties among all his films: most of them star his wife, Stéphane Audran, and even repeat the same names for corresponding characters from film to film (the love relationship of an Hélène and a Charles is generally disrupted by a Paul).

Chabrol's films since *La Femme Infidèle* have often been criticized for their obvious relationship to the films and temperament of Alred Hitchcock (particularly by American critics, who often disapprove of the suspense thriller in general). Significantly, while both Hitchcock and Chabrol have worked in many genres of the suspense thriller, Hitchcock has never been especially interested in the triangular relationship of husband/wife/lover, which is Chabrol's primary interest. Chabrol does not merely re-create Hitchcock; like Hitchcock, he develops ideas and images in the genre which is amenable to his own *Weltanschauung.* The suspense thriller provides the framework for an examination of the psychopathology of murder and passion.

While murder is always a violent act, for Chabrol it is rarely an act associated with thugs, but with the bourgeoisie. The violence in Chabrol's films is always initially repressed, lurking beneath the respectable veneer of upperclass society, almost unnoticed by the eye seduced by the rich decor, the perfectly-formed flowers in the vase on the breakfast tablecloth, and the stylish high-fashion walk of Stéphane Audran. Chabrol's suspense thrillers are all carefully photographed films: the colors controlled, the camera movements elegant and precise. Indeed, he has often been attacked for a kind of formalism because of his overt interest in decor and structure. To me, Chabrol's interest in style reflects no more than his mastery of the language of cinema; his films represent a kind of art-house thriller, synthesizing a self-conscious style, an intellectual sensibility, and suspenseful stories.

The importance of Chabrol to the development of the thriller of murderous passions cannot, I think, be overestimated, for his films consistently push outward the genre's boundaries. Indeed, at least ten of Chabrol's films are explicitly constructed around the primary triangular relationship of wife/husband/lover, although in many of the earlier films, the emphasis is on a fourth character who is resentful of some aspect of the triangular relationship and whose intervention propels the plot. In *A Double Tour,* for instance, the husband's lover is killed not by his rather colorless wife, but by the son who feels his mother has been betrayed. In *L'Oeil du Malin,* a fourth party jealous of a wife's relationship with her husband discovers that the wife has a lover; by revealing that fact to the husband, the outsider is able to catalyze the husband's murder of his wife. *Ophélia,* directed in 1962, recognizes one source of the murderous triangle in *Hamlet* (through the characters of the deceased king, his queen Gertrude, and Claudius). *Ophélia* represents a rather elaborate modern variation with the Hamlet character (played by André Jocelyn, who also played the son in *A Double Tour*) out for revenge against his stepfather and mother, who he feels are responsible for the death of his father. The film ends with the stepfather taking poison—not because he is guilty, but because he wishes to escape the constant harassment and hell imposed by his stepson.

Two other Chabrol films—*Les Biches* and *Ten Days' Wonder*—represent variations on the traditional thriller of murderous passions. *Les Biches,* directed in 1968, presents a bisexual triangle composed of Jean-Louis Trintignant, Jacqueline Sassard, and Stéphane Audran—each of whom in the course of the film has a sexual relationship with the other two characters. The suspense in *Les Biches* builds unusually slowly; our knowledge of the genre allows us to anticipate some inevitable violence, and ultimately our expectations are not foiled. In *Ten Days' Wonder,* directed in 1972, the traditional triangular structure (in this case represented by husband, wife, and stepson-lover) is mediated by a character who represents the detective element. The visual style of *Ten Days' Wonder* is remarkably expressive: the colors are controlled and exuberant, the camera is continuously gliding and swooping. In one particularly

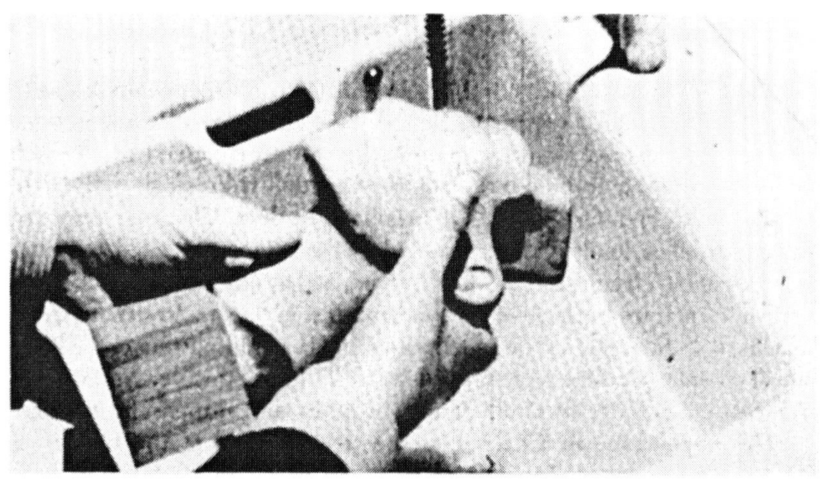

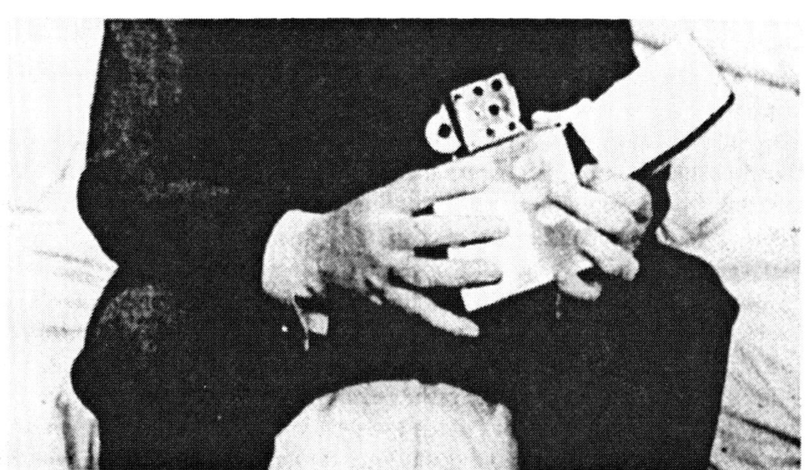

striking flashback, the wife and her stepson confess their love as they stroll along an unearthly clear lake which reflects trees and an upside down world. Like most thrillers of murderous passions, *Ten Days' Wonder* ends tragically, with Hélène killed and her husband and stepson committing suicide. If this film has more the temperament of a mystery than a suspense thriller, it is because much of the actual murderous plotting is kept from the spectator until the final sequence.

In this genre, the most consistent critical approval of Chabrol was accorded that series of films which began with *Les Biches* and *La Femme Infidèle* in 1968, and continued with *Just Before Nightfall (Juste Avant la Nuit)* in 1971, *Wedding in Blood (Les Noces Rouges)* in 1973, and *A Piece of Pleasure (Une Partie du Plaisir)* in 1976. In *La Femme Infidèle,* the husband (played by Michel Bouquet) kills the lover of his wife (played by Stéphane Audran); that the crime serves to renew the couple's love and their marriage can be seen as an evolution of the genre's typical attitude toward crime.

In the final shot of *La Femme Infidèle,* accompanied by Pierre Jansen's exquisite music, the camera subjectively reveals the point of view of the husband as he is being taken away by the police. The camera dollies away from the wife and child, but since the husband's love for them is increasingly strong, the camera simultaneously zooms in to a closer shot of the wife and child. The shot is thus beautiful and mysterious in the complex way it works as a stylistic culmination of the issues of passion, love, and grace examined so consistently within the film. If *La Femme Infidèle* is centrally evolutionary, it is because the recriminations and betrayals so typical to the genre have been most fascinatingly replaced with love and renewed commitment.

Other of Chabrol's suspense thrillers present variations. In *Wedding in Blood,* the wife (again played by Stéphane Audran) and her lover plot to do away with her husband. They kill him in a car accident similar to the one in *The Postman Always Rings Twice* and are finally brought to justice only by the intervention of the wife's daughter, who was merely trying to help the mother avoid any suspicion. Although this film ends with the wife and her lover about to be taken to prison, the final image is again a complex and ironic one which emphasizes the relationship between the two remaining characters of the murderous triangle: handcuffs join them together—their love greater than ever, their passion to be stifled indefinitely.

Just Before Nightfall may be Chabrol's most ironic thriller of murderous

Objects in Claude Chabrol's *La Femme Infidèle* take on symbolic dimensions in these frame enlargments: top, the statue used as the murder weapon represents Stéphane Audran's cool presence and indirect responsibility for the murder. Middle: the huge lighter held by the cuckold Michel Bouquet represents the sexual passion his wife has now given her lover. Bottom: her son's puzzle that Stéphane Audran struggles to complete represents the fragmentation of her marriage and family.

passions. In this film, a husband (played by Michel Bouquet) strangles his mistress in passion and confesses his crime to his wife (again played by Stéphane Audran). The wife forgives the husband, but the husband is unable to expiate his guilt. He confesses to his lover's husband, but even he is easily able to forgive the husband. The husband finally decides that he must go to the police and confess the whole murder publicly; his wife, in order to avoid the scandal, quietly poisons him, so that their respectable bourgeois appearance can remain intact.

In *A Piece of Pleasure,* more than in any of Chabrol's recent films, the thriller format which Chabrol has so unabashedly embraced is virtually elided; it becomes, rather, a repressed substructure which suggests that at any moment passions may erupt beyond the characters' control. Like the rest of these films, *A Piece of Pleasure* can be perceived as an extension of Chabrol's fascination with the triangle as well as of his interest in the dictum of Oscar Wilde: "Each man kills the thing he loves." In *A Piece of Pleasure,* there are two intersecting triangles: Philippe, Esther, and her lover Habib; Esther, Philippe, and his lover Sylvia.

From the very beginning, Chabrol's examination of the relationship between Philippe and Esther is at once psychologically unflinching, yet formal. The film begins with a sequence at the Ouessant Island beach, where their relationship seems relatively untroubled. The foghorn on the soundtrack (repeated later in the film in the parallel scene between Philippe and Sylvia) signals the beginning of the dissolution; the image of Philippe and Esther sitting placidly on their boat in a tumultuous sea works as a surprisingly direct symbol of the tenuousness of their relationship. Philippe may be a boorish character: he may insult his wife, correct her pronunciation, humiliate her in front of friends, and call her crazy, yet his love is absolute and obsessive, his confession of extramarital affairs more a product of ego rather than of any suppressed hatred. At the table, while eating and watching television, Philippe tells Esther that if she had an affair, he would kill her: he then suddenly reverses himself and urges her to have one. (Later in the film, after Philippe marries Sylvia, this scene, like the scene on the island, will also have a precise parallel.) When Esther, always the dutiful woman defined in the image of her man, does begin an affair, it becomes clear that the dominating Philippe was actually far more dependent on Esther than she was on him. The decay of their relationship is accompanied by a kind of flowering of Esther's resources.

Typically for Chabrol, the psychological violence is played against images of great beauty: characters are constantly framed against flowers or flowered wallpaper, flowered pillowcases, or flowered mattresses. Indeed, the flower motif remains constant even when the latent violence erupts and

The surprising beginning of *Just Before Nightfall* shows Michel Bouquet after having accidentally murdered his mistress in the heat of passion: now what?

the relationship of Esther and Philippe is irrevocably ended at the grave. The passing of time is another motif underscored again and again as Esther and Philippe's relationship evolves to the point of no return: the constantly ticking clock as they essay a reconciliation, the ticking of a metronome, the daughter's constant habit of counting aloud—three times stopped by Philippe, who is made nervous by it. Perhaps the film's most expressive sequence has Philippe trying a reconciliation with Esther: the camera watches in a very formal and slightly meandering long shot. The failure of their lovemaking to win back Esther for Philippe is made clear with a striking close-up of Esther's impassive face. The sequence ends with a graceful camera movement; the camera retreats through the crack in their doorway, reducing the image (and, by implication, their relationship) to a meager vertical slit, surrounded by darkness. The next time we see Esther and Philippe, they have permanently separated.

Ultimately, the tensions in the film explode: in a remarkable scene at the cemetery, in which Philippe, jealous of Esther's relationship with Habib and incensed that she is no longer able to love him, literally kicks her to death at a gravesite. The whole film can be seen as moving from the open spaces of the Ouessant Island beach and the walnut farm to the more crowded city and the restricted final image of the geometrically framed bars in Philippe's jail door, accompanied on the soundtrack by the voice of their little daughter continuing to count aloud, this time, up to 600 million. Philippe's love for Esther, obsessive and crazy, has reached the logical evolution of the Wilde dictum. The triangle is destroyed: Esther is gone, and Philippe is in jail, all the time in the world stretching out before him.

As usual for Chabrol, *A Piece of Pleasure* is filled with images and symbols which are often foregrounded—many of them of death and decay: the wax museum figure of Landru which seems to work as a foreshadowing device, the beautiful yet horrifying image of a spider consuming a ladybug, the image of Philippe covered by a windswept black veil, and, of course, the final images of the cemetery. "I believe in transcendence," says Philippe as he walks among the dead; yet unlike the husband who is taken away from his wife at the end of *La Femme Infidèle,* Philippe does not transcend; he has learned nothing. In one sense, it is Esther that cannot be killed and who transcends through the personality of her daughter, who, like her mother, can pronounce correctly neither the word *"chocolat"* nor *"pêches."* Shall the cycle never end: Can love exist and evolve naturally into a mutually beneficient equilibrium without the eruption of obsession and violence?

If Chabrol can be considered an art-house director with a surprisingly popular temperament, he is not the only art-house director who has turned to the thriller of murderous passions for inspiration. Other directors, like Michelangelo Antonioni or Roman Polanski, have used the genre's framework in the service of various intellectual or personal interests which

In the cerebral and theoretical *L'Avventura*, Monica Vitti and Gabriele Ferzetti search for their missing friend in a crowded ocnophilic environment (above) and a deserted philobatic environment (below).

the framework naturally supports. *L'Avventura*, for instance, directed in 1960, deals with three primary characters: Sandro, his mistress Anna, and a third woman, Claudia, with whom he enters into an affair. The (potential) triangle is generically attacked, but not by passion; nothing erupts, but Anna does mysteriously disappear. The other characters, particularly Sandro and Claudia, spend the rest of the film more or less searching for Anna—but since Antonioni is uninterested in "plot" in the traditional sense, no explanation of Anna's disappearance is ever given.

In a sense, a suspense thriller framework is used here precisely in order to show that it has no relevance to modern life, that modern man is too alienated to feel emotions strong or clear enough to precipitate the kind of murderous crises we generally associate with films constructed around triangular relationships. The characters, therefore, are fated not to discover the whereabouts of Anna, but to wander against bleak landscapes in various subtle degrees of despair, anxiety, guilt, and ennui. Other Antonioni films, particularly *Blowup* and *The Passenger,* show an even clearer relationship to the suspense thriller, and are discussed in more detail in subsequent chapters.

Roman Polanski's *Knife in the Water* is similar to *L'Avventura* in that although a suspense thriller, it has an art-house sensibility and almost no thrills whatsoever. To call *Knife in the Water* an art-house film is, on a very simplistic level, to relate it to a certain modern style in which dialogue is kept to a minimum, the spectator is constantly aware of the ambience and the volume of the intermittent sound effects, and the most minor actions seem portentous and symbolic. Because of *Knife in the Water*'s generic framework, there is the constant implication that thrills, in the form of murder or adultery, might at any point erupt. (Significantly, later films of Polanski, such as *Chinatown* and *Rosemary's Baby,* reveal explicitly his attraction to popular genres.)

The opening shot of *Knife in the Water* is that of a car windshield which alternately reflects the trees above and reveals the faces of the husband and wife who are driving to their sailboat for a weekend sail. We don't hear their dialogue at first, although it is clear they are arguing, and the man eventually takes the wheel from his wife, who remains impassive even when he kisses her on the neck. Almost immediately, the husband nearly hits a hitchhiker, who is standing in the middle of the road, refusing to move. Thus, from the very beginning of the film, Polanski presents his two major themes of violence and passion—both of which are so far explicitly repressed and are to remain so throughout most of the film.

The husband gives the young hitchhiker a ride, leaves him off at the beach, and then calls him back to invite him to accompany the two of them sailing. "I knew you'd call me back," says the boy, "You want to carry on the game." A competition develops between the two men. While the boy knows nothing about sailing, the husband is an expert sailor who claims that on any boat one man must always be the captain. The competition becomes increasingly ambiguous, and we are not really sure how to judge who is ahead. The husband claims that one must never whistle while on board; the boy breaks the rule, but then later on, so does the husband. Although the boy constantly criticizes the husband and his sailing methods, his criticisms are consistently false: at one point the boy burns his hands on the soup bowl when he doesn't follow instructions, at another point the boy's own rowing succeeds only in propelling the sailboat in circles. And yet, it is the husband whose error causes the boat to go aground in the shallows.

Much of the competition between the two men appears to be politically allegorical—with the husband representing the conservative, repressive, hard-line orientation, and the boy representing the freer, more liberal orientation. Significantly, when the husband, wife, and boy all play pick-up sticks, the game (an allegory for postwar Poland?) is easiest for the husband and hardest for the boy. Ultimately, it seems that the competition's victor will be rewarded with the sexual conquest of the wife. At one point, the sexual and political tensions seem almost to surface: the husband puts on earphones to listen to a fight, while his wife sings to the boy a song that can be interpreted as a comment on the basic lovelessness of her marriage as well as on the ennui of the film's social context.

If the husband seems to be the most consistent victor in the series of confrontations, the boy seems always to have a potential edge: the knife, which he opens to the accompaniment of an extraordinarily loud sound effect, and with which he plays constantly. The husband tries, without much success, to duplicate the tricky game with the knife, in which the boy rapidly and alternately strikes the blade between his outstretched fingers against the flat deck. Aware of the traditional theatrical dictum that one doesn't show the audience a gun in the first act unless it's going to be used in the third act, we expect that the knife will be eventually used; indeed, it even appears in the title. And yet, although the film is amazingly spare, with no more than three characters and few objects, there is only one camera movement into the knife. What will happen—will the boy eventually kill the husband? Will the husband take the knife and kill the boy? Will the wife show any emotion? Will the repressed violence in this film erupt at all?

At the film's climax, the husband provokes a confrontation, and the knife goes overboard. There is a scuffle; the boy goes overboard, as well, and disappears. After an unsuccessful search for the boy, the husband and wife argue. She calls her husband a murderer and sends him to swim for the police. After he leaves, the boy returns to the ship, for the first time alone with the wife; he had been hiding behind the buoy. The wife slaps the boy and tries to call her husband back, but he cannot hear her. "You're just like him, only half his age and more stupid," says the wife to the boy. "He was just like you, you want to be like him."

The two of them make love, but not particularly passionately. The boy leaves; when the wife returns the boat to the dock, she finds that her husband has not yet gone to the police and is waiting for her. She tells him that the boy is alive and that she was unfaithful. Her husband doesn't believe her and thinks she is just protecting him—for if the boy were alive, he wouldn't have to go to the police. In any case, he doesn't want to hear anything about her faithlessness, which he calls a joke. They stop the car at an intersection, and his wife reminds him that he never finished the story he had started earlier about a particular sailor. "I don't know what happened to him," responds the husband, in the film's last line of dialogue which as well refers to his own situation regarding the boy. The film ends with the image of their car in the middle of the intersection in the rain. One route leads to the police station, the other route leads back to their home. The ending is much like that of "The Lady or the Tiger." Which way will the husband go? What will he choose to believe?

Not only does *Knife in the Water* repress the usual violence promised by the thriller, but it ends its narrative with violence's opposite: a scene of total stasis, in which no action is perfectly acceptable to the husband protagonist. A film like *Knife in the Water* makes clear the remarkable range of the thriller of murderous passions: not limited to the sordid *films noirs* of the forties like *The Postman Always Rings Twice*, nor to the bright and polished thrillers of Claude Chabrol, the genre can even embrace those virtual antithrillers which select generic structures only in order to make clear the genre's basic incompatibility with certain aspects of contemporary life and the modern temperament.

As the American films of the forties and fifties influenced and inspired the New Wave thrillers of the sixties, so too did these art-house films inspire a variety of subsequent American films. *The Honeymoon Killers*, an independent film written and directed by Leonard Kastle in 1970, begins by stating that the "incredibly shocking drama you are about to see is perhaps the most bizarre episode in the annals of American crime." Based on the true story of Martha Beck and Raymond Fernandez, *The Honeymoon Killers* is a combination of *The Postman Always Rings Twice* and Chabrol's *Landru*. This low-budget, black-and-white film, made on location, has an urgency and attention to detail both perceptive and disturbing. Its story is that of a very fat and unattractive nurse who falls in love with a very oily Mediterranean man; the nurse becomes the man's lover, and, while posing as his sister, helps the man gruesomely murder a series of women he marries for their money.

As played by Shirley Stoler (who would later notably play the Nazi commandant in Lina Wertmüller's *Seven Beauties)*, Martha is a sullen, inexpressive, petty, unhappy woman, who loves passionately, if unwisely; as played by Tony Lo Bianco, Ray is a foppish, lying, ethnic stereotype. Their love affair is sordid and incredibly unromanticized, although director Kastle counterpoints the subject matter with an ironic soundtrack taken from Mahler. Perhaps only an independent film would have the audacity to present such an unabashedly unsympathetic portrait; indeed, the very girth of Shirley Stoler's protagonist stands as a kind of anomaly to decades of mainstream filmmaking in America.

One murder, which is presented particularly graphically, has Martha hitting a woman over the head with a hammer, and then allowing Ray to strangle her brutally. *The Honeymoon Killers* is quite remarkable for the milieu it observes and its unflinching portrayal of the emotionally disenfranchised. By the end of the film, after several triangular relationships, Martha ultimately betrays Ray, because she realizes that he has been sleeping with his various wives and thus betraying her. They both go to jail, stand trial, and are sentenced to death. In prison, Ray writes Martha a letter in which

Murderous passions: Jack Nicholson and Jessica Lange in the 1981 remake of *The Postman Always Rings Twice.*

he states that, "You are the only woman I will ever love—now and beyond the grave." The final image of the film shows Martha reading his letter while sitting under an American flag—an image which comments obliquely on the social context of their criminal activity.

By the 1980s, the American cinema, responding to the French celebration of American thrillers, had itself returned to forties forms. *The Postman Always Rings Twice* was itself remade by Bob Rafelson with Jack Nicholson and Jessica Lange. This remake—less romantic than the original—emphasized the seaminess of the stars' love scenes. *Against All Odds*, a remake of the *film noir Out of the Past*, constructed a significantly less complex narrative than its predecessor, but presented a woman who becomes involved in a triangular relationship with two lovers. In the film's final scene, the woman kills one of the men in the triangle before he can kill the other. If *Against All Odds* does not seem to have the sensibility of a thriller of murderous passions, it may be because the romantic triangle is overshadowed by the film's milieu of corruption in Los Angeles zoning policies. Even unlike the typical *film noir*, *Against All Odds* presents a woman who, though she may attract evil, is actually morally superior to the men around her.

Against All Odds was an unsuccessful attempt to duplicate the commercial and critical success of *Body Heat*, the film directed and written by Lawrence Kasdan in 1981, which worked definitively to redefine *film noir* (if in color) to the American audience and provide an extremely powerful thriller of murderous passions. *Body Heat* marked the impressive debut of Kathleen Turner starring as *femme fatale* Matty Walker opposite William Hurt's Ned Racine; together, Turner and Hurt provide a steamy team which rivals the original pairings of Stanwyck and MacMurray in *Double Indemnity* and Turner and Garfield in *The Postman Always Rings Twice*. *Body Heat* is a film in absolute control: from the striking cinematography which is dark and atmospheric, in the best *film noir* tradition, yet in color, with touches of red as violent punctuation, to the carefully constructed narrative. I feel certain *Body Heat* will come to be regarded as one of the classic Hollywood films of the last twenty years, an example of the "kind of film they don't make anymore," but which, on this rare occasion, they actually did.

Body Heat's credits begin over undulating flames and a body—immediately introducing the themes of heat and passion, which are consistently evoked throughout the film. One of the first images is that of a fire on the horizon which Ned Racine watches in his underwear. "My God, it's hot," says his one-night-stand. When Ned meets Matty Walker, fireworks erupt. Kasdan's dialogue is brisk, short, filled with double entendres which recall the dialogue of forties films.

"My temperature runs a couple of degrees high—around 100," says Matty, "I don't mind—the engine or something."

"Maybe you need a tune-up," says Ned.

"Don't tell me . . . you have just the right tool."

Or later, when Ned comes on to Matty:

"You shouldn't dress like that."

"What do you mean? It's a blouse and a skirt."

"You shouldn't wear that body."

"I'm gonna get out of here. I gotta go home."

"I'll take you."

"I've got a car."

"I'll follow you."

When Ned arrives at Matty's huge home, he tells her, "You're not so tough after all, are you?" "No, I'm weak," she answers, as she kisses him passionately, then goes inside the house, locking the door behind her. He listens to the wind chimes, then goes to the door himself. She stands inside, looking out at him longingly, but unwilling to unlock the door to let him in. In a moment charged with eroticism, Ned breaks the door's window with a chair, charges in, and embraces Matty. To the accompaniment of the extremely sensuous and romantic theme music of John Barry, they tear at each other's clothes and make passionate love right there on the floor. Even after beginning their affair, Matty and Ned remain hot: in one scene, they take a bath in ice cubes to try to cool down. Eventually they both realize, during one steamy love scene, that they're going to kill Matty's husband: the camera pulls up as they embrace in a dark and shadowy room.

Right before the murder, Ned sees a clown in a red convertible, which works as a *Döppelganger.* If the clown represents Ned, who also drives a red convertible, it does not augur well for Ned's involvement in the murder plot. Matty has a double too: a high school friend who greatly resembles her and who turns out to be rather important to the plot. Matty and Ned do kill her husband: Ned hits him over the head, and then, using a bomb, sets a fire—which relates to the film's motifs of passion and heat.

But does Matty really love Ned? Behind his back, she purposely makes out a will with legal errors which will be attributed to Ned's status as a second-rate lawyer, in an attempt to circumvent her husband's intentions and get all of his money, rather than just half. The pressure on Ned increases. "I don't blame you for thinking I'm bad," says Matty, "I am, I know it." The film proceeds with scenes of recrimination typical to the genre. The ocnophilic object— in this instance, the husband's glasses—apparently turns against them. Ned discovers that Matty may have set him up and is perhaps going to kill him too. She sends him to get the incriminating glasses in the boathouse, but will a bomb she may have placed there kill him? But Ned doesn't do what he's supposed to do and challenges Matty instead to a kind of test not unlike the one at the climax of *The Postman Always Rings Twice.* Matty wears a white dress, as she did when we saw her for the first time: the dress blows in the wind, in the darkness, as they confront each other. Ned asks Matty to get the glasses herself, and she tells him, "No matter what you think, I do love you." A solitary figure in white, she turns and disappears in the blackness of the frame. Moments later, there is one final explosion, one final burst of flame.

So Matty is dead . . . or is she? The film ends with one last twist which shows that the film has been much more carefully plotted than the spectator might have imagined. In any case, the triangle is destroyed, with only one of its members—though solitary—successful and happy.

Another thriller of murderous passions, influenced somewhat by *Body Heat,* is the independent film *Blood Simple,* made by Joel and Ethan Coen in 1984. *Blood Simple* is a low-budget, slow-moving thriller filled with black humor. It builds inexorably to a suspenseful climax. The cinematography is extraordinary and filled with little "tricks": there is a wonderful shot, for instance, of a newspaper in slow-motion hitting a window and sounding like a gun shot; as well, there are numerous tracking shots, including one alongside a walking dog, which are almost surreal in their intensity. These almost "purple patches" are used like punctuation devices to highlight the thrills. The Coens take the genre's typical triangle and alter it by elevating in importance a fourth character: Loren, the corrupt investigator, played by M. Emmet Walsh.

The film begins with a number of poetic shots of the Texas landscape accompanied by Loren's voice-over saying that "The world is full of planners . . . something can always go wrong." From here we move to the heart of the triangular conflict, as an early scene, certainly inspired by *film noir,* shows the two lovers, Ray and Abby (played by John Getz and Frances McDormand) driving in the rain on a dark night, the windshield wipers clicking obsessively. Abby seems remarkably ordinary for a *femme fatale.* Her husband Marty (played by Dan Hedaya) is weak and nasty; he hires Loren to kill his wife and her lover for $10,000. Loren often talks comparatively about the political system in Russia: "People look out for each other, but make only fifty cents a day"—thus relating the characters' actions to a political and social context of critical examination. Loren agrees to kill the two lovers and goes to their bedroom at night. He returns to the husband and shows him pictures of their bloody bodies in bed. "Count it," says the husband as he gives Loren the $10,000. "I trust you," says Loren and immediately shoots the husband with the wife's gun.

Of course, the woman and her lover are not dead; Loren's plan was to take the husband's money, kill him, and pin the crime on the illicit lovers. As the plot proceeds, however, things get even more complicated. The lover finds the wife's gun and the husband's body and assumes that the wife has killed him. He tries to clean up the bloody mess in a scene which is quite horrifying: the rag sopping with blood, blood dripping from the husband's nostrils, blood spreading on the floor even more severely as the lover tries to clean it up, blood washing down the sink. The husband puts the body in his car, leaves it in fear, and then, when he returns, discovers that the body is gone. How? Because the husband is not dead, and is, rather, painfully and slowly crawling down the deserted highway in the dark of night. The lover retrieves the husband and proceeds to bury him alive.

Later, the wife says to her lover, "I haven't done anything funny," using the same language that the husband had earlier warned the lover she would use and which would indicate that she would now be betraying him, too, as she had her husband. The lover suddenly fears that Abby may be trying to pin "their" murder of the husband solely on him. Together, they fear that the husband may not really be dead. The phone rings—there is no one there: is it the husband? At one point, the husband, alive, returns to the wife and vomits blood—though this reappearance is revealed as an extraordinary dream. But neither Abby nor Ray can know definitely that the husband is truly dead. The climactic scene is extraordinarily riveting. By this time, the lover has lost faith in the wife. Suddenly, the lover is shot dead—presumably by the husband. Through an open window, the wife uses a knife to impale the hand of the killer she cannot see; the killer then shoots through the wall which separates them in a beautifully photographed scene recalling the climax of Fritz Lang's *Ministry of Fear.* Then the wife shoots the killer through the wall, all the time thinking that she's killed her husband. Her last line, to the dying man in the other room is "I'm not afraid of you, Marty." Loren, the investigator, laughs as he expires: "If I see him, I'll sure give him the message."

Thus, to the end, the wife has assumed that the corruption and evil has derived solely from the passion associated with the romantic triangle. The irony and cynicism of the film is that the corruption extends beyond—to the fourth character, that of the investigator, who, in other times and other subgenres of mystery, would have been the hallmark of integrity and justice, but who in this film becomes the most folksy and ordinary symbol of everyday decadence and evil.

Dance with a Stranger, the 1984 British film written by Shelagh Delaney and directed by Mike Newell, stars Miranda Richardson as Ruth Ellis, the last woman to be hanged in Britain. *Dance with a Stranger* is oddly similar to *Blood Simple* in the way it strongly emphasizes the social milieu within which its characters live. Ruth Ellis comes from a lowerclass background; a no-nonsense kind of woman, she recognizes, when others can speak of a finishing school as a place "where girls go to finish their education," that it is really a place where "girls learn to cook and sew and fill in divorce papers." Ruth, too, is involved in a triangle: in this film, the tragedy is that her obsessive relationship with her lover, the upperclass race driver who mistreats her, cannot attain any kind of mutually sustaining equilibrium. It is Ruth who kills her lover; although even she, like so many of these ill-fated lovers, can—only shortly before she is hanged—write to the mother of the man she killed that "I shall die loving your son." Although a British production, *Dance with a Stranger* is part of that recent renaissance of thrillers which show the influence of the *films noirs* of the forties.

Although *Blood Simple* and *Dance with a Stranger* were moderately successful at the box office, neither managed to reinvigorate the genre as did the electrifying *Fatal Attraction.* Directed by the British Adrian Lyne in 1987, *Fatal Attraction* was a box office sensation that garnered the attention of the industry and the public from the first day of its commercial release through to the 1988 Academy Awards ceremony where it competed for the distinction as best film of the year (losing, incidentally, to Bernardo Bertolluci's epic *The Last Emperor*). Indeed, *Fatal Attraction* served the overall suspense thriller genre as *The Exorcist* had served the horror genre over a decade earlier: making it respectable for critical commentary and sophisticated taste. Essentially a thriller of murderous passions with a traditional triangular construction, *Fatal Attraction* tells the story of an American bourgeois couple, Dan and Beth (played by Michael Douglas and Anne Archer), whose marriage has gone somewhat stale. Attracted to the dynamic and erotic career woman Alex (played by Glenn Close), the something of a milquetoast Dan begins an adulterous affair with her. As their relationship evolves, Alex reveals herself as increasingly psychotic and dangerous. Although Dan wishes nothing more than to dispose conveniently of this now troublesome one-night-stand, Alex threatens to reveal Dan's infidelity to his wife, or worse, to commit a violent act which would effectively destroy Dan's traditional nuclear family. The adulterous triangle thus continues because Dan is too fearful to end it.

What made *Fatal Attraction* the box office sensation of the year was the almost naked way in which the film revealed a basic premise of thrillers of murderous passion: namely, their invariable criticism of social norms and their commentary on the values of the dominant ideology. *Fatal Attraction* especially benefited from a careful construction and uncanny timely release which allowed it to function as a Rorschach test in which each spectator saw in it the value he or she psychologically projected.

Is *Fatal Attraction* a feminist film? Perhaps so: since the strongest and most interesting character in the film is Alex—who is an intelligent, self-possessed career woman who acts aggressively. It is the woman Alex who turns the man Dan into a passive victim; uncharacteristically unmacho for a hero, Dan is incompetent at controlling Alex's increasing aggressiveness and unpredictability.

Is *Fatal Attraction* an antifeminist film? Perhaps so: since Alex, although a career woman, is ultimately revealed to be a psychotic who is unable to sustain a mature relationship or to conform to recognizably "normal" human behavior. Her status as monster seems to validate the ideological position of the bourgeois wife, who is ultimately revealed as the moral center of the film's universe.

On one level, issues of feminism/antifeminism compete with the issue of AIDS, which hangs over the film like a dim specter—never quite visible except over-the-shoulder, peripherally. In the era in which Nancy Reagan's "Just Say No" dictum against drugs has become the watchword of a generation and *Zeitgeist* of the decade ("Just Say No"—to drugs, cigarettes, alcohol, sex, abortion, insider stock trading, cholesterol, foreign imports—indeed, "no" to *everything*), *Fatal Attraction* becomes a clear, cautionary tale. Sexual intercourse can literally kill as surely as can Alex's knife-wielding psychopath. Dan's original sin, certainly, is that he *didn't* just say no. Thus, *Fatal Attraction* seems to suggest that we must retreat from the Sexual Revolution and the New Morality and return to a happier and simpler time in which the nuclear family prospered—a time in which a well-appointed home in the suburban country remained the ideal, and a woman's place was clearly there, taking care of her obedient and well-mannered children.

And yet, one can never truly go back home. The moving finger writes, and having writ, moves on; what has been thought or done cannot be unthought nor undone. If *Fatal Attraction* can be read as embracing the nuclear family, it can as easily be read as a stunning condemnation of the nuclear family's shortcomings. The relationship between Dan and Beth that we see at the beginning of *Fatal Attraction* is by no means a horrific one. They love each other, definitely; but like perhaps too many traditional marriages, their marriage is taken for granted, ultimately unfulfilling, and devoid of excitement and passion. That Dan is so easily willing to sleep with Alex in the first place is testament to the film's primary truth: that all the excitement and passion in life is truly to be found outside the nuclear family, outside the boundaries of the kind of behavior proscribed by the dominant ideology.

The two different endings of *Fatal Attraction* themselves testify to the ambivalence of the film's message and values. The original ending—truer in integrity to the internal logic of the expertly crafted script by James Deardon which allowed each character to achieve his or her own central fantasy—had Alex fulfilling her Madame Butterfly fantasy. After a violent attack on Dan, Alex commits a glorious and romantic suicide so that it will appear that Dan is guilty of her apparent "murder." Thus, in the original ending, although the passion associated with the illicit relationship is revealed as ultimately destructive, the nuclear family is destroyed nevertheless and itself revealed as an archaic and impotent institution. And certainly, there are a great number of internal clues within the film (discussion of *Madama Butterfly*, the use of operatic music on the soundtrack, a scene where the characters go to the opera, and so forth) which prepare the audience for this ending.

Reportedly, preview audiences were upset with the original ending, disturbed that the strong woman played by Glenn Close should—even in death—achieve a Pyrrhic victory; disturbed too that the film's denouement should come about with the male protagonist failing to take a decisive action and instead remaining a passive victim to the end. Although the original ending was used in Japan, where passivity is not necessarily regarded as a dramatic or psychological failure, a second ending was shot and appended to the film for distribution in the United States and elsewhere. In this second version, Alex no longer commits suicide, but instead lashes out aggressively at the nuclear family in one last attack directed specifically at her ex-lover Dan. This new ending finally allows Dan to take aggressive action for perhaps the first time in the film. It also provides the audience the opportunity to cheer on, rather enthusiastically, an act of cathartic male violence directed toward a woman. So despite all Alex's cunning and aggressiveness, Dan finally manages to kill her.

Or does he? Homages to the bathtub scene of *Diabolique*, to the ending of *Halloween*, and to the coda of *Carrie* (all horror films, rather than thrillers) extend the narrative proper; and the wife Beth makes a belated, surprise appearance as she *herself* kills the monstrous Alex once and for all. Are thus the traditional values of American motherhood shown to be more powerful than the modern values of the liberated woman? This ending is one of those increasingly frequent examples of a film deformed by the system which produced it: its interior logic contradicted by a studio-mandated "happy ending" which allows the issues to be apparently, if simplistically, resolved so that the spectators can return home, undeterred from their uncritical attachment to the dominant ideology and the values associated with it. Or is *Fatal Attraction* already so ambivalent and contradictory ideologically that even the new ending contributes to its ambiguity?

The second ending shows that the nuclear family is at the center of American life *precisely* because it powerfully incorporates (as reflected in the brutal actions of both Dan and Beth) the violence and the coldly excluding energies which have always supported the most enduring reactionary values of American society. And certainly there is an irony here: in the most typical thriller of murderous passions, it is the adulterous lovers who, sinfully and coldbloodedly, kill the hapless spouse; in *Fatal Attraction*, it is the marriage partners who savagely and in concert kill the adulterous *outsider*. But can any film be seen truly to uphold traditional marriage, if that marriage is held together primarily because the man has developed such sexual guilts and fears that he is too cowardly to act honestly according to his instincts? Is fear the only enduring foundation for a marriage? With either ending, *Fatal Attraction* is one of the most interesting examples of the thriller of murderous passions since Claude Chabrol's oddly similar *La Femme Infidèle* two decades earlier, as well as a testament to the genre's ability to express effortlessly and energetically the tensions in contemporary society.

6
The Political Thriller

Jack Lemmon, as Ed Horman in *Missing,* has journeyed to Chile in order to find his son, who disappeared shortly after the military takeover. Optimistically at first, and then more cynically, Ed has followed one lead after another—from official to official and now to rooms filled with the unidentified dead bodies of innocent men and women killed by the military. So tightly packed are the corpses that Ed and his daughter-in-law Beth must walk gingerly, almost on tiptoes, to avoid stepping on them. The sordid spectacle of death both overwhelms and stuns them. Suddenly, Beth gasps and breaks down as she spies the corpse of a friend who had also disappeared. Clearly, he has been killed by the military. Ed can barely comfort Beth; his own trust in institutions makes it difficult now for him to comprehend how the American government could somehow be accomplice to such violence and horror. At the ceiling and visible as dark shadows through the skylight are more dead bodies—these corpses on the floor upstairs. "What kind of world is this?" asks Ed, shaken by the answer he knows he will have to face. . . .

The political thriller is composed of those films which are organized around a plot to assassinate a political figure or a revelation of the essential conspiratorial nature of governments and their crimes against their people. These films generally document and dramatize the acts of assassins, conspirators, or criminal governments, as well as the oppositional acts of victim-societies, countercultures, or martyrs. These films may be completely fictional or based on fact; they may also include an actual investigatory force (often represented by a reporter) which works virtually to narrate the revelations.

Certain thematic ideas which are integrated in this generic structure again and again include (1) the tendency of power to corrupt, (2) the inescapability of politics, (3) the moral necessity to examine and question government and social institutions, (4) the conspiratorial nature of repressive government and society, (5) the distinction between the apparent and the actual, which can be generalized into a distinction between the public history and the people's truth, (6) confidence in the people's judgment in open-minded investigators or journalists, or in politicians

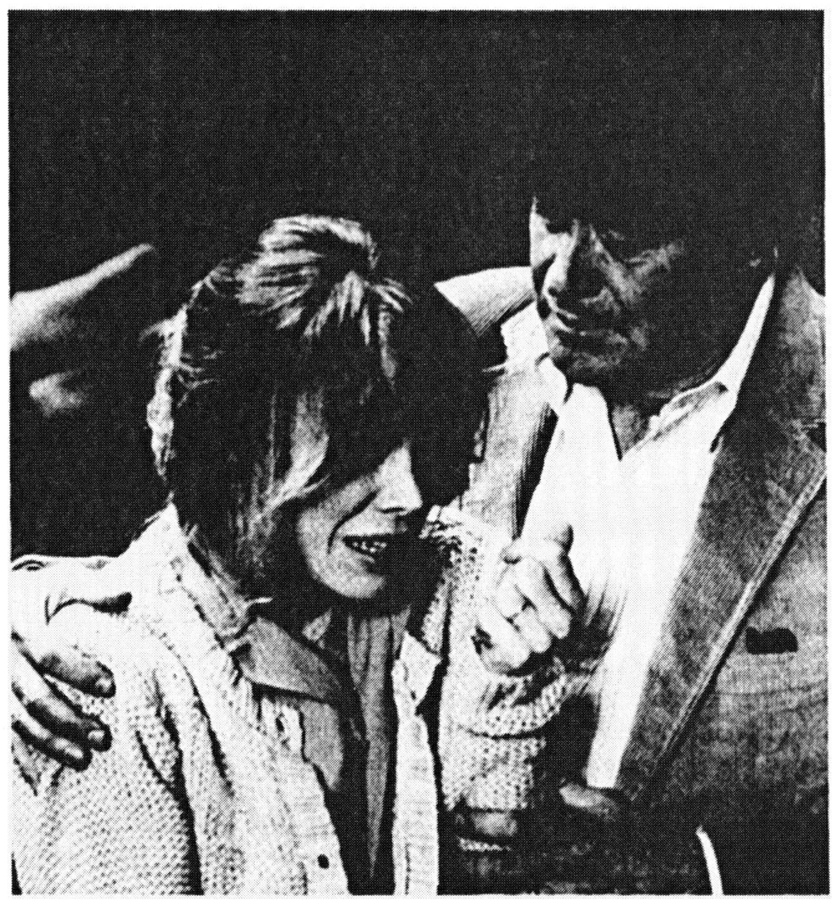

Jack Lemmon and Sissy Spacek search among the corpses in *Missing*.

whose strength and integrity derive from their attempt to serve the people rather than to acquire power, and (7) the potential of individual heroism to bring about social and political change.

A list of political thrillers would include the following:

The Tall Target (1951)
Suddenly (1955)
Intent to Kill (1959)
Three Came to Kill (1960)
The Best Man (1960)
Advise and Consent (1962)
The Manchurian Candidate (1962)
Nine Hours to Rama (1963)
Seven Days in May (1964)
Rush to Judgement (1967)
The Chairman (1969)
Z (1969)
Topaz (1969)
The Confession (1970)
The Groundstar Conspiracy (1972)
State of Siege (1973)
The Day of the Jackal (1973)
Executive Action (1974)
The Missiles of October (1974)
Nada (1974)

Special Section (1975)
The Day of the Dolphin (1976)
All the President's Men (1976)
The Domino Principle (1976)
The Eagle Has Landed (1977)
Washington: Behind Closed Doors (1977)
The Trial of Lee Harvey Oswald (1977)
The Lincoln Conspiracy (1977)
Sleeping Dogs (1977)
Black Sunday (1977)
Capricorn One (1978)
The China Syndrome (1979)
Winter Kills (1979)
The Kidnapping of the President (1980)
Rollover (1981)
Blow Out (1981)
Missing (1982)
Under Fire (1983)
The Year of Living Dangerously (1983)
Special Bulletin (1983)
Silkwood (1983)
Hanna K (1983)
The Star Chamber (1983)
Marie (1985)
The Official Story (1985)
Under Siege (1985)
Acceptable Risks (1986)
Salvador (1986)
Power (1986)
Defence of the Realm (1986)

Although political thrillers are extremely wide-ranging and in continual evolution, they can nevertheless also be recognized by the presence of various other elements, including conspiracies, assassinations, terrorism, government institutions, the press as a heroic social institution, explicit dates and the names of places—often printed in on-screen titles, ambitious and hypocritical villains, actors portraying historical personages or characters loosely based on historical personages, military men, homosexuality, government repression, surveillance, invasions of privacy, official acts of physical or psychological torture, a perception that the object of assassination is a martyr, an assassin with whom the spectator is invited to empathize or one who is either an innocent patsy or not completely culpable, a scene of interrogation, nuclear threats, virtuous reporters or photographers, kidnapping, a high-powered rifle, "what if" premises, legislatures in progress, a sense of exposé journalism, historically real locations, narration, and a printed prologue which lays in a historical framework or an epilogue which projects a historical future.

In a psychoanalytic perspective using Michael Balint's terminology, the typical political thriller is constructed upon a psychoanalytic imbalance and a conflict which cannot be peacefully mediated. One social group may be so overwhelmingly ocnophilic and repressive that objects, customs and conventions become fetishes which conflict with the more anarchic impulses of another social group that embraces new political ideas and the freedom of philobatism. Because the point along the ocnophilia-philobatism axis representing maximum psychological health is by no means objectively fixed, the assessment of psychological health (and whether, for instance, one is considered an assassin or a freedom-fighter, an upholder of tradition or a reactionary) must derive from specific psychoanalytic premises. The conflicted groups compete for the privilege

privilege of identifying the optimum point, which the narrative may itself identify in an attempt to become the psychoanalyst and affect the values and perceptions of the spectator.

The political thriller was not born fully-formed, as the list of examined titles might seem to indicate. Though this chapter does not discuss them, there are significant political thrillers from as far back as early sound cinema, films such as William Wellman's *The President Vanishes* and Gregory La Cava's *Gabriel Over the White House.* If this chapter commences its survey *in media res,* it is because the fifties seems an appropriate place to begin. The end of World War II signalled an end to the dichotomous political conflict of Hitler's fascism versus the democracies and the beginning of the newly focused conflict of Marxism versus capitalism, of the Soviet Union versus the United States.

Reflecting this second conflict, fifties thrillers were fueled by the growing paranoia which would erupt in the sixties. Certainly the political thrillers of the last thirty-five to forty years can and should be related to specific political events or *Zeitgeist,* particularly the activities of Joseph McCarthy, the Cold War, the Kennedy assassination, the Johnson/Nixon/Vietnam/Kent State repressions (and the various left-wing responses), and Watergate—all of which tended to contribute to an overall sense of the conspiratorial nature of recent political history. Certainly, the activities of Joseph McCarthy made abundantly clear the existence of demogogic politicians who were interested only in their own power and self-perpetuation; their ambitions conspired against the people they were supposed to serve. At the same time, McCarthy's suggestion that the government and society could be secretly overrun with Communists met with great public support. Thus, whether one were right-wing or left-wing, Senator Joseph McCarthy offered a relevant conspiracy. (It is interesting to note the way *The Manchurian Candidate* manages to take advantage of both these conspiratorial ideas.)

The Cold War probably contributed most overtly to the spy films of the sixties, but is reflected as well in the way so many of these political thrillers hinge on keeping the balance between the United States and the Soviet Union (especially in the right-wing suspense thrillers and the thriller novels of Allen Drury). The John F. Kennedy assassination was just one in a series of spectacular assassinations, including those of Robert Kennedy and Martin Luther King, Jr. For each assassination, one lone assassin has been held primarily responsible: Lee Harvey Oswald, Sirhan Sirhan, and James Earl Ray, respectively; yet for each assassination there have been countless counter-explanations suggesting conspiracies and multiple culpabilities.

The various Kennedy conspiracy theories include among their villains the CIA, the FBI, the KGB, the Mafia, rich Texas oilmen, and Cuban Communists out for revenge at Kennedy's attempts to assassinate Fidel Castro. And since Lee Harvey Oswald seems to have had concrete connections of one sort or another with the FBI, the CIA, the Russians, and the Cubans, speculation seems hardly extraordinary. Indeed, Gallup polls now show that the majority of Americans disagree with the official Warren Commission Report, which found Oswald singly responsible. This conspiratorial notion of American society was not limited to the assassins and their friends: certain theories (although definitely the more *outré*) held that various objects of assassination or accident were not dead, after all. Radio talk shows in the late sixties and early seventies paraded various authors and eccentrics who claimed that John Kennedy was still alive in a hospital in Dallas, John Dillinger had never been killed in Chicago, and Amelia Earhart had never crashed and was now living a quiet life as a housewife under an assumed name.

The Vietnam War, as waged by Johnson and Nixon, provided a continuing source of conspiratorial thought: secret bombings, the Pentagon Papers, the revelations of My Lai, the establishment's culpability for the killing of four students at Kent State University in Ohio. And finally, of course, there is Watergate. The term has come to stand for an assortment of evils including presidentially sanctioned burglary, improper use of funds, the drawing up of enemies lists, the collection of thousands of secret files on law-abiding citizens, and sundry illegal and immoral actions by the CIA and the FBI.

Certainly not to be underestimated in the propagation of this conspiratorial notion was Nixon's illegal buggings and his routine taping of conversations in the Oval Office without the knowledge of those participating in the conversations: the public image created was one of a foul-mouthed president who, so uninterested, cynical, or out of touch with the morality and integrity of democracy, developed a Mafia-like obsession with the conspiracies and petty politics necessary to realize his own selfish ambitions. Needless to say, the constant questioning of the actions or ethics of governments and their politicians was not limited to the United States: witness the remarkable French general strike of 1968, as well as the frequent topplings of governments throughout the world.

In the early political thrillers of the fifties, there is little, if any, emphasis on the conspiratorial nature of government; the films more simply use assassination or its threat as content. *The Tall Target*, for instance, directed by Anthony Mann in 1951, deals with the train journey of Abraham Lincoln to his inauguration in Baltimore. A crawl tells us that the film will be "a dramatization of that disputed journey"; the film proceeds to tell the story of a government agent (played by Dick Powell) who fears an assassination attempt on Lincoln. Much of the film is actually organized around mystery constructions, for there is a group of suspicious characters among whom the government agent must ferret out the assassin(s). "There is a difference between murder and political assassination," says one of the conspirators.

Although there may be perhaps forty gentlemen, primarily, if not exclusively Southern, who are planning to assassinate Lincoln in Baltimore, their plot does not seem particularly conspiratorial because we are aware of the Southern concept of honor and recognize that Southern separatism has by now acquired almost a mythological romanticism. If the assassins' plot is secret, their allegiances are not; it does not come as a revelation to us that Southerners, before the Civil War, should try to destroy the republic. More interesting, because of its slight ambiguity, is the film's attitude toward slavery. At one point, a Harriet Beecher Stowe–like writer asks one of the slaves on the train, "What does it feel like to be beaten?" It seems we are not meant to share the writer's sentiments, but to question them; clearly this fat, self-satisfied woman knows little about the South or about slavery, and of course, the slave in question has never been beaten. In a later scene, however, this same slave suggests that even though she likes her masters, she desperately wants her freedom; she even helps the government agent in his attempt to prevent the assassination.

When the narrative reveals that Lincoln has cancelled the speech during which the assassins were planning to kill him, the film seems about to come to an early end. We know the assassination attempt is doomed to failure, although we are equally aware of the irony that "Mr. Lincoln's a tall target; there'll be another day." It is not until this point that the film's protagonist, the antagonists, and the spectator, are all allowed to discover that Lincoln himself is actually on the train; mystery structures finally give way to suspense structures. As the train begins to pull away, one of the villains writes a message on the outside of one of the train windows to try to communicate this knowledge to one of the interior assassins. Suspense takes over completely: Will the government agent realize what is going on and prevent the assassination before the Southern assassin on the train finds Lincoln's compartment and kills him? Our knowledge that Lincoln was not assassinated on this particular train trip does not attenuate our anxiety.

Other films of the period use the theme of assassination in much the same way. *Suddenly*, directed in 1954 by Lewis Allen, stars Frank Sinatra as a would-be assassin who takes over a small house the president plans on visiting for a fishing vacation. Ultimately, the film emphasizes the confrontation between the assassin and the woman hostage who stands up to him. The president is never seen, and at the film's climax, his train is signalled to go through the town without stopping. *Intent to Kill*, directed in 1958 by Jack Cardiff from a screenplay by Jimmy Sangster, deals with an assassination attempt on a president of a South American country. *Three Came to Kill*, directed by Edward L. Cahn in 1960, deals with an assassination attempt directed toward an ex-premier of a Far Eastern country.

What is significant in all three of these films, as well as in *The Tall Target*, is that the assassination attempts fail. Generally, the attempted assassination in these films also seems removed from the contemporary

American temperament; Lincoln, for instance, is set apart from us by time and romantic myth; and certainly most Americans perceive both South America and the Far East as inevitably insecure places marked normally by government intrigues and revolutions.

Of all these films, *Suddenly* comes the closest to connecting with any roughly contemporary sensibility, at least because the object of assassination is ostensibly the president of 1955. And although the psychotic assassin is presented as a definite aberration, he can be seen as a product of his own country because his disturbance derives from his inability to deal with civilian life after having been brainwashed by the military sensibilities that so rewarded his wartime killings.

The popular expression of the conspiratorial theory of politics can perhaps be traced to the seminal series of six novels by Allen Drury which exposed the machinations and conflicts behind the scenes of Washington, D.C. The first, *Advise and Consent,* was published in 1959, remained on the bestseller list for two years, and won the Pulitzer Prize. Before embarking on his career as a novelist, Drury had worked as a Washington correspondent. Further novels in the series were not as well received, perhaps because they made increasingly overt what in *Advise and Consent* was only latent: the right-wing viewpoint of Drury. Indeed, running through all six of the novels and stated explicitly in various prefaces is "the continuing argument between those who would use responsible firmness to maintain orderly social progress and oppose Communist imperialism in its drive for world dominion; and those who believe that in a reluctance to be firm, in permissiveness and in the steady erosion of law lie the surest path to world peace and a stable society."

Although *Advise and Consent* was received as a "serious novel," all of Drury's novels in this series are popular suspense thrillers, using suspense, symbolic ideological confrontations, and the various other elements so typical to the genre. I find it particularly fascinating that the first wholesale examination of government and its participants should come from a highly literate conservative. Aside from Drury's crisp, clean writing, and constant suspense, one of the things that makes his work so entertainingly readable is that no matter what one's political persuasion, one can recognize in the books parallels to real historical figures as well as to current political issues. In the course of the novels, Drury deals with the Senate, the United Nations, a nominating convention, the Cold War, civil rights issues, the Third World, American involvement in armed ideological struggles in other countries, assassination, civil disobedience, and even nuclear war—and in every instance Drury presents a convincing exposé of what takes place behind the scenes.

Drury's conservative viewpoint seems particularly interesting in relation to the generally liberal (or Marxist) orientations of most contemporary political thrillers—at least on film. Although Drury was initially attacked for

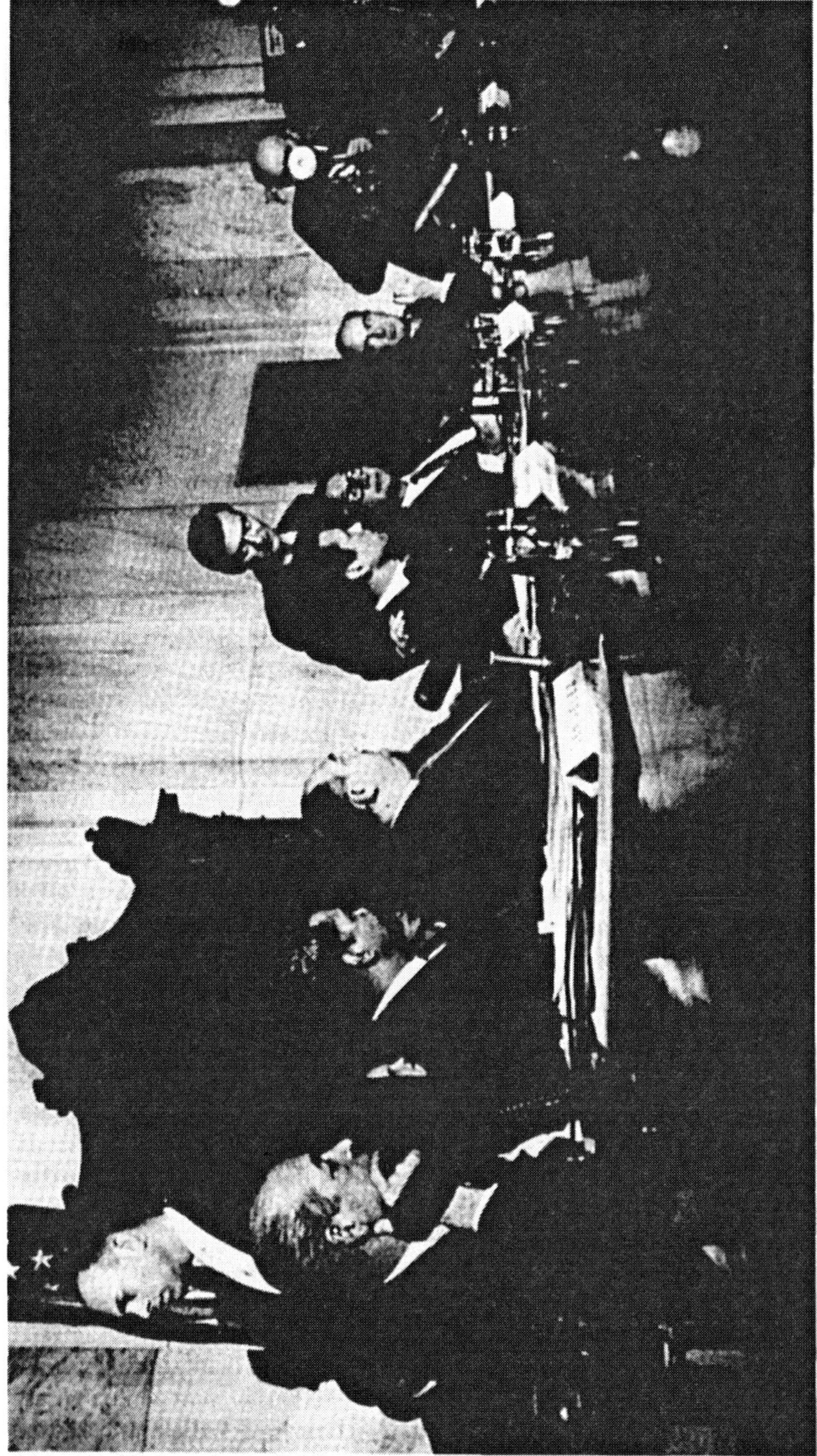

being un–American, it is clear he is quite patriotic and has never lost his faith in the American Dream. In fact, Drury is today attacked for being jingoistic. The film version of *Advise and Consent,* the only novel in the series to be made into a movie, was directed by Otto Preminger in 1962 and has a different sensibility: as usual, Preminger's interest in a variety of viewpoints transforms Drury's plot from a suspenseful thriller into a less suspenseful, if fascinating, "serious" drama. *Advise and Consent* deals primarily with the Senate and the various issues involved in the ratification of the president's nominee for secretary of state, a man thought to be soft on Communism. The film ends with the president's sudden death and the vice-president taking over, events which irrevocably alter the outcome of the ratification process.[1]

Shortly after the publication of *Advise and Consent,* Gore Vidal's popular play, *The Best Man,* was produced on Broadway. Like *Advise and Consent, The Best Man* represents an exposé of political intrigue, this time from a liberal perspective, as two potential presidential nominees jockey for the support of the president. The president resembles Truman; the liberal, courageous presidential aspirant resembles Adlai Stevenson; and the over-ambitious, villainous presidential aspirant resembles both Joseph McCarthy and Richard Nixon. The film version was directed in 1960 by Franklin Schaffner and works as a fascinating complement to Preminger's film. Like *Advise and Consent, The Best Man* includes evil and hypocritical villains, a central character of conscience and integrity, various conspiracies and political plots, and revelations of homosexual conduct (in each case, a single wartime experience by the sympathetic protagonist). Both films end fairly optimistically with evil vanquished—if in *The Best Man* not necessarily by the inherent goodness of the system, at least by the heroic actions of those few individuals of integrity who are determined to make the system work.

The Manchurian Candidate, directed in 1962 by John Frankenheimer (from a script by George Axelrod based on the novel by Richard Condon), is one of the most significant political thrillers in that it is one of the first to unite the theme of assassination with that of the basic conspiratorial nature of politics. Self-conscious in style, *The Manchurian Candidate* offers a terrifying version of United States politics. The would-be assassin (played by Lawrence Harvey) is, typical to the genre, not really responsible for his actions; while in Korea during the war he had been unknowingly brainwashed and programmed by a group of Chinese Communists. The surprising revelation is that his own mother masterminded the entire plot in an attempt to get her husband (who has adopted a rabid anti–Communist stance only out of expediency) elected president.

***Advise and Consent:* the archetypal board of inquiry so typical of the political thriller.**

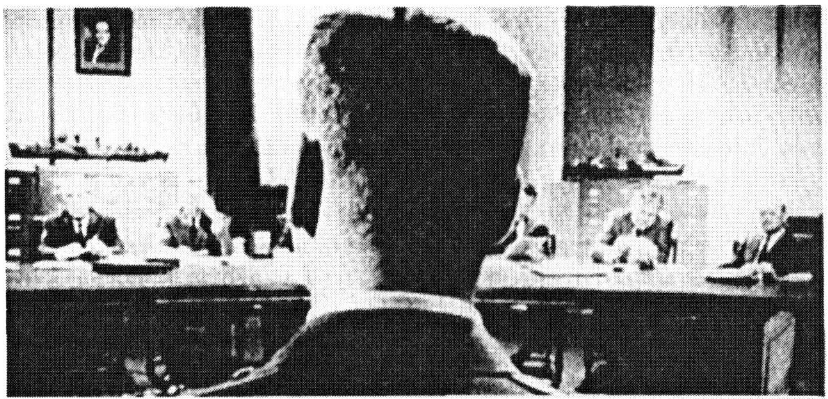

Burt Lancaster as a military officer who plans a coup in *Seven Days in May*. Note how the camera placement and his position in the frame emphasize his power.

"Things" are always important in suspense thrillers, and the political thriller is no exception: in *The Manchurian Candidate*, the assassin is brainwashed into obeying only those commands which follow the image of a queen of diamonds. The film climaxes with the generic scene of the assassin about to disrupt a political event as he sets the sights of his high-powered rifle on the man he is about to kill. *The Manchurian Candidate* was a very controversial film in its time. Although almost all critics agreed it was suspenseful and stylishly shot, they thought many of its premises farfetched, including the Communist brainwashing, the characterization of the "anti-Communist" senator, and especially, the whole idea of political assassination as a realistic possibility in American politics.

The assassination of President Kennedy in 1963 worked in part to alter the public's perceptions as to what was and was not possible or probable; *The Manchurian Candidate* was thus transformed retrospectively from a wild and creative fantasy into a sober, although stylish, speculation. Rereleased theatrically in 1988, *The Manchurian Candidate* was greeted with rave reviews.

Frankenheimer's 1964 film, *Seven Days in May*, can be seen somewhat as a companion piece to *The Manchurian Candidate*, presenting a different version of America's potentially apocalyptic future. With a screenplay by Rod Serling based on the Fletcher Knebel novel, *Seven Days in May* deals with a conspiracy by military men to take over the government because they oppose the president's nuclear treaties with the Soviet Union. The narrative includes the gradual revelation of the conspiracy, various suspenseful confrontations and plot twists, the threat of nuclear war, the protagonist of integrity and courage (in this instance, the president himself), and the final grandstand play by which the conspiracy is squelched. Significantly, the military men in *Seven Days in May* are not presented simplistically as as power-lusting villains, but as men who act out of patriotism to the country, if not to the country's Constitution.

Not surprisingly, assassination became a subject increasingly popular and relevant in film and fiction. Across the country, thousands sent away for the various albums memorializing the four days in November, 1963, which culminated in John F. Kennedy's interment in Arlington Cemetery. Americans needed to own their own images: the president's head being propelled backwards, Jackie in a black veil, the tortured grimace of Oswald as he is shot by Jack Ruby, the eternal flame. . . . Film director Brian De Palma anticipates in *The Phantom of the Paradise* the possibility of coast-to-coast assassination as real entertainment. Indeed, many Americans might concur with De Palma's admission that, "The Kennedy assassination is probably the most entertaining thing I ever saw. It riveted me, held me emotionally, and I watched the television set for days and days, and that is entertainment on a scale that no one could ever come up with."[2]

The theme of assassination found its way into numerous films of the period, including many, like Arthur Penn's *The Chase* (1966), which are not really suspense thrillers, but which nevertheless include parallels to certain aspects of the Kennedy assassination. The sense of conspiracy permeated popular entertainments as well. A science fiction television series like *The Invaders,* which ran from 1967 to 1968 and was about a man who discovers that alien beings—in preparation for an eventual takeover—have infiltrated the planet as supposedly normal citizens, relates to the growing conspiratorial notions.

Films of this period include *Nine Hours to Rama,* a 1963 film directed by Mark Robson about the assassination of the nonviolent Mahatma Gandhi which emphasizes the moral righteousness of Gandhi's position, and by implication, the uselessness of violence as a political act; *Rush to Judgement,* a 1967 documentary made by Mark Lane and Emile De Antonio which criticizes the integrity of the Warren Commission and offers evidence in favor of a conspiracy theory of assassination; *The Chairman,* a completely fictional 1969 film about the struggle for control of a wondrous agricultural formula and which ultimately emphasizes the hypocrisy of all the governments because of their intention to use the formula as a political weapon rather than as a humanitarian service to feed the poor; and *The Groundstar Conspiracy,* a 1972 film, set in the vague future, which is interesting not only because of its geometric compositions and stylish electronic music, but because of its overt thesis that an increasingly multi-tentacled government is stripping its citizens of privacy and attaining social goals at the expense of human decency. Indeed, in this last film (as in *The Domino Principle*), the way the government forces the protagonist to take on a particular identity relates directly to various of the assassination theories by which an innocent dupe is made to take on the responsibility for the assassination.

Certainly one of the most significant developments in the political

A journalist typical to the genre encounters military repression in Z.

thriller was the arrival of Z in 1970, the first of a series of films directed by Costa-Gavras, this one from a screenplay by Costa-Gavras and Jorge Semprun based on the novel by Vassilis Vassilikos. The story itself is based on the assassination of Gregorios Lambrakis, a pacifist who was run over by a delivery truck in May of 1963 while protesting the installation of Polaris missiles in Greece. Although his death was officially listed as an accident, evidence uncovered by the magistrate Christos Sartzetakis showed that the accident was premeditated and that high-ranking Greek politicians and military men were involved in the assassination. The resulting scandal was responsible for the downfall of the Greek government of Constantine Karamanlis and the rise of the party of George Papandreou, whose government subsequently fell to military takeover.

Although Costa-Gavras tends not to use any of these names (instead, using labels such as "the deputy," "the examining magistrate," and so forth), his story is based on the assassination of Lambrakis. Eschewing traditional documentary techniques to tell the story (although occasionally using a quasi-*vérité),* Costa-Gavras embraces instead the techniques of the consummate suspense thriller, including a rhythmic soundtrack, much montage, a fast pace, a high-speed chase, and traditional suspense constructions. The mainstream critical response was overwhelmingly positive; indeed,

Hollywood was so taken by *Z*'s combination of traditional structure and revolutionary content that the Academy of Motion Picture Arts and Sciences nominated it as best film of the year, alongside *Hello, Dolly!*, *Anne of the Thousand Days*, *Butch Cassidy and the Sundance Kid*, and *Midnight Cowboy*. Perhaps even more unprecedented is that the film actually won the Academy Award for the best editing from voters generally so provincial that they rarely give the award to a New York–based editor, much less a foreign editor (in this case, Françoise Bonnot).

Z begins with a pow-wow of its military generals, one of whom gives a speech emphasizing the need to rid the country of pacifists and Communists, while indoctrinating everyone else. As the generals talk, the camera emphasizes their age: we see their ugly reflections in their own eyeglasses, their blotchy skin tones, their wrinkles, their moles. Throughout its first half, Z follows a roughly parallel structure. Thus, from the pow-wow of the generals, Costa-Gavras cuts to the pow-wow of the pacifists. No single pacifist demagogically gives a speech; they all democratically discuss the problems of getting a hall and the murder threat on the deputy's life. Says one pacifist, "It's safe to blame the Americans. The fact is, they're always guilty if the truth were known." Unlike the generals, the pacifists tend all to be young and uniformly good looking—with not a mole among the bunch.

We are introduced to the eventual target of the assassination, the deputy played by French leading man Yves Montand. The deputy is portrayed as an absolute hero: a former Olympic champion and surgeon who has now entered politics and embraced pacifism for the good of the unspecified country (Greece). He is further glamorized through the use of almost subliminal, New Wave flashbacks which show that, although the deputy loves his wife, he has had love affairs. The deputy is contrasted with Vago, the primary assassin played by Marcel Bozzufi. Vago is simple-minded, authoritarian and without a conscience. Costa-Gavras includes one scene in which Vago gawks at a young boy in his underwear in order to indicate that Vago is homosexual, which we are meant to take—rather bigotedly—as a shorthand sign of his villainy. (In many ways, including its characterizations, Z is almost a New Wave version of *Open City*, a film whose melodramatic structure becomes increasingly apparent with each passing year and a film which could itself usefully be analyzed as a political thriller.)

After giving his speech in the midst of demonstrations and counter-demonstrations, the deputy is assassinated (as we feared he would be). His wife Hélène, played by Irene Papas, arrives at the hospital amidst flashbacks of her husband. In one sequence as she and others hesitatingly approach her stricken husband, the camera peers around the corridor toward the operating room until its view is shut out by a door. Another striking sequence takes place in the wife's hotel room; the walls are white, the bed is white, the wife's dress is white. How can she be anything else but the wife of a martyr? Only when she breaks down do we see a flashback of her being told that her husband is dead. The sequence ends as the journalist comes in the room and asks her for a statement. Although at this point, the journalist is mostly being insensitive, he does eventually become one of the primary vehicles by which the film's subsequent investigation is carried out. The fact that he is later responsible for uncovering one of the most important connections in the conspiracy makes clear his role as the typical crusading journalist who appears in so many political thrillers, including *State of Siege* and *All the President's Men.* The first part of the film ends with the pacifist demonstrators being beaten up and arrested; defiantly, they publicly paint a white Z, which signifies "He is alive!"

The second part of the film begins with the investigation carried out by the character Costa-Gavras calls "the examining magistrate," based on Sartzetakis and played by another French leading man, Jean-Louis Trintignant. The magistrate is presented as a methodical and orderly man who is unbiased; only as he gradually compiles the evidence against the government does he come to realize the importance of his commitment to the truth. His interviews with generals and pacifists, witnesses and participants, are handled by Costa-Gavras through fast-paced montage which suggests that the movement of justice is inexorable. In the bravura climax, the magistrate unemotionally charges with murder—one by one—all the high officials involved. The editing is very rapid: we see the close-up of the typewriter ball typing out the charges; the medals on the chests of the generals, each chest weighted down heavier and sillier than the last; and each general trying to make a respectable escape from the reporters and foolishly using the wrong door. The pacifists, of course, are elated, for they take the indictments as a sign of a more open and less repressive government.

The crawl epilogue, so typical to the genre, tells us the awful truth by projecting the real historical future. Although trials were held, the charges against the four top officers were dropped. Eventually all the surviving "good guys" were punished or killed. In a coup, the military took over and expanded their repressions, outlawing, among other things, the books of Dostoyevsky, the plays of Ionesco, modern music, the music of Theodorakis (who scored Z and was, at Z's release, living in Greece under house arrest), freedom of the press, and above all, the letter "Z."

Although theoretically a revolutionary film, Z is certainly traditional in its style and consistent to conventions of the suspense thriller in general and the political thriller in particular. Its structures are predominately parallel, particularly in the way the subjective first view of the assassination (which provides the apparent history) is contrasted with the objective second view of the assassination as revealed by the investigation (which provides the actual history). Typical too is the way the object of the assassination is

Yves Montand at the beginning of his long ordeal in *The Confession*

presented as a Christ-like figure who is resurrected symbolically, so as to engage the spectator's sympathies. If Z aims at a greater support for left-wing revolutionary causes, it does so in a framework in which individual heroism is still more relevant than either the will of the masses or revolutionary violence.

The Confession, the second film in this series, was directed by Costa-Gavras in 1970, again from a script by Jorge Semprun. *The Confession* is based on the 1952 Slansky trial in Czechoslovakia in which Artur London, a Jewish Communist, was charged with conspiracy against the Communist Party. Although innocent, London was subjected to countless tortures as a result of the Communist purge and forced to admit guilt for crimes he did not commit. As usual, a dominant theme of *The Confession* (as in *Z,* and in *State of Siege* to follow) is that the people never engage in conspiracies; it is, rather, governments that engage in conspiracies in order to propagate their own power.

The Confession begins in 1951 Prague, as the protagonist realizes that he is being followed. As in Z, Costa-Gavras again refrains from giving his characters their real historical names; the protagonist elaborated from Artur London's autobiographical account is herein called Gérard and again played by Yves Montand. Two cars filled with agents from Prague Intelligence suddenly surround Gérard's car on the street. Gérard is blindfolded, handcuffed, arrested, and put in prison. While in prison he is forbidden to sit or stand still; whenever he stops walking back and forth, he is beaten. His feet become bloodied as he marches in the various small cells filled with excrement and urine. His experience in prison quickly becomes horrifying and absurd, resembling nothing so much as a Kafka fiction. "You're nothing! You're a number!" yells one of his interrogators.

Gérard is accused of being a Trotskyite, a Titoist, a Zionist, and an ally of an American spy. He is even accused of having been in collaboration with the Gestapo, because, as a Jew, he survived the Nazi concentration camps. As a result, his family is moved to a woefully decrepit apartment in punishment for his "crimes." Gérard is allowed no food and forced to sleep on a wooden plank only on his back. Black blinders are put over his eyes when he is taken from place to place so he can't tell whether it's day or night. He is repeatedly asked to confess. "Confess?" asks Gérard, "But confess what?" His interrogators offer him a choice: confess or die. They threaten him with hanging, and at one point actually drag him outside and put a noose around his neck; but even that doesn't make him confess, because he still doesn't know what he was supposed to have done.

In the course of the film, more of Gérard's friends are arrested, and many of them sign confessions which implicate Gérard in the fictional crimes. The interrogations are horrifying; the interrogators—who constantly question him, badger him, and scream—use words independently of their true meanings in order to confuse and distort. When Gérard gives his autobiography, Costa-Gavras juxtaposes this testimony with one of the interrogators repulsively eating a sandwich and burping, the camera (just as in Z) coming in closer than necessary in order to dwell on the villain's facial eccentricities. (Earlier, the "villainous" party members who arrest Gérard can be visually recognized by the similar trench coats and hats which make them look silly.) The frenzy of Gérard's questioning is highlighted by numerous zoom-in/dolly-out shots of the interrogators behind their desks, the visual perspectives distorting as the people's truth is altered into a properly public history. Gérard is told that confession is the highest form of self-criticism; finally, he breaks down and admits that "I participated in the conspiracy against the state."

In preparation for the Soviet-backed public trial, Gérard is injected with drugs and forced to memorize and recite his testimony word for word. The state is prepared for all eventualities: when a defendant forgets a line, the defendant's pre-recorded testimony is broadcast so that the people listening to the trial on the radio will have no idea that anything is amiss. All

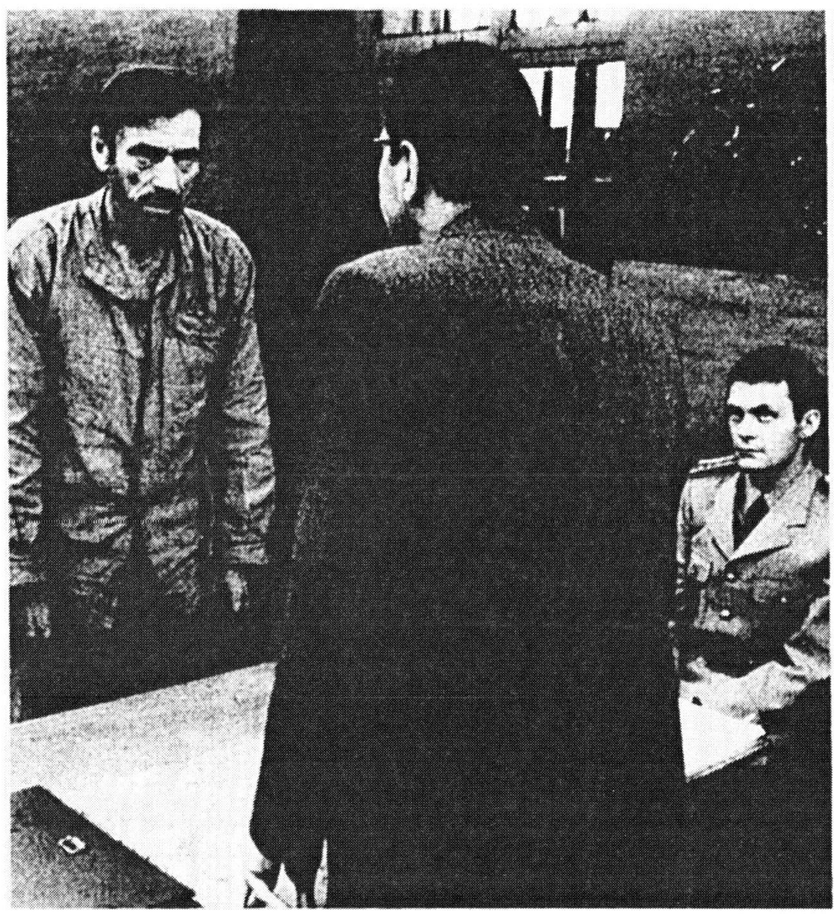

Montand being grilled by his captors in preparation for the public "show trial," in *The Confession.*

the defendants are made to understand the futility of retracting anything. Thus, the outcome of the trial is completely predetermined, the entire event absolutely fictional. At one point the court laughs when one of the defendants drops his pants; the hysterical laughter is juxtaposed with the image of the ashes of the executed defendants being spread over a slippery road. Except for Gérard and two others, all the defendants are sentenced to death.

Like Z and *All the President's Men, The Confession* ends with an epilogue. We learn that after the death of Stalin, Gérard was released from prison and moved to Paris. In defense of his actions, the investigator Kahoutek, unconsciously mimicking the officials of Nazi Germany, says simply: "I was following orders." By 1968, the Stalinists in Czechoslovakia were ousted; because Gérard sees the government of the liberal Alexander Dubček as the sign of an open era and a new Communist Party, he returns to Prague. The very day he returns, the city is invaded by Russian tanks and the government is overturned. In the context of Gérard's previous tortures and his present hopes, the new repression is both ironic and unbearable; documentary still and moving images of the heartbroken Czechoslovakians as the tanks roll in are quite moving. A group of students write in paint on a public wall (as in Z): "Lenin, wake up—they have gone mad!" The film ends with still shots of Gérard which emphasize his red eyes as he watches what is happening in horror, pain, and disbelief, knowing that his martyrdom was apparently in vain.

State of Siege, the third film in this series, was directed by Costa-Gavras in 1973 from a script by Costa-Gavras and Franco Solinas. Like Claude Chabrol's 1974 *Nada, State of Siege* accords a very sympathetic treatment to the "terrorists" at the center of its narrative. Specifically, the film is based on the abduction and eventual assassination of Daniel Mitrione, an official of the United States Agency for International Development (AID), by the Tupamaro guerrillas in Uruguay in August of 1970. Of all Costa-Gavras' films, *State of Siege* is probably the most controversial. Originally scheduled to premiere at the American Film Institute theatre at the Kennedy Center in Washington, *State of Siege* was cancelled when AFI director George Stevens, Jr., decided that the film would be inappropriate to show at a theatre dedicated to an assassinated president because the film rationalized political assassination. The cancellation caused an outcry in the international film community.

State of Siege begins with the message that "The events in this film actually took place in South America." We are then presented a rather mysterious image of the front, and then back of a car. Police are searching, but for what we are not told. When they finally find the car we have been shown and open the trunk, they discover the dead body of Philip Santore, the name Costa-Gavras gives the character (again played by Yves Montand) based on Daniel Mitrione. At a funeral service, a priest calls Santore "an innocent, sacrificial victim," a statement which turns Santore into a martyr and shows how the government and its institutions are already beginning to propagate an official, public history.

Most of *State of Siege* is made up of flashbacks which reveal the events leading up to the assassination of Santore and provide the means by which the people's history may be elaborated. The film is structured according to days, which are explicitly named on the screen, consistent to the political thriller's usual emphasis on specific times and places.

The flashbacks begin with a sequence of traditional suspense as the Tupamaros prepare to assassinate Santore. As in Z, Costa-Gavras uses parallel structures: here he juxtaposes the actions of the Tupamaros with those of the police. In one sequence, both the Tupamaros and the police are shown expropriating cars; interestingly, some of the victims of the Tupamaros tacitly agree with the terrorists' ends, if not their means. The Tupamaros' sense of justice and enlightenment is, if simplistic, humorous: after stealing a car from a rich woman, they let her out at a garbage heap in a bad section of the city to indicate her responsibility. When they kidnap Santore (in a sequence very similar to the arresting of Gérard in *The Confession*), they wound him in the process. Significantly, we are not shown the gun being shot, nor Santore's immediate response. When, however, the army's courses in the administration of electric shocks are revealed, we are graphically shown the wires attached to groins and genitals.

A structure of parallels (if with sympathy for the Tupamaros) is evident throughout *State of Siege*: the mobilization of the police and the military as they search for Santore is juxtaposed with the mobilization of the terrorists as they attempt to elude detection; the statements issued by the government are juxtaposed with the bulletins issued by the Tupamaros; and the Tupamaros' interrogation of Santore by which they attempt to get at the people's truth is juxtaposed with a scene in which the police destroy one loudspeaker after another on a college campus in an attempt to prevent the people's truth from being disseminated. This last scene, which is quite extended, becomes a metaphor for the stupidity of all repressive orders and the attendant military belief that ideas can be stilled.

The Tupamaros interrogate Santore in their makeshift hideaway in front of walls covered with newspapers headlining the revolutionary struggle. The interrogation of Santore is primarily undertaken by a Tupamaro in a mask—the mask working not to turn the guerrilla into a monster, but into a symbol of objective truth which implies the inevitability of the people's justice. The interrogator serves much the same narrative function as the magistrate in Z, although in *State of Siege,* he is ideologically committed. Presenting Santore with evidence he is unable to dispute, the Tupamaros want an admission that he has been an accomplice in South American repression, that his participation in AID was basically a front for reactionary activities, and that his primary advice was instruction in the use of political assassination and torture. At this point we are shown various police assassinations of Tupamaros or their sympathizers; in one assassination which has a particularly documentary quality, the grainy-imaged witnesses run swiftly and fearfully to the fallen body. Once again, Costa-Gavras presents the idea that it is not the people who involve themselves in conspiracies, but their governments, who do so in order to squelch the people's will.

Not surprisingly, Santore is overwhelmed by all the interlocking information that is used against him. "You can't build a thriller around foreign car sales!" he protests at one point; but that is what Costa-Gavras is doing—that is, making clear the connections between South American repression and the American military-industrial complex. Significantly, Santore was first presented as a man with a loving family and children; his involvement in the various crimes against the people gradually transform our attitude toward him, making us aware of the dichotomy between the actual and the apparent, and of the importance of continually questioning the surface reality in order to discover the often disturbing, underlying truths.

Another important character in *State of Siege* is Ducas, an older reporter who, like the opposition party in the Parliament, agrees with the aims of the terrorists and is anxious for the president to resign. Even the terrorists would prefer the resignation of the government to their own execution of Santore. Ironically, the government seems on the brink of resigning until an important terrorist is caught by a man who was actually trained by Santore. Thus, in a significant sense, Santore is responsible for his own execution. When the president then gives a speech on television and does *not* resign, Costa-Gavras emphasizes the flipping of the cue cards (which suggests that the speech is not truth, but a written fiction) as well as the ease with which the president is able instantly to turn on his sincerity.

The inevitability of Santore's fate is presented most strikingly in the sequence in which Ducas, in reply to an announcement by the foreign affairs minister of government action against the Tupamaros, says that Santore will therefore be executed in a few hours. Costa-Gavras cuts to a close-up, a medium shot, a long shot, and then back to a close-up of the minister all from the same angle. In the final close-up, the minister breaks the silence and asks: "What is the question?" Ducas responds quietly: "There is no question"—no question as to the culpability of the government, no question as to the fate of Philip Santore. Significantly, the actual act of assassination is not shown the spectator; to show it would give the act status as violence, to omit it gives the act status as justice and allows us to keep our sympathies with the apparently peace-loving Tupamaros. Only in the public history will the act be called assassination; in the people's history, it will simply be an execution.

If *State of Siege* rationalizes terrorism, it is only, according to Costa-Gavras, because "The word 'terrorism' is a word invented by the reactionary press to poison the minds of its readers and hide the justifiable acts to which all the revolutionary movements are forced to resort."[3] *State of Siege* ends with the casket of Santore sliding inexorably onto the United States Air Force plane; this is immediately followed by the arrival of Santore's replacement, who is already under the unnoticed surveillance of anonymous Tupamaro guerrillas working at the airport. Costa-Gavras' final images are close-ups of the vigilant eyes of these nameless men dedicated to the ongoing ideological struggle against the conspiracy of government.

Special Section, a fourth Costa-Gavras film made in 1975 from a script by Jorge Semprun and Costa-Gavras, deals with the Law of August 14, a retroactive antiterrorist statute promulgated by the Vichy Government in 1941 to allow it to bring to trial and guillotine Communists, Jews, and anarchists in order to impress the Germans. Although little seen in this country, *Special Section* reflects much the same preoccupations as the other Costa-Gavras films—all of which, particularly Z, worked tremendously to influence other political thrillers. Some of these subsequent thrillers, such as *The Day of the Jackal,* merely reflected the interest in terrorism and assassination popularized by Costa-Gavras. Others, such as *All the President's Men,* borrowed Costa-Gavras' high-powered style and dealt with government conspiracy. Few of the political thrillers influenced by Costa-Gavras operated from anything approaching his committed radical political position. The result was that none of the American films assayed a wholesale attack on American capitalism or imperialism and were thus assured the more widespread acceptance of middle-class audiences.

The Day of the Jackal, directed in 1973 by Fred Zinnemann, opens with a narrator who informs us that in August of 1962, extremists vowed to assassinate Charles de Gaulle for "giving away" Algeria; to achieve their goal, the reactionary OAS members hired an outside assassin—his code name, "the Jackal." If most of Zinnemann's film seems to be a historical reënactment rather than a suspense thriller, it may be because *The Day of the Jackal*'s temperament is generally restrained; there are many scenes of well-dressed officers talking English with a French accent in front of maps in clean rooms. Still, the film exhibits the typical concerns of the thriller, particularly in its emphasis on real places, time, and parallel structure—here, a structure in which the Jackal, who meticulously prepares the assassination, is contrasted with the police commissioner, who tries to uncover the OAS conspiracy and stop the Jackal.

Most of the film deals with the Jackal's attempts to go undetected as he carefully (and often mysteriously) plans the assassination. Although he is a charming assassin, he is completely without conscience: he kills a beautiful woman he made love to, he kills a homosexual he allowed to pick him up, he even knocks unconscious a nice old concierge who was about to give him a drink. The final sequence in which de Gaulle and the Jackal come together is an extended and principally silent montage. In the midst of the military demonstrations and parading for de Gaulle, the Jackal gets through security by making an appearance as an old war amputee on crutches; before long, he has managed to take his place at a window overlooking de Gaulle. It is fascinating to see how all the Jackal's preparations finally come together (as in a heist film); how, for instance, through the Jackal's ingenuity, the medals he bought twenty minutes into the film pay off ten minutes before the film's end. The assassination attempt fails, of course; although the Jackal shoots with a telescopic rifle from a window, his shot misses as de Gaulle chooses precisely that instant to bow. The Jackal does not get a second chance, since the film ends as the police commissioner bursts into the room in the proverbial nick of time and kills him.

Many political thrillers strive for an almost documentary sense of immediacy. Above is the real Charles de Gaulle.

In *The Day of the Jackal*, actor Adrian Cayla-Legrand is virtually indistinguishable from the real de Gaulle.

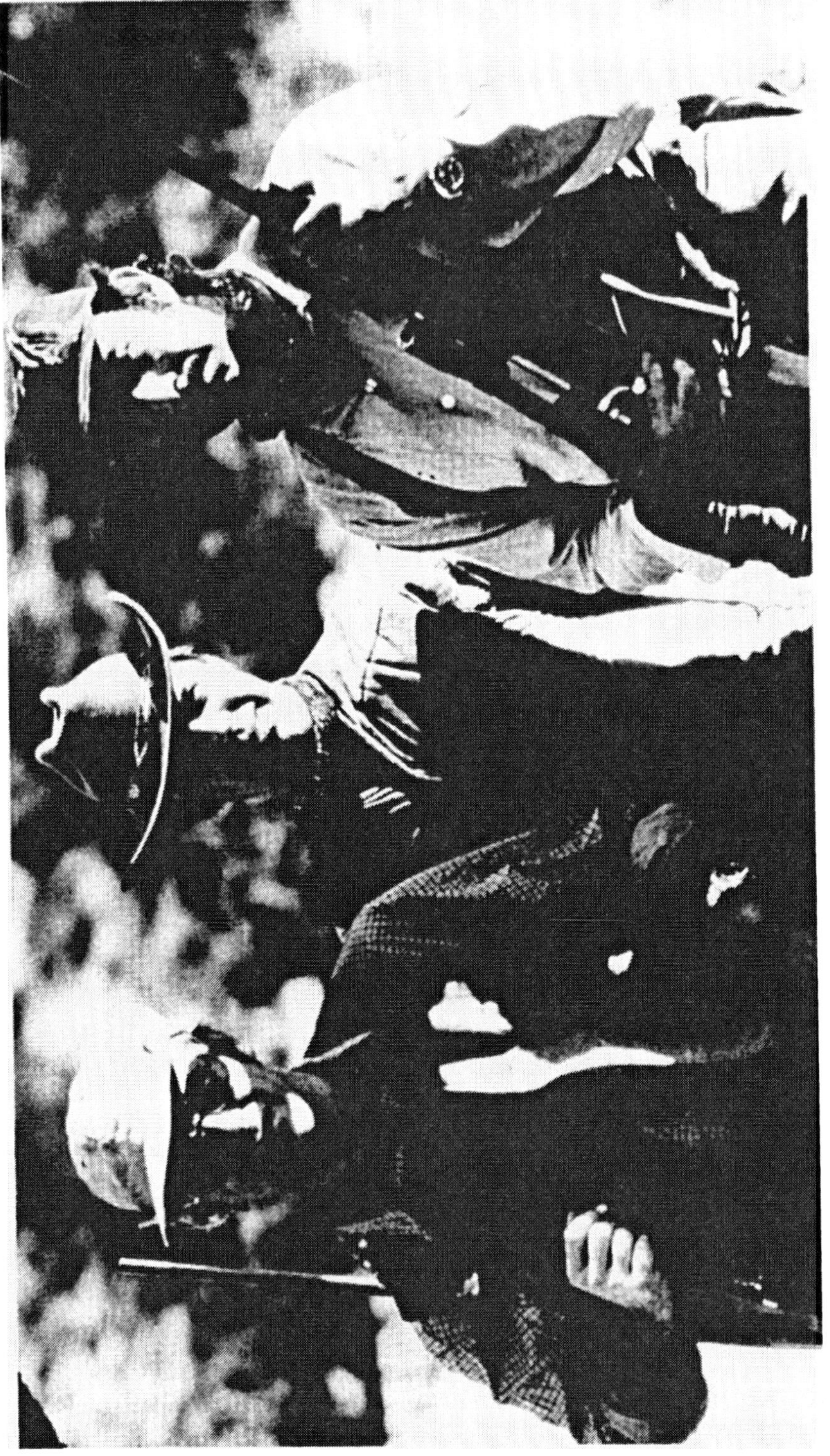

Day of the Dolphin, directed in 1973 by Mike Nichols from a script by Buck Henry, is a combination animal story and political thriller dealing with a scientist's attempts to develop a communication system with dolphins and his realization that a conspiratorial counter-intelligence agency is trying to use one of his dolphins to assassinate the president of the United States. Typical to the genre, the film climaxes with the assassination attempt. Ultimately, it is the dolphins themselves—anthropomorphically speaking in cute, babyish voices, or more naturally swimming about in an expressive montage—which engage the spectator and perhaps fatally upstage the film's political and suspenseful content.

Executive Action, directed by David Miller in 1974 from a script by Dalton Trumbo, represents an attempt to offer a conspiratorial version of the Kennedy assassination. The film begins typically with a preface, which states that although in a television interview Lyndon Johnson himself actually expressed a belief in a conspiracy theory, this controversial portion of the interview was deleted and never broadcast. As in so many political thrillers, the events that take place in this film are constantly tied to a specific time and often a specific place—all of which serves to propel inexorably the narrative to the November 22, 1963, assassination of President Kennedy.

Executive Action claims that Texas oil millionaires were behind the assassination because they were unhappy with Kennedy's campaign promises and fearful that he might work for civil rights or end the war in Vietnam. The conspirators spend much time trying to convince Ferguson (an oil millionaire played by Will Geer) to help underwrite the assassination's cost. Ferguson seems to spend most of his time watching television and getting increasingly upset with the political and social trends in the country; he finally decides to invest in the assassination after seeing a Buddhist monk set himself aflame in Vietnam.

The sections of the film dealing with the conspirators are primarily composed of talking heads photographed in wood-paneled studies, which makes much of *Executive Action* rather static. Other sections of the film are comprised of news footage and other actualities—including speeches by Kennedy, Adlai Stevenson, and Martin Luther King, Jr., as well as a slide show (of apparently original documents) on Lee Harvey Oswald's life. The juxtaposition of the fictional color footage and the black-and-white news footage adds interest to the film, although surprisingly the filmmakers have chosen not to use uninterrupted the famous Zapruder film of the assassination, preferring instead to intercut their own reconstruction.

The four basic features of the assassination conspiracy put forward by *Executive Action* include, first, its organization by oil millionaires; second, the participation of three assassins firing from three different locations; third, the theory that Oswald was set up as a patsy and that an Oswald

***Executive Action:* Portrait of the "real" assassins of John F. Kennedy?**

look-alike was hired to go around Dallas to make psychotic statements which would later incriminate the real Oswald; and fourth, the hiring of Ruby by the conspirators in order to assassinate Oswald. Much of the film's conspiracy theory doesn't make absolute sense: Why, for instance, didn't Ruby talk about what he knew? And how could the country (including utility companies, evidently) be so completely manipulated by a small handful of people?

Perhaps the most chilling, suspenseful scene takes place during a presidential motorcade on September 25 when the three assassins practice for the upcoming assassination using cameras instead of rifles. Ironically, the helicopter shot of Dealy Plaza near the end of *Executive Action* seems to have more drama and tension than most of the narrative, so fraught is that site with its historic significance. Similarly, a brief image of a flag being lowered to half mast after the assassination is equally moving. The film ends with word that Farrington (a primary organizer of the assassination, played by Burt Lancaster) has had a "heart attack"; we are to presume that he was killed by another of the conspirators in order to tie up loose ends. A printed epilogue reveals that as of 1973, eighteen material witnesses to the assassination had died, and that the odds of that happening in ten years are one hundred thousand trillion to one—which is given as irrefutable proof that a cover-up conspiracy existed as well.

An interesting analysis of *Executive Action* is offered by Joan Mellen, who claims that

> In the very process of showing that Farrington has access to individuals in the CIA, but is not a member himself, the film indirectly absolves the government agency of all knowledge of the killing. This technique is used at every point to stress that the government was innocent of complicity in Kennedy's murder. . . . Its task, thereafter, is to show the American people that six or seven cranks rather than the one, Lee Harvey Oswald, were responsible for the President's death. The film begins by attesting to the sincerity of Johnson. It moves on methodically to exonerate the CIA, the FBI, the Cabinet . . . and the Secret Service. . . .[4]

Thus, for Mellen, *Executive Action* involves itself in its own conspiracy and cover-up by trivializing objective and persuasive evidence in order to put forward a particular conspiracy theory which is patently absurd.

All the President's Men, directed in 1976 by Alan J. Pakula and based on the account by Woodward and Bernstein (the *Washington Post* reporters who broke the Watergate story), can be seen as the American Z. Not only was *All the President's Men* critically well received and nominated for many Academy Awards, it was embraced wholeheartedly by the public as an exciting and significant entertainment. The film begins with news footage of President Nixon at the peak of success, being applauded in Congress following his landslide election. The white printed titles begin silently over a black background (a style reserved generally for films of some pretension) and continue over the discovery of the Watergate burglars during their break-in by the hotel's guard (played by Frank Wills, the guard who caught the burglars in real life).

The two reporters, Bob Woodward and Carl Bernstein, are played by Robert Redford and Dustin Hoffman respectively. They decide to work as a team because they complement each other: Woodward is the more reasoned of the two, Bernstein the better writer. They first realize something is strange about the break-in when counsel is arranged for the burglars in a way that suggests the burglars had been working for someone else; the reporters' subsequent discovery of E. Howard Hunt's name in one of the burglar's address books sets off their extensive investigation which will implicate increasingly higher authorities, ending ultimately with President Richard Nixon. Again and again, the investigation by the two reporters, despite its objective basis, seems almost fictional, so consistently does the film follow typical suspense thriller constructions. When, for instance, Woodward tries to contact one of his special sources, he gets a letter instructing him to put a red flag in his flower pot, after which the source will respond by leaving Woodward further instructions on page twenty of Woodward's *New York Times.*

The intrigue of the investigation is partially represented by a continuing series of objects: the geranium, the *New York Times*, address books, library cards, and so forth. At one point, Woodward asks Deep Throat (Woodward's name for his secret source) about the Department of Justice's investigation of the Watergate affair; just after Deep Throat implies there is a very high White House connection, a car in the parking garage screeches away loudly, and Deep Throat disappears. Woodward walks off, his footsteps solitary, the city of Washington suddenly turned into an ominous place of total conspiracy, the entire investigation no longer an adventure, but a potentially dangerous nightmare.

Later in the film, Woodward falls asleep when he is supposed to be meeting Deep Throat to obtain an extremely important piece of information; there is much suspense as to whether he will get to the parking garage in time. Fortunately, he does, and Deep Throat gives Woodward the final verification: that the FBI, the CIA, and the Justice Department are all involved in a cover-up conspiracy initiated by the White House. Eerily aware that his own reality has become a suspense thriller plot, Woodward visits Bernstein at his apartment where he puts on loud music before he types out the message that they have been bugged and that their own lives are in danger.

The visual style of *All the President's Men*, photographed (as was Pakula's *The Parallax View*) by Gordon Willis, is consistently distinguished. The press room of the *Washington Post* is predominately white and brightly lighted, implying the relationship between the press and the truth. The downtown parking garage where Woodward finds out so much of his information about the conspiracy is dimly lighted, implying the sinister nature of

Nixon and his men. At one point early in the reporters' investigation, a sympathetic clerk in the Library of Congress gives them library cards to examine tediously; there are three shots, one dissolving into the next, each taken from a position increasingly further above the two reporters in the circular library room. The shots work to put Woodward and Bernstein in the heroic context of history. In another sequence in which the two reporters painstakingly check for leads on a list of names of the members of the Committee to Re-Elect the President, the reading of the names which don't pan out is accompanied by the image of the darkening Washington sky.

There are constant ironic juxtapositions: at one point we see Nixon on television receiving the nomination at the Republican convention just as Woodward and Bernstein are being told that they have come to a dead end. Perhaps one of the film's most exciting shots is one near the end of the film: it is a long moving shot, which begins on Bernstein talking on the telephone and then follows as Bernstein runs excitedly to Woodward, who then runs equally excitedly into the editor's office. After all the static shots and quick montage up to this point, the moving camera suggests that Woodward and Bernstein are now at the center of the universe, their investigation gathering irresistible momentum. And of course, the spectator in the movie theatre is aware of the historic importance of what Woodward and Bernstein are discovering—not only because he or she may have lived through the Watergate experience in actuality, but also because the spectator hears from Ben Bradlee, the editor who has been trusting the instincts of the reporters all along, that "Nothing's riding on this—except the first amendment, the freedom of the press, and the future of this country."

The primary narrative of the film ends with a symmetrically constructed shot: a television on the left side of the frame in the foreground, balanced by the two reporters, separated by pillars, typing at their desks on the right side of the frame in the background. (See page 24.) On television we see Nixon being administered the oath of office for his second term. The camera zooms in slowly to Nixon's image; we hear the sound of a twenty-one gun salute. The image abruptly changes to that of Woodward and Bernstein typing; the twenty-one gun salute has become the sound of their typewriters, for it is their reporting which shall provide the ammunition Nixon is next fated to encounter. The public history shall be balanced by the people's truth.

All the President's Men ends typically with a coda which outlines the historical outcome. A close-up of the teletype informs us with machine-gun rapidity of the various actions taken against the government officials as a result of the two reporters' successful investigation. The dates and names appear almost faster than the spectator can perceive them and climax with the result on August 9, 1974: "Nixon resigns." There is the overwhelming sense that the corrupt status quo has been completely toppled. The film ends on a freeze frame celebrating Nixon's resignation and then returns, in its end credits, to its simple (and yet pretentious) white lettering on black background.

The Domino Principle, directed in 1976 by Stanley Kramer and completely overshadowed by *All the President's Men,* is in many ways a more fictional *Executive Action* which takes the Kennedy assassination as its inspiration. The film begins with Roy Tucker (played by Gene Hackman) in prison, having been sent there for murder. Because Tucker has been in the army, in Vietnam, and in prison, he claims that he is able to live by anyone's rules. When an intelligence official named Tagge (played by Richard Widmark) contacts Tucker and offers him a chance to begin a new life in exchange for some unspecified service, Tucker accepts the offer and is given a new identity. His cellmate (played by Mickey Rooney) warns Tucker about the government officials, whom he refers to simply as "they." When Tucker asks him who "they" are, the cellmate says, "They're never anything you can identify. They're just they." Later, when Tucker asks Tagge, who has gotten him out of prison, "Who are you people?" Tagge only responds, "Did you ever hear of Franz Kafka?" For *The Domino Principle,* the society of Kafka is synonymous with the United States; conspiracy and absurdity are no longer aberrations, but parts of the American way of life.

Although Tucker convinces the officials to free his cellmate as well, the cellmate is shot after the two of them are released. Not surprisingly, Tucker hears later on the news that he is being sought for the murder of his cellmate. Tucker is now unable to go to the police and is totally in debt to the government officials (who can only be villains). Later, in a helicopter, Tucker is told what he must do in exchange for the opportunity to live freely the rest of his life in another country. Although this scene is presented in a way which prevents us from hearing what Tucker is to do, by this time we can certainly guess. Tucker refuses to cooperate; only after the officials kidnap and threaten his wife does he finally give in.

Flying in a helicopter with Tagge over a San Clemente–like estate, Tucker is given a rifle and instructed to assassinate the president who lives there (although strictly speaking, the target's identity and office are left ambiguous). The president is killed; as in *Executive Action,* the assassination is juxtaposed with the image of the American flag at half-mast. Later, however, Tucker claims that he shot short, that he couldn't have killed the president; we then learn that there were two shots fired from the ground as well, one of them by Tucker's cellmate, who is alive after all. (Thus, the assassination here takes advantage of the three-gun assassination method put forth by *Executive Action.*) At this point, we still don't know exactly who "they" are.

As Tagge puts Tucker onto a plane to take him to sanctuary, Tagge remarks, "The bigger the stink, the more the cover-up; and if the guy who ordered it panics, the dominoes start to fall." By this time, we almost like the character of Tagge, perhaps primarily because he is juxtaposed favorably with his ruthlessly robotized assistant, Pine (played by Edward Albert). From his position on the plane, Tucker sees a man deliver a suitcase to Tagge's car. As the plane taxies slowly down the runway, Tucker tries to warn Tagge through the window; but Tagge doesn't notice, gets in the car, and is blown up; the dominoes have begun to fall. Thus, Tagge's fate parallels that of Farrington in *Executive Action*, who is also killed by one of his fellow conspirators.

In the foreign country where Tucker is reunited with his wife, Tucker admits to her that he didn't kill the man he was originally sent to prison for, but went to prison willingly because he had thought that she had killed him herself. To his surprise, she is innocent as well; the nebulous "they" had been setting Tucker up even then. The final sequences of this bleak film liquidate all the underlings involved in the conspiracy. Tucker's wife is run over by a truck; in retaliation, Tucker shoots the ruthless Pine and his murderous cellmate before they can shoot him. The last lines of the film belong to Tucker. "I can't give up," he says. "I never learned how." The film's last image is that of Tucker walking down a beach; the camera pulls back and reveals a rifle about to assassinate our protagonist as well. The image turns into a freeze frame before the assassin fires.

The ending can be seen as a parallel to the coda in *Executive Action*—both of which chronicle the continued and surprising violence related to the initial assassination. In many ways, *The Domino Principle* can be analyzed as an innocent-on-the-run thriller; most of Tucker's predicament derives from his and his wife's failure to be honest with each other. This film ends where the typical innocent-on-the-run thriller begins: with the protagonist (in this case finally becoming a total innocent) about to go on the run and explore the source of the conspiracy that has involved him.

Nineteen seventy-seven brought a spate of political thrillers, including *The Eagle Has Landed, Nasty Habits, Twilight's Last Gleaming, Washington: Behind Closed Doors, The Trial of Lee Harvey Oswald, The Lincoln Conspiracy,* and *Sleeping Dogs.* Strictly speaking, *Nasty Habits* could be excluded from this list, because although it uses many of the elements of the political thriller, it is clearly a comedy which significantly excludes suspense. Still, its point-by-point adaption of the Watergate affair to the improbable setting of a convent embroiled in the election of a new Mother Superior makes *Nasty Habits* relevant to the other films discussed here.

Based on the Muriel Spark novel, the film sets up parallels between the nuns in *Nasty Habits* and the male Republicans of Watergate: thus, Glenda Jackson plays the conspiratorial Mother Superior (based on Richard Nixon) who bugs the convent, Geraldine Page and Anne Jackson play the high-ranking nuns (based on Haldeman and Ehrlichman) who smoke cigars and support the Mother Superior, Anne Meara plays the nun (based on Gerald Ford) who likes nothing better than swimming in the convent pool, Melina Mercouri plays the Catholic missionary (based on Henry Kissinger) who refuses to bail out the Mother Superior, Susan Penhaligon plays the young and liberal nun (based on George McGovern) who is Mother Superior's adversary, and Sandy Dennis plays the nun (based on John Dean) who is used as a flunky. *Nasty Habits* ends, appropriately enough, with the convent's scandal made public and the Mother Superior being summoned to Rome in order to explain herself to the Pope.

The Eagle Has Landed, directed by John Sturges, deals with Hitler's supposed attempt to kidnap Winston Churchill during World War II. The would-be kidnapper and protagonist is played by Michael Caine; he is presented not as a German Nazi, but as a Pole who understands the complexities of loyalties and who agrees to kidnap Churchill only so that the death sentences imposed on the protagonist and his men for having saved a Jewish girl from the concentration camps can be commuted. Altan Löker would probably be particularly pleased with the way *The Eagle Has Landed* carefully manipulates us to empathize with the protagonist. Our empathy grows even stronger when this "villain" we like is contrasted with an absolutely unsympathetic "hero"—a jingoistic and stupid American general who wants all the glory of halting the assassination plot himself.

The Eagle Has Landed especially takes on the sensibility of a suspense thriller at the precise point that some of the British townspeople realize that the protagonist and his men are working for the Nazis. Even though ideologically we may not want the assassination of Winston Churchill to take place, we at least partially welcome it. Ultimately, the protagonist is no longer motivated to kidnap Churchill just so his own death sentence will be commuted, because, as he says, "The time has come when I no longer control events; they control me." The film becomes increasingly concerned with the sweep of history; indeed, one character even quotes Jung's concept of synchronicity. As the film approaches its suspenseful conclusion, almost all of the protagonist's men are killed; the protagonist, determined to kill Churchill if he cannot kidnap him, sneaks up to the place where Churchill is staying. We expect, of course, something to happen at the last moment which will prevent the protagonist from succeeding, but amazingly, nothing unforeseen develops, and the protagonist shoots and kills Churchill! Later we discover that the man the protagonist shot was not really Churchill after all, but a variety artist who was hired to impersonate Churchill, who was in reality in Teheran secretly meeting with Roosevelt.

The plot twist here is interesting in the way it reflects in general on the representation of famous people in movies. We are all too willing to assume that the particular actor we see at the end of *The Eagle Has Landed* actually represents Churchill even though the resemblance may not be precise, because we are used to the conventions and limitations of fictional representation and know that the resemblance cannot be precise. That the faulty aspect of the resemblance is actually significant surprises us and shows that the filmmakers are slyly using a convention they are actually

Charles Durning (at far left) as the president surrounded by his advisors in *Twilight's Last Gleaming.*

subverting. *The Eagle Has Landed* ends with one of the superior American officers announcing that officially the whole plot to assassinate Churchill did not occur—thus compounding ambiguity but allowing the spectator to believe that the whole episode may really have happened but has been covered up for the last thirty years to avoid possible embarrassment to the Americans.

Twilight's Last Gleaming, directed by Robert Aldrich and based on the novel *Viper Three* by Walter Wager, combines the threat of nuclear destruction with the revelation of government misconduct. In this film (which seems to take its inspiration from the release of the Pentagon Papers by Daniel Ellsberg), a dismissed United States Air Force officer, played by Burt Lancaster, seizes a nuclear missile site in order to force the president to disclose publicly the real motive behind the United States involvement in the Vietnam War: the government's desire to prove to the Soviet Union that the United States was equally capable of inhuman acts and should therefore not be underestimated. Once again the dominant theme is the dichotomy between the apparent and the actual, the latter being that which is informed by the conspiratorial theory of government. Although *Twilight's Last Gleaming* does not deal overtly with the subject of assassination, it builds to an ingenious climax whereby the president is assassinated. The film derives considerable interest from its style—particularly Aldrich's use of split-screen, which creates suspense and reflects the film's complexity of viewpoints, and the score by Jerry Goldsmith, which often powerfully evokes the Americana of Aaron Copland.

Washington: Behind Closed Doors was produced as a miniseries for ABC television. It ran for six consecutive days for a total of twelve-and-a-half hours and presented, in fictional form, the abuses and excesses of the Nixon administration. Nixon is represented by President Richard Monckton, played by Jason Robards, Jr. Robards imitates and exaggerates Nixon's mannerisms almost to the point of parody; the sneering, psychotic, ambitious, megalomaniacal portrait which results is an archetypally evil villain. Although many of the incidents in the film are taken directly from Watergate tapes or related revelations, other incidents are completely contrived; it thus becomes virtually impossible to separate the real abuses of Nixon from the fictional abuses, so inextricably are they intermingled.

As in other political thrillers, the characters are based on historical personages, although some may be more obscure than others. The Haldeman-Erlichman duo, for instance, combines into one character called Frank Flaherty, played by Robert Vaughn as an absolutely cool, unfeeling, professional hypocrite, completely loyal to the president. It is interesting to compare the Vaughn performance in *Washington: Behind Closed Doors* to his performance between 1964 and 1968 in the spy series *The Man from U.N.C.L.E.*, in which he played an American pseudo–CIA agent with a similarly cool and professional persona. The difference between the moral attitudes embodied in these two works is overwhelming: the Vaughn persona which was acceptable and even laudable in the mid-sixties becomes, in 1977, unacceptable and inhumanly evil. What makes *Washington: Behind Closed Doors* particularly significant is that it reached a wider audience than any of the other thrillers discussed in this chapter and yet there was little public outcry against its obvious exaggerations. Many Americans didn't care that this work was not an objective dissertation reasonably analyzing Nixon's wrongdoings. Indeed, they welcomed a popular entertainment which turned Nixon into a simple and unambiguous symbol of evil.

Also inspired by real political history, *The Trial of Lee Harvey Oswald*, another television movie made for ABC, is based on the supposition, What if Lee Harvey Oswald had not been assassinated and had instead been able to stand trial for the murder of President Kennedy? The film begins, typically, with a printed introduction; this one claims that although much in the film is fictionalized, many events have been reconstructed at the actual sites at which they occurred. As in *Executive Action*, the emotional climax of *The Trial of Lee Harvey Oswald* is in its reconstruction of the assassination. We know what is going to happen, yet hope against hope that it won't; we are allowed to witness the great course of history, as the moments tick away, the important times even flashed across the screen. After the assassination, the film continues chronologically, and Oswald is arrested. On the day of Sunday, November 24, 1963, at 11:20 a.m., Oswald is moved from his cell.

The famous televised murder of Oswald seems about to be reconstructed as the actor playing Oswald walks toward the (unseen) camera. Just at that moment when in real life Oswald was shot and his face suddenly contorted, we hear a sound: but it is not the shot of a gun, just the click of a camera. The picture and sound freezes for a few moments, demarcating clearly the point at which the "what if" premise of the film takes hold. The court prosecutor of Oswald, who is at first skeptical that Oswald acted alone, is played by Ben Gazzara. Ultimately, the prosecutor aligns himself with the official Warren Commission Report, but additionally puts forth his own ingenious and far-fetched theory that Oswald killed Kennedy primarily because once when Oswald had wanted to make love to his wife, she had insisted on watching Kennedy on television instead.

Oswald's defense attorney is played by Lorne Greene, which was an astute and sly piece of casting, because after more than a decade as the heroic American patriarch in *Bonanza*, Greene built up such audience empathy that subsequent characterizations could not help but be imbued with authority. The defense attorney aligns himself consecutively with a variety of alternatives implying government conspiracy, but finally settles on the particular theory that Oswald was a patsy of the CIA and the Mafia, both wanting to assassinate Kennedy so that the new president would presume a Cuban plot and therefore invade Cuba. The supposedly "objective" portions of the film itself seem to support this theory: Oswald is shown shaken when confronted with the murder of one of the supposedly involved Mafia figures as well as when confronted with this theory itself.

In one of the prison scenes between Oswald and his wife, the actor's portrayal of Oswald seems to suggest clearly that Oswald considers himself a martyr who has been undergoing an undeserved trial. Further, when taking the stand, Oswald vehemently denies he killed Kennedy, but refuses to confirm or deny that he was unwittingly part of a conspiracy. Other events and flashbacks presented in visual terms throughout the film also make inadequate the explanation of the Warren Commission and require some sort of conspiratorial theory.

Presenting a conspiratorial theory of its own is *The Lincoln Conspiracy*, a "Sunn Classic" produced by Charles E. Sellier, Jr. The film is virtually a documentary and almost humorous in the way it uses the assassination of Abraham Lincoln to deal obliquely with the assassination of Kennedy and the Watergate crimes of Nixon. The film begins with a white-lettered crawl on black background, as the narrator tells us that we have a right to know the facts and that the story of the Lincoln assassination is really "a story of corruption, treachery, and cover-up." Once again we immediately get the dichotomy between the apparent and the actual; before long, we get the emphasis on particular places and specific dates, as well. The primary narrative begins at the conspiracy trial of eight people linked with John Wilkes Booth's supposed assassination of Lincoln. The narrator asks us portentously: Were they really guilty?

Although in *The Lincoln Conspiracy,* John Wilkes Booth does kill the president, his intentions are known and approved of by many high officials, including Lincoln's secretary of war, Edwin M. Stanton, who had virtually hired Booth to kidnap Lincoln so that Stanton could extend the Civil War for political reasons. "Victory would be a calamity," says Stanton, which suggests an obvious modern-day parallel to the extension of the war in Vietnam. After Stanton and his fellow conspirators finally give up on Booth as a total incompetent, they hire a jailed Confederate spy named Boyd to kidnap Lincoln from the theatre; unfortunately, Booth intercedes and assassinates Lincoln before the kidnapping could be effected. Boyd and Booth both try to escape; Booth knowing that the whole country (particularly the North) would be after him, Boyd knowing that the conspirators would want him dead so he could not reveal the extent of the conspiracy. *The Lincoln Conspiracy* contends that the man who was so famously shot while hiding in a barn was not Booth, but Boyd.

Led by Stanton, the conspirators falsify various records and arrange for the whole country to assume that Booth has been killed, so that no questions will be asked as to why Boyd was similarly fleeing the assassination site. When the narrative returns to the trial in which Booth's friends and acquaintances are tried for treason, the narrator points out which of the witnesses are perjuring themselves and suggests that their lies were part of a massive cover-up to link Booth to a Southern conspiracy involving Jefferson Davis, a conspiracy which would then divert attention away from the real conspiracy and allow a harsh postwar treatment of the South.

Booth's diary, which had been found by an Indian guide and which implicated all the high officials who had implicitly or explicitly approved of his plots against Lincoln, had been stored away in the government archives. When, in 1868, an investigation of the Lincoln assassination was undertaken and the diary was retrieved for examination, eighteen of its pages were missing.

"What became of the eighteen missing pages!?" asks the investigating Mr. Rogers in a line that invariably brought the 1977 audience to laughter so obvious was the parallel to the eighteen-and-a-half erased minutes on the Watergate tapes. Where is Booth now? asks the narrator. "No one knows." The last image of Booth shows him running—perhaps in Canada, perhaps in India—from the assassin that he knows the conspirators have sent after him. The film ends uniquely with a bibliography (!) listing the film's sources, which include published books, letters, and diaries. The bibliography, shown in white printing on the black screen, works to impress the spectator that this delightfully preposterous and seemingly too relevant political thriller may be accurate revisionist history, after all.

Watergate was a culminating conspiratorial event of a tumultuous period in American history, a period which *The Lincoln Conspiracy* in many ways accurately reflected. Although by the release of *The Lincoln Conspiracy* in 1977, Nixon had already been out of office several years, the accompanying cultural energy resulting from such pervasive conspiracy worked to unleash an extraordinary number of political thrillers throughout the next decade. Indeed, one could argue that during this period, most of the thriller's energy was reserved for the political thriller. Certainly no other subgenre seemed somehow so relevant, so immediate, so filled with a righteous sense of issues to be explored, of tantalizing headlines to be dramatized. What may seem somewhat paradoxical is that although conspiratorial notions tended to disappear from other thriller subgenres (such as the innocent-on-the-run films) in the seventies and eighties, conspiratorial notions remained strong and powerful in the political thriller—even as the United States entered the more conservative Reagan era. It was as if these political films (at least those with a left-wing bias) served to provide a release for those minority tensions needing to be worked out; planted in the sixties and seventies, these tensions bloomed in the late seventies and eighties, even as street demonstrations and radical public expression of dissent became unfashionable.

Those years from 1975 to 1985 saw an extraordinary variety of political thrillers, works which can be usefully described as conforming to one of several different orientations. One whole series of political thrillers, for instance, examined in harsh and critical detail the United States policy toward Latin America or the policies of specific right-wing Latin American countries. Uruguay had already been examined in 1973 by director Costa-Gavras in *State of Siege*. Chile was examined in 1982 by Costa-Gavras in *Missing;* Nicaragua was examined in 1983 by Roger Spottiswoode in *Under Fire;* Argentina, in 1985 by Luis Puenzo in *The Official Story;* and El Salvador, in 1986 by Oliver Stone in *Salvador*. Each film in this series seems extraordinary, filled with the crackle, excitement, and anger that comes when a work is highly structured and propelled from a central and sincerely felt moral position.

Missing was the most successful of these films, nominated for an Academy Award and based on a script by Costa-Gavras and Donald Stewart. *Missing* deals with the political turmoil in Chile during the military takeover of September 1973. The film begins with a title which tells the audience: "This film is based on a true story. The incidents and facts are documented. Some of the names have been changed to protect the innocent and also to protect the film." Incredibly compelling is the general atmosphere of the film, the way Costa-Gavras communicates what it feels like to live in a police state. *Missing* opens with the American young man Charlie

Horman (played by John Shea) waiting to pass a military roadblock on his way to his Chilean home and then forced to stay in a hotel because of the curfew. The military police are everywhere, and everyone scurries to get off the street. The next day Charlie is reunited with his wife Beth (played by Sissy Spacek), and they joke together to calm their nerves while from outside the sound of gunshots indicates that the military troops are killing people in the street.

Justified paranoia continues: later while Charlie and Beth wait for a bus, the military remove people from the bus line, including a woman whose only "crime" is wearing slacks, which the military disapproves of. In the first section of *Missing*, Charlie and Beth are constantly in danger, harassed by the military, searched, and in a state of anxiety as around them the streets fill with people being arrested or shot. Perhaps the most suspenseful scene is one in which Beth, unable to get a bus, is stranded outside after curfew. Military men are everywhere, and dead bodies pile up all around. Beth, unable to find sanctuary, is forced to sleep in an alley. At one point, she sees a beautiful white horse charging through the dark streets, followed by a military tank driven by men who are shooting after it. The image is very beautiful, almost surreal: the horse a symbol, perhaps, of the spirit of the Chilean people—strong, graceful, pure. The next day, when Beth returns to her home to be reunited with her husband, her house has been ransacked and her husband is gone: has he been arrested or killed by the military?

The rest of the film gradually and inexorably answers that question. The narrative cuts to Ed Horman, Charlie's father, played by Jack Lemmon. The characterization of Ed is crucial to the film's structure: he is a decent American, perhaps slightly right-wing, a devoutly religious Christian Scientist who believes in his government. Ed has attempted to enlist all kinds of aid in finding his son, including the State Department and various congressmen. When he arrives in Chile, it is Ed who is the innocent, and the young counterculture Beth who is his "mature" guide. Ed regards Beth with suspicion and resentment. "I don't want to hear any of your anti-establishment paranoia," he tells her; and many wonderfully-written scenes between them show the subtle tensions underneath the obvious tensions. Although Ed's Bible is taken away from him temporarily at the airport, and he later sees a woman being taken away violently by the military, Ed's transformation into an enlightened man cognizant of Chilean repression and American complicity is a gradual one. The government insists that Ed's son may be on the side of the leftist revolutionaries and in hiding; Ed is the man in the middle, not knowing what to believe.

One of the things that makes *Missing* so extraordinary is Costa-Gavras' facility with style. Just as we begin to feel definitively that Charlie must be dead, the film cuts to Charlie. Is he alive after all? But the scene is gradually revealed as a flashback: the day of the beginning of the military coup when Charlie accidentally became acquainted with a retired American Navy man

who was involved. Later, as Beth receives testimony from people in the countryside, Costa-Gavras shows us different versions of events dissolving in and out of a long shot, allowing us to pick the version we prefer. In this scene, as in others, Beth must teach Ed. "Where are you going?" she asks him at one point inside their hotel when he storms off angrily. "For a walk." "You can't. It's curfew. You'll get shot." Her tone is matter-of-fact, almost like a mother teaching a child not to go out in the rain. Later, when Ed begins to acknowledge that he has been too closed to Beth's point of view, she reads him the section of *The Little Prince* that was Charlie's favorite. "It is only with the heart that one can see rightly. What is essential is invisible to the eye." Ed is moved and asks her, "What is essential?" She says, "The stuff you can't see." And what Ed cannot yet see is the profound goodness of his son or the insidious evil of the military regime and the American involvement in it.

That the government constantly changes its story helps Ed to realize how much lying is going on: now they suggest that Charlie was actually picked up by leftists posing as military. When Ed, upset at Charlie's interest in what was going on in Chile, says that Charlie should have stuck to the basics, Beth replies bitterly, "What are the basics? God, country, and Wall Street?" Ed's knowledge of the repressions grows as he learns of the great numbers of people who have disappeared. His phone is tapped openly by an arrogant military worker who does not even feel the need to keep the act secret. In a variety of offices hang the ubiquitous portraits of President Nixon, implying American complicity. At one point, an American embassy official asks Ed what Christian Science is all about. "Faith," says Ed. "In what?" asks the official. "Truth," Ed replies, suddenly noticing that their car is being followed, realizing that he is being regarded as a troublemaker.

Typical to the genre, there is an investigative reporter, Kate Newman (played by Janice Rule), who helps to propel the narrative and organize some of its revelations. And there are certainly many of them. At a hospital, a patient cries, "Another one," and we see a dead body floating down the river, an everyday occurrence. Still Ed wonders what his son must have done to have been arrested. "You Americans," he is chastised, "You always assume you must do something before you are arrested." In a stadium in front of thousands of prisoners, Ed makes a general appeal on the off chance that his son is there; one man comes forward—whom Ed momentarily thinks is his son—and gives a speech to the effect that since *he* isn't American, *his* father can't come and make an appeal for him.

Perhaps the emotional climax for Ed, his psychological turning point, comes when Ed sees military men on a tank killing someone for writing

Costa-Gavras' *Missing:* a country under military siege. Left: A vulnerable John Shea. Right: Surrounded by the horror, Jack Lemmon makes an emotional appeal in the center of an amphitheatre filled with political prisoners.

graffiti on the wall; Ed's moral outrage is suddenly so great that he tries to stop the killing and almost gets himself, Beth, and Kate Newman killed. Kate tells Ed that she witnessed almost the exact same scene earlier with his son Charlie; and Ed realizes now that Charlie was not really a revolutionary, but a common man of great moral decency who came to sympathize with the revolutionaries for good, solid reasons.

Before long, the officials offer yet another explanation: Ed's son was found dead on the street, but there is no evidence he was killed by the military. Shortly thereafter, there is an earthquake, and as Ed and Beth start to run out to the street, military men begin shooting people outside because it is after curfew: the horror has become completely absurd. Finally, the investigation uncovers the truth: Charlie *was* killed by the military, probably with the tacit approval of the Americans, who were involved in the military coup. The officials stop denying it, yet inflict upon Ed one final indignity: a shipping bill for $931.14 which Ed must pay to those officials responsible for the murder of his son, before the body can be mailed back to the United States. In an epilogue we discover that Ed Horman later sued eleven officials, including Henry Kissinger, but that the suit was dismissed, because the information needed to prove complicity remained classified. If the United States provides the official history, which claims the coup as an independent action of the Chilean military, the United States cannot designate *Missing* as classified. This film provides the real history and documents proving the Chilean and United States involvement in repression and murder.

Under Fire, made in 1983, deals with the spring of 1979 when the Sandinista opposition to Nicaraguan dictator Anastasio Somoza was about to climax, a time when the country was seesawing between two radically different political fates. A prologue to the Nicaraguan narrative is set in Chad in 1979: color moving picture footage of military and animals freeze-frames into black-and-white still photographs, as director Roger Spottiswoode introduces us to the film's protagonist, Russell Prince (played by Nick Nolte) who is a photojournalist. We also meet Oates (played by Ed Harris), an American mercenary who goes from one war-torn country to the other, fighting for the highest price. Although he is hired to work for the military government, the reactionary pragmatist Oates has, out of his own ignorance, actually been fighting *alongside* the rebels, unable to distinguish the black revolutionaries from the black military. We discover too that the CIA is aiding the military in Chad, just as it aided the Chilean military in *Missing*.

The film then takes us to Nicaragua, where we get to know the two other important characters—a radio correspondent, Clara (played by Joanna Cassidy), and her ex-lover Alex (played by Gene Hackman), a Walter Cronkite–like journalist who is widely respected. *Under Fire* is very skillful, as is *Missing*, at showing what it is like to live in a country in political turmoil—here, one on the threshold of a revolution. In a nightclub, Sandinistas burst in, kidnap a fascist, and accidentally detonate a hand grenade, which causes death and destruction. At one point, Russell is arrested by the military, put in jail and beaten up; a priest is his unlikely cellmate. In the war zone, we see F.S.L.N. signs everywhere, signs of the Sandinistas' political movement. Clearly, the film romanticizes the Sandinistas, coming down squarely on the side of their "revolution of poets" and opposing the military, who are presented as dumb and oafish brutes.

In an attempt to get good photographs, Russell attaches himself to a group of Sandinistas, putting himself in danger as he gets caught numerous times in cross-fire between them and the military. At one crucial point, when Russell runs into his mercenary acquaintance Oates, who is fighting in South America, but at the moment pretending to be dead on a pile of military casualties to avoid capture or death, Russell keeps quiet; later, Oates himself shoots Pedro, one of Russell's Sandinista companions. The moment of the killing is a turning point: up until then, Russell, despite his sympathies toward the Sandinistas, has tended to remain objective and distanced from them and their cause. Suddenly, when Pedro is killed, Russell feels, as do we, that Oates' action has been dishonorable, that the unspoken premise of Russell's silence which allowed Oates' life to be spared was that Oates would not himself use Russell's silence to his own violent advantage. In a sense, Russell has become responsible for the death of a man whom he regarded as honorable. Later, Russell says that although he didn't want to get involved, he realizes he made the wrong choice, he *should* have helped the Sandinistas rather than Oates. Russell and Clara make love: two journalists surrounded by the strife of an exciting and passionate war. "Something's happening to us," says Russell to Clara.

And indeed it is, for as the film proceeds, both Russell and Clara find themselves increasingly committed to the Sandinista cause. Living in Nicaragua has opened up their eyes to the repressions and corruption of the government. Somoza owns one-fifth of the land, the shipping industries, and the Mercedes dealership; he is corrupt, acquisitive, manipulative, violent, oafish, and uninterested in his people. When Clara interviews him, Somoza, who is more interested in his affair with the beauty queen Miss Panama than in the suffering of the poor, asks Clara to record in the interview that he conscientiously visits his father's grave. As the narrative progresses, the central issue of the film revolves around whether the Sandinista's revolutionary leader "Rafael" is, indeed, dead, as Somoza has announced. If so, the United States will ship more arms to support Somoza, for without the charismatic leadership of Rafael, the revolutionary cause may fizzle. If, however, Rafael is not dead, the State Department may more definitively conclude that Somoza's cause cannot be won and abandon Somoza.

Seeking Rafael, Russell and Clara journey into the Sandinista-held territory of the Northern province of Matagalpa, almost getting themselves

killed. At the Sandinista camp, they discover that Rafael *is* dead, after all, but the Sandinistas, needing momentum and realizing that Russell is a fine photographer who sympathizes with their cause, ask him to take a picture of the dead Rafael in such a way that he will appear to be alive. Clara says to Russell, "Sure would be a prize winner." "I've won enough prizes," says Russell. "But you haven't won a war," says Clara.

Russell is thus put in that critical position where he is asked to make a commitment. Although they represent the investigatory force so typical to the genre, Russell and Clara are asked to participate in a lie toward the service of what they believe to be a greater truth. What should they do—say Rafael is dead? Say Rafael is alive? Say "we fell in love with the guerrillas?" But Russell and Clara are no longer merely journalists, they are partisans: they take the picture, which becomes an international sensation, makes Russell's reputation, and—more importantly—is immediately copied and distributed all over the country, spurring the Sandinistas to victory. Children run down dirt roads waving pictures of Rafael and shouting, "Rafael vive! Rafael vive!" There is a kind of implicit *hommage* to Z in the central construction of *Under Fire;* just as the letter Z came to signal, "He is alive," expressing the martyrdom of the Greek minister, so too does the picture here come to signify the same sentiment.

The various and subtle implications of this scene are noteworthy. Certainly, the scene implies the need for commitment to politics above all else, upholding Russell and Clara's decision. As well, it implies that "objectivity" is not a supreme value, that it is not always correct to remain distanced, that politicization requires learning with both the head and the heart. As well, this scene questions the validity of all news coverage. Even though *Under Fire* presents us with heroes who use their reporting media in order to lie, the implication is that any or all news coverage can lie and that we must always see beneath the coverage to the underlying truth. This message recalls the one communicated by Beth in Costa-Gavras' *Missing:* "What is essential is invisible to the eye."

As Rafael's status grows, he becomes a folk hero. As someone says rather cynically, they want to do a musical on him in America, his face is on T-shirts, he's bigger than Farrah Fawcett. The international stir attending Rafael's "reappearance" causes Alex to return to Nicaragua in order to have Russell set up an interview with Rafael. Meanwhile, Russell discovers that if his photograph of Rafael has aided the Sandinistas, his other photographs have aided the military government. In one horrible scene where Russell is surrounded by dead bodies, he again sees the mercenary Oates, who is using copies of the many photographs Russell took in the

Joanna Cassidy and Nick Nolte as the investigative journalists who come to embrace the Sandinistas' Nicaraguan revolution in *Under Fire* (here with Hamilton Camp and Halim Camp).

Sandinista camps as his own guide to identify Sandinistas to murder. Thus, Russell becomes indirectly responsible for military killing and torture.

To explain what they did, Russell and Clara bring Alex to a statue of Somoza on horseback which stands on the square. It is actually a statue of Mussolini with a different head, erected because it was cheaper than building a whole statue. "They switched heads—you can't tell, can you?" The statue, of course, is a symbol of Somoza's fascism as well as of what Russell and Clara themselves did with the picture of Rafael: "Things aren't exactly what they seem to be." Russell tries to explain further in terms which emphasize the romantic, almost fictional nature of their dilemma. "Here we are, two guys in love with the same dame in the tropics, bullets flying. . ." Alex, when he is told about the deception, is just furious, but later when he is asked by another reporter to verify that the photo may have been faked, he backs up Russell and Clara—not happy about it, but loyal to his friends and their careers.

In the most horrible scene of the film, Alex and Russell get lost in a war zone dominated by the military, which has become increasingly paranoid as the revolutionaries appear closer to success. At one point, Alex walks down the street to ask directions. While Russell watches from a distance and takes pictures, Alex is casually stood up against a wall and shot. The emotional impact of seeing a Cronkite-like journalist killed so brutally is electrifying; and the offhand suddenness with which the act takes place reminds one of the death in *Open City* of Magnani at the hands of the Fascists. With his camera and his film of the killing, Russell runs from the military men until a sympathetic peasant woman provides him a hiding place. Ultimately, Russell is saved when a scared kid in the military who perhaps has Sandinista sympathies, lies to save Russell's life (and maybe his own).

Up until this point of the film, there has been virtually nothing anti-Sandinista or pro-Somoza. At the height of the action, director Spottiswoode allows the French character played by Jean-Louis Trintignant—who has been surreptitiously helping Somoza even though he doesn't completely approve of him—to defend his pragmatic position rather eloquently. While three terrified Sandinista children threaten to shoot him, this urbane Somoza partisan says calmly to Russell and Clara:

> I like you people, but you are sentimental shits. You fall in love with the poets, the poets fall in love with the Marxists, the Marxists fall in love with themselves. The country is destroyed with rhetoric, and in the end we are stuck with tyrants. Somoza—he is a tyrant, too, of course, a butcher. But finally, liberty is not the point. If we wish to survive, we have a choice of tyrants. And for all the right reasons, you poets chose the wrong side.

In a sense, the French Somoza partisan is the character who can see into the future, who can anticipate what many will call the Sandinistas' betrayal of their own revolution with a totalitarian system similarly rigid and repressive. But neither Russell nor Clara buy his arguments; and as the three boys assassinate the Somoza partisan, Russell refuses to take the picture. Russell's refusal seems to signify his own tacit acceptance that in Nicaragua he is no longer a journalist: he could photograph the military's assassination of Alex, which would aid the Sandinistas, but he cannot photograph the Sandinistas' assassination of the Somoza partisan, which might help Somoza.

Later, when Clara sees photo by photo each moment of the assassination of Alex, she breaks down—the historical document of Russell working to put her in touch with her heart and implicitly affirming the ability of radical journalism or political thrillers to function politically and connect with an audience. However, lest Clara or the spectator be too moved by the photographs, a Nicaraguan woman interrupts Clara's grief to remind her, "50,000 Nicaraguans died and now one Yankee. Maybe we should have killed one American journalist fifty years ago." For the typical Nicaraguan victim there is neither a *Time* magazine cover nor international outrage. The film ends shortly after the civil war is resolved when, on July 17, 1979, Somoza flees to Miami with the exhumed bodies of his father and brother, and the Sandinistas take over control of the country.

At the street celebration, Russell and Clara see the mercenary Oates, who is now pragmatically joining in the festivities. "See you in Thailand," he says, reminding them and the spectator that there are other conflicts, other wars. Clara turns to Russell and asks rather rhetorically, "Did we fall in love with too much?" Although *Under Fire* was not financially successful in this country, it created controversy and garnered some very good reviews. What is remarkable about the film is that, in the anti–Sandinista Reagan era, it was made at all: partisan and slanted, romanticizing the rebels, a surprisingly courageous film.

Luis Puenzo's Argentine *The Official Story*, directed in 1985, was as well a courageous film. One of the biggest foreign-language commercial successes in recent years, Puenzo's film also won an Academy Award as the best foreign film of 1985. *The Official Story* stars Norma Aleandro as a history teacher in Argentina, who, very much like Ed Horman in *Missing*, sheds her initial conservative, almost reactionary attitudes as she discovers and admits the true horror and conspiracy of the military government. What makes the protagonist's initial naïveté all the more ironic and indefensible, however, is her career as a teacher of history. In her class, she states that, "History is the memory of the people." A radical student who is one of her best, if one she disapproves of, interrupts to claim that history is written by assassins. His point is that the course of history is changed—and in Argentina it would be for the good—by assassinating those in power. An alternate interpretation of his point which would be both more subtle and astute is that those who have political power can determine the content of the history books; thus, history is not necessarily objective truth as much as it is a record of who has been in power; and in Argentina, those who write the history that the protagonist teaches are indeed assassins.

What *The Official Story* takes as its primary issue is the most highly publicized horror perpetrated by the Argentine military—its killing of those opposed to its rule and, in particular, its killing, kidnapping, or "re-allocation" of the children of adversaries. Demonstrations take place daily by "los madres"—those mothers fighting to regain their missing children. The protagonist in *The Official Story* comes to realize that her own adopted daughter is indeed a stolen child, the adoption arranged by her husband and her priest, who are all involved in the government conspiracy to punish those opposed to the military and to reward those supporting the military. Typical to the conventions of the political thriller, Puenzo's film contrasts "the official story"—the history given by the government, with the actual story—the history uncovered by the people. It is the latter which this history teacher gradually embraces, as her world is turned upside down and she is forced to commit herself in opposition to the fascist values of those around her.

A fourth film on Latin America is *Salvador*, released in 1986 and directed by Oliver Stone. *Salvador* deals with the events in El Salvador in 1980 and 1981 in the wake of the Nicaraguan revolution, when El Salvador was itself plunged into chaos. Thousands of people were killed or disappeared, and the government feared a people's revolution similar to the one of the Sandinistas. True to the political thriller genre, *Salvador* constantly interrupts its apparently fictional flow with a title caption that indicates some ostensible "fact"—showing us, for instance, the identity of "Colonel Figueroa" by superimposing his name on the screen, or of the "El Playon" death site, or of "Ramón Alvarez" of the Revolutionary Democratic Front, or of "Thomas Kelly, U.S. Ambassador to El Salvador," and so forth. These captions give the film an immediacy and sense of documentary realism that make the film all the more compelling.

As usual for this kind of political thriller, there is an investigative force: this time, again a photojournalist. What makes *Salvador* rather unique (and different certainly from *Under Fire*) is that its protagonist, the photojournalist Richard Boyle (played by James Woods) is one of the most unromanticized protagonists ever to appear in a political thriller. He is basically a sleazy, selfish jerk who alternates between amorality and insensitivity; that, by the end of the film, Boyle is somewhat redeemed by what he has learned about the people's suffering in El Salvador, makes *Salvador* surprisingly affecting.

The primary political horror of El Salvador that this film exposes is the existence of violent death squads, controlled by the right wing, which terrorize the peasants and kill indiscriminately. One moving and horrible scene shows Boyle visiting "El Playon," the dump site for the death squads. In images recalling Holocaust footage, we see hills covered with dead and mutilated bodies. In the context of this horrible carnage committed by the military right-wing, a televised Ronald Reagan speech within the film about the dangers of the Communist guerrillas rings both hollow and stupid. In fact, Boyle calls Reagan "straight man to a chimpanzee." The most outrageous villain in *Salvador* is Major "Max," the right-wing presidential candidate who orders his followers to kill Archbishop Romero and then in his television commercials for the presidency proclaims his support for the church and for law and order. Virtually all the officials in El Salvador are presented as corrupt bribe-takers.

In one of the central scenes of the film, Archbishop Romero delivers a sermon at a Mass: "We are poor. You in Washington are rich. Why are you so blind?" Romero's sermon is a fiery one (the kind of liberation theology officially disapproved of by the conservative Pope John Paul II) which attacks the American support of the death squads and decries the violence in the country. After the sermon, Boyle and the Salvadoran woman he loves take communion; shortly thereafter, a military assassin spits at the host that the Archbishop offers, then kills the Archbishop violently in the church. Like this assassination, there is another horrifying scene based on historical fact which shows nuns being raped and killed by the right-wing death squads—an incident which the Salvadoran government in real life had long tried to deny. Ronald Reagan is held clearly responsible for the increased activity of the death squads. And responsibility too (as well as ridicule) is accorded reporters like the fictional Pauline Axelrod, a news correspondent who misunderstands everything, refuses to see the truth, is concerned primarily with her own career, and allows herself to be part of government deception.

One of the most suspenseful scenes occurs late in the film, when Boyle and his fellow photographer John Cassady (played by John Savage) gleefully take great risks to get romantic pictures of peasants on horseback charging the military the way the cavalry would in an American western. When the peasants later brutally shoot their right-wing prisoners, Boyle says to them somewhat bitterly, "You'll become just like them." They answer simply: "You have no stomach for war!" For them, an all-out war is indeed what they are involved in. The American ambassador, weak and manipulated, advises that military aid be released, effectively squelching the civil war and propping up the military government. Boyle's friend Cassady is then killed as he tries to take a picture of an American helicopter participating in the military offensive and killing peasants. Shockingly, it is the American helicopter which guns down Cassady; and Boyle tries to save Cassady's film so that he will not have died in vain and so that the true story of the American involvement in the repressive violence can be reported.

In the film's final irony, after Boyle has risked his life and gone through countless trials to get the film and the Salvadoran woman he loves out of the country, just as he arrives in California, bragging about the kind of free lifestyle available in the United States, border patrol guards insist on sending the Salvadoran woman back to El Salvador—oblivious to the potential torture and death that await her.

Another group of suspense thrillers made in the last ten years takes basically the same approach as the four films dealing with Latin America, but attack countries outside the Americas as being repressive. The two most notable examples in this group of thrillers are Peter Weir's *The Year of Living Dangerously*, which examines Indonesia, and Costa-Gavras' *Hanna K*, which examines present-day Israel. Also relevant here is the David Puttnam production *Defence of the Realm*, which looks beneath political scandal in Britain to examine government corruption, cover-up, and assassination.

The Year of Living Dangerously, directed in 1983 and featuring a very atmospheric score by Maurice Jarre, takes the theme typical to other Weir films: an individual who must come to terms with an environment and a culture which are alien to him. From the beginning, the news correspondent Guy Hamilton (played by Mel Gibson) finds himself in a mysterious and dangerous country about which he knows little. The title credits of *The Year of Living Dangerously* are superimposed against exotic Indonesian puppets, imagery which early on raises the theme of being controlled by others. The first scene of the narrative shows Billy Kwan at his typewriter; Billy is a dwarfen news correspondent, half Chinese and half Australian.

What is remarkable about Linda Hunt's Academy Award–winning performance as Billy is not only the actress' masquerade in a male role, but the strange, androgynous quality and authority she brings to the role, perfect for the character of Billy, who is as much a metaphor as a person. Billy has a wisdom and perception that is greater than anyone else's; he is the moral center of the film, the only person who passionately cares about the fate of the Indonesians. He also idolizes President Achmed Sukarno, who he believes has been successful in walking that tightrope between the military on one side and the Marxist revolutionaries on the other. "Sukarno tells the West to go to hell, and today he is the voice of the Third World," says Billy. When Guy Hamilton arrives in Indonesia, Billy is attracted by his potential. In a marvelous scene, Billy leads Guy through one of the most destitute sections of the country. "Most of us become children again as we walk into the slums of Asia," says Billy as we see an unforgettable image: emaciated Indonesians walking toward us from out of the mist.

When Guy and Billy discuss political action, Guy is rather cynical. Billy urges him to give all his money to the poor—or at least to give away five dollars, which would be a fortune to an Indonesian. Guy argues that the suffering and poverty are so great that five dollars would make no difference. Billy says that he has himself gone beyond that kind of reasoning: "You just don't think about the major issues; add your light to the sum of the light!" Billy is urging Guy to get involved, to act. Later we discover that

Billy has himself "adopted" an Indonesian woman and her child in an attempt to shed some light of his own. Billy, who is a photographer dealing in light, tells Guy, "I can be your eyes," thus leading him to a more profound understanding of Indonesia. The other Western journalists, if sophisticated and intelligent, are largely insensitive—both to the political nuances as well as to the genuine suffering of the Indonesian people. "The great advantage of being a dwarf," says Billy, "is that you can be wiser than other people and no one envies you."

In the central metaphorical scene of the film, Billy shows Guy the exquisite, Indonesian shadow puppets: but one is supposed to watch the shadows cast by the puppets rather than the puppets themselves. The puppet plays, says Billy, are based on balance between the right and the left—just as Sukarno balances the political right and the political left. Billy shows Guy three specific puppets: the prince, who is the hero, but who can be fickle and selfish; the princess, who is noble and proud, but who can be headstrong; and the dwarf, who serves the prince. It is clear that Billy sees himself as the puppet master and manipulator as well as the dwarf, and that he considers Guy to be the romantic "prince." As the dwarf, Billy will serve Guy by getting him good stories and by setting him up romantically with Jill Bryant, the well-bred woman (played by Sigourney Weaver) who works at the British consulate and whom Billy admires, the "princess" who is the only other non–Indonesian with any sensitivity to the country's suffering. In keeping with the theme of puppetry and manipulation, Billy keeps files on everyone he comes in contact with. If Billy successfully manipulates Guy and Jill, and Sukarno manipulates the country, so too does the military manipulate Sukarno—who is revealed as little more than a puppet himself.

Billy continues his manipulation. In his residence, he says, "Here I am master, stirring my prints in the magic developing bath," a pun, because not only does Billy stir photographs, he also stirs his "prince," that is, Guy, in the developing bath of understanding and sensitivity. At one point, moved by her increasing love for Guy, Jill breaks a top secret clearance as she is about to leave the country when she tells Guy that an arms shipment is coming to the Communist revolutionaries. Jill knows that when the shipment reaches the revolutionaries, the country will be in turmoil and dangerous, a revolution possible. To Jill's surprise and disappointment, Guy is more interested in his career than in leaving the country with her, and he decides to use the piece of information in one of his increasingly influential news reports. Billy feels that his prince, like the puppet, has shown himself to be fickle. "You are capable of betrayal. You make your career a fetish. Why can't you learn to love?"

After the betrayal of Billy's ideals and Jill, Guy and an American reporter dance in an Indonesian club: both of them insensitive louts, oblivious to how they are degrading the Indonesian women by their own brazenness. Guy cannot understand Billy's reaction and asks, "How far are my loyalties to Jill supposed to go?" Billy says, "I would have given up the world for her. You wouldn't even give up one story!" Of course what is also significant about Guy's use of the story is that it also contributes to the military cause by providing them information about the revolutionaries. Thus, just as in *Under Fire* the journalist's photograph, though false, tipped the scale toward the Sandinista cause and brought about the revolution, in *The Year of Living Dangerously,* Guy's news report, verified and true, tips the scale toward the military and helps to defeat the revolution. Billy's opprobrium falls on Guy because Guy has failed to examine the moral implications of his actions.

The horrifying climax begins as Billy discovers that the young child of the woman he adopted has died; later he witnesses starving Indonesians rioting over some rice. One image in particular, that of a child hurriedly stuffing uncooked rice in his mouth before others can take the rice, is a haunting one indeed. In his own residence, surrounded by his heartrending photographs of pleading, starving Indonesians staring out at him, Indonesians incapable of helping themselves rise above their abject misery, Billy, crying and listening to the beautiful strains of Richard Strauss' *Four Last Songs,* asks as he types out the words spasmodically on his typewriter: "What/then/must/we/do?/What/then/must/we/do?"

Billy knows what he must do. Sukarno has betrayed him, as Sukarno has betrayed his people. Billy goes to a high floor of a high-rise, and out of a window he hangs a banner which reads, "Sukarno, feed your people," a banner which Sukarno should see when his motorcade passes by. Billy thus remains true to his own principles: of trying to add to the light, however insignificant that light may seem to be. But Sukarno never sees the banner, for just before his car pulls around the corner, military supporters remove the banner and push Billy out the window to his death many stories below. The image of Billy's small, dead body, an enigmatic half-smile on his face, is an unforgettable one; perhaps only now can we comprehend the significance of the Hermann Hesse text of Billy's beloved Strauss: "Hands, leave off your deeds; mind, forget all thoughts; all of my forces now yearn only to sink into sleep. And my soul, unguarded, would soar on widespread wings, to live in night's magical sphere more profoundly, more variously. . ."

When Guy attempts to go to the palace to check on the revolution, a revolution which the film now clearly supports, a military man hits Guy in the eye with the butt of a rifle. Severely injured and wounded, Guy may suffer a detached retina if he moves or uncovers his eyes. In the suspenseful final scene, Guy goes to the airport despite the risk, casting off the fetish of his career and aware only that he must show his allegiance to Jill by leaving the country with her. On the dangerous ride to the airport, it becomes clear that the military has accelerated its repression and violence: people are being shot openly in the street. At the airport, as the ultimate symbol of his commitment to Jill, Guy loses the mantle of an objective reporter as he effectively abandons his tape recorder to the military men. Not surprisingly, the Communist coup fails, and the political situation ends up even more repressive than before, with Sukarno deposed by the military, who then place the country under virtual siege.

The specter of military siege hangs over Israeli society in Costa-Gavras' *Hanna K,* directed in 1983 from a screenplay by Franco Solinas and Costa-Gavras. *Hanna K* is one of Costa-Gavras' least strident films, not at all histrionic or flashy like Z or *State of Siege. Hanna K* seems an attempt to synthesize his political films with the more personal impulse from his earlier and lovely *Clair de Femme;* what results is a kind of melodramatic, political soap opera, very sensitively handled. *Hanna K* was virtually ignored or dismissed by critics. There are several reasons for this: one, because however subtle and sensitive, *Hanna K* is nevertheless hostile to the state of Israel for what it regards as its institutional terrorism against the Palestinian people; and two, because the film does not hesitate to explore the romantic life of its female protagonist Hanna Kaufman (played by Jill Clayburgh in an exquisitely understated performance). Without apologies, *Hanna K* explores the love life of this woman, who, for much of the film, is rather unhappy in a way recalling Antonioni's women. Male critics especially tended to call Hanna's problems mawkish soap opera—failing to recognize that it is the very genre of soap opera which tends to deal with the political implications of personal and sexual relationships; and Hanna's personal relationships are related to the greater political issues that Costa-Gavras and Solinas explore.

The plot of the film has the American-born Israeli Hanna finding herself repeatedly defending a Palestinian accused of terrorism. Whether or not Selim Bakri (played by Muhamad Bakri) is indeed a terrorist is never made explicitly clear, although by the end of the film we may gradually come to believe that those Palestinians who do resort to violence are somewhat justified. The film's background of the Holy Land is both ritualistic and compelling, as well as at times strangely anachronistic—as, for instance, when Hanna considers an abortion and the need to go to a European country where abortion is legal. "There are fine specialists among those Aryans," says her Israeli lover; and Hanna, responding negatively to the increasing knee jerk conservatism of the Israelis around her, responds sarcastically: "Even the Chinese are Aryans."

Perhaps the most moving scene in the film is one in which Hanna goes to the village of Koufar Romaneh in an attempt to discover whether or not Selim and his family did indeed live there, as Selim has claimed. When Hanna tries to find the village, an Israeli military sentry claims that the city doesn't exist; he's been on duty a long time, and knows the area well. Hanna retorts that the village has only been there since the fifth century; upon reflection, the Israeli sentry concludes that maybe she wants to go to Kfar Rimon (the name the Israelis gave to Koufar Romaneh when they occupied it). Once Hanna arrives in the town, she meets a Jewish Soviet immigrant who has been there five months and is very proud of her new house, which she and her husband built with their hard work. "What about the old village?" asks Hanna, "Is there anything left of it?" "What village?" answers the woman. The Soviet woman is herself intelligent and kind, yet there is nevertheless an insensitivity about her to the land and to the plight of the Palestinians—not a hostility, but a truly terrifying indifference.

Hanna finds out that there is one house remaining from the old village: a house being used as a museum for the largely Israeli tourists. When Hanna visits the house, she discovers definitive proof that it was indeed Selim's family home. The tourist guide, who can talk knowingly about its architecture, is oblivious to the moral implications of this Palestinian home being used as an attraction for sightseeing Israelis. As Hanna leaves the town, she comes across in the countryside an Arab crazily pointing to each and every tree, saying over and over, "This is *Koufar Romaneh,* this is *Koufar Romaneh.*" Of course, the Israeli sign reads differently, for after fifteen hundred years, the town has now become "Kfar Rimon." Typical to the political thriller, a central scene in *Hanna K* is its trial concerning Koufar Romaneh—in which we learn of Selim's repeated attempts to get his home back through legal means, his appeals to various ministries, the bigotry and prejudice of the Israelis, and even the hypocrisy of the legal system which would allow Selim to "immigrate" to "Kfar Rimon" providing he first take on South African citizenship so that his case cannot appear to set any precedent which might recognize a Palestinian claim.

The final and exquisitely filmed scene of *Hanna K* is one in which the personal and political spheres come together. Hanna, disenchanted with much in her life, has allowed Selim to live with her in her home in Jerusalem. This living situation began because she wanted to take care of him after his hunger strike, but it continued because Hanna enjoyed his company and because Selim provided a rather useful babysitter to her child, worth putting up with the constant taunts of the right-wing Israelis who harass and threaten her. Under her roof all at the same time in the final scene are Selim, the right-wing Israeli prosecutor (played by Gabriel Byrne) who is the father of her child, and her relatively apolitical French husband (played by Jean Yanne) from whom Hanna has been separated, despite her continuing affection.

When a television news report indicates that an act of terrorism has just been committed nearby, the prosecutor assumes the culprit must be Selim and calls the police. There is much tension in the room as Hanna and all three men must confront the situation and their feelings for each other. Then, Selim, after saying goodbye to Hanna's child, runs off. Angrily Hanna asks the prosecutor to leave. When he has gone, she then asks her husband to go back to France and give her a divorce. She is now alone. Hanna goes into the bathroom and begins to undress for a bath, when there is a ring at her doorbell. It has only been several minutes since the three men left; on her way to the door, she stops briefly at the hall mirror to see how she looks. And which man will have returned—Selim? Her Israeli lover? Her French husband? As Hanna opens the door, Costa-Gavras shows us her face in close-up. She looks out, stunned; and Costa-Gavras holds on her face for a relatively long time as she looks to the right, to the left, slowly taking in what she is seeing.

Finally, Costa-Gavras shows us the point-of-view shot: a single medium-long shot in which almost thirty Israeli military men carrying weapons fill virtually every portion of the frame. No one moves; no words are spoken. The film ends with a drumroll as Costa-Gavras cuts to black, and the credits roll. Costa-Gavras' criticism has been made: a harsh one, if subtly presented, about Israel being increasingly dominated by a strident military sensibility which is threatening to destroy the Israelis' compassion and humanity. *Hanna K* thus becomes one of the very few English-speaking films to offer a sympathetic treatment of Arabs.

Another kind of political thriller important in the last decade is typified by those films which are more clearly fictional entertainments than ideological calls to action, films which explore a fictional premise that has some relationship to politics. *Sleeping Dogs*, for instance, directed by Roger Donaldson in 1977, is not based on historical fact, but uses a what-if premise to examine what would happen if a right-wing repressive regime were to take control of New Zealand. A television movie, *The Kidnapping of the President*, directed by George Mendeluk in 1980, uses the obvious what-if premise implied by its title. Similarly, *Under Siege*, another television movie, this one directed in 1985 by Roger Young, uses a what-if premise to examine what would happen if the terrorism so common in Europe were to begin taking place in the United States. Related to these films which use what-if premises about some future event are those films which speculate, often wildly, about some past event. Two of the more interesting examples include *Winter Kills* and *Blow Out*, both dealing in fictional terms with the Kennedy family.

Winter Kills, directed in 1979 by William Richert from the novel by Richard Condon, has one of the most eccentric casts in recent memory, including Anthony Perkins, John Huston, Jeff Bridges, Dorothy Malone, Toshiro Mifune, Richard Boone, and Elizabeth Taylor. Its credits are superimposed over a chess board, a motif suggesting royal families. In a coded way, *Winter Kills* deals with the mythology of the Kennedys, particularly the assassination of John. Jeff Bridges plays Nick Kegan, the brother of Timothy Kegan, who was the United States president assassinated on February 22, 1960, in Philadelphia. At the time of the assassination, a judicial commission reported that the assassin was Willie Arnold, who was himself assassinated before he could be brought to justice.

The film's action begins as a contrite assassin admits he was the "second gun" on the Kegan assassination and then dies in Nick's presence. Nick finds the rifle and decides to bring it to the FBI (he says, "They probably built it") but his colleagues are killed; and the rifle and the dead bodies all disappear. In this film, Nick Kegan's primary relationship is with his father, a rich industrialist like Joseph Kennedy, President Kennedy's father. The older Kegan is presented as a total capitalist monster—a pragmatist who bugs conversations, owns most of the country, and changes his blood every six months. In the course of the film, Nick and his father examine most of the famous theories about the Kennedy assassination. As Nick's father says, "Should I point my finger at the Russians, the Cubans, some goddamned industrialists?" And of course, there is always the CIA and the FBI. One "new" explanation offered by *Winter Kills* is that "Federal Studios" may have ordered the assassination because the president's ending his affair with a famous movie star who subsequently committed suicide deprived the studio of huge profits (this theory, of course, a clear reference to Kennedy's affair with Marilyn Monroe, which, true or not, has certainly become a part of the Kennedy mythology).

In the course of the film, Nick comes in contact with a variety of odd characters: a crazy general who plays war games with tanks on his ranch; a maid who violently tries to kill Nick; a group of clichéd Mafia men who look like they belong in a B-movie. At the end of the film, Anthony Perkins, playing the man who heads the think-tank conglomerate owned by Nick's father, tells Nick, "They will pile falsehood on top of falsehood until you can't tell a lie from the truth and you won't even want to. That's how the powerful keep their power. Don't you read the papers? You've got to accept that there is a world outside of you and that you affect that world!"

Ultimately, the climax upholds the one assassination theory which had not yet been seriously put forth in real life: that President Kegan was assassinated by his own family, specifically by his father, who, having bought the presidency for his son, became disenchanted when the president refused to use the office only for amassing corporate power and instead began developing genuine democratic concerns. *Winter Kills* ends with a deliciously surreal image: the billionaire father trying to hold onto a huge American flag hanging out of the penthouse floor of a skyscraper and then sliding slowly off the flag to his death.

Blow Out, directed in 1981 by Brian De Palma, continues the fictionalizing of the Kennedys. In this film, which combines *Blowup* with *The Conversation*, the protagonist Jack (played by John Travolta) is a motion pictures sound recordist who needs to record, among other sounds, an excellent, emotionally-felt scream for a cheap horror film. Outside one night

In an image of suspension in *Winter Kills* typical to the suspense thriller, John Huston slides to his death from a huge American flag.

as Jack is trying to record some wind ambience, he unexpectedly records an accident in which a car—with a politician and his apparent girlfriend inside—goes off a bridge and sinks into the water below. The incident here is obviously based on the Chappaquiddick incident, in which Ted Kennedy's car sank when it went over a bridge and resulted in the drowning of his passenger, Mary Jo Kopechne, bringing about an apparent end to Ted Kennedy's chances to become President. In *Blow Out*, Governor McRyan (the Kennedy parallel) is presented as ahead in the polls in the presidential primaries, but it is *he* who drowns rather than his girlfriend.

The truth, as Jack discovers, is that this was no accident: his sound recording of the event proves that a gunshot was fired into the tire of the car, causing the blow-out. The accident was thus a specific attempt by others to make a political gain. As the film proceeds, Jack discovers that a photographer made a motion picture of the accident; when frame-by-frame photos are published in a magazine, Jack cuts out the pictures, puts them together and photographs them (in a scene resembling the central scene in *Blowup*), and then syncs the film footage to his sound to create a persuasive documentary record of the accident. The photographer says that his footage will be "the biggest thing since the Zapruder film." Jack, in his tacit way recognizing the increasingly conservative mood of the country, says perceptively, "No one wants to know about conspiracy," which—except for characters in political thrillers—seems to be quite true in Reagan's America.

The climax of *Blow Out* has Jack trying to save a woman involved in the conspiracy, with the background of the Liberty Day Parade in Philadelphia adding a level of irony; for as people celebrate democracy with demonstrations and fireworks, they are oblivious to the fact that the rich and powerful, through conspiracy and assassination, really control things. When, horrifically, Jack fails to save the woman and instead hears her anguished screams as the assassin kills her, Jack has, inadvertently, finally recorded a scream which could be used for the cheap horror film. The final scene shows Jack watching that film: drained, emotionally spent, almost impassive as he hears again the scream which will remain on the soundtrack for all time—a symbol of his failure, of violence, of the conspiracy in America.

Also a part of this Kennedyana are two significantly earlier films, both of which deal with Kennedy's Cuban missile crisis: *Topaz,* directed by Alfred Hitchcock in 1969, and *The Missiles of October,* directed by Anthony Page in 1974. It is interesting to note that Hitchcock, who has worked in so many different genres of the thriller, has only once attempted a film which could be called a political thriller. Based on the Leon Uris bestseller, *Topaz* attempts to provide the human story as to what might have taken place behind the scenes of the Cuban missile crisis, laying out in human terms the tremendous personal tolls state conspiracies of intelligence-gathering exact. In many ways, *Topaz* is Hitchcock's most experimental film, containing an unusual structure in which the narrative contains no single character with whom we can easily identify. In fact, the narrative moves from one character to another in a way which predates Buñuel's *The Phantom of Liberty.* The most striking scene in *Topaz* is the murder of an anti–Castro Cuban woman who is involved in a passionate affair with an American agent; when she is shot by her Cuban Communist lover, her brightly colored dress opens surreally like a flower as her lover lowers her limp body to the chessboard-patterned floor, the queen taken by the knight in the game of international political intrigue.

Surprisingly, another thriller of sorts, the television drama *The Missiles of October,* also provided a behind-the-scenes account of the Cuban missile crisis—although in this film the actors all play the important *public* personages involved in the event: John Kennedy, Robert Kennedy, Nikita Khrushchev, Adlai Stevenson, Dean Acheson, Robert McNamara, and McGeorge Bundy, among others. This film, slow-moving and inexorable, with a documentary quality totally unlike the other films in this category, attempts to reconstruct almost hour by hour the escalation of the crisis which brought the world to the brink of nuclear confrontation.

Two other important and significant films which fit into the category of fictionalized political thrillers are *Capricorn One,* directed in 1978 by Peter Hyams, and *Black Sunday,* directed in 1977 by John Frankenheimer. Both of these films seem to me absolutely first-rate thrillers: exciting, suspenseful, and thought-provoking. *Capricorn One* itself derives from a what-if premise, based on the popular myth, discussed everywhere if ridiculed, that the original Apollo moon landing in 1969 did not really take place, but was stage-managed in a television studio. The idea was preposterous, of course, but so overwhelming was the archetypal mystery of the moon and its importance in human folklore, that the realization that the moon was becoming colonized and mundane provoked, perhaps, the subconscious hope that the moon landing had not really taken place. With the revelations of Watergate and secret Vietnam War bombings, the idea of pervasive conspiracy being present in *all* agencies of government proved to be compelling and made its way into this creative thriller.

Three astronauts—Charles Brubaker (played by James Brolin), Peter Willis (played by Sam Waterston), and John Walker (played by O.J. Simpson)—are scheduled to make the first landing on Mars. As they wait in their capsule for the blast-off, we watch corrupt Congressman Hollis Peaker (played by David Huddleston) attempting to throw his weight around; later, he and the vice president speak to each other with a phony, insincere deference symptomatic of the conspiracy and power struggle which undermine all government endeavor. When the three astronauts are suddenly and secretly whisked out of the rocket which then flies to Mars without them, Dr. Jim Callaway, the head of the Space Administration (played by Hal Holbrook) gives them a speech explaining what has happened. Holbrook is a master at playing this kind of sincere villain; Callaway talks movingly about the dream of space and all that it has meant to him. Unfortunately, he says, there is no longer interest from the public; after the first moon landing, the public became blasé; as a result, there has been less and less money available. And as well, Con-Amalgamate delivered the commissioned life-support system, but the company took too much profit and cut corners, and the system just doesn't work. Although Callaway doesn't propose to overturn the system, his speech implicitly attacks the method of military and government spending. Callaway implores the astronauts to go through with the charade in order to rekindle interest in the space program. Brubaker says, "If the only way to keep something alive is to become everything I hate, then I'm not sure it's worth keeping it alive." When Callaway threatens to kill the astronauts' families if the three men don't go along with his plan, they reluctantly agree.

Several months later, when the ship lands on Mars, we see that the Space Administration has created a replica of the Mars landscape and the spaceship in a television studio. On live television, Brubaker exits the spaceship with the line, "I take this step in the journey of peace for all mankind." There are moving close-ups of the astronauts' wives, who are watching. The irony is fetching: as the president sends the astronauts a message ("You, the men of Capricorn One, have shown us how wonderful we can be. You have shown us what we are. You are the basic truth in us. You are the reality. . ."), the camera pulls back to reveal the phony, unreal set, and we become strikingly aware of the discrepancy between what is true and what the government tells us. Several months later, when the space ship is coming back to the earth and the men are supposedly now close enough to make radio contact, there is an incredibly suspenseful scene as the various wives talk to their husbands and we wonder whether any of the astronauts will break down and tell the truth. "You sound so close. It's hard to believe you're really so far away in space," says one of the wives, whose husband says, "It's hard for me to believe, too." Brubaker's wife reads her husband an essay written by their son which talks about his father's selflessness and integrity. The essay is shamelessly sentimental; and the suspense grows almost unbearable as we wonder whether Brubaker, the clear protagonist of the film, will confess or whether the government will interrupt the transmission. "There's something I have to tell you," he finally says to his wife, but then talks instead of a vacation they took, a reference which turns out to be a coded message.

Much later, when the real spaceship re-enters the atmosphere, a surprising development occurs: the heat shield burns up and the ship is destroyed. Whereas the government had previously planned on having the men "return," now there is no way the astronauts can participate in the charade, for the re-entry would have killed them. The conspiracy must grow, and the government realizes it must kill all three astronauts. The astronauts manage at least temporarily to escape their desert prison; they fly off in a plane which crashes, and then they go off in three different directions as the camera pulls up and away: three different chances for the conspiracy to be revealed and for the truth to come out. Will the astronauts succeed? Or will the government?

Peter Hyams fills *Capricorn One* with wonderfully-created scenes and images. One notable scene shows Brubaker's wife (played by Brenda Vacarro) reading her children the tongue-twisting nonsense words of a Dr. Seuss book as she struggles to hold back the tears over the great loss of her husband. Meanwhile, her husband is chased by two government helicopters, which are at one point photographed like evil dragonflies, at another point, like vultures. One set piece which is especially clever has Peter Willis, the comedian of the three astronauts, exhausted and climbing up the sheer wall of a mountain, but telling himself a joke the whole time to distract himself from the danger of falling and the probability of being caught. When he tells the punch line—"She's on the roof"—which in the joke indicates someone's death, the telling coincides with Willis reaching the "roof" of the mountain upon which wait the helicopters carrying the government agents to kill him.

Running through the film and typical to the genre is the character of an investigative journalist (here played by Elliott Gould), who is the catalyst in unmasking the conspiracy. One set piece in *Capricorn One* involves the journalist in an exciting high-speed car chase using many point-of-view shots which create (at least on a large movie screen) a strong visceral sense of involvement for the spectator. A later scene uses reflexive movie dialogue between the journalist and his less-than-totally supportive editor. For instance, Journalist: "The assignment editor is supposed to say, 'You've got forty-eight hours, kid!' I saw it in a movie. 'But your job is on the line!'" Editor: "I'll give you twenty-four. *I* saw the movie, too!" It is difficult for the journalist to prove anything, because the conspiracy is so great and because crucial evidence keeps disappearing. The final set-piece is a suspenseful chase in which the journalist enlists the aid of an eccentric man (played by Telly Savalas) who runs a crop-dusting service. The reference is clearly to *North by Northwest;* but here the crop-dusting plane rescues the protagonist from the desert and is then pursued by the two government helicopters, Brubaker the whole while hanging precariously from the wing.

In the moving final scene, Callaway's villainy is just about to be exposed as Brubaker and the journalist—in slow motion—bound up to the memorial service which is being held in the astronauts' honor. Today, years after its initial release, and in the context of the Challenger tragedy and NASA's irresponsibility and negligence in relation to the commissioned O-rings responsible for the fuel leak and attendant explosion which killed all the astronauts aboard, *Capricorn One*'s conspiracy and cover-up have a greater resonance than ever before.

Like *Capricorn One, Black Sunday,* directed by John Frankenheimer in 1977, takes advantage of Balint-derived concepts of philobatism and ocnophilia, as characters grab onto objects while suspended over enormous, hostile spaces, the objects alternating between offering danger and providing rescue. *Black Sunday* was one of the first films to deal with terrorism in the United States; its narrative is a tight one, slowly and inexorably building to a spellbinding climax. *Black Sunday* takes as its inspiration the killing by Arab terrorists of the Israeli athletes at the German Olympics, imagining an even more horrific act of terrorism at an American sporting event. Throughout the film, dates and the names of places are superimposed on the screen, until we arrive, finally, at that destined place and time reserved for the supreme act of violence the film promises.

The film opens in Beirut, where we meet our protagonist, Dahlia (played by Marthe Keller), a member of the Black September pro–Palestinian terrorist group. Almost immediately she watches on an old news film the explicit political statement given by Michael Lander (played by Bruce Dern) when he was an American prisoner of war captured by the Vietnamese, a statement in which he confesses to war atrocities against the Vietnamese and attacks the United States. We do not immediately understand

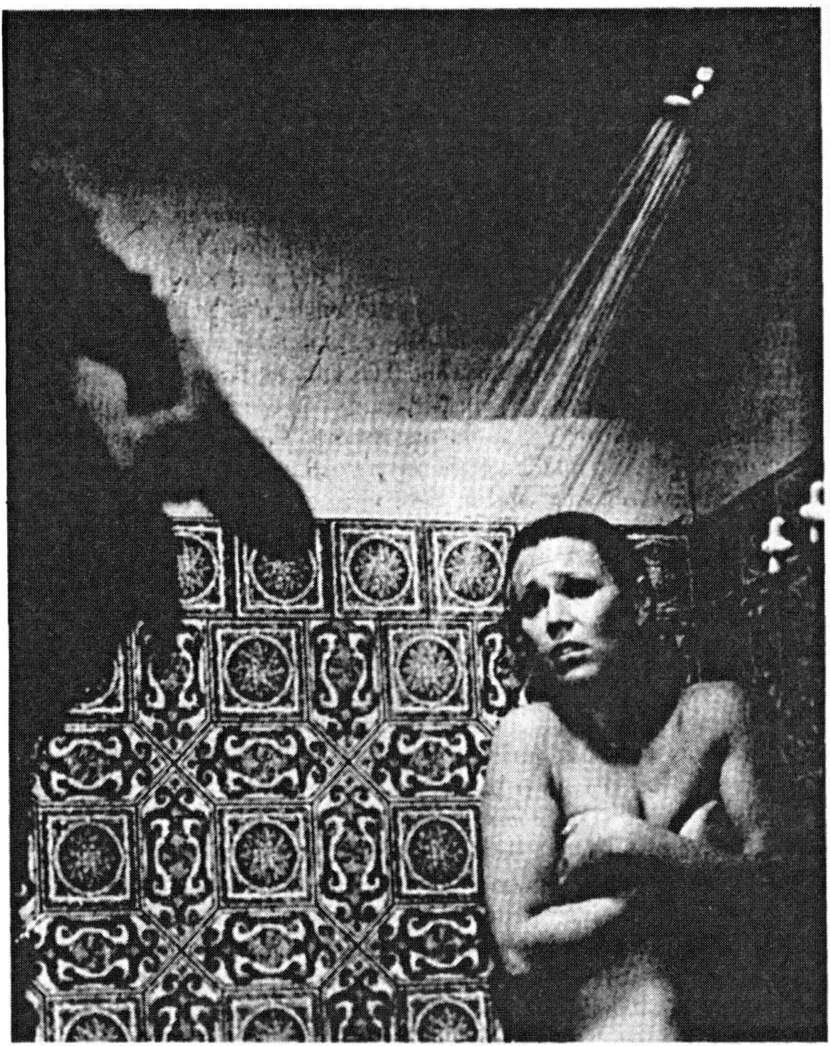

Counter-terrorist Robert Shaw confronts terrorist Marthe Keller at the very beginning of *Black Sunday;* antagonist and protagonist, they will meet again only at the film's conclusion.

exactly what it is that Dahlia plans to do in concert with this psychotic, now-released war veteran, only that it will involve 220,000 steel rifle darts, and that, as articulated in the audio tape that Dahlia makes to be played after the terrorist event, it is to force Americans to share the suffering, because "Americans have remained deaf to the cries of the Palestinian nation." There is considerable tension when Israeli commandos storm in, because our empathies are at least partially with the terrorists, who are interesting and committed and led by Dahlia, who is a beautiful and self-possessed woman. Violence ensues, and the Israelis shoot and kill most of the gang. But when Kabakov, the Israeli in charge (played by Robert Shaw), bursts into Dahlia's shower and discovers her naked, there is one electric moment between them: at that moment, Dahlia is completely defenseless, and perhaps because she is defenseless, Kabakov does not kill her.

As a result, Dahlia is able to escape and to proceed with the terrorist plot, which we gradually learn more and more about, including the involvement of the Goodyear blimp, which the psychotic Michael pilots at football games. The narrative, constructed according to dualities, alternately follows Dahlia's actions and Kabakov's actions. Both of them have in their backgrounds incidents in which their family members have been subjected to great political injustice and violence. For all his bravado, Kabakov is the more sensitive of the two. At one point he confesses to an ally, "For thirty years, I have been killing, and what has it accomplished?" The ally realizes that Kabakov has perhaps reached a point where he can no longer kill, because "Doubt has entered in." If this doubt makes Kabakov the "good" character, and Dahlia's total lack of doubt makes her the "bad" character, they gradually change positions: a structure which strongly suggests that of the typical thriller of moral confrontation. When Dahlia cold-bloodedly masquerades as a nun and kills Kabakov's partner, Kabakov realizes the necessity of stalking his prey with no mercy and repressing all his human impulses; as Dahlia becomes more involved with the psychotic Michael, who falls desperately in love with her, she breaks down and weeps, gradually becoming a human being and no longer a total automaton.

True to the genre, *Black Sunday* is filled with a variety of significant objects: thousands of statues of the Madonna which are actually plastic explosives, a telephone which is also a bomb, a blimp which is more than a blimp. In one fascinating scene, Dahlia and Michael go to the Mojave Desert to test Michael's explosive device in a deserted hangar. Michael has placed thousands of darts in a contraption of his own making which the two of them mount on a tripod inside the hangar. A stupid caretaker volunteers to stand heroically next to a plane inside for their "picture." They exit and detonate the device; the explosion immediately and grotesquely kills the caretaker, but even more spectacularly, propels outward the thousands of darts in perfect geometric arcs. When Michael and Dahlia return inside the hangar, its walls are filled with holes; thousands of shafts of sunlight create beautiful patterns on their faces. Finally, we discover definitively their plan. With the help of the Goodyear blimp, they will use the 220,000 steel darts to try to kill 80,000 people—detonating a larger version of Michael's device over the fifty yard line of the football field in Miami during the Superbowl Game. And since the Superbowl is going to be attended by the president of the United States, their elaborate plot will incidentally accomplish an assassination as well. When Kabakov, discovering that the Superbowl is the

Unusual love scene in *Black Sunday* between Bruce Dern and Marthe Keller after they test their strange and violent weapon.

target, suggests the game be cancelled, he is told, "Cancel the Superbowl? That's like cancelling Christmas."

Black Sunday seems to be a film tailor-made to Altan Löker's theories of suspense. Certainly the small-scale test of the murderous device is, in its odd way, very beautiful. Our curiosity, our desire to witness the spectacle of such an apparently ludicrous thing—220,000 steel darts exploding outward from beneath a blimp to kill 80,000 people simultaneously—is so great that we rather want to see the destruction and we almost root for the horrible act to take place. As the film races to its conclusion at the Superbowl, the suspense, which has begun slowly, is now overwhelming. When we see the president of the United States looking like the then President Jimmy Carter (through the courtesy of skillful cutting and an

The surreal image of the Goodyear blimp looming perilously close to the stands at the climax of *Black Sunday*.

actor look-alike), a rather stunning moment is created which lifts the film beyond the "fictional" into the realm of the real; the documentary footage of the Superbowl game, clearly not staged by the filmmakers, also lends a veracity to the final sequence. The football game itself is between the Pittsburgh Steelers and the Dallas Cowboys; one ominous sign in the stands reads, "Doomsday for Pittsburgh."

Ultimately, the narrative has everything and everyone finally coming together in that one place, to that final moment: the terrorists, the Israeli commandos, the explosives, the Goodyear blimp, the football fans, the president. And of course, there is much irony associated with all the Americans (sportscasters, newsmen, fans, the blimp crew) oblivious to the real drama being played out before them, giving their attention only to the football game, their own unison screams of excitement unwittingly accompanying the battle of wits between the terrorists and counter-terrorists as well. As Michael and Dahlia are almost stopped at the blimp's landing field, the suspense is almost unbearable, and our sympathies are with the terrorists. Have we come this far only to have the spectacle withheld from us?

What makes *Black Sunday* such a fine piece of filmmaking is that its slow build-up has been so well-constructed that by this climactic scene the film's incredibly improbable premise seems probable, indeed, even likely. As Kabakov chases the blimp in a helicopter, Frankenheimer shows us great shots of Kabakov clinging onto the line descending from the helicopter as he swings and flies through the great open spaces. Finally, when Kabakov in the helicopter catches up with the blimp and sees Dahlia—for only the second time in the film, the first time since that initial encounter in Beirut—there is another electric moment between them, the two of them hundreds of feet in the air moving inexorably to the fifty yard line. But this time, it is Dahlia who hesitates, as she recognizes him; in that instant of hesitation, Kabakov shoots her, thus bringing to an end her participation in terrorism, which could have been prevented at the very beginning had he been less compassionate. But Michael is not quite killed, and the blimp continues its way toward the fifty yard line of the Superbowl. Can Kabakov prevent the horrifying catastrophe from taking place? There are incredibly surreal images of the blimp as it silently descends over the stands; and then . . . mass pandemonium as 80,000 people, prisoners in that space, suddenly realize they may be in danger; as Kabakov struggles to intercept the blimp; as Michael lights the fuse to the explosive which will shoot the darts into the stands; as the blimp approaches ever-closer the fifty yard line . . .

Having made thought-provoking and suspenseful films like *The Manchurian Candidate* and *Seconds,* John Frankenheimer, one of the thriller's most distinguished artists (along with Claude Chabrol and Alfred Hitchcock), in *Black Sunday* again creates an achievement of rather dazzling virtuosity: dazzling not only in the complexity of the apparatus of blimp and helicopter effects; not only in its incredibly skillful final montage, which works like Eisenstein's "Odessa Steps" sequence to create tensions; but also on the theoretical level—providing a psychological drama of philobatism and ocnophilia which rivals all others and which manipulates the spectator to such a degree that he or she is willing to consider, indeed, perhaps even wish for, the gruesome simultaneous deaths of 80,000 Americans at the hands of terrorists whose cause, by the typical spectator, is barely understood. A distinctive achievement, indeed.

A final category of suspense thrillers which has come into increased play in the last ten years are those films which expand the basic concept of conspiracy to include institutions beyond the government. These films squarely face the truth that governments alone no longer single-handedly dominate institutional life; conspiracies to acquire and expand power can be found everywhere. Thus, *Rollover,* for instance, directed by Alan J. Pakula in 1981 and starring Jane Fonda, is a political thriller which examines the international banking community. Its premise is that the billions of dollars made by the Arabs after the oil embargo has contributed to an extreme volatility in the international banking community; were the Arabs, or presumably any conspiratorial elements, to choose to remove money from Western banks rather than to allow the money to "rollover," the total destruction of the world economy could result. *Silkwood,* directed by Mike Nichols in 1983 and starring Meryl Streep, deals with the real-life plutonium factory worker Karen Silkwood, who blew the whistle on the nuclear industry and was, as many have claimed and the film suggests, possibly assassinated by conspirators within that industry.

Special Bulletin, a television movie directed by Ed Zwick in 1983, uses a fictional story about terrorists threatening to detonate an atomic bomb to achieve their goal of nuclear disarmament as a way of criticizing the television news industry rather savagely. *Special Bulletin*—which, like Orson Welles' *War of the Worlds* radio broadcast, used a structure that tried to simulate *how* an event of this kind would be covered—strongly criticizes the network television news not only for its stupidity, but also for the incredible arrogance of those newscasters who have the power to decide every night exactly what is the news and thereby what is the truth, in many instances, preventing, rather than compelling our profound understanding of the issues.[5]

Marie, directed by Roger Donaldson in 1985, starred Sissy Spacek as Marie Ragghianti, an extradition officer in Tennessee who fights the system when she discovers corruption and conspiracy in the penal system. *Acceptable Risks,* a television movie directed by Rick Wallace in 1986, deals with the tremendous power and lack of responsibility of the chemical industry, as a Bhopal-like tragedy befalls a typical American city, bringing home to American audiences the human cost of corporate corruption and irresponsibility. *Power,* a very underrated and ignored film directed by Sidney Lumet in 1986, attacks the very practice of American electoral democracy by exposing the actions of high-paid and pragmatic media consultants who manipulate the truth and the issues in order to sway public opinion.

Perhaps the most interesting of all the thrillers which expand the scope of conspiracy in America is *The China Syndrome,* directed in 1979 by James Bridges, a film which attacks the nuclear industry as corrupt and which had the good fortune (if we might use that term) to be released at the time of the Three Mile Island nuclear accident. *The China Syndrome* stars Jane Fonda as Kimberly Wells, a television newscaster, and, like so many Jane Fonda films dealing with social issues, the emphasis is not so much on the issues as on Fonda's ability to affect the issue and thus become a role model for others who might engage in social activism.

The first image of the film is that of a woman with red hair whose face is obscured by a round mirror. Off-camera, we hear voices in the control room: "Red hair was a good idea, but we talked about cutting it," and the response: "We haven't talked to her about it, but she'll do what we tell her." On that line, Kimberly lowers the mirror in alarm, revealing her face to the audience for the first time. Thus, from the very beginning of the film, the dramatic question clearly set up is, "Will Kimberly Wells do what she's told and be a toady of those who have power?" *The China Syndrome* is very critical of television news, particularly its impulse to sanitize all issues so as not to offend and its tendency to sully the airwaves with what is popularly called "soft news"—garbage journalism whose primary purpose is to amuse or entertain in an attempt to get higher ratings. Indeed, perhaps the most fetching strength of *The China Syndrome* is the persuasiveness with which it presents the ubiquitous stupidity of television. Kimberly is, however, interested in breaking out of the soft news beat and getting into hard news. In one of her first hard-news broadcasts on atomic power, she slips and says "selfish sufficiency" instead of "self-sufficiency"—a kind of Freudian slip which suggests the truth about the nuclear industry long before the film demonstrates that truth dramatically.

Early in the film, Kimberly and her cameraman Richard (played by Michael Douglas) happen to be in an observation room at the plant during an accident which almost melts down the core of the reactor. This accident sequence is very suspenseful; almost immediately, the plant and utilities officials begin a cover-up. Richard, aware of the cover-up, aware too that the station manager is all too willing to participate in it, accuses Kimberly of being "a piece of talking furniture." Like the Jane Fonda protagonists of *Coming Home* and *9 to 5*, Kimberly is a relative innocent who comes only gradually to a mature and committed position. *The China Syndrome* particularly charts her evolution into an activist; because of the public's knowledge of Fonda's off-screen activities, the role here seems to have special resonance. There is great irony that in the midst of the cover-up Kimberly should be forced to report on "one of the basic principles of physics" in a news story which deals amusingly with an errant balloonist's accident rather than seriously with the nuclear accident. In the course of the broadcast, Kimberly, in an exchange of what the industry calls "happy talk," jokingly tells the male news anchor that he's "filled with hot air"—another Freudian slip which is indicative of the very serious charge made by the filmmakers about television's abrogation of its responsibilities to the public.

When the official report on the accident soft-pedals the significance of the event and excuses the workers, a nuclear engineer in the plant, Jack Godell (played by Jack Lemmon), is disturbed, because he knows that culpability has not been properly accorded. The federal government's hearings into the safety of the atomic reactors are presented clearly as *pro forma* hearings, controlled by the nuclear industry and never leading to any restraint on the expansion of nuclear power. At one point, men who work in the plant ridicule a housewife on television who is protesting nuclear power because she is afraid: Jack Godell himself begins to realize how arrogant his fellow workers are and begins to sympathize with the housewife's point of view, because he feels fear himself—a justified fear.

As it proceeds, *The China Syndrome* presents the parallel stories of Kimberly and Jack—both of whom gradually acquire an activist position; she from outside the industry, he from within. Certainly, Godell is aware of the significance of the meltdown which almost occurred. The "China Syndrome" itself describes the phenomenon of a meltdown by which radiation would theoretically bore through the earth all the way to China, unless (as would happen in reality) the radiation hit ground water, at which point it would then shoot into the environment, potentially killing thousands. The bottom line is financial: the company loses a half million dollars every day that the plant is down; and as Godell discovers more corruption and cover-up, including falsified welding x-rays, he knows that the plant is unsafe and must be closed down. The greed of the company and the extent of the conspiracy become so great that the villains even attempt murder, at one point running an investigative reporter off the road to prevent the release of crucial evidence—an incident which recalls the fate of Karen Silkwood, the activist whose life was later specifically documented in *Silkwood.*

In the film's climactic scene, Jack Godell takes the nuclear plant hostage in order to get the truth to the people, with the help of Kimberly Wells. The owners of the plant, with no moral or ethical concern for anything but their own profit, simulate an accident to distract Godell; a SWAT team then bursts into the chamber and assassinates him. As Godell dies, he feels a *real* accident, one he predicted might have been possible, if not yet a meltdown. This climactic murder scene, with its emphasis on the importance of getting out the truth before those in power succeed in hiding or revising it, is compelling. Of course the nuclear industry lies about what has happened, but Kimberly struggles to get the truth out, shouting down the oily company spokesman, Mr. Gibson, in order to ask a hard-hitting question of Jack Godell's friend, Ted Spindler, who also works in the plant.

"Jack thought this plant should be shut down. What do you think?" asks Kimberly urgently. "It's not my place to say," answers Spindler. But Kimberly refuses to relent; although her friend Jack Godell has just been murdered before her eyes, although she has just experienced her second atomic accident, although she is on the verge of an emotional breakdown in front of thousands of viewers, although company spokesmen are trying to

The China Syndrome.* Top: Nuclear engineer Jack Lemmon urgently concerned that a major nuclear accident be averted. Bottom: Journalist Jane Fonda urgently concerned that the truth about the nuclear industry be revealed. Compare the composition, angle and actor expression in the two photographs. Jean-Luc Godard would perhaps claim that both expressions are flawed by a bourgeois countenance which prevents political change—that the emphasis should not be on the sensitivity of the one who looks, but on the political reality of what is looked *at*.

**For a detailed analysis of Jane Fonda's countenance, see Godard's film* Letter to Jane *or the illustrated, published text of its screenplay.*

shout her down and end her broadcast, she presses on: "If it's not your place, Mr. Spindler, whose is it? Whose is it?" And then when the company spokesman interrupts, she interrupts loudly back, "Mr. Gibson, if there's nothing to hide, let him speak!" and then asks again, "*Whose place is it,* Mr. Spindler? *Whose place is it?*" Finally, her sheer intensity breaks Spindler down and he is willing to speak: "Jack Godell was a hero," he proclaims, seconding Godell's story and destroying the credibility of the atomic industry spokesman. The truth has come out.

Kimberly gives a final, moving speech, barely, but heroically retaining her composure; after the live broadcast ends, she breaks down, and we hear again the off-camera voices we heard at the beginning of the film—"She's incredible. She did a hell of a good job," and "I can't say that I'm surprised"—comments which again clearly put the film's focus on Fonda's performance as an activist. From Kimberly's final speech, the station cuts to a commercial for a microwave oven, a not too subtle irony which continues the attack on television. Perhaps surprisingly, although the film was attacked by many in the nuclear industry, it—along with the Three Mile Island incident—did work truly to effect a change in people's attitudes toward atomic reactors and to slow the expansion of the nuclear power industry.

One final thriller worthy of comment is *The Star Chamber,* directed by Peter Hyams in 1983. *The Star Chamber,* unlike Hyams' ideologically liberal-to-left film *Capricorn One,* seems for the most part in the service of the ideological right, which makes it, as a thriller, rather notable. *The Star Chamber* begins by presenting two incidents which suggest that justice is no longer possible in the United States because the court system is excessively protecting the rights of criminals. In the first incident, an undercover cop chases a killer of elderly women who puts the incriminating weapon in his garbage can; although the cops, who do not have a search warrant, do *not* search the garbage can's contents until they have been put in a public garbage truck, the judge throws all the evidence out and releases the killer, because the cops did not wait until the contents of the garbage were completely mixed with the garbage already in the truck. In the second incident, the cops catch two men who apparently mutilated and killed a five-year-old boy, but this case is thrown out because of a clerical error: although the cops had initially stopped the men's vehicle because of an outstanding traffic ticket, that traffic ticket had actually been already paid, thus rendering any arrest warrant invalid.

As in the most typical political thriller, the central image in *The Star Chamber* is the courtroom; although the public trials are shown to be unfair (as indeed are public trials in most political thrillers), in this film the unfairness results not because the system is reactionary, but because it is too liberal. Michael Douglas plays Steve Hardin, a judge within the system who becomes cynical about what the law forces him to do and who subsequently joins forces with Judge Benjamin Caulfield, again played by the marvelous Hal Holbrook. Caulfield is the chief justice of the "Star Chamber," a group of nine judges who, realizing the grievous errors of the official system, hold additional, private trials in order to effect justice—hiring a paid hit-man to carry out sentences. Except for the politics involved, these second trials are not all that dissimilar from the second trials instigated by radicals to get at the truth and effect justice in films such as *State of Siege*. The situation changes, however, when Hardin discovers that the Star Chamber he has joined and participated in has made a mistake; from that point on (relatively near the end of the film), he then works to reveal publicly the Star Chamber's actions (i.e., its executions or assassinations, depending upon your point of view).

All the energy of Hyams' *The Star Chamber* seems clearly directed toward the side of the reactionary judges; although we realize their methods may not be democratic, the narrative stacks things in their favor so that we abhor the criminals they vote to dispatch. Because Peter Hyams could not quite bring himself to make a film which champions without reservations government officials who violate the law, Hyams' protagonist does ultimately arrive at a more liberal position in opposition to the reactionary justices. Still, the energy of the film remains so completely with the Star Chamber that Hardin's change of heart seems more perfunctory than sincerely felt—reminding one of the typical "woman's melodrama" of the forties, in which the narrative's energy was clearly on the side of the subversive woman protagonist up until the concluding minutes which punished her for breaking conventions.

The irony of *The Star Chamber* is that its ending can be read in several ways, although it is not clear to this writer whether ambiguity was intended: for when Hardin decides to turn in the Star Chamber by taping their secret conversations, one might wonder whether he is carrying out the bugging in such a way that accords them the same opportunities and loopholes to escape punishment as were accorded the common criminals earlier in the film. The single shot which indicates Michael's betrayal of the Chamber does not provide us with enough information to come to a definitive conclusion, although I think most spectators would interpret the ending as containing no ambiguity and simply affirming the due process of the law by suggesting that the members of the Star Chamber will soon be behind bars. The final image is that of a close-up of Hardin who is surreptitiously listening to the words of a Star Chamber justice who asks, "Are there any questions? I would like a verdict." Thus, the film ends as it invites the spectator to arrive at his or her own verdict on the Star Chamber.

No discussion of the political thriller can be complete without some comment on the relationship of the political thriller to the specific politics which underlie so many of these films. To what extent do political thrillers use propaganda or aim to persuade their audiences? According to

Costa-Gavras, "Propaganda is the victory over the mind. Through the mind you can convince people, but in order to vanquish them you must prevent them from thinking. Propaganda is based on false or transformed events. . . . Propaganda is not the truth—at best it's only the truth of an ideology for certain people. But my films are basically the truth, they're based on the facts."[6] It is evident that Costa-Gavras rejects the view that his films are propaganda, because of his sincere belief that they are indeed objective truth—but this is obviously because his films are informed by a political perspective he personally advocates. Probably, Allen Drury would deny just as heartily that his books are right-wing propaganda; he too would claim that they represent an attempt to educate his audiences to contemporary political realities, which affirm the values of democracy, capitalism, and a limited American imperialism.

Costa-Gavras' statement that propaganda must be based on untruths seems to me an attempt to exempt his work from that label. Such an exemption is, however, unnecessary. If we accept the common dictionary definition that propaganda is "that which serves to propagate doctrine or principles," works such as *State of Siege* seem clearly to be at least partially propaganda, but this fact does not invalidate them as art. What seems more interesting than arguing over the definition of propaganda is understanding how it is possible that political thrillers can be enjoyed even by those resistant or indifferent to a specific political thriller's propaganda content, and what this may mean in regard to the genre's usefulness as a revolutionary instrument.

Jean-Luc Commolli and Jean Narboni claim that "every film is political, inasmuch as it is determined by the ideology which produces it (or within which it is produced, which stems from the same thing). . . ."[7] These writers characterize political thrillers such as Z as "films, increasingly numerous today, which have an explicitly political content . . . but which do not effectively criticize the ideological system in which they are embedded because they unquestionably adopt its language and its imagery."[8]

This same line of reasoning is continued by Guy Hennebelle, who claims that generic forms cannot be innocent. Quoting an article by Jean Fièschi and Emile Breton in *La Nouvelle Critique,* Hennebelle reiterates that political thrillers "derive fundamentally from the same reasoning which consists of injecting an ideological theme into commercially successful forms. What usually happens, however, is that these forms, being far from innocent, revenge themselves. In the Z movies, for instance, 'politics' is generally reduced to a clash between a solitary hero and a vast oppressive structure before the dumb-founded gaze of a simple and submissive throng. . . . [T]he ideological characteristics of these films are anarchism of the right or left, vague humanism, moralism and psychologism."[9] In other words, because the forms and structures of these films (with their plot revelations, traditional heroes, and palpitating suspense) derive from popular American capitalist genres, any revolutionary content is automatically rendered null and void.

Of course, any reasoning along these lines is ultimately proscriptive and implies that the primary and passionate interest of the makers of political thrillers should be the propagation of Marxist revolutionary politics, not the production of popular films. Fortunately or unfortunately (depending on your political persuasion), this is certainly not the case—perhaps not even for those directors, like Costa-Gavras, whose Marxist sympathies are obvious. If it were, perhaps only a few films (by Godard?) would pass the test. In a revealing interview in *Cinéaste,* Costa-Gavras was asked whether he feels free to choose any subjects he wishes for his films. Significantly, Costa-Gavras overlooked the question's implication: are there any *political* subjects that are so inflammatory he would encounter difficulty in raising money from his bourgeois backers? He answered instead, "I feel a pressure from some people to make only one kind of film, only political films."[10] Thus, for Costa-Gavras, some censorship pressures come not from the establishment, but from the revolutionary left which will not allow him to make a love story like his solitary and exquisite *Clair de Femme* or maybe another whodunit like his very first film, *The Sleeping Car Murders.*

Perhaps for many directors who have worked in the genre of the political thriller, directors whose policies range from the left to the right, Hitchcock's famous statement to François Truffaut can be taken as a basic attitude informing their work and as their relevant answer to political criticism: "My love of film is far more important to me than any considerations of morality."[11] And yet, how could this chapter end without an admission that for many of us it is precisely that passionate political vision which makes this subgenre so attractive, that it is precisely that ideological cause sincerely felt which distinguishes the best political thrillers from their less compelling relatives on the thriller family tree?

7
The Thriller of Acquired Identity

Everything in the North African setting of *The Passenger* appears somewhat bleached out: the sky a light blue, virtually all else the flesh-color of the desert, which extends for miles and miles, immutable, mysterious, unknowable. Jack Nicholson as Locke moves about that landscape restlessly—from one point to another, watching, responding, coming almost imperceptibly to the realization that his life has come somehow to that same nothingness as the sand. When he discovers the dead body of another man who has been staying in the same bare hotel, Locke somberly, though with fascination, puts his face only inches from the dead man's head—noting that the man's facial features are very much like his own. Locke understands at that moment, as perhaps do we, that he will begin a new life, that he will take on the identity of that dead man in an attempt to free himself from his own . . .

The thriller of acquired identity is composed of those films which are organized around a protagonist's acquisition of an unaccustomed identity, his or her behavior in coming to terms with the metaphysical and physical consequences of this identity, and the relationship of this acquisition to a murderous plot. The protagonist is often a villain wanting a better life, many times a murderer; and the new identity is that of someone who is dead or nonexistent. Generally the protagonist is killed or punished, although often not as a result of his or her real identity or crimes, but as a result of a murderous plot against the acquired identity or crimes attributed to it. Thus, these films, which are constructed along explicitly ironic lines, consistently raise questions as to what in our lives is meaningful and what in our personalities has value.

Certain thematic ideas integrated into this generic structure again and again include the existential search for a better life, the inability to escape what is central to one's character, the pervasiveness of cynicism, sadness, and ennui, and the objective cruelty of fate.

As these themes might indicate, this subgenre of the thriller, perhaps because of its negative and disturbing world view, has never been among the most popular of the suspense thrillers. A list of thrillers of acquired identity would include the following:

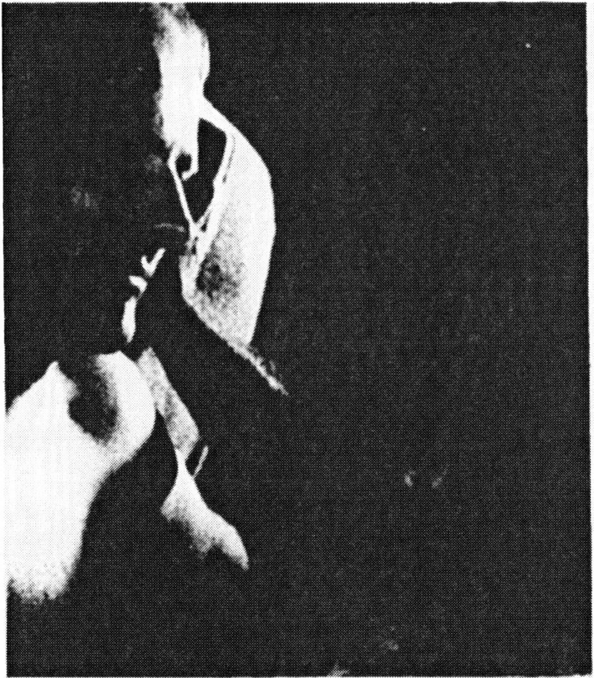

Jack Nicholson (right) confronts his alter-ego (left) in *The Passenger*.

Demoniaque (1957)
Purple Noon (1960)
The Third Voice (1960)
The Running Man (1963)
Dead Ringer (1964)
Seconds (1966)
Someone Behind the Door (1971)
The Passenger (1975)

These films can also be recognized by the presence of various other elements, including subsidiary characters who promote the masquerade, the protagonist's belated wish to reject the identity, material goals, lies and deception, cold-blooded characters with no values, exchanged clothes, police officials, unhappy but just endings, the manipulating protagonist being manipulated, large sums of money, blackmail and extortion, the revelation of the false identity, faked suicides and deaths, and a troubled love affair or marriage.

Related to the genre of acquired identity as a kind of subset are those films in which an amnesiac searches for his or her real identity, which is now unfamiliar or alien. These films are generally a more optimistic inversion of the others in that the protagonist survives and discovers that his or her life has value or that it may be satisfactorily amended. Because the films in this subset often climax with a revelatory flashback, they exhibit a relationship to the psychotraumatic thriller as well. A short listing of films in this amnesiac subset would include the following:

Mirage (1965) *Mister Buddwing* (1966)
The Third Day (1965) *Jigsaw* (1968)

In a psychoanalytic perspective using Michael Balint's terminology, the typical thriller of acquired identity presents a protagonist who feels straitjacketed by the ocnophilic universe and loaded down with attachments. The protagonist tries to escape such ocnophilic constrictions by discarding his or her identity along with the objects, places and people attached to that identity. For a while, in an environment which is more open and philobatic, the protagonist feels happy, but as his or her new identity grows, often in association with a psycho-epistomologically doomed attempt to gain new possessions, other ocnophilic associations begin once again to constrict the protagonist. These associations generally lead the protagonist to a fate more bleak and limited than that from which he or she was originally attempting to escape.

Of course, the acquired identity, although central to this genre, is reflected as an element in the other varieties of suspense thriller as well, particularly in certain political thrillers such as *The Groundstar Conspiracy* and *The Domino Principle.* In the former, for instance, a CIA-like government agency virtually brainwashes the protagonist into taking on a new identity in order that he may be used in an intelligence-gathering operation. In *The Domino Principle,* the protagonist is similarly forced to take on a new identity. These films suggest that the government is immoral precisely because it robs us of our identity and forces us to become something we are not. Films like these are significantly different from the thrillers of acquired identity because the protagonist's rebaptism does not represent his or her own conscious moral choice, but the coercive efforts of one or more antagonists.

The innocent-on-the-run thriller is another suspense genre which sometimes includes an acquired identity; in these films, the protagonist may acquire an identity mirroring his or her moral evolution in the course of adventures with the villains. (Examples include Roger Thornhill's significantly becoming George Kaplan in *North by Northwest,* or Johnny Jones becoming Huntley Haverstock in *Foreign Correspondent.)* If the mainstream innocent-on-the-run thrillers are optimistic, the mainstream thrillers of acquired identity are definitely pessimistic; in the latter, fate cruelly manipulates the protagonist, offering a chance here and there only so fate can more completely punish the protagonist and make him or her suffer later.

Two French-made thrillers of the late fifties both derive from works by thriller theorists. *Demoniaque,* directed by Luis Saslavsky in 1957 from a screenplay primarily written by Boileau-Narcejac, has its protagonist Gervaise taking on the identity of his deceased friend Bernard in order to wed Bernard's mail-order-styled fiancée, Hélène. Hélène's household includes her sister Agnes (played by Jeanne Moreau) and eventually Bernard's real sister, who goes along with Gervais' masquerade. After Bernard's sister and then Agnes are killed, Gervais realizes (but alas, as in so many suspense thrillers, too late) that all the women—particularly Hélène—were actually just trying to get Bernard's money. The film ends with Gervais married to Hélène, but dying the poisoned death intended for Bernard. *Purple Noon* (or *Plein Soleil,* in French) was directed in 1960 by René Clément from the Patricia Highsmith novel *The Talented Mr. Ripley.* In this film, the protagonist Ripley (played by Alain Delon) brutally kills his friend Philippe and then acquires his identity so that he can take over his rich friend's life of leisure. When his masquerade is uncovered, Ripley is forced to kill again, and suddenly realizes that the prime suspect will be Philippe, whose identity he has taken over. The plot twists continue until, ironically, Ripley's complex scheme unravels at that precise point at which it seems to have reached its absolute success.

A variety of English-language thrillers made roughly in the same period present largely similar plots. *The Third Voice,* directed and written by Hubert Cornfield in 1960, has a protagonist (played by Edmond O'Brien) taking on the identity of a rich man in order to swindle him out of a fortune with the help of the man's private secretary (played by Laraine Day). The rich man is killed, the protagonist tries to betray the secretary, and the film ends with a most ingenious twist as the protagonist's careful plotting backfires. *The Running Man,* directed by Carol Reed in 1963 from a screenplay by John Mortimer, deals with a protagonist (played by Laurence Harvey) who fakes his own death in an airplane crash and then adopts a new identity so that he can collect and enjoy the insurance money. The film develops a cat-and-mouse structure as the protagonist becomes increasingly certain that an insurance investigator is hot on his trail. The film ends, in typically ironic fashion for the genre, with the protagonist fleeing potential arrest in a small, unfueled airplane which crashes into the water. Thus, fate intercedes in the most ironic yet just way imaginable; by making the protagonist's insurance claim legal, fate takes away even his acquired identity.

Dead Ringer, directed in 1964 by Paul Henreid, offers Bette Davis a double role as Edith Philips and her own twin sister Margaret de Lorca. (Indeed, the idea of twins seems particularly apposite to the suspense thriller, which so consistently is constructed around elaborate dualities. One wonders why more thrillers have not taken advantage of this device. In fact, Nora Sayre has suggested that the archetypally frightening thriller image would be twin nuns.[1] Imagine the potential anxiety that image could create: nuns, black-robed and silent, one good, one evil . . .) In *Dead Ringer,* Edith Philips kills her rich sister Margaret after the death of Margaret's husband, whom Edith had also loved. After the murder, Edith takes on the identity of her sister and begins to live her sister's rich life in the mansion. Gradually, Edith discovers that Margaret had herself poisoned her husband, and Edith finds herself being sent to the gas chamber for the murder committed by Margaret. Thus, Edith is properly punished by an ironic but just fate.

Perhaps the two most critically celebrated thrillers of acquired identity, primarily because of their self-consciousness, are *Seconds* and *The Passenger*. *Seconds* was directed in 1966 by John Frankenheimer from a screenplay by Lewis John Carlino. The acquired identity in *Seconds* reflects the identity crisis of an entire age: youth in the late sixties were turning on, tuning in, and dropping out; parents were finding themselves on the far side of a generation gap, no longer sure about their American dream or the desirability of a house and a barbecue in the suburbs; and women were in the process of articulating questions for which women's liberation would soon be providing answers. *Seconds* offers the spectator a very specific fantasy: Supposing you had the chance to reject your present lifestyle, take on a new identity, and start over. Would you do it? And more importantly, what would you do differently than before? Unlike those protagonists in the other thrillers of acquired identity, the protagonist in *Seconds* is not a villainous character, but an everyman. Even the casting reflects this, for Hamilton is played by the then middle-aged actor John Randolph, a plodding, empathetic, talented performer whose face is comfortable and familiar, but whose name has never been recognized by popular audiences.

Seconds begins with a title sequence designed by Saul Bass. The film's first image is that of an eye anamorphically changing shape. Other parts of a face then stretch and become distorted, turning into something potentially terrifying. The final credit image is that of a face covered with a mask, the camera dollying in to the blackness of the mouth hole as the symbol of this suspense thriller's journey. The first sequence shows Hamilton at a train station being followed by a man who gives him an address. The many point-of-view shots invite audience identification with Hamilton. The camera emphasizes his hands, his nervousness. Frankenheimer cuts back and forth between two images photographed through the train window: one revealing the countryside which is coming up, another revealing that which has just been passed. These dichotomous images symbolize the basic quest of the film: the past versus a future. And yet, at the same time, the similarity of the images foreshadows already the failure of the experiment that has as of yet not even been revealed. Through visual means alone, Frankenheimer thus relates the address given Hamilton to Hamilton's very identity.

The protagonist is clearly an everyman, having a wife, a daughter, a son-in-law, a station wagon, and a secure life in suburbia. And yet, what Hamilton has is not enough: he feels an ennui, a discontent. His marital relations are no longer satisfactory, his job is tedious. When Hamilton gets a call from an old friend, presumed dead, who offers him the opportunity of a lifetime, Hamilton finds himself irresistibly drawn to the mind-boggling offer. As Hamilton begins his adventures, the image of steam from a

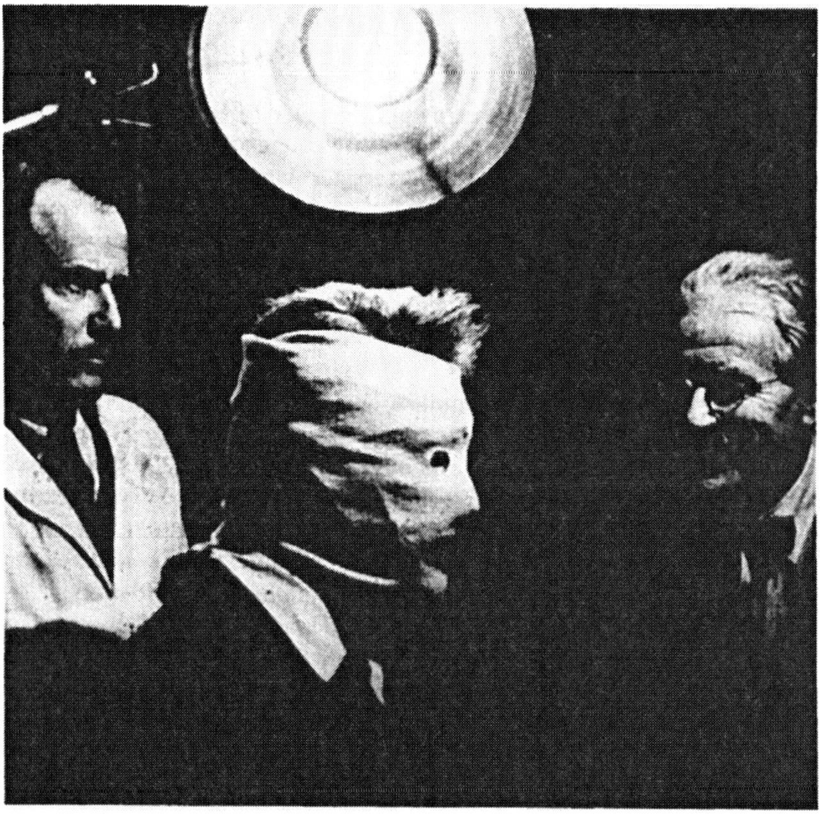

cleaning establishment fills the screen. Now there is no turning back: will the protagonist's journey represent a descent into hell? The front for the Company is the appositely titled Hi-Pro Meat Packing Company. In his meeting with the Company executive, Hamilton is told that the Company will provide him with a new identity for $30,000; the CPS (Cadaver Procurement Section) will easily fake his death as soon as Hamilton is ready to go forward. The sequence is very grisly, filled with black humor such as the Company executive gobbling down chicken while discussing Hamilton's death.

Still, Hamilton is not sure whether he wants to trade in his life. Typical to the genre, blackmail is involved: unwilling to allow a client who has come this far to change his mind, the Company is quite willing to blackmail Hamilton with film footage of him in a violent sexual encounter with a woman not his wife. How this footage came about is left ambiguous, although it seems to have been engineered by the Company. Hamilton's distorted memory of the encounter—taking place in a nightmarishly elongated room with bright checkered tiles—is vivid and horrifying. To aid Hamilton in making his decision, the Company executive allows him to talk to an old man (played by Will Geer). Hamilton's monologue to the old man is remarkably cathartic; while trying to explain his life he begins to cry as he realizes that there is very little left that offers him meaning or still provides him pleasure. The paternal figure (unnamed even in the credits except as the "Old Man") says simply, "There never was a struggle in the soul of a good man that wasn't hard." This sequence promotes an interpretation of *Seconds* as a religious parable. The old man represents God—the father, who gives people identities and then kills them. Although obsessed and committed to the dream of a good life for man, God is unable to comprehend that the problem with the dream resides in the very construction of the human organism, that man's fundamental "lack" is what comprises man's very essence. In this context, new things, places, and experiences may temporarily distract man, but they cannot succeed in making man happy.

The operating room sequence clarifies what is entailed in Hamilton's new identity, particularly the radical plastic surgery which will physically transform him from Hamilton into "Wilson." The operation climaxes with the newspaper article announcing Hamilton's "death" in a hotel fire. Significantly, Hamilton's new "Wilson" identity is not played by John Randolph, but by Rock Hudson—a device which plays upon the wish-fulfilling impulses of the spectator. A symbol of American masculinity, Hudson is (or at least, was, in the sixties) the perfect dream object: the lover of Doris Day,

Top: An unhappy John Randolph riding on a commuter train and contemplating the speeding blur which represents his unfulfilling past; Bottom: Faustian reworking in *Seconds* as surgery allows the protagonist, at this stage of the film played by Rock Hudson, to take on a new identity.

***Seconds:* After the surgery, Rock Hudson contemplates his former identity as John Randolph within a characteristic composition using mirrored reflections.**

the strapping American hero, and the granitic Hollywood construction of physique, face and name. The Company proceeds to set up Hamilton/Wilson in a new life created according to his own subconscious wishes gleaned while he was under the influence of sodium pentathol. Because he had always wanted to do something creative, the Company sets him up as a painter; since (as they tell him) they have made him a successful painter, he will be able to paint whatever he wants and his work will automatically be accepted. "You are alone in the world," he is told, "absolved of all responsibilities except to your own interests. Isn't that marvelous?"

After the protagonist's transformation into Wilson, *Seconds'* photography often takes advantage of mirrors; there is a small circular mirror in the office of Wilson's guidance counselor, a mirror in the airplane, a triple mirror when the blindfold finally comes off, and another triple mirror in Wilson's new bedroom (perhaps foreshadowing Wilson's longing for yet a third identity). Set up at a studio at Malibu and given a manservant from the Company to take care of his needs, Wilson soon meets Nora Marcus (played by Salome Jens). Nora asks the question, "Who and what is Tony Wilson?" Certainly the ungiven answer is complex. She describes her own past life as "a happy family, a husband, two boys, a microwave oven." Four years ago she walked out on them all, but certainly (she says ironically), Wilson wouldn't understand that. She takes him to a wild wine party in Santa Barbara dedicated to Pan, in which everyone strips and jumps into a vat of grapes. At first, Wilson cannot join Nora in the vat because the patterns of his old life are perhaps inextricably programmed into him. It is horrifying when the crowd rips off his clothes against his will and throws him into the vat.

After a while, Wilson begins to enjoy himself; covered with grapes, he jumps up and down orgiastically, yelling "Yes! Yes!" as he embraces the naked Nora. At this point, the wish-fulfilling upward movement of *Seconds* is consummated, the spectator having witnessed the transformation of a tense, complexly unsatisfied, middle-class everyman into a free spirit who can enjoy celebrative orgies. But in none of the suspense thrillers of this genre is an acquired identity easy; in its examination of the insurmountable problems of the protagonist's identity, *Seconds* begins its tragic downward movement.

Except for the one moment of acceptance in the vat of grapes, Wilson has still not been able to come to terms with his new life. At a party he gives for his neighbors, he begins to get drunk. Nora says to him, "Don't drink so much. It's not like you." But what exactly *is* like him? The party is attended by an assortment of odd characters, including one woman whose group changes sects every month (this month they're into virgin sacrifice). If one can change sects every month, can one ever really be in any sect at all? Can lives be exchanged like merchandise? Wilson gets drunker and mentions his previous identity as Hamilton, as well as aspects of his former life. The guests appear increasingly diabolical, and Frankenheimer photographs them from low angles. They carry Wilson into his bedroom and hold him down. Wilson discovers that the guests are all "reborns" from the Company and begins screaming and crying. An irritated Nora comes in and begins to swear; even she is a Company employee who has been paid to associate with him.

Upset and uncomfortable with his new identity, Wilson visits his former wife. She doesn't recognize him; Wilson pretends to be an old friend of Hamilton's who wants to paint his posthumous portrait. His wife's description of "Hamilton" surprisingly reveals that she was much more sensitive to his nature, problems, and needs than he had ever realized. "Arthur had been dead a long, long time before they found him in that hotel room," says Mrs. Hamilton, adding that what she remembers most about her husband was "his silences." (Indeed, the whole film moves finally to one grand silence—in which neither Hamilton nor Wilson are allowed to exist). Shaken by the experience with his wife, Wilson returns to the Company and asks for yet another identity; the Company asks him for a referral, which he refuses to provide. While waiting for the Company's decision, Wilson finally meets the friend who had referred him to the Company and discovers that his friend's new identity didn't work out either: the failure rate of the Company is very high. Wilson claims that the Company didn't understand what was important in life any more than he did, and that his bohemian, artistic lifestyle was—although seemingly antithetical—just the same as his suburban lifestyle: the "things" in one's life don't matter. "This time I've got to be allowed to make my own decisions!"

But Wilson can't go back again. As the old man says to him very kindly, "We can't let the mistakes jeopardize the dream." Wilson is strapped down and taken toward the operating room. As an all-purpose minister begins to comfort him, Wilson realizes that he is going to be killed. The minister intones, "No man can see me and live," lending credence to a view of the old man as God. In this horrifyingly violent scene, Wilson continually struggles and screams as he is wheeled into the operating room to his death. Wilson's cadaver is then to be used for someone else's "rebirth" (which finally explains where the Company got the corpses for their fictional deaths). The narrative implies that had Wilson provided a referral, he would not have been killed. Thus, the actions of Wilson's friend can be seen as betrayal, since the friend may survive at the cost of Wilson's life.

The sequence ends with a sedated, almost unconscious Wilson watching as the doctor brings a whirring drill towards Wilson's skull. The camera dollies in to the image of the operating room light; and then there is the image of a beach and at least one figure there—Hamilton? Wilson?—an image of peace, contentment, and serenity, which almost immediately distorts, blurs, then disappears. Typical to the genre, the protagonist is finally visited by the cruel, if just, fate and is punished for the insolence of asking for another identity by being forced to embrace the death he had earlier only pretended. Certainly contributing to the power of *Seconds* is its construction according to dualities. In fact, just as the first third of the film can be divided into three sequences relating to the protagonist's home, his visit to the Company, and his operation, so too can the last third be divided into three sequences relating to his return to his initial home, his return to the Company, and finally, his return to the operating room for his second (and real) death. Undoubtedly this kind of structure creates unconscious expectations in the spectator that propagate suspense.

Perhaps even more than Frankenheimer, Michelangelo Antonioni is a director supremely interested in form and film language. Antonioni's *The Passenger*, directed in 1975 from a script by Mark Peploe and Peter Wollen, emphasizes semiotic codes and a style which seem often to extend the language of the cinema. The frame is used unusually; the camera will often move past a walking character who will later catch up with the camera movement and re-enter the frame; "present" narrative and flashbacks can coexist within one uninterrupted shot. The color scheme of *The Passenger* seems completely controlled, with oranges and blues dominant. One image

The ageless sands in Antonioni's *The Passenger:* the angle of the truck and Jack Nicholson's gestures bespeak an archetypal alienation.

of a blue truck against orange sands stands out particularly vividly. And yet, despite *The Passenger*'s self-conscious "artiness," the film provides the genre with a relatively accessible work.

By making the protagonist who acquires the new identity a neutral rather than a villainous character and one subtly rather than obviously disillusioned with his own life, Antonioni creates an everyman who invites audience identification even as the stylish conceits surrounding him promote aesthetic distance. Antonioni's protagonist is a man who suffers from ennui, a man who is *not happy*, rather than one who is *unhappy*. If *The Passenger* is in any sense an antithriller, it is not because it subverts the conventions of the genre, but because Antonioni is so uninterested in or antipathetical to the concept of plot that he is unwilling to provide the explanations and motivations we have come to expect in popular forms. We never really know why Antonioni's characters act the way they do or what their precise relationships are; he knows that our understanding of the suspense thriller and its conventions will allow us to create our own expectations. If *The Passenger* represents a search for meaning, it is a search which demands the spectator's participation. Antonioni's part is to chronicle a certain organization of objective movement, color, and incident; ours is to isolate and identify the significance within the panorama provided.

Jack Nicholson plays the protagonist Locke, a reporter who is gathering information on African revolutionary groups. When a Mr. Robertson, a man staying at the same hotel, dies, Locke decides to take over Robertson's identity—not because Locke is involved in a complex and murderous plot, not because he is financially ambitious, not because his own wife is a hateful shrew, and not because Robertson's life is superior to his own. Indeed, words cannot adequately explain Locke's motive—which has more to do with the constant blue walls, the angle of the stuck jeep against the eternal orange sands, the weird and unsettling architecture of Gaudí, and the ambiguity of the African landscape. As Locke begins living Robertson's life, he discovers that Robertson had been a gunrunner; for Locke, for Robertson, even for Locke *as* Robertson, to escape politics and the pragmatic complexities of twentieth century life becomes impossible.

If *The Passenger* were a Hollywood film, Locke would continue living Robertson's life in order to do an exposé (and perhaps win a Pulitzer Prize?). But since this is not a Hollywood film, Locke's motivations remain ambiguous. As he finds himself involved in mysterious conversations with Robertson's associates, the words of his wife are recalled in a flashback: "You involve yourself in real situations, but you have no dialogue." In his new identity, Locke again has no dialogue: not knowing what Robertson would say or should say, Locke must constantly improvise.

The love interest in *The Passenger* is provided by Maria Schneider. Although Locke sees her for the first time in London while following Robertson's itinerary, neither of them speaks to the other. He meets her again in Barcelona. Although they begin a relationship, it is not clear whether either recalls seeing the other; nor is it clear whether Schneider (who plays only "the girl") is Robertson's wife, lover, or a mere stranger whose double appearance was coincidental. Antonioni fashions *The Passenger* out of images of constant travel: Locke traveling across the barren desert landscapes in Africa, the girl strolling through the Gaudí architecture in Barcelona, the two of them escaping from the police who pursue them, Mrs. Locke tracking down Robertson to find out information about her own husband's "death."

Peter Wollen has suggested a crucial difference between Antonioni's films and Hollywood's; whereas Hollywood photographs the confrontations between characters and omits their movements as they travel from place to place to arrive at those confrontations, Antonioni by and large seems to omit their confrontations and photographs only characters' movements. The suspense thriller's generic emphasis on locations and on the travel or flight of a protagonist explains its occasional use by Antonioni as an apposite framework within which to work out his related preoccupations.

The Passenger builds to a climax in which everyone is pursuing Locke: his wife (played by Jenny Runacre), who realizes that Locke is still alive and desperately wants to understand what has been happening; the police, who have been enlisted in her assistance; the two men in a white car, who may in actuality be after Robertson. The girl, who remains enigmatic, tells Locke that "Robertson believed in something. Keep his appointments." Locke does. When Locke checks into a hotel, he is surprised to discover that "Mrs. Robertson has already arrived." But does this mean the real Mrs. Robertson, the girl pretending to be Mrs. Robertson, the girl who is actually Mrs. Robertson, or Mrs. Locke pretending to be Mrs. Robertson? Locke knows only that even in Robertson's identity, he is tired. He tells the girl the story of a blind man whose sight was restored, but who killed himself three years later because the world was uglier than he had imagined; before he committed suicide, he had retreated voluntarily into darkness in order to avoid contact. What more can be said?

Locke asks the girl to leave and then lies down on the bed. The bravura shot that follows has been widely discussed and is almost impossible to describe properly. The shot, which runs several minutes uninterrupted with the camera constantly, but very slowly, moving, provides much the same fascination as looking out a real window onto a courtyard—only every casual detail or action is taken by the spectator as potentially significant. The camera pans about Locke's room and then moves outside through the window grate, revealing what is going on in the courtyard. A car goes by twice; the girl walks out of the frame; a boy enters the frame; a white car enters the frame, two men get out; one man sees the girl and talks to her (Does he know her?); the white car drives out of the frame; a police car comes into the frame; the white car, revealed again, is stopped before it can drive off; another police car arrives with Mrs. Locke . . . By the end of the shot, the camera has moved completely around, ending on the image of Locke still on the bed—now dead. Did he kill himself (as the story about the blind man might have implied)? Was he killed by the two men because they thought he was Robertson, or because they knew he wasn't Robertson? Was the girl an accomplice? Antonioni does not provide us the answers, although the conventions of the genre suggest that the death—whether

An image from the end of the celebrated long-duration shot in *The Passenger:* Maria Schneider and Jenny Runacre standing at left, Jack Nicholson dead on the bed at right.

suicide or murder—was properly Robertson's and Locke took it on. The film ends with a further ambiguity which, nevertheless, emphasizes this generic interpretation. "Do you recognize him?" the police ask Mrs. Locke in reference to her dead husband. "I never knew him," she answers, suggesting on one level that she never really understood her husband; and on another, that his transformation into Robertson was absolutely complete.

Although Antonioni is discussed time and again in the context of the unique creator colonizing new filmic territory, *The Passenger* nevertheless reflects—almost point by point—the generic conventions so typical to the thriller of acquired identity: the protagonist's acquisition of an unaccustomed identity, subsidiary characters who promote the masquerade, exchanged clothes, police officials, an examination of values, the protagonist himself being manipulated, large sums of money, the revelation of the false identity, the just and ironic fate which destroys the protagonist, and so forth.

A film like *Someone Behind the Door,* directed in 1971 by Nicolas Gessner, can be seen as a suspense thriller combining the acquired identity conventions with those of its amnesiac subset. In *Someone Behind the Door,*

Gregory Peck as the amnesiac wandering about the bleak landscape of *Mirage*.

Lawrence, a psychiatrist (played by Anthony Perkins) discovers a stranger suffering from amnesia (played by Charles Bronson) who he has reason to believe has already committed at least one brutal murder. The psychiatrist then tries to convince the amnesiac that the latter is actually Lawrence, in the hope that the amnesiac will again go off the deep end and kill the lover of Lawrence's wife.

One particularly workable amnesiac idea was that devised by Peter Stone based on a novel by Howard Fast—which was first used in the 1965

Mirage (directed by Edward Dmytryk) and used again as the basis for the 1968 *Jigsaw* (directed by James Goldstone). *Mirage* is a remarkably eclectic film and could easily be discussed as a psychotraumatic thriller, an innocent-on-the-run thriller, or a political thriller (with its sense of conspiracy), as well as an amnesiac film. Certainly its relationship to the innocent-on-the-run films like *North by Northwest* is very strong, for *Mirage*'s protagonist is chased by villains, set up as a murderer, and romanced by a *femme fatale.* As well, he searches for a MacGuffin (in this case, an equation for "a method of neutralizing nuclear radiation") which will make sense of his adventure.

Gregory Peck plays David Stillwell, the protagonist who realizes that he has amnesia and feels it has something to do with the death of Charles Calvin, a pacifist who fell (jumped? was pushed?) out of a window in a skyscraper. At one point when Stillwell comes home on the subway, the memory image of Calvin falling to his death is replaced by an image of a watermelon splattering as it hits the pavement. Stillwell's dilemma is to discover the secret of his own identity. When Stillwell is attacked by one of the villains who is after him for reasons he does not yet understand, the fight between Stillwell and the villain is replaced on the screen by a bout on a television wrestling program. "Now that all the westerns have gone psycho," says one character, "this is the only place you can tell who the bad guys are." This comment, of course, self-reflectively refers to the villains in *Mirage* as well.

Later, while out walking, Stillwell sees a book entitled *The Dark Side of the Mind* and consults one of its psychiatrist contributors. "Do you know the difference between right and wrong?" the psychiatrist asks him. "I can give you five minutes on good and evil," responds Stillwell. But the psychiatrist is uninterested: "Good and evil are theological terms." Succinctly summing up the contemporary moral crisis, the psychiatrist claims that he can't treat a dying man in the street without fear of a legal reprisal. Thus, "in today's complicated world, right becomes wrong, and wrong becomes right." The psychiatrist, if a genius, is presented as a moral coward, afraid to help Stillwell because he doesn't want to get involved or find out what Stillwell is repressing. Stillwell is thrice rejected as he seeks help: first by the police (an agent within society), then by the psychiatrist (an agent of enlightened society), and then by a detective (an agent outside society) who is killed while tracing Stillwell's past.

Mirage ends as Stillwell discovers that he is not a murderer and that his amnesia was caused by the shock of having witnessed the accidental death of his pacifist idol Calvin, who exhibited his true nature and fell while trying to grab the secret formula out of Stillwell's hands in order to gain a financial profit. In its revelation of the traumatic encounter witnessed by Stillwell, *Mirage* becomes the bridge between acquired identity films like *Seconds* and psychotraumatic thrillers like *Marnie.* Ultimately, Stillwell realizes that his life has value, recovers from his amnesia, and resolves to abide by his values even if Calvin was too weak to do so. "Commit!" says Stillwell. "If you're not committed to anything, you're just taking up space. . . ." The protagonist and the love interest who has aided him in his endeavors embrace. "We'll help each other. That's really what it's all about, isn't it?" Thus, the existential crisis of the sixties is solved by commitment to social causes and human values.

The very loose 1968 remake of this story as *Jigsaw* seems to me more interesting than *Mirage* itself, largely because of Goldstone's stylistic elaboration of the *mise-en-scène. Jigsaw* opens with Jonathan Fields (played by Bradford Dillman) waking up in a strange apartment. His memory gone, he washes blood off his hands and discovers a dead girl. Scattered memories of what happened come to him disturbingly in almost subliminal New Wave–styled cuts. His hand and head quiver as he tries to call the police and suddenly realizes he can't remember his name. The sequence is punctuated by constant jump cuts; Fields, still shaking, trying to find his identity, begins checking credit cards and frenziedly examines the telephone book to search for his address. Almost by itself, the book opens to a page advertising a detective agency; as the phone suddenly rings, the page tears off into Fields' hand and he runs from the room. The whole opening sequence is remarkably expressive in the way it communicates to the spectator the horror of amnesia. (Indeed, one wonders if Claude Chabrol was at all familiar with *Jigsaw* considering the way the beginning of his own film, *Ten Days' Wonder,* resembles it.)

Fields works for a think tank called the "Thought Corporation"—a pseudogovernmental agency much taken with playing military games, manipulating possibilities, and reducing everything to an objective and nonpersonal level. The settings of the corporation are all sterile, modernistic, and color-coordinated; Fields' girlfriend Helen (played by Hope Lange) wears white as she walks amid silver desk ornaments and past white walls. The romance between Fields and Helen has been unsatisfying because Fields is so cold. Helen needs a more emotional response; next time she gets involved with a man, she says, it will be with an ape-man. In one confrontation she bitterly screams at Fields that "One day you'll be able to tell me 'I love you' in this computer world we're making here!" After this outburst, she leaves Fields' office; he then takes off his black jacket and replaces it with a white jacket, becoming even more a part of the sterile, impersonal system. Even the detective that Fields hires (played most amusingly by Harry Guardino) calls Fields "a home-made, do-it-yourself robot." This soulless sensibility compares with that of Antonioni, whose alienated figures roam similarly blank landscapes.

Unlike Stillwell's amnesia in *Mirage,* Fields' amnesia does not derive from a psychotrauma, but from having been given LSD without his knowledge. Ironically, it is the drug experience that allows him to transcend

Dazzling color imagery from *Jigsaw* which this black-and-white still can only suggest: a wounded villain who collapses against a paint shelf and then drips paint, rather than blood, as he proceeds to exact his revenge.

his robot-like character. Later in the film when Fields is given LSD by the detective to help him relive the former experience, the screen explodes with beautiful and mysterious colors and images, including a red rose which opens up and turns into an atom bomb explosion. Like the opening sequence, Fields' flashback while under the influence of the LSD is most expressive. The flashback repeats itself, goes forward in time, backs up a bit in a narrative spiral, and takes advantage of montage and special effects, establishing a visual relationship between one of the film's villains, the blood on the dead girl, the flower, and Fields' job as represented by the atomic bomb. One striking but very brief shot shows Helen (in a black and white image) trying to comfort the hero, who (in a color image) is unknowingly taking the LSD which has been put in the sugar cubes stored in the refrigerator.

The search for Fields' identity and the accompanying analysis of that identity's value comprise the crux of *Jigsaw*. In this film (unlike *Mirage*), the detective is not killed; the emblem on the detective's door—that of a bloodshot eye—works as a symbol of identity imperiled, of the search for a soul. Not too far into the film, director Goldstone reveals that Lew Haley (played by Pat Hingle), a fellow worker in the Thought Corporation, is the true villain and has been trying to manipulate Fields into taking on the identity of murderer. When Fields and the detective finally learn the truth, they attempt to manipulate Haley in the same way Haley tried to manipulate Fields. They arrange events so that Haley and his evil associate Arnie will turn on each other.

In one of the recesses of the Thought Corporation building, Haley shoots Arnie, who backs into a shelf of paint cans and is completely covered with brightly colored paints. On a simple level, the image works to avoid the cliché; instead of blood, Arnie drips paint. The already striking image takes on a more profound meaning later when Arnie, who is not quite dead, comes staggering after Haley through the white hallways of the Thought Corporation, his dripping colors violating irrevocably the sterile space. Finally, Arnie catches on fire, envelops Haley, and the two of them fall off the building to their deaths. With the murderous plot of Haley destroyed, and more importantly, with the psychological sterility of the Thought Corporation violated, Fields is now free to amend his life and invest it with value. *Jigsaw* ends with the implicit suggestion that as a result of the psychological self-examination precipitated by the accidental LSD trip, Fields may yet be transformed into a warmer human being capable of commitment.

It is perhaps not accidental that *Jigsaw*, like so many of the films dealing with an acquired or forgotten identity, was produced during an introspective period of American history and was derived from an impulse rooted in the sixties. That in the late seventies and eighties the acquired identity films have largely been eclipsed is itself a reflection of an era which values narcissism over introspection and regards identity crises as anachronisms.

8
The Psychotraumatic Thriller

Tippi Hedren as *Marnie* appears to be the model of decorum: her clothes are stylish, her hair swept back in a sophisticated manner, her features patrician. As a secretary, she is exemplary: responsible, proper, efficient. On this weekend morning, she has arrived at the Rutland Building to take dictation from Mark Rutland, who is planning a book on zoology, and she waits patiently for the small talk to end so she can begin work. When a storm begins outside with a clap of thunder and lightning, Marnie gives out an unexpected scream. As the storm intensifies and a huge branch breaks through the office window, she begins running hysterically from one spot in the office to another, her calm reserve completely evaporated as she is transformed into a different person: one who is vulnerable, out of control, mysterious. Everything appears to go red, and she closes her eyes to shut out the horror. Confused by her reactions, but fascinated and attracted, Mark reaches out to try to comfort her. Romantic music erupts on the soundtrack, and in the midst of the confusion—surprisingly—they kiss; and a huge close-up of their lips fills the screen . . .

The psychotraumatic thriller is a film organized around the psychotic effects of a past trauma on a protagonist's current involvement in a love affair and a crime or intrigue. The protagonist is always a victim—generally of some past trauma and often of real villains who take advantage of his or her masochistic guilt. The protagonist may occasionally be a criminal as well. There is rarely a detective; when there is a force of inquiry, it is generally undertaken by the narrative itself or by the romantic interest of the protagonist, who applies a Freudian psychoanalytic method. This genre of film takes considerable advantage of mystery structures as well as of suspense structures, in that the source of the past trauma or the truth behind the present crime is not revealed until well into the narrative.

Certain thematic ideas integrated into this generic structure again and again include the duality of masochism/sadism, the destructive nature of guilt, the precariousness of the psyche, the importance of the subconscious, the inherent romanticism of mental disorder, the importance of facing unpleasant truths, and the potential for mental health and integration.

More specifically, the psychotraumatic thriller tends to proceed along the following lines: the introduction of the protagonist, the manifestation of his or her trauma, involvement in a present crime (of which the protagonist may be ignorant, its perpetrator, or its victim), involvement in a love affair; one or more re-enactments of the trauma, some of which may appear in symbolic forms; the revelation of the source of the past trauma or the truth behind the hidden crime (at least one of these effected through a flashback), a resolution of the love affair, and the actual or potential psychological integration of the protagonist.

A list of psychotraumatic thrillers would include the following:

Spellbound (1945)
The Locket (1946)
Under Capricorn (1949)
Vertigo (1958)
Marnie (1964)
Hush, Hush, Sweet Charlotte (1964)
Obsession (1976)
Body Double (1984)

These films can also be recognized by the presence of various other elements. These include an obsession, a trauma, guilt, climactic flashbacks, psychoanalysis, overt Freudian symbolism (generally sexual), a romantic love affair; various psychological disorders such as kleptomania, frigidity, acrophobia; an insane asylum or its threat, dreams and nightmares, the adoption of a false identity by the protagonist or the love interest, an accidental death, a suicide or its attempt, unhappy children, single characters portrayed by two actors one of whom appears only briefly in a flashback, a conflict between a protagonist and a symbolic or real stepparent, and a totem pursued by the protagonist.

In a psychoanalytic perspective using Michael Balint's terminology: the typical psychotraumatic thriller presents a protagonist who suffers from an unresolved conflict which has as manifestation an abnormal relationship with objects. The objects become either fetish objects to which the protagonist is unusually attached or such icons of fear that the protagonist spends most of his or her time working out elaborate defense mechanisms which would allow escape from them. The complex is often sexually rooted, which provides a potent if repressed sexual dimension to all that the protagonist experiences.

Ultimately, the protagonist must summon up the courage, usually with the help of another character who functions as psychoanalyst, to destroy the unhealthy ocnophilic association in order to face a more philobatic universe, which, for the first time, can be seen as life-affirming and filled with possibilities.

Alfred Hitchcock, who has always been interested in psychoanalysis and abnormal psychology, has made several of the most moving psychotraumatic thrillers. Certainly, Hitchcock is interested in dreams; many of his films, like *Vertigo* or *Psycho,* unfold with the almost surreal inevitability of dreams. What makes *Spellbound* unique is that the

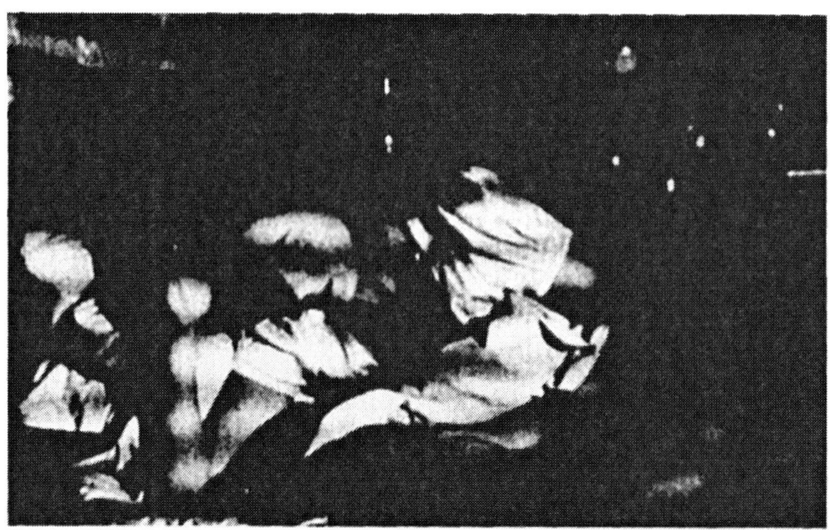

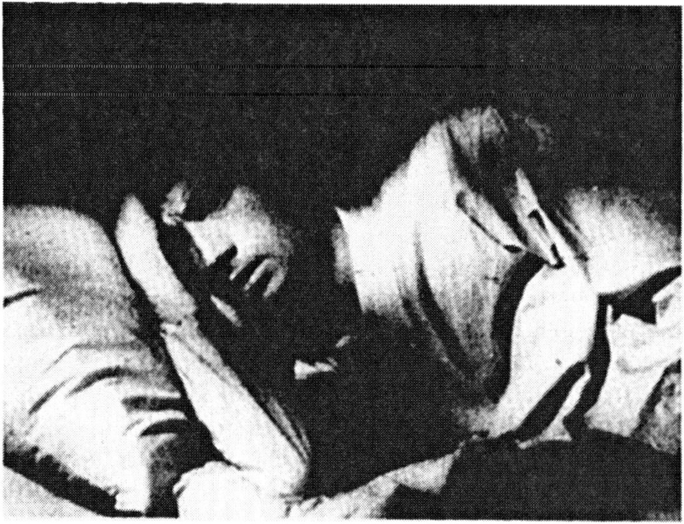

The suspense thriller tends consistently to take advantage of parallel structures, as evident in these two frame enlargements from *Spellbound*. Although it is Gregory Peck (bottom) who is under suspicion, note that it is the sexually unfulfilled Ingrid Bergman (top) who is photographed with imprisoning shadows across her face.

central dream sequence was designed by that notable surrealist, Salvador Dalí, and becomes the central clue, which, once decoded, solves the mystery and reveals the murderer. *Spellbound* begins with a crawl telling us that the film we are about to see deals with psychoanalysis: "The fault is not in our stars, but in ourselves." Indeed, in all psychotraumatic thrillers, events rarely proceed as a result of some objective or cruel fate which attacks from without (as in the thrillers of acquired identity), but as a result of subconscious urges from within.

Ingrid Bergman plays the role of Dr. Constance Peterson, a psychiatrist who works at the hospital clinic Green Manors. Her psychiatrist friend and would-be lover criticizes her, because she is, like so many suspense thriller heroines, cool: "Your lack of human emotional experience is bad for you." After embracing her, all her friend can add is that "It's rather like embracing a textbook." Leo G. Carroll plays the head of the clinic, Dr. Murchison, who, although hero-worshipped by Constance, is due to be replaced by a Dr. Edwardes, whose latest work, *The Labyrinth of the Guilt Complex*, could be used as a theoretical textbook for the psychotraumatic thriller.

When Constance meets Gregory Peck, who arrives as Dr. Edwardes, the romantic music comes up and we know that despite her cool and distancing inclinations, she has instantly fallen in love with him. She cannot consciously understand the mechanism herself, but it seems only just that the psychiatrist must now come to terms with her own subconscious impulses. Later, a restless Constance in her nightgown roams about the halls of the clinic; there is the most remarkably expressive moving point-of-view shot, as Constance comes up a stairway and sees a light shining from the bottom crack of the library door. The first love scene between Constance and Edwardes, for Constance a fulfillment of a lifetime of subconscious longing, is extraordinary: a series of opposing alternate long shots, medium shots, and then close-ups of their eyes. As they kiss, we see the surreal image of a series of doors beyond doors opening magically: a symbol both sexual and spiritual.

But their love affair is not smooth. There is a disturbing incident even at their first meeting: when Constance, sitting at a table, makes a mark with a fork on a tablecloth in order to show Edwardes a certain shape, he tries quietly to erase the fork marks. After they kiss for the first time, Edwardes becomes similarly disturbed at the lined pattern on Constance's robe. Later, the lines in a bedspread affect him in the same way. Constance takes it as her job to discover the meaning behind Edwardes' irrational fear. It is significant, therefore, that when Constance and Edwardes take a walk early in *Spellbound*, before all the problems with Edwardes' psyche are known, Hitchcock allows Constance to trip over a wire fence — symbolically implying the importance for Constance to confront Edwardes' line fixation in order to cure him of his psychosis and her of her coldness.

Edwardes' fear of lines turns out to be only one symptom of what appears to be a disturbed, and perhaps murderous personality. While performing surgery, Edwardes demands that more lights be turned on, yelling crazily, "What do you know of guilt complexes?!" Constance discovers that Edwardes is not Dr. Edwardes at all, but an imposter suffering from

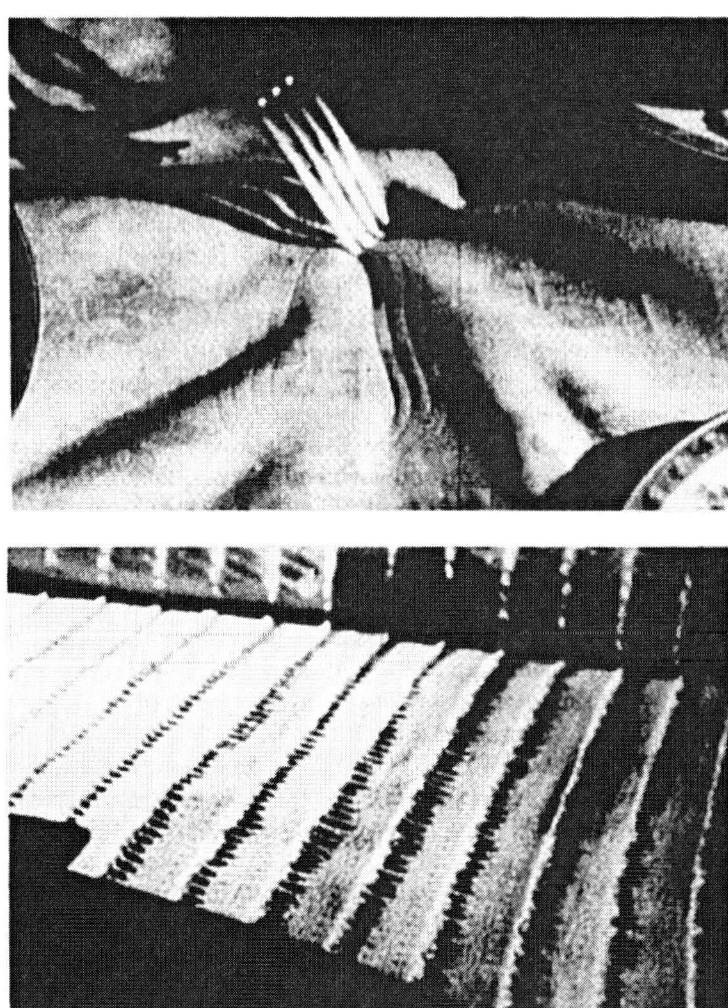

Objects that conspire against us: different manifestations of the parallel lines which so terrify Gregory Peck in *Spellbound*.

amnesia; further, the real Dr. Edwardes is missing. Has "Dr. Edwardes"—ultimately revealed as John Ballentine—killed the real Edwardes and repressed the details? To help get at the truth, Constance takes John to her old psychiatrist mentor, a typical Freudian with a German accent and a pointed beard. When they arrive, two men are already there waiting for the psychiatrist to return. "So how's your mother been lately?" says one to another—a line which invariably makes the audience laugh, so accustomed are we to the popular belief that crazy people always have fixations on their mothers. Hitchcock's joke ultimately implies the relevance of psychoanalysis to everyone, when the two men are revealed to be not psychiatric patients, but policemen trying to track down the murderer of Edwardes.

After the police have gone, Constance and her returned mentor discover that John is also afraid of the color white. One particularly suspenseful sequence has John suddenly disturbed by the white shaving lather, then the white sink, the white counter, the white bathtub. Distraught, he turns with his razor toward the unsuspecting, sleeping Constance. Perhaps he has killed once; will he kill again? He passes by her and instead goes down the stairs to the Freudian psychiatrist, who tries to calm him down by giving him something to drink . . . a glass of white milk, which, as he drinks, completely whites out the image. The color symbolism here presages the more complex *Marnie*, in which Hitchcock periodically suffuses the image with a bright technicolor red, which works as the expressive symbol of the heroine's guilt.

The next day, John tells Constance and the psychiatrist his dream. Typical of Dalí (and surrealism), the dream images, although often grotesque, are sharp and not presented unrealistically using distorting lenses or obvious special effects. The dream sequence begins with John in a gambling house. There are eyes on all the curtains; a man with scissors walks about cutting all the eyes, and then a young woman comes in and kisses all the men. The scene changes: John is now playing cards with a man with a beard. John deals the seven of clubs, so "that makes twenty-one"; the man's cards are blank. A proprietor with no face accuses John of cheating. The scene changes once more: John is on a high building. A man falls off; the proprietor who is now standing on the roof behind a chimney drops a distorted wheel; and John runs away, chased down a hill by a pair of wings.

After telling the dream, John notices through the window that it is snowing; he becomes scared as he sees ski tracks on the hill. Constance and the psychiatrist both realize the relationship between the tracks and his fear of parallel lines and conjecture that his amnesia relates to some recent skiing. For some reason, John has chosen to believe he murdered Edwardes rather than to remember his own painful past. After Constance deduces that the winged angel in his dream stands for the San Gabriel Valley, she forces John to go back there. In a very suspenseful scene, the two of them ski down the mountain toward the cliff at its bottom. With the traumatic conditions re-created, will John now remember his past or try to kill Constance? In the midst of the thrill, John finally recalls the horrible accident in his youth, in which while sliding down an outside bannister, he slid into his brother, who fell from the bottom of the bannister and was impaled on a sharp metal fencepole. This memory, communicated through the flashback so consistent to the genre, uses brief but stunning montage and a child actor to portray John as a boy.

But what was it that happened recently—in relationship to John and Dr. Edwardes—which made John associate it to the event in his childhood and then repress both? When the real Dr. Edwardes is subsequently found dead in the snow with a bullet in him, Constance uses John's dream to solve the mystery and discover why John was associating his childhood trauma with Edwardes' disappearance. The gambling house represents the clinic, Green Manors; the eyes on the curtains represent the guards. The young woman who kisses all the men represents John's sexual fantasy of Constance. The card playing sequence represents the fact that John and Edwardes (the man with the beard) had met at the Twenty-One Club (the comment "that makes twenty-one") and on that occasion were interrupted by the psychotic behavior of Dr. Murchison (the proprietor), the present director of Green Manors.

Because Murchison did not want to be replaced by Edwardes, he followed them both to the ski slopes (the roof of the house) where, hiding behind a tree (the chimney), he shot Dr. Edwardes with a revolver (the wheel). The wings which then chase John represent again Constance, this time as a kind of archangel determined to make John face the repressed truth and regain his mental health. Murchison can be seen as the symbolic stepparent who is put into conflict with the protagonist, in this case, Constance; as in *The Locket, Marnie,* and other films in this genre, the protagonist can achieve happiness only when she or he is completely freed of the stepparent's influence. Thus, Murchison's ultimate suicide frees Constance from her hero-worship and allows a completely happy ending in which John is purged of his guilt over his brother's death, absolved of responsibility in the murder of Edwardes; and Constance is finally able to face her formerly repressed subconscious need for love.

The Locket, directed by John Brahm in 1946, is a psychotraumatic thriller which is rarely discussed. The narrative is particularly complex and presents a flashback within a flashback within a flashback. In a sense, *The Locket* is like a Chinese box which is taken apart and reassembled. The ambiguous ending, in which the heroine perhaps destroys the life of yet another man, suggests that the narrative may yet expand, with the entire Chinese box as a flashback in another narrative container were the story allowed to continue.

The film begins with the party being held for Nancy (played by Laraine Day), who is about to get married. While her fiancé John Willis says, "I'm in a dream world," unaware that his dream world will soon be destroyed, the partygoers sing, "Nancy, Nancy, what'll you do to him now; he's only a fish in a gilded pan, he's going to be fried anyhow. . . ." A psychiatrist by the name of Dr. Blair arrives at the mansion, demands to see Nancy's fiancé, and then tells him about his own destructive marriage to Nancy years ago. Thus, the first flashback begins. Just like John Willis, Dr. Blair used to be a happy man . . . and then he married Nancy. Some time after they were married,

Dr. Blair was visited by Norman Clyde, an artist (played by Robert Mitchum) who demanded to talk to Blair just as Blair had demanded to talk to Willis.

The second flashback begins as Clyde tells the psychiatrist his own unhappy story. Clyde used to be a happy man . . . and then he met Nancy. "Are you in love?" he asks her. "Nope," she replies, "and I don't intend to be for a long, long time." Fascinated by her, Clyde painted a surreal portrait which he called Cassandra, described by Nancy's boss as "a madwoman, a woman with prophetic eyes." Gradually, Clyde discovered that the woman he was falling in love with was a kleptomaniac. "Why did you take the bracelet?" he asks her. "Because I wanted it," she responds. "You must be out of your mind. Don't you realize what you've done?" But Clyde insisted on a more complete explanation as to why Nancy took the bracelet, why the bracelet tempted her.

The third flashback begins as Nancy starts to tell her story. We discover that Nancy's mother used to be a housekeeper in a mansion, and that Nancy used to play with Karen, the daughter of the rich woman who owned the mansion. At a birthday party for Karen, Nancy became unhappy when, because she was the housekeeper's daughter, she was the only girl who didn't get a present. To cheer Nancy up, Karen gave her the very expensive locket she had been given for her birthday, although when Karen's mother found out, Nancy was forced to return it. Later when Karen herself temporarily lost the locket, Karen's cruel mother made Nancy cry and falsely confess that she stole it. Perhaps that's why I steal things, suggests Nancy.

The third flashback ends, and Clyde continues with his story. At a party, Nancy's boss was murdered: and although Nancy killed him in conjunction with a theft, she didn't speak up, and a valet was unjustly convicted of his murder. The second flashback ends as Dr. Blair continues with his story. In the psychiatrist office, Clyde asked him to intercede to save the valet before he was executed, but Blair didn't believe him. Clyde responded by giving Dr. Blair his painting of Nancy and then committing suicide by jumping through one of the skyscraper's windows. Although Dr. Blair was shocked, he went ahead and married Nancy. When in London during the blitz, Dr. Blair discovered that Nancy had stolen a very expensive diamond necklace, he became so distraught at the realization that he had allowed the innocent valet to be executed and had himself no real understanding of his wife, that he had a nervous breakdown and was confined to a sanitarium.

The first flashback finally ends, and Dr. Blair leaves Nancy's present fiancé Willis with the ominous sentiment: "There can be no happiness for you—ever." At this point in the film, we really don't know exactly what to believe. In a sense, all the flashbacks have been told by a man just out of a sanitarium; we tend to believe him, but should we? And will John Willis believe him? Will he proceed with the marriage? Will Nancy? The film saves for its conclusion its final twist—which cements perfectly the relationship between Nancy's present behavior and her past trauma, reinforces the conflict between her and the stepparent figure as represented by Karen's mother, and makes evident Nancy's lifelong pursuit of the totem locket. The film's narrative climax comes with the revelation that John Willis, Nancy's fiancé, is actually the brother of the now deceased Karen; Karen's mother, soon to be Nancy's mother-in-law, unaware of her former relationship with Nancy, gives her Karen's old locket as a wedding present.

Since *The Locket* deals with the psychopathology of personality, the narrative structure chosen by Brahm and his screenwriter Sheridan Gibney seems remarkably apposite. The constant enclosing flashbacks suggest a series of secrets, stored in the minds of the various characters:

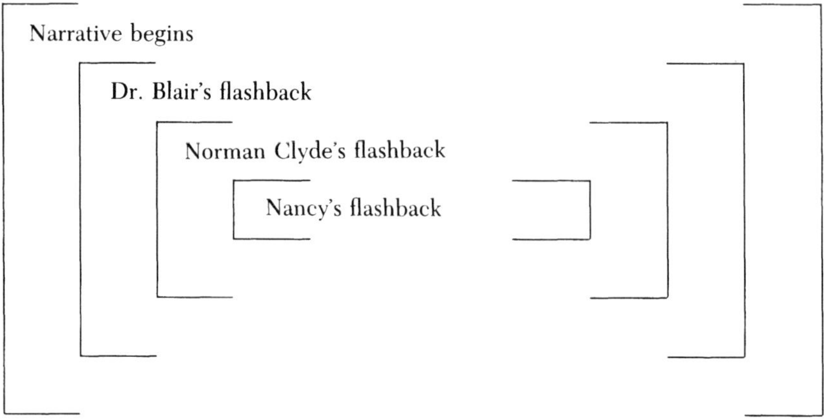

The central clue to Nancy's monstrous past is the locket of the title—and the locket is hidden away from the spectator in both time and space. In fact, in the central flashback the locket is revealed in the hem of the dress which is in the house of Karen's mother, Mrs. Willis. Yet the memory of all this is in the mind of Nancy, who is telling her story to Norman Clyde in his studio, who is in turn telling his story to Dr. Blair in his office, who is in turn telling his story to John Willis, Nancy's fiancé, who is paradoxically in the house of Mrs. Willis. Thus, like the house in Edward Albee's avant-garde *Tiny Alice*, the house in *The Locket* manages narratively to enclose itself. As in a similar film, *Marnie*, *The Locket* augments its unusual narrative by foregrounding various objects which also enclose spaces—most noticeably, the purse (which is in part sexual in its imagery), the treasure box, and the music box.

Each of the three enclosed flashbacks handles its exterior space in a more visually constricted manner: the first flashback the least constricted;

the second flashback a bit more constricted; and the final flashback completely constricted. Indeed, the climax of constriction takes place in the absolute center of the film, in the third flashback, when the little girl Nancy is shown literally pushed into a corner and towered over by Mrs. Willis. At this point Nancy is physically surrounded, as well as fictionally surrounded by the four different narratives. At another point in the central flashback, Nancy is framed within a thin vertical slit of light, as she and Karen hug in the closet, surrounded on either side by darkness. In this third flashback, we see nothing of the outside (exterior) world. Rather we are always inside the house, inside rooms in which doors are being closed. Although rooms contain windows, the windows hold curtains which effectively keep out any sense of any outside space.

The second flashback, unlike the third (which the former encloses), does allow us some glimpse of the exterior world—although that glimpse usually suggests an exterior world that is flat, a backdrop not to be used. In this second flashback, although windows are generally large and unencumbered by curtains, the outside world cannot be seen perfectly clearly, since the view through windows is often partially obscured by either rain (as in many scenes in Clyde's studio) or by night. On the few occasions when we do see panoramas of the city through a window, the panoramas often appear to be fairly obvious two-dimensional backdrops; there is never the implication of a "real exterior location" which may become three-dimensionally usable. Perhaps this flatness ties in somewhat with Clyde's occupation as a painter. One striking example of this purposive two-dimensionality takes place in the Italian restaurant where Nancy and Clyde have several meetings. Whereas in the first flashback, the psychiatrist was shown meeting Nancy against some exotic background of open sea and trees, Clyde courts Nancy in the restaurant against an exotic scene *painted* on the restaurant wall.

The overall progression from the first flashback to this second flashback is obviously of a gradual constriction. The one scene between Nancy and Clyde which is supposed to take place outside shows the two of them looking at one of Clyde's paintings on sale in the window of an art gallery. Yet this shot is photographed in a way so that we can see none of the exterior; we get no sense of the three-dimensional open space of the street, merely the intimations of cars reflected in the two dimensions of the window.

The differences between the second flashback and the first relatively unrestricted flashback (which encloses the second) is made obvious by the manner in which space is handled shortly after the second transition between them. Not long after Clyde finishes telling the psychiatrist his story, he rushes out of the office and throws himself through the window. The camera shows us what looks like a two-dimensional representation of the city, and then suddenly dollies through the window and down to reveal a striking

Laraine Day and Robert Mitchum in his artist's studio in *The Locket*, the film with a flashback within a flashback within a flashback.

image from a skyscraper-high perspective which creates a vertiginous illusion of three-dimensionality. As the first flashback continues, we see for the first time many scenes taking place outdoors—especially in the England sequences, in which there are scenes outside an English mansion, another scene implying three-dimensional space on the road leading to the mansion, and a scene in which real (albeit back-projected) trees and gardens are glimpsed through train windows. In short, as we move further away from the central constricted flashback of Nancy's youth, in both time and space, scenes are consistently photographed in ways which suggest more freedom and more open space.

It is only when we return to the original narrative, with all the flashbacks expended, that the constriction of the central flashback returns. This is only right, for the house at the beginning and the end is in actuality the same home as that appearing in the central constricted flashback. When Nancy moves down the stairway in her wedding dress through the crowded room and sees all the time and space in her life superimposed on the floor in front of her at the source of the original trauma, she screams and faints because she can no longer go on. Her past finally exposed, Nancy is taken away by her fiancé to an asylum to recover. The film's final image—that of Mrs. Willis' front door closing to exclude Nancy from the enclosed space—finally separates her physically from the source of her problem.

Often, psychotraumatic thrillers are criticized for being naive psychologically. This seems itself to be a naive criticism. Any film which, in approximately two hours, tries to deal in a popular narrative with the relationship between Freudian theory and actual behavior, must inevitably be simplistic; that *Spellbound, The Locket* and *Marnie* are simplistic does not diminish their relevance or interest. Psychotraumatic thrillers are not realistic psychological case histories, but stylized models. One sequence in *The Locket* self-reflectively addresses itself to precisely this criticism. At one point, the psychiatrist goes to a movie which he terms a "melodrama." "Was it ghastly?" asks Nancy half-hopefully. "It was about a schizophrenic who kills his wife and doesn't know it," he responds. "Of course, it may not be sound psychologically." If a fictional psychiatrist can understand the exigencies of art and respond to filmic events symptomatic of human behavior, so should we.

While Brahm's work remains, even today, relatively unknown, Hitchcock's work, of course, is extraordinarily well known. After *Spellbound*, Hitchcock was to make at least three more psychotraumatic thrillers: *Under Capricorn* (1949), *Vertigo* (1958) and *Marnie* (1964). *Under Capricorn*, the least consequential of the three films (though especially admired in France), may be as much a costume drama as a suspense thriller, but it certainly follows many of the conventions of the psychotraumatic thriller. Ingrid Bergman plays Lady Considine, an alcoholic brought to Australia and suffering from the secret trauma of having murdered her brother. When Lady

Considine finally confesses her past crime, she cries out, "What a release! What a blessed release!" The climax of *Under Capricorn* offers too the revelation that lady Considine was the object of a murderous poisoning plot. Bergman's protagonist is thus transformed into the genre's archetypal victim: a victim of her own masochistic guilt, as well as of a sadistic villain.

Vertigo has been much discussed elsewhere and is almost universally considered one of Hitchcock's masterpieces. Although the film remained out of release for over a decade, its reputation during that period grew steadily, and now—back again in distribution, the film continues to cement its reputation as one of the key films of world cinema. *Vertigo* begins immediately by establishing the trauma which will propel its narrative: because of his fear of heights, Scotty Ferguson, played by Jimmy Stewart, allows a fellow policeman to fall to his death. After resigning from the police force, Scotty is hired privately by Gavin Elster to follow his wife Madeleine, played by Kim Novak. Scotty finds himself falling in love with Madeleine and even saves her when she tries to drown herself in the ocean. When she finally does commit suicide by throwing herself off a tower, Scotty is absolutely crushed and suffers a nervous breakdown, particularly because his fear of heights prevented him from following her to the top of the tower to save her.

Unknown to Scotty, Elster had actually involved him in a plot to kill his wife; the woman Scotty had been following was really Judy Barton, working with Elster, who was only impersonating Madeleine Elster. When Judy ran up to the top of the tower, a waiting Elster had thrown off the real Madeleine Elster, whom he had already killed. After recovering from his breakdown, Scotty sees Judy Barton on the street one day and (not realizing it is the same woman) falls in love again. Completely obsessed, Scotty methodically tries to turn Judy into the Madeleine he had earlier loved. Hitchcock's decision to reveal the murder plot and Kim Novak's dual identity halfway into the film (when Judy confesses in a letter she subsequently destroys) rather than at the film's end again obeys his dictum that the spectator should always be given more information than the characters so that suspense, rather than mystery, is created. Scotty finds himself re-enacting his trauma yet again: finally realizing exactly how the plot must have worked, Scotty forces Judy up to the top of the tower. Scared by the sudden appearance of a nun, Judy falls off the tower—attaining the death that she had earlier only pretended. The film ends with Scotty on top of the tower, able finally to look down, his fear of heights gone.

The terminology of Michael Balint seems particularly relevant to *Vertigo:* Scotty must move away from the fearful ocnophilia brought on by his trauma; his rejection of the security represented by the brassiere-designing career woman played by Barbara Bel Geddes reflects Scotty's innate understanding that despite his fears, he must develop his philobatism and arrive at a balance. By following through with his obsession, coming to terms with his nightmares, and reliving his traumas, he does precisely that. If *Vertigo* seems to have the temper of a tragedy, it is because the integration of a personality is a complex and tortuous process; the crucial truths we learn upon self-examination are not particularly pleasant. If *Vertigo* is, indeed, a masterpiece, it is certainly in part because of the extraordinary beauty and expressiveness of its images. Large portions of the film are virtually silent, colors and costumes are carefully orchestrated, and constant point-of-view shots take advantage of the most sensuously moving camera.

Although *Vertigo* is the film considered Hitchcock's masterpiece, *Marnie* is nevertheless my favorite. Discussing one's favorite film is always a tricky proposition; one would so prefer to show the film and say simply, "Behold!" Has Hitchcock's narrative ever found a more apposite and expressive style? *Marnie* profits from multiple viewings, and particularly when viewed on a large screen, continuously offers up new insights, subtle images, unnoticed details. All is expressive: the systematic fades-to-black which divide the film into its component acts (often deleted on television showings); the complex and stylized use of color; the ingenuity with which the scenario is constructed; the integrity of each image and angle so that everything relates significantly, with nothing extraneous; the power of the consistent sexual symbols—from the images of concavity (such as Marnie's closed purse, her various suitcases, the safes and vaults that she robs) to the liquid images associated with her mother's prostitution (the sailor, the ship at the end of her street, the porthole, the drops of blood, the swimming pool into which Marnie tries to commit suicide); the rhythms of the montage; and the sensuousness of the camera movements.

Marnie takes as its subject the psychotic behavior of a young woman (played by Tippi Hedren) who suffers from frigidity and kleptomania, and the attempts to help her by the man (played by Sean Connery) who falls in love with her. Although *Marnie* appears to be one of Hitchcock's most personal films, its narrative conforms nevertheless to the conventions of the psychotraumatic thriller, including the heroine's involvement in a series of ongoing crimes as a result of a past trauma; her lack of awareness of the cause of the trauma (when she was a child she murdered a sailor being entertained by her prostitute mother); her reenactment of the trauma in symbolic form by shooting her horse; the revelation of the original trauma through a climactic flashback in which a child actress portrays the young heroine; and the potentially happy future in which the heroine begins to purge her subconscious, masochistic guilt and integrate her personality. Other generic elements include Marnie's obsession that sex is dirty, her husband's attempt to use explicitly Freudian psychoanalysis, her kleptomania, her constant nightmares, her attempted suicide, her unhappy childhood, and her pursuit of her horse as totem.

A recitation of the film's generic elements simplifies *Marnie* by ignoring

Tippi Hedren as the victimized *Marnie* longing for mental health and sexual fulfillment.

its style, for sequence after sequence is constructed in stylized images pregnant with meaning: the horrifying beauty of Marnie's honeymoon night in which her husband virtually rapes her; the riding sequences in which the back projection appears so disturbingly flat and noncathartic; the unbearable extension through montage of her horse's failed jump over a fence; and the final revelatory flashback which correlates Marnie's present crimes, her past trauma, her frigidity, and her fear of the color red. If indeed *Marnie* is a great film, it is also because its story is ultimately heart-breaking and moving. Its hopeful message is that although life is hard and unfair, wreaking great psychological violence and depriving us of love, compassion, and understanding, we may yet, with the help of the (however impure) love and trust of others, overcome all obstacles to become psychologically balanced and sexually fulfilled.

Although I have emphasized the style of *Marnie,* psychotraumatic thrillers in general seem to have more stylistic flourishes, narrative tricks, camera movements and montage than any of the other suspense genres. Perhaps because these films inevitably deal with obsessions, psychoses and other intangible maladies of the mind, their directors are forced to invent specific and symbolic visual and narrative means to communicate these psychological states. A fairly recent example of the psychotraumatic thriller which similarly reflects this inventiveness of style is *Obsession,* directed by Brian De Palma from a script by Paul Schrader. *Obsession*'s specific relationship to *Vertigo* has been noted by critics as well as by De Palma himself. Certainly *Obsession* can be seen as De Palma's first attempt to refashion *Vertigo* (the second would be *Body Double,* eight years later). A great number of critics were, therefore, unusually harsh on this De Palma film, responding as if it were only a self-conscious homage to Hitchcock, or—much worse—simple plagiarism. Few critics were willing or able to acknowledge that De Palma was also working within the conventions of a popular and expressive genre, a genre to which Hitchcock, despite his successes, did not own exclusive rights.

The opening credits of *Obsession* are juxtaposed with ominous tracking shots toward a church and still slide images of the protagonist Michael Courtland (Court, played by Cliff Robertson) and his wife Elizabeth (played by Genevieve Bujold) in Florence in 1948. The narrative proper begins with a tracking shot into the New Orleans home of Court and his wife. It is 1959, and they are showing slides of their trip to Florence. One slide says, "And they lived happily ever after," which suggests, of course, that they won't. The photography by Vilmos Zsigmond is glistening and misty; the dancing in their home seems almost like a ball in a fairytale.

One complex camera movement begins by showing Court and his wife dancing happily; when they dance off into the background, a waiter walks into the picture, approaches the camera, and offers a drink; as he raises his arms, the gun hidden beneath his coat fills the screen for one surprising moment and then disappears when he turns and goes off, the happy, oblivious dancers once again coming into view. Thus, this one elaborate shot has suggested most expressively that something awful may shortly take place. One purpose of this opening sequence seems to be to establish the almost delirious love between Court and his wife.

In another shot, the lyrical camera pivots almost 360 degrees: while Court dances with his wife, the moving camera reveals in long shot their little girl Amy at the top of the stairway; as she joins them in their dance, the camera ends on a close-up of the faces of Court and Amy as they dance happily. (Significantly and consistent to the generic dualities, *Obsession* ends with Court and his daughter embracing, this time the camera itself dancing around them.) As the camera continues its expressive movement in Court's bedroom after the party, where it tracks into the eyes of his wife, filled with longing, Bernard Herrmann's score comes up powerfully.

The fantasy-like happiness ends abruptly when the wife and little girl are kidnapped. Following the advice of the police, Court decides against paying the ransom and instead allows a magnetic beeper to be attached to the ransom briefcase. De Palma constantly juxtaposes the evil and the horror of the kidnapping with images of innocence: the newspaper boy who delivers the tape-recorded message from the kidnappers, the troop of boy scouts who swarm over the boat Court takes when he makes the "pay-off," and Amy herself. When the police arrive at the kidnappers' hideout, we see the kidnappers dragging Court's wife into their car and carrying the figure of Amy wrapped in a blanket. A chase ensues, the car crashes into the Mississippi River and explodes, and the bodies are never found. The sequence ends with the mausoleum—built in the likeness of the church in Florence—being lowered onto a large expansive plot of land: Elizabeth Courtland, 1931–1959; Amy Courtland, 1950–1959. An amazing 360 degree pan follows, with an almost imperceptible cut on the mausoleum; at the end of the shot, sixteen years have gone by, and we see Court years older, still guilty, unrecovered from his trauma.

The second act of the film begins Court's ritualistic re-enactment of this initial trauma and his innocent involvement in a murderous plot. With his partner Bob, Court decides to go back to Florence and visit the church where he and Elizabeth first met. As Court goes into the church, twin priests come out (which works partially as a reference to De Palma's own *Sisters,* a film about twins, but primarily as an indication of the doubling so common to the suspense thriller which will propel the rest of *Obsession*'s narrative). Inside the church, the camera tracks in to an image of a girl moving her brush in a lyrical slow-motion, then Court's expressive eyes: the girl is a virtual image of Elizabeth. When Court returns to the church, he introduces himself to the girl (played too by Bujold). Her name is Sandra; she had been hired to help restore the painting of the Madonna.

A while ago, it was noticed that moisture had seeped into the altar piece and the washing away of some of the paint began to reveal another, although perhaps cruder, painting underneath. The dilemma: whether to uncover the painting underneath, or hold onto and restore the painting of the Madonna? Court agrees with the experts: "Hold on to what you got." Unknown to Court (and perhaps to the spectator at this point), the painting of the Madonna serves as an explicit symbol of the narrative's movement: the seepage of the water, for instance, relating specifically to the earlier crash into the Mississippi River. It is Sandra's real identity that Court should hold onto, not that identity he is projecting onto her (his former wife). So obsessed is Court with Sandra's resemblance to his wife, that he immediately falls in love and convinces her to come back to New Orleans to marry him. He is determined to regain his lost happiness.

When Sandra goes back to New Orleans with him, she becomes just as obsessed with Elizabeth as Court. Sandra visits the crypt and cries when she touches Elizabeth's inscription. Three tracking shots into the portrait of Elizabeth alternate with shots of Sandra's dark brown eyes staring at it intently. Another bravura tracking shot follows the key in Sandra's hand as she walks with it to Elizabeth's bedroom, which had been locked since 1959; inside, she reads Elizabeth's diary and the newspaper account of the

Genevieve Bujold in *Obsession* comes to terms with the past; note how the mirror reflection serves to reinforce the film's underlying obsession with identity.

crime. Court dreams of getting married again; in his dreams, Sandra has the same hairstyle as Elizabeth, and the wedding cake is built in the shape of the Florence church, the shape of Elizabeth's mausoleum. The image of the church is always accompanied by the same maddeningly obsessive theme of Bernard Herrmann's score, repeated over and over. In a sequence which is only ambiguously a dream, Sandra/Elizabeth comes into Court's room and says, "Now I am your wife, I am Elizabeth . . . I came to give you a second chance to prove your love."

In the morning when Court goes to the locked room, Sandra is gone, and the clipped copy of the kidnapping note from 1959 is again attached to the bed. A frantic Court raises the ransom money by selling an important plot of land to his associate Bob La Salle. The earlier trauma is thus being reenacted, this time with Court determined it be concluded differently. To this end, Court willingly delivers the ransom briefcase (this time filled with real money) to the deserted landing. After Court leaves, a car races to the landing and Sandra jumps out and opens the briefcase: amazingly, it is filled only with paper. When Court's associate, Bob, gets out of the car as well, we realize that Bob and Sandra had joined in a plot to swindle Court; the treacherous Bob, who primarily wanted Court's land to develop it for financial gain, then switched the briefcase with the ransom money as well. Had the second kidnapping failed to get Bob the land, Bob was certain the whole experience would have so unnerved Court that Bob could have had him declared mentally incompetent. "Court just can't come up with the money," says Bob cruelly to Sandra, "Not for her and not for you!"

While in *Vertigo* it is the letter Judy writes that triggers a flashback which reveals the murderous plot to the spectator, here it is Sandra's shock at not getting the ransom money: "Mommy, Mommy," says Sandra, suddenly regressing, as we realize that Sandra is actually Court's now grown-up daughter Amy and we again see the kidnappers' 1959 hideout just as it is being surrounded by the police. In this flashback, Genevieve Bujold herself plays the terrified daughter as well as the mother. We see what really happened: although the kidnappers took Elizabeth with them in the car, the wrapped-up bundle did not contain Amy, who therefore never died in the accident. Bob, who had masterminded that kidnapping as well, saved Amy himself by taking her out a back exit.

The flashback ends as Bob drags the hysterical Sandra/Amy to the airport to return her to Italy. A contrite Amy, however, who has now developed real affection for her father, wants to go back and ask for Court's forgiveness. The duality so consistent to the genre is reflected in the remarkable airport sequence which is simultaneously the narrative present and a flashback. The little girl Amy (played still by Bujold) is dragged by her "Uncle" Bob and another kidnapper; Uncle Bob is the 1959 Bob with shorter hair, and he expresses genuine sorrow because he never intended the original kidnapping plot to end with Elizabeth dead. The 1959 Amy was then adopted by a family in Italy and prepared for a possible revenge, thinking always of her Uncle Bob as a stepparent and her father as a villain directly responsible for the killing of her mother. This sequence serves too to get the grown-up Amy on the plane back to Italy, where she is presumably half-dragged by a 1975 longer-haired Bob.

A suspense scene follows on the airplane, when a suicidal Amy starts to write a letter to her father, changes her mind, and then goes into the washroom. Later, the stewardess walks by and sees a puddle of red blood seeping from underneath the door; the airplane is turned back so Amy can get medical help. Meanwhile, after finding out about the plot from Bob, as well as about "Sandra's" involvement (but not realizing Sandra is actually Amy), Court kills Bob with a pair of scissors and then races to the airport with the real briefcase of ransom money and a gun. The film ends with a tremendously exciting set-piece: there are alternate tracking shots of Court running through the airport toward the returning airplane, and Amy being wheeled down the ramp of the embarkation tunnel. When a policeman notices Court's gun and tries to stop him, Court hits him with the briefcase and the ransom money flies about. The suspense is almost unbearable as at this point, De Palma switches to slow motion and Amy rises out of her wheelchair and begins to approach her father. Will Court shoot her? He points the gun at her, she runs toward him, he runs toward her. As Amy embraces the incredulous Court, she says: "Daddy." There is a pause, and the camera begins to revolve around Amy and Court. The music comes up full, and Court suddenly realizes the whole truth, as for the first time he calls his daughter: "Amy." In a final apotheosis of style, the camera revolves dizzyingly, endlessly around their frantic embrace—as Court cures his obsession and sheds his guilt, and as father finds daughter, and daughter finds father.

Interestingly, *Obsession* originally was to have been entitled *Triple Ransom* and to have ended quite differently. In screenwriter Schrader's original version, Court was not reunited with his daughter after the second kidnapping and ransom. Instead, as he runs to the airport, he is arrested by the police and sent into a mental institution for ten years. A third act to the film, taking place ten years later (presumably in 1985) follows. Upon release from the institution, Court gets a gun, the briefcase of money, and goes a third time to Florence, where, inside the church, he sees once again Sandra/Amy/Elizabeth. Amy, now approximately the same age as Elizabeth when she died, does not recognize Court since she has been catatonic ever since the second kidnapping experience with Uncle Bob. The nuns taking care of Amy suggest a kind of hypnotherapy, and the kidnapping is reenacted yet again—with Amy thinking it is the first time, and Court thinking it is the second time. Only this third time with the ransom money finally in the right place are the father and daughter reunited. Certainly, this fascinating third act might have proven too obsessive for an audience to bear; perhaps, however, some of the plot-related rough edges around *Obsession's* climax result from De Palma's cutting of Schrader's original script.

With *Body Double*, Brian De Palma returned once again to the basic structure of *Vertigo*. Although the response to *Obsession* had been varied, critics this time responded almost unanimously with a viciousness which was rather astounding: their hostility divided somewhat between anger at what they regarded as plagiarism and distaste for what was, at the emotional center of *Body Double*, one of the most violent acts directed against a woman ever filmed in the American cinema. In one sense, *Body Double* can be seen as De Palma's *ne plus ultra* of style: a film in which the manner is so elevated that the subject seems almost irrelevant.

The opening of the film immediately employs several visual tricks. The credits are in the style of a low-budget horror film, with the credits dripping red blood. The camera tracks from a stylized moon to a vampire in a coffin. Ultimately, we realize that this is not a horror film; we are, rather, watching a Hollywood horror film *being made*. Shortly, another shot, that of a mountain vista, turns out to be a painted backdrop. Thus, De Palma raises the questions: What is real? And can we trust what we see? The "vampire" is actually the actor Jake (played by Craig Wasson), who ruins the scene and is fired because he is claustrophobic and unable to move or speak when under stress.

Later, in an acting class, Jake—doing a psychoanalytic sense-memory exercise directed by his acting teacher—recalls his significant youthful trauma: while playing a game called "Sardine," he hid behind the freezer in the basement, and had become stuck and afraid, unable to move. Remembering his fear that his brothers would call him a baby if he cried out, Jake becomes emotionally distraught in the acting class, but is unable even in the present to cry out or move. Instead, he stands paralyzed in front of the acting class, a pitiful child-adult who has not yet conquered juvenile fears. We see that Jake, like *Marnie* or Scotty in *Vertigo,* suffers from an emotional trauma which prevents the integration of his personality and blocks success in his endeavors.

Down on his luck, Jake is set up temporarily in a wonderful house by his friend Sam, who shows him that the house has a telescope which is trained on the home of a woman across the way, who every night dances provocatively in a skimpy outfit. Fascinated by the spectacle, Jake begins to spy on the woman. Here De Palma is reworking the same theme of voyeurism that so fascinated Hitchcock in *Rear Window* and which has been present in some manner as well in virtually all of De Palma's films. In this film, however, unlike *Rear Window,* the voyeurism seems disturbingly pornographic, for as Jake watches the woman masturbate, he finds himself aroused and emotionally moved.

Perhaps the most accomplished and expressive sequence in *Body Double* is an almost twenty-minute long, virtually silent, set-piece which is patterned after the sequence in *Vertigo* in which Scotty follows Madeleine. Here, Jake follows the object of his desire, Gloria (played by Deborah Shelton), who goes to a shopping mall. She is dressed in white, which offsets her flowing black hair. In a beautifully expressive montage with music, we can see, almost *feel,* Jake's growing obsession with her. Jake knows that an Indian has been following Gloria, and although he catches up with her in an elevator, he cannot tell her of his feelings nor of the man following her, because he has another attack of his claustrophobia. He continues to follow her to a multi-terraced, beachfront complex; and she becomes increasingly vulnerable and in need of human contact.

After a pursuit amidst sixteen perfectly geometric cabanas, Jake finally reaches her and tells her that "Someone's following you." "I know," she says, looking at him longingly. Before he can explain, the Indian steals her purse; and Jake follows the Indian into a tunnel where, overcome again with claustrophobia, he proves himself impotent, unable to act. The Indian lets out a long scream (like Jake's as the vampire at the beginning of the film), and Jake himself must ultimately be rescued by Gloria. Again outside the tunnel, Gloria seems both vulnerable and beautiful, and De Palma shows us an incredibly passionate kiss between Jake and Gloria (recalling the final image of *Obsession*) as the camera revolves around them three times while they spin around as well. Successfully created, at least on the wide screen of the movie theatre, is a sensuous feeling of ectasy which is quite impressive.

Later, while spying on Gloria again with his telescope, Jake watches as the Indian intrudes on Gloria and tries to kill her. The Indian first tries to strangle her—in a scene which recalls Hitchcock's *Frenzy*—and then, when that fails, horribly and obscenely attacks her with a huge power drill. The violence is so extreme, the defilement of Gloria so great, that it is very difficult for audiences not to respond to the scene as a misogynist attack, by De Palma himself, on all women. Just as it appears that the Indian is going to succeed in impaling Gloria, who pleads pathetically for mercy, the electrical cord of the drill is extended too far and pulls out of the wall. Downstairs, the would-be hero Jake is able to get into the house—in the nick of time?—but as he does so, a guard dog attacks *him* as the intruder, preventing him from saving Gloria. While Jake fights with the vicious dog, he looks up and sees, above his head, the huge drill bit coming through the ceiling, dripping blood, as Gloria has been savagely drilled through to the floor of the upstairs bedroom. The violence is so great, the suspense so protracted, the manipulation so unabashedly embraced rather than disguised, that it is unusual for an audience not to feel some measure of violation.

Inevitably, as the film proceeds, there are the prerequisite narrative surprises: for it turns out the murder was not quite what it appeared to be, that Jake was, as was Scotty in *Vertigo,* set up to provide the real killer with an alibi. In the second half of the film, Jake gets involved in the pornography industry, as the film becomes increasingly sordid and satirical. Jake discovers Holly Body, a porno star (played by Melanie Griffith) who has been a double of sorts, indeed, a body double, for Gloria. Like Scotty in *Vertigo,* Jake now begins to pursue this second woman and ultimately expose her part in the murder. And again, as in *Vertigo*, there is a narrated flashback which reveals exactly how the murder plot was supposed to have worked.

Like Court in *Obsession,* Jake is given a second chance. Can he save Holly, who, despite her pornographic career, is actually an innocent, or will she be killed as was Gloria? Will Jake's claustrophobia again cause his failure? The villain, counting on Jake's traumatic responses, attempts to bury Jake alive in a sequence which seems to be a real-life version of the beginning of the film when Jake, as the vampire, needed to escape from his coffin. In the suspenseful climax, Jake psychologically relives the incident at the beginning of the film, accepts his fear, and, for the first time, transcends it—thus able to save the woman and triumph over the villain. Because he was given yet another chance, Jake overcomes his psychotrauma, exorcised of the demons of his past.

One final psychotraumatic film requiring comment is *Hush, Hush, Sweet Charlotte,* directed by Robert Aldrich in 1964. *Charlotte* deals with a woman who, traumatized by the murder of her lover (which she may have perpetrated), descends into madness. Charlotte (played by Bette Davis) regains her sanity only after reliving the trauma and discovering the surprising truth about both the present and the past. If strict psychotraumatic thrillers are few, there are nevertheless a significant number of films, particularly horror films, which share many of the genre's characteristics. *Hush, Hush, Sweet Charlotte* seems to me to be a thriller which comes very close to a horror film—with its old, dark house; characteristic visual style dense with shadows; and emphasis on the horrific excesses of the protagonist's madness.

In fact, there is a large group of horror films, which I have called horror-of-personality films, that reflect a great interest in trauma and psychotic behavior—horror films I discuss in detail in my own book, *Dark Dreams: A Psychological History of the Modern Horror Film.*[1] Most of these films, like *Psycho,* emphasize the psychotic personality's identity as a virtual monster who kills, wreaks havoc, and perpetrates violence, rather than as an archetypal victim of his or her own masochistic guilt. Yet these films—and there are a very large number of them, from *Strait-Jacket* and *What Ever Happened to Baby Jane?* to *Homicidal* and *Pretty Poison*—are certainly very close relatives to the films described in this chapter.

Also related to the psychotraumatic thriller are those dramas, like *The Three Faces of Eve* (1957) and *Sybil* (1976), which deal with multiple personalities, often of real individuals. If these films do not come across with the sensibility of suspense thrillers, it may be because they lack an overt criminal element or murderous plot and because the protagonist's romance is replaced with a more systematic investigation of the protagonist's past, an investigation which at times resembles a documentary case-history.

Yet significantly, the score of *Sybil,* for instance, is rhythmically insistent in the best tradition of the suspense thriller and undoubtedly helps to underscore the anxiety and horror of the protagonist's past. Like the psychotraumatic thrillers, these multiple personality films proceed towards revelatory flashbacks as well. I suspect the success of these films may derive more from their relationship to the psychotraumatic thriller than from any less simplistic or more documentary approach to psychoanalysis that they may offer.

9
The Thriller of Moral Confrontation

Farley Granger as Guy Haines, the tennis pro in *Strangers on a Train*, is a fundamentally decent and moral man, an innocent with a good heart who has been repeatedly cuckolded by his duplicitous wife, Miriam. At a telephone booth at a railroad station, Guy telephones Ann, the moral and kind woman with whom he has fallen in love. As he tells Ann the bad news that his wife will in all probability continue to refuse him a divorce, he admits, in an offhand way, that he's so angry with Miriam that "I could kill her myself," his hands clenching in reflex.

Later, on an island used as a lovers lane by couples brought there by an amusement park ride, Robert Walker as the evil Bruno Anthony, out of a misguided and psychotic motivation, has tracked down Miriam, who has come to the amusement park on an excursion with her two boyfriends. Miriam knows that Bruno has been following her; and when Bruno finally approaches her, lighting a cigarette lighter in greeting, Miriam acts coy and shows interest. There, on that dark island, surrounded only by those making love, Bruno puts his hands around Miriam's neck and slowly begins to strangle her. When he is finished, he lowers her inert body to the ground, anxious to tell Guy, who is innocent and oblivious, that it is now Guy's turn to commit a murder in exchange . . .

The thriller of moral confrontation is the film organized around an overt antithetical confrontation between a character representing good or innocence and a character representing evil. These films often are constructed in terms of elaborate dualities which emphasize the parallels between the victim and the criminal. The detective force, if present, is inevitably subsidiary.

Certain thematic ideas integrated into this generic structure again and again include the inevitable evanescence of innocence, the struggle between good and evil, and the ultimate ambiguities of moral issues.

More specifically, these films tend to proceed along the following lines: the introduction of the protagonist and his or her adversary; the assignment of the victim/protagonist to the role of an observer or witness who could potentially endanger the adversary; the gradual estrangement of the protagonist from those who could provide assistance; the elaboration of the symbiotic relationship between the protagonist and the adversary; the transformation of the protagonist from passive victim into an active fighter who struggles to defeat the adversary; a series of increasingly tense cat-and-mouse encounters between protagonist and adversary; often a distinct moment at which the protagonist becomes absolutely conscious of the adversary's power and retaliates by adopting new, more powerful methods to achieve victory—often the adversary's own methods; a final confrontation in which the protagonist emerges victorious; and a concluding scene of stasis in which the protagonist reflects on the complex meaning of the struggle.

A list of thrillers of moral confrontation would include the following:

Shadow of a Doubt (1943)
The Window (1949)
Stage Fright (1950)
Strangers on a Train (1951)
Dial M for Murder (1954)
Rear Window (1954)
The Desperate Hours (1955)
Night of the Hunter (1955)
Step Down to Terror (1958)
Cry Terror (1958)
The Singer Not the Song (1961)
Cape Fear (1962)
The Boy Cried Murder (1966)
Blowup (1966)
Wait Until Dark (1967
The Bride Wore Black (1968)
Le Boucher (1969)
La Rupture (1970)
Sudden Terror (1970)
Duel (1971)
Straw Dogs (1971)
Outrage (1973)
Death Wish II (1974)
The Eyes of Laura Mars (1978)
Eye of the Needle (1981)
The Fan (1981)
Death Wish II (1982)
Victims (1982)
10 to Midnight (1983)
Red Dawn (1984)
Perfect Strangers (1984)
The Mean Season (1985)
Death Wish III (1986)
Blue Velvet (1986)
The Stepfather (1987)

Related to these thrillers of moral confrontation as a kind of distinct subset are a group of "women's thrillers" which include:

Rebecca (1940)
Suspicion (1941)
Gaslight (1944)
Sorry, Wrong Number (1948)
Midnight Lace (1960)
The Naked Edge (1961)
Jagged Edge (1985)

It should be noted that of all the thriller listings in this book, those above may be the most selective in that the thriller of moral confrontation may itself be the most common of all the thriller subgenres. Particularly common are films which use a protagonist who is a member of a professional police force but which otherwise follow thriller conventions (such as Clint Eastwood's *Tightrope* in 1985); or films which use the thriller plot of moral confrontation in the service of a radically different genre (such as the science-fiction thriller *The Terminator,* directed by James Cameron in 1984).

Perhaps not surprisingly, the thriller of moral confrontation is not as iconographically consistent as, say, the political thriller or the innocent-on-the-run thriller, but it can sometimes also be recognized by the presence

To emphasize the genre's theme of voyeurism, protagonists in thrillers of moral confrontation are often photographed as they look through windows, like the innocent children in Charles Laughton's *Night of the Hunter.*

of various other elements. These include a child or boyish protagonist, windows, a central sequence of pursuit, an interest in voyeurism, an evil protagonist who sometimes remains largely unseen or who adopts a civilized persona, and a fictional time span which rarely extends beyond a week and which often is limited to a few hours.

In a psychoanalytic perspective, using Michael Balint's terminology: the typical thriller of moral confrontation presents a protagonist who is initially ocnophilic, imprisoned by ignorance, fear or custom to a mental state and lifestyle which is unnaturally repressive or limited. As a result of the actions of a criminal philobat, the protagonist is forced out of that ocnophilic world to experience philobatic thrills and danger—in fact, to experience the entire three-act philobatic drama, returning to the home base at narrative's end, though changed irrevocably: more mature, open to new experience, and unwilling to allow ocnophilic attachment to prevent the healthy expression of a more balanced, synthesized personality.

Shadow of a Doubt, directed in 1943 by Alfred Hitchcock and written primarily by Thornton Wilder, is one of the most typical thrillers of moral confrontation and a film which seems increasingly one of Hitchcock's two or three greatest. Particularly successful is the film's juxtaposition of a disturbing, murderous plot with the comedy and local color inherent in its quaint *Our Town*–like setting. Its structure is organized by dualities, carefully balancing the antagonist criminal (the Merry Widow killer, played by Joseph Cotten) with the protagonist victim (his teenage niece, played by Teresa Wright); even their names—Uncle Charlie and the young Charlie named after him—alert the spectator to their symbiotic relationship.

Hitchcock's first image of Uncle Charlie shows him lying on his back quietly in bed and being visited by his landlady, who enters through a door on the left side of the frame. As she pulls down the blind, we see a close-up of Uncle Charlie's face as darkness covers it, the landlady having correctly, although unconsciously, characterized him. Because we are allowed to share his thoughts when he sees the two detectives tailing him ("They're bluffing, they've got nothing on me . . ."), we presume that Uncle Charlie is a guilty man, although we don't know exactly of what. Uncle Charlie runs until he successfully eludes the two detectives, who walk as if they are twins. As he stands unseen above them, the two detectives come together from opposite sides of the screen, their two figures creating one combined shadow—the most striking visual representation of the film's theme of "two becoming one."

Uncle Charlie then sends a telegram to his Santa Rosa relatives which states: "Will arrive Thursday and try to stop me." The message is ironic, for it is precisely that which his niece Charlie will eventually attempt to do: stop him. Hitchcock's first image of Charlie is parallel and shows her lying on her bed quietly and being visited by her father, who enters through a door on the right side of the frame. Charlie feels her life in Santa Rosa is torpid and wants to send a telegram to her uncle inviting him to come and visit. When the uncle's train comes to town and Charlie goes to the station to meet him, billowy black smoke fills the sky; Uncle Charlie sits unseen behind a dark curtain in his compartment. The train is transporting a virtual devil into town. Quite properly, *Shadow of a Doubt* will not end until Charlie and Uncle Charlie return to the station for another train.

Charlie is overjoyed at the visit of her uncle. Recognizing their mutual and almost mystical second sight of each other, Charlie tells her uncle that she knows he has a secret and that she intends to find out what it is. Her claim that the two of them are really like twins coincides perfectly with this genre's constant elaboration of the relationship between its protagonist and antagonist in terms of the good object and its identical, but perverted reflection. During this conversation, Charlie and her uncle are photographed facing each other within the same shot—she on the right, he on the left. Uncle Charlie's presentation of a ring to his niece amounts to a symbolic marriage between them. Hitchcock then dissolves from Uncle Charlie to the image of the dancers waltzing to the Merry Widow theme which is associated with Uncle Charlie's murderous crimes (and which represents what Charlie will be symbolically—that is, a widow—by the end of the film). When, almost immediately, in another instance of the marvelous thought transference between the two of them, Charlie begins singing the incriminating tune, her sister recites: "Sing at the table, marry a crazy husband"—which is, indeed, what in the previous scene Charlie has metaphorically done.

Charlie gradually picks up on all the various clues. One particularly suspenseful sequence has Charlie racing to the library before it closes, so she can see what it was Uncle Charlie had cut out of the newspaper. After convincing the librarian to let her in, Charlie discovers that the purloined article dealt with the Merry Widow Murderer, and furthermore, that the initials inscribed inside her ring correspond to those of one of the victims; the truth that her uncle is a murderer is thus inescapable, the ring the generic object which symbolizes her relationship to that evil. As Charlie walks out of the library, the camera pulls back and isolates her: a solitary figure in the creeping darkness. The image of the protagonist/victim alone in the dark recurs in this genre: one thinks of the little boy Tommy in *The Window*, Suzy in *Wait Until Dark*, and David in *Straw Dogs*, among others.

The structure of *Shadow of a Doubt* proceeds by twos. First of all, the film takes place in two cities: *Saint* Paul (one of the twin cities) and *Santa* Rosa. Twice while being escorted by a man through town, Charlie is confronted by two of her friends: the first time her escort is Uncle Charlie, who is still her symbolic partner; the second time her escort is the detective who will eventually literally take her uncle's symbolic place and marry her. There are two scenes at the dinner table: in the first, Charlie is still her uncle's biggest fan; in the second, she tells her uncle a dream which strongly implies he should leave. Twice Uncle Charlie makes revealing speeches: in the first, he talks about the uselessness of greedy, fat widows, while the camera dollies in slowly to a tight close-up of his smug and cruel face; in the second, he expresses his cynicism by claiming that "The world is a foul sty; the world's a hell . . ." Twice Charlie bumps into the traffic cop. Twice Charlie gets locked in the garage. Twice Uncle Charlie sets up "boobytraps" in attempts to kill his niece. Twice Uncle Charlie and the entire family go to church—first, when Uncle Charlie arrives in Santa Rosa; and second, when the family mourns his climactic death. And twice suspects have encounters with deadly vehicles: first, when a second suspect—in an East Coast city— is run over by a plane; and second, when Uncle Charlie—in a West Coast city—is run over by a train.

Shadow of a Doubt is constantly setting up expectations which it later fulfills. Early in the film, Charlie's worldly younger sister characterizes her sister's modesty as "Just putting on, like girls in books who don't ask for anything and always get more in the end than anyone else." Ironically, Charlie does get much more than she bargained for: the shattering of her illusions and the end of her innocence. When in the bank, Uncle Charlie says, "I guess heaven takes care of fools and scoundrels," the banker assumes that Uncle Charlie is referring to himself as a fool, when actually he is referring to Charlie as the fool (that is, the innocent) and himself as the scoundrel; ultimately, heaven takes care by saving the former and damning the latter. Later, when Charlie and Uncle Charlie go to a tavern, the waitress who admires Charlie's ring intones, "I'd just die for a ring like that, I'd just about die." And Charlie just about does.

Increasingly in a dilemma, Charlie cannot go to her family with her knowledge, because she knows it would break her mother's heart; she thus becomes estranged from those who would help her (at least until she is able to trust one of the two policemen who are investigating her uncle). Finally, Charlie can no longer be a passive observer; she must take a stand, not only because she is in danger, but because she is righteous. In one of the film's central scenes, she confronts her uncle at night; aware of his tremendous evil, she is herself now willing to adopt his own tactics in order to vanquish him. "Go away," she says coldly, "or I'll kill you myself." In the final suspenseful scene in which Uncle Charlie struggles to push his niece off the train which is starting to take him away from Santa Rosa, the strong uncle is himself pushed off by Charlie—which, if incredible, nevertheless fulfills Charlie's prophecy. The film ends with a scene of stasis typical to the genre, as Charlie and her detective boyfriend stand outside the church and talk very quietly, attempting to make sense of all that has happened. "He said people like us have no idea what the world is really like," says Charlie wistfully, irrevocably changed and not really having wanted to know so much about the world and its wicked, wicked ways.

The Window, directed by Ted Tetzlaff in 1949 and based on a story by Cornell Woolrich (the author of *Rear Window*'s original story as well), has developed quite a reputation as a quality "B" film. *The Window* deals with a little boy, Tommy (played by Bobby Driscoll), who witnesses a murder, but cannot convince anyone he is telling the truth, even when he is inexorably pursued by the two killers. Much of the film is depressing and works incidentally to examine the grim (if worthwhile) life in a New York tenement. The movie opens with a moving shot into the darkness of a tenement window. In one early sequence, the camera pans from Tommy's parents in a window photographed through the bars of a fire escape to another window with Tommy behind it. The constant darkness and "prison bar" treatment symbolize the immurement of their lives. Yet even the anxious trap of the tenement is better than nothing, and Tommy's family lives in constant fear of eviction into the street.

The Window opens by quoting Aesop's fable about the Boy Who Cried Wolf. The film's first sequence, in which Tommy's alarming tears are revealed as part of his cops-and-robbers game, displays Tommy's active imagination and ironically apposes the rest of the narrative in which the cops and robbers are for real. Like the typical thriller-of-moral-confrontation protagonist, Tommy takes on the role of potentially threatening witness when he views the upstairs neighbors scissors-stabbing a man they have robbed; we see the murder from Tommy's point-of-view as he stares at the scuffling feet through the window from the fire escape. Tommy gradually becomes estranged from those who would help him, as his mother, father, and policemen all refuse to believe his story. When his father disapproves of Tommy's behavior, Tommy finds himself in a moral predicament of his own: Should he stick to the truth of what he knows took place or should he lie about what happened and paradoxically become the good son his father can be proud of?

The Window is constructed around two related themes: the second class status of the child imprisoned in the adult world which refuses to accord him trust, and the plight of the innocent in a world that is threatening and evil. Like other protagonists in this genre, Tommy cannot remain a witness forever; because the neighbors are aware of his knowledge and determined to silence him, Tommy must flee or fight.

The last sequences of *The Window* are continuously suspenseful, as Tommy is left alone and locked in his room by his father, while the neighbors begin their all-out pursuit. In the course of his trials, Tommy is scared, confronted, chased, kidnapped, knocked out, and dangled precariously off a high fire escape. Naturally, the process of Tommy's torture is drawn out by numerous near escapes, unfortunately obtuse policemen, and split-second off-timings. Ultimately, Tommy is victorious precisely because the power of his goodness (and the cunning therein) has been underestimated by the villainous neighbors. After a final cat-and-mouse chase, Tommy finds concrete evidence to support his accusation of murder and maneuvers the primary murderer into a position in which he is crushed by a collapsing beam. Thus, Tommy conquers the evil, proves his righteousness, and gains the respect and pride of his father.

Stage Fright, directed by Alfred Hitchcock in 1950, demonstrates the range of the thriller of moral confrontation by using the genre to examine concepts of reality versus fiction, or truth versus illusion. In a sense, *Stage Fright* is a mystery; although it ostensibly sets up a protagonist-adversary relationship linking Jane Wyman with good and Marlene Dietrich with evil, the film's climax undoes the truth of this relationship. Thus, by emphasizing how difficult it is to distinguish between good and evil, *Stage Fright* examines too what is true, what is not, and what are the moral meanings of our confused perceptions.

The film's first image is that of a safety curtain rising to reveal, not a stage, but (supposedly) real life. We are introduced to our protagonist Eve Gill (played by Jane Wyman). Although Eve serves the generic role of the innocent, good character who confronts the immoral adversary, the Biblical reference of her name indicates that the confrontation she so courageously accepts may not be clear cut; and sure enough, Eve's erroneous moral perceptions of the forces supposedly opposing her transform her unknowingly into more of a sinner than a crusader. Strictly speaking, Eve is not the victim. The apparent victim is Jonathan Cooper, the man wanted for murder, who convinces Eve that Charlotte Inwood (played by Marlene

Dietrich) is the guilty party. Where Hitchcock pioneers is in his translation of Jonathan Cooper's lies into the precise images of a flashback which is perceived by the spectator as veracious by convention. Significantly, within the flashback Charlotte takes on the traditional color coding of popular genres: she is initially dressed in a white which implies innocence; presently, Jonathan brings her a black dress to change into and tells her that "You're an actress; you're playing a part." Thus, the real murderer has in his lying flashback turned Charlotte into the villain by literally redressing her in the symbolic color appropriate to a fictive mode.

The film's flashback works to set up the conflict between innocent Eve (standing in for her friend Jonathan) and guilty Charlotte Inwood—even though this conflict is faultily dichotomous. Appropriately (at least in retrospect), it is Eve who continuously plays roles and adopts a fictive mode; an acting student, she ruthlessly takes on disguises in order to clear her friend. Even the characters within *Stage Fright* cannot tell what is real and what is false. Eve's father kiddingly calls her a gunman's moll, which later turns out to have been precisely what she was. "One thing I cannot bear is insincerity," says the father, even though he is not always sincere himself. When he finally tells his wife the truth about Eve's adventures, Mrs. Gill claims that this time he's gone too far and refuses to believe anything—a statement which can be interpreted also as a self-reflective comment on Hitchcock's false flashback. And yet, Charlotte is virtually honest and certainly morally superior—refusing, for instance, to wear black in mourning because she simply doesn't want to.

Truth is inscrutable. When Charlotte finally tells her version of the murder, it sounds fictively melodramatic; yet, it is her version which is true (and Charlotte's predilection for white dresses continues). At the garden party, Eve, determined to play the moral innocent, herself dresses in white. Although we sympathize with Eve, the dishonesty with which she has secured her job with Charlotte makes us uneasily feel that Eve has betrayed Charlotte. The true climax of *Stage Fright* takes place after all the deceptions have been revealed and Charlotte's moral superiority made clear. Almost as if in retribution for her behavior, Eve is made finally to confront the true evil, the true murderer, her friend Jonathan Cooper. And if Eve is not a true force of good, she is nevertheless a true force of naive innocence.

Like the other thrillers of moral confrontation, *Stage Fright* finally progresses to the point where the protagonist must confront evil alone, estranged from those who would help her. The confrontation takes place backstage in an old-fashioned coach being used as a theatrical prop. Eve's eyes, lit to look like a bright white mask on a dark face, widen in quiet horror at all she has done and at all that now faces her. The conversation between her and Jonathan, so quiet, so slow, resembles a similar scene at the climax of Claude Chabrol's *Le Boucher,* in which a woman also finally faces a man who is a homicidal maniac. Eve carefully leaves the coach; as in a nightmare, its door opens weirdly in apparent slow motion. When Eve saves herself by later shutting another door on Jonathan, it is not clear whether it represents a victory over evil or yet a further betrayal. Because *Stage Fright* opens with a raised curtain unveiling Jonathan's evil, it ends appropriately with a lowered curtain killing Jonathan and extinguishing his evil. In the coda, Eve and her new boyfriend walk off backstage illumined by a series of spotlights, each pool of light increasingly distant. The two are now absolute fiction, a romance uneasily contrived for the sake of the inevitable fictional requirement: the happy ending.

Hitchcock followed *Stage Fright* with a series of thrillers of moral confrontation, including *Strangers on a Train, Dial M for Murder,* and *Rear Window. Strangers on a Train,* directed in 1951 and based on the novel by Patricia Highsmith, deals with the confrontation of two men: one a psychopath, the other a tennis pro. The psychopath (played by Robert Walker) suggests that he murder the wife of the tennis pro, and the tennis pro murder the psychopath's father in exchange. Although the tennis pro (played by Farley Granger) refuses to go along with the idea, the psychopath performs his murder anyway, thus freeing the protagonist tennis pro to marry his girlfriend. Most of the film deals with the protagonist's attempt to remain technically innocent as it becomes clear that the psychopath is going to try to conceal his own evil and pin the murder on the protagonist.

The theme of fate and the sense of events criss-crossing in time and space which pervades *Strangers on a Train* is consistent with the suspense thriller's generic dualities. In *Strangers on a Train,* as in *Stage Fright,* Hitchcock again emphasizes the ambiguity of the moral forces that confront each other. While the tennis pro certainly does not murder his wife, he does consciously wish his wife dead—and in a real sense, takes on the guilt. The murderer, on the other hand, is so clearly psychopathic that he becomes more a slave to urges he cannot control than a conscious exponent of evil. Thus, the final confrontation in which the protagonist emerges victorious is both satisfying and disturbing.

Dial M for Murder, directed by Hitchcock in 1954, was based on the play by Frederick Knott (who also wrote the play *Wait Until Dark,* another thriller of moral confrontation). In this film, the confrontation is between the evil tennis player (played by Ray Milland) and his virtuous wife (played by Grace Kelly), although the wife doesn't realize her husband is evil until toward the end of the film. To inherit her money, the husband hires someone to kill his wife; when his wife most unexpectedly manages to kill the assassin with a pair of scissors, the husband slyly arranges for her to be tried for murder. The plight of the wife in *Dial M for Murder* is much like the plight of Stéphane Audran's Hélène in *La Rupture:* neither knows that awful

The opening sequence of Hitchcock's *Strangers on a Train* is dominated by the theme of "criss-cross" and the characteristic triangular shape: the diamond on the side of the cab, the diamonds on the floor of the railway station where paths

criss-cross, the criss-crossing railroad tracks which create diamond shapes, and the criss-crossing strings on the criss-crossed tennis rackets on the cigarette lighter.

things are being plotted against them. In both films, however, the spectator is let in on everything so that suspense is created.

Dial M for Murder departs from the typical thriller construction in that there are at least two detective figures who try to help Kelly: a novelist friend played by Robert Cummings and a police inspector played by John Williams. Thus, the one-on-one confrontation is inevitably de-emphasized in that the innocent victim is not herself responsible for her ultimate victory. In this regard, *Dial M for Murder* resembles a more traditional detective work, although of the inverted variety with mystery replaced by suspense.

Rear Window, directed in 1954, is critically considered one of Hitchcock's towering achievements. Virtually the entire film is constructed of predominately static shots in which the protagonist and his primary adversary appear in neither the same frame nor the same location. Jimmy Stewart, playing Jeff, the photographer protagonist with a broken leg, looks out his window and before long begins spying with binoculars on his neighbors across the courtyard. In the course of his spying, Jeff discovers that one of the neighbors, played by Raymond Burr, has killed and dissected his wife. Hitchcock has often referred to *Rear Window* as an example of pure cinema: almost completely visual, it is composed of people watching other people. With its emphasis on Jeff's voyeurism, the entire film works as a metaphor for the voyeurism of the spectator who vicariously participates in the suspense thriller's thrills.

Like the typical thriller-of-moral-confrontation protagonist, Jeff moves gradually from the role of the passive observer to the role of the witness who can endanger the adversary; in the climax, when he is finally pursued by the murderer, Jeff graduates to the role of the active fighter. In his own way, Jeff too becomes estranged from those around him; to his girlfriend Lisa, played by Grace Kelly, he is disturbingly monomaniacal. Jeff's broken leg works as a symbol both for his separateness and his essential helplessness. When in the final confrontation Jeff is forced to face directly the murderer who is advancing into his room, Jeff tries to blind him with the light of his flashbulbs and thereby counter the blackness of the evil with a whiteness of his own.

Although satisfying, *Rear Window* is finally disturbing not just because we have been given a glimpse into the struggle between good and evil, but because we have been forced to face the essential humanity of the murderer and to question the integrity of Jeff's motives. Voyeurism, no matter what its ultimate end, is not very nice. To use Löker's terms, although we share Jeff's guilt and are afraid of punishment, we want him nevertheless to continue spying because we inevitably accept the package deal and want to satisfy our desire for spectacle. And although Jeff is the victor in his confrontation with evil (thus satisfying our desire for success as well), he is nevertheless punished for his voyeurism by breaking his other leg in the process.

Visual correlatives in *Strangers on a Train* tend to suggest psychological states: the pin-stripes on Robert Walker's suit and the shadows across his face suggest a jail cell and imply his guilt.

The Desperate Hours, directed in 1955 by William Wyler from a script by Joseph Hayes, presents—unlike the preceding three Hitchcock films—a confrontation between good and evil that is not particularly ambiguous. *The Desperate Hours* does, however, depart from the usual one-on-one confrontation and instead pits a nether-family of criminals against a family of upstanding citizens. Other generic conventions remain stable: the victim protagonists witness the deeds of the criminal antagonists, become estranged from those who could help them, and must ultimately fight for their very lives.

The film opens with a graceful dolly shot down the street and into the house of the family which will be taken over by the criminals; this shot parallels another shot later in the film taken through the window of the criminals' car as it approaches the house. When the crude, ill-dressed, and unshaven criminals come in, break things, and hold the Hilliard family hostage, the house seems perverted by their presence. Griffen is the hardened criminal and cynical father figure (played by Humphrey Bogart); Robish is the menacing, almost retarded brute (played by Robert Middleton); and Hal is the young hoodlum who still retains some vestige of innocence (played by Dewey Martin).

Wyler then directly opposes each villain with a different protagonist. Griffen is counterpoised with the father of the Hilliard family (played by Fredric March), who represents all that is good in the American dream.

Robish is counterpoised with the young son Ralph (played by Richard Eyer); and just as Robish is not intelligent enough to show caution, Ralph is not mature enough to show fear. Hal is counterpoised with the teenage daughter Cindy (played by Mary Murphy), the potential object of Hal's love. In a significant sense, the unseen gun moll that Griffen so anxiously awaits is counterpoised with the Hilliard mother (played by Martha Scott). That the gun moll is never seen suggests that it is the absence of love and feminine affection that is partially responsible for the cynicism of the nether-family.

The Desperate Hours consistently raises moral questions about courage. What is the moral response to evil? One interesting scene has the brutish Robish chasing Ralph in order to get his toy airplane; the boy breaks the plane himself rather than give it to the criminal. Because he is the most naive, Ralph is the most traditionally "heroic." Later in the film, Ralph laughs out loud at Griffen's fears and even attempts to singlehandedly attack him.

The film takes advantage of a notable deep-focus style. Compositions throughout unite the innocent victims in the same frame as their evil adversaries, including as well doorways and windows potentially useful as exits from the frame and from the horrific situation. The style adds to the suspense by allowing the spectator to observe the spatial relationships between the characters and their threatening environment and thereby to anticipate potential courses of action. Numerous sequences are based entirely upon suspense structures: a sequence in which Cindy and her father develop on the spur of the moment a ploy to escape which almost succeeds; a sequence in which Cindy's boyfriend successfully rescues her from the besieged house; and a sequence in which the garbage man takes away the garbage while the wife and the villains watch, knowing full well that if the garbage man notices the strange car in the garage, he will forfeit his life.

At one point in the film, Hilliard turns to Griffen and says, "I never understood how a mind like yours works, but I do now." Hilliard's vow to kill Griffen should anything happen to any member of his family represents that generic moment when the good protagonist is willing, at least theoretically, to accept the methods of his adversary. At the very climax of the film when Hilliard has managed to train a loaded gun on Griffen, the moral dilemma is presented quite forcefully. "You ain't got it in you, Pop," says Griffen. "I got it in me," says Hilliard. "You put it there!" But Griffen is right; although Hilliard does have courage and strength, he does not have violence or vengeance.

It is interesting to compare *The Desperate Hours* with *Straw Dogs*, made sixteen years later in 1971. In *Straw Dogs*, Dustin Hoffman's David undergoes a similar ordeal as his house and family are besieged by a nether-family of

The protagonist family in *The Desperate Hours* before it is shattered by the intrusion of evil: Martha Scott and Fredric March play the wife and husband, Mary Murphy and Richard Eyer play the son and daughter.

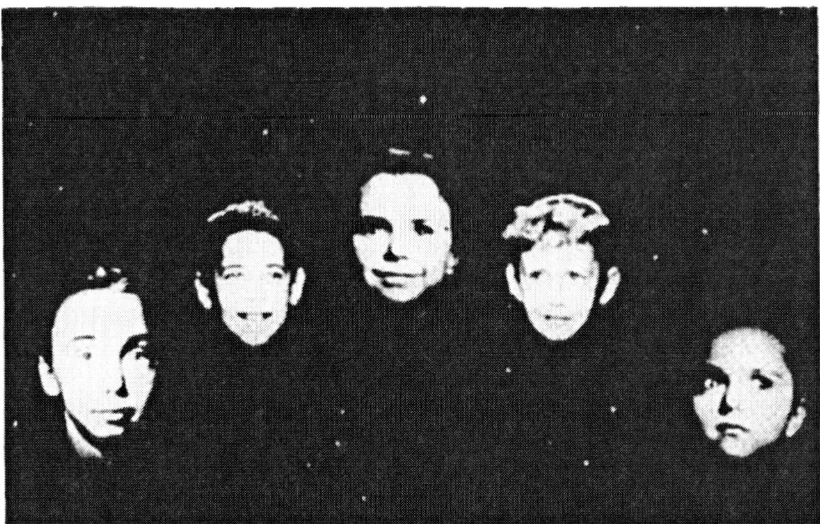

Expressive images from the prologue of *Night of the Hunter* which show Lillian Gish and children as archetypally innocent, almost heavenly entities.

petty criminals. David's world, however, reflects the violent sensibilities of the Nixon era (and the vision of Sam Peckinpah, the film's director), and therefore David *does* find the violence within him—and when it is unleashed, it is stronger than the violence expressed by his adversaries, stronger perhaps because it had been repressed for so long. But Wyler's moral and decent 1955 protagonist inhabits an America not yet defined by its repressed violence; violence is still only aberration. *The Desperate Hours*

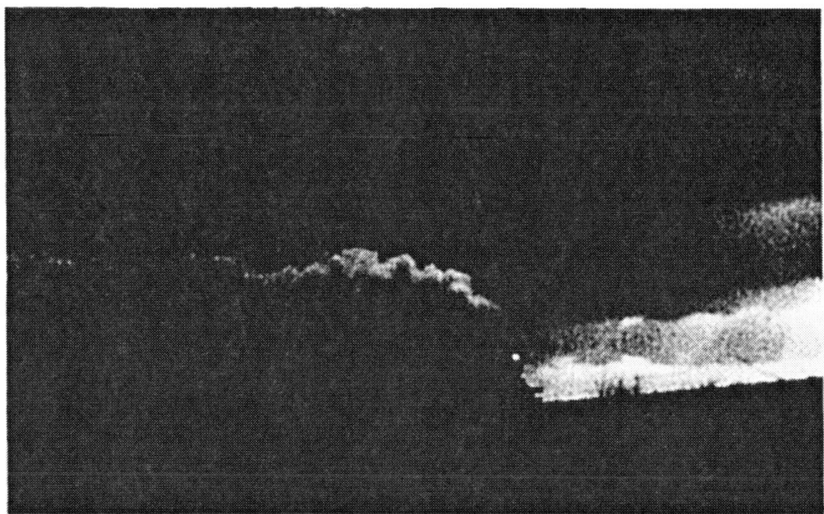

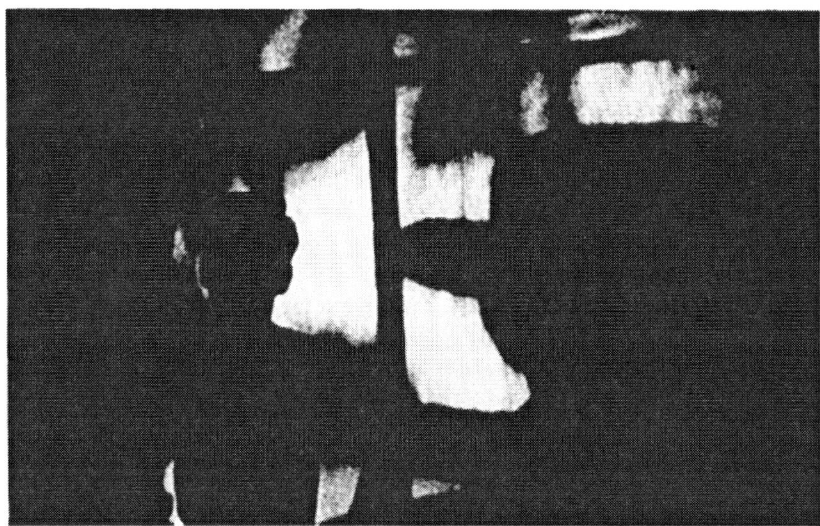

Symbolic images from *Night of the Hunter* which represent Robert Mitchum's evil: (top) as a dark and shadowy train racing into town, and (bottom) as a huge and ominous shadow on the innocent protagonist's bedroom wall

ends with a quiet scene as the victorious family embraces in their front yard before returning to the salvaged comfort and protection of their home.

Released the same year as *The Desperate Hours* was *Night of the Hunter*, the very notable, and in fact only, film directed by actor Charles Laughton. Based on a script by James Agee constructed of atypically short scenes, *Night of the Hunter* portrays in the most expressive and expressionistic terms the plight of innocence in a world of cruelty. The film begins with the image of twinkling stars in the sky. Loud and anxious orchestral music is suddenly quieted by the image of Lillian Gish, who, floating in the sky like a guardian angel, quotes the Bible: "Blessed are the pure of heart, because they shall see the Lord . . . Beware of false prophets . . . A good tree cannot bring forth evil fruit."

The protagonist victims of *Night of the Hunter* are the two children, John and Pearl, whose father has robbed a bank and hidden the money in Pearl's doll. The first image of the children shows them surrounded by flowers on a meadow: tranquil, innocent, at one with the nature around them. When their father is executed for his crimes, an evil preacher, Harry Powell, marries their widowed mother and torments the children in an attempt to find out where the money has been hidden. Robert Mitchum plays Powell, the false prophet warned of by Gish in the credit sequence.

Powell is consistently associated with evil. When Willa, the children's mother (played by Shelley Winters) says that she doesn't want another husband, Laughton cuts to the image of the speeding train carrying Powell into town, its black smoke filling the sky, the loud orchestral theme coming up full volume. The image itself seems to be a self-conscious reference to *Shadow of a Doubt*. When John tells Pearl a bedtime story which is allegorically about the death of their father, the ominous and gigantic shadow of Powell's head suddenly appears on the wall just as John tells of the return of his own story's villain. After Harry Powell convinces Willa to marry him, Laughton photographs the two of them at revival meetings from behind the flames of torches, suggesting a vision of hell. The metaphysical nature of the struggle between the children (the hunted) and Powell (the hunter) is made clear by Powell's hypocritical public ritual: a fight between his right hand and left, the former tattoed with "LOVE" across its knuckles, the latter tattoed with "HATE."

With the insight of the innocent who can see through all pretense, the children know inherently that Powell is a bad man and become the witnesses to his evil. Consistent to the genre, the confrontation between the protagonist and the adversary cannot be personally meaningful unless the protagonist is estranged from those who could help. Thus, the children (especially John) are set apart from everyone else by their compulsion to keep the secret of the doll. They cannot turn to the Spoons, who spoonerismically confuse moral issues. Nor can they turn to their theoretical protectress, their mother, who first falls under Powell's spell and then is taken away from them completely. In one striking sequence, Willa's bedroom is photographed like a temple, the windows in the triangular garret-like roof allowing the light to stream in. The sequence ends as Powell coldly brandishes his knife and approaches Willa, who is lying peacefully on the bed, her arms folded like a corpse or an angel. The final image of Willa reveals

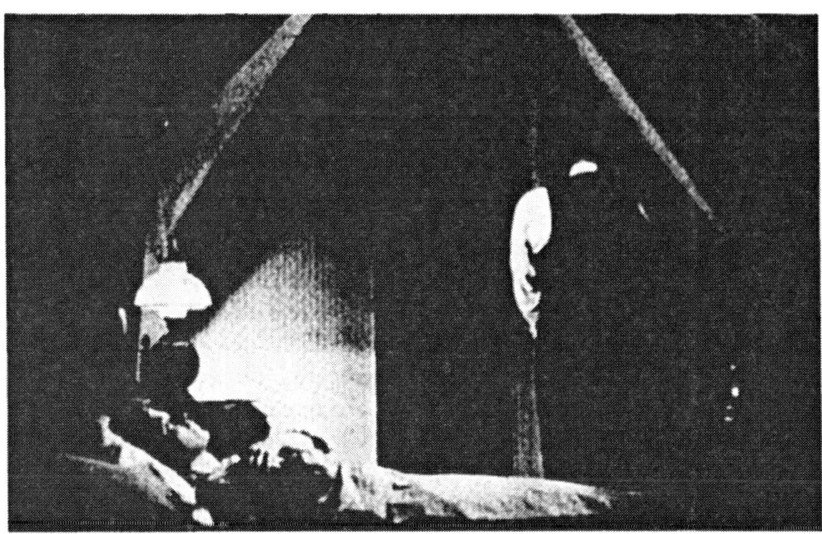

In *Night of the Hunter*, Robert Mitchum struggles with the conflict between good and evil. Although his bedroom resembles a temple with his wife Shelley Winters on an altar, the final resting place for her murdered body is underwater.

her tied to a jeep underwater, her hair waving like seaweed, her dead body floating slightly—an image simultaneously beautiful and horrifying.

Once Willa is dead, the confrontation between the two innocents and Powell is unencumbered. In a wonderfully suspenseful sequence in the basement of the house, John knocks Powell in the head with a collapsing shelf; as John and Pearl run up the steps to escape, Powell rushes after them, his arms and hands extended like some archetypal zombie from a child's nightmare. When John manages to slam the basement door on Powell's hands, Powell emits a horrifyingly animal growl. The children continue their escape by running to the skiff they have hidden in the water; the suspense heightens as Powell catches up with them, falls in the water, takes out his knife, and barely misses killing them both—this time letting out a chilling growl which constantly rises in pitch by measured increments.

Although Powell continues to pursue the children, John and Pearl have, in one sense, already won. Their trip down the river is beautiful: the moon glistens, the water ripples. The children are repeatedly photographed in ways, as from behind a spiderweb or a frog, which suggest they are again at one with nature. Indeed, for most of their boat trip, John and Pearl don't even row, but sleep; the boat itself seems part of a fateful plan to transport them to their proper destination. At one point, Pearl sings herself a lullaby, her strange and evocative voice breaking the stillness of the night.

The last third of the film serves to counter Powell's false prophet with the true prophet represented by Miss Cooper (played by Lillian Gish). Miss Cooper takes the children in and tells them Bible stories which parallel their own situation: the baby Moses who had to float down the river, the baby Jesus that Herod would destroy. While she sings "Leaning on Jesus," an owl attacks a rabbit and Miss Cooper realizes profoundly that "It's a hard world for little things." Like John, Miss Cooper recognizes instantly that Powell is neither the children's father nor a true preacher; with her help, Powell is vanquished once and for all.

When the police come for Powell just as they came for John's father at the beginning of the film, John says "Don't" in exactly the same tone and relives the earlier experience. As if Powell were his father, John beats him with the doll containing the money. "Take it back!" he screams, not wanting the burden of keeping the secret, not having wanted to have grown up so suddenly and to have lost his innocence. The film ends as the same guard who executed the children's father prepares to execute Powell, while the townspeople (led by the Spoons, who were formerly Powell's biggest fans) try to lynch him. Like a guardian angel, Miss Cooper leads the children away from the townspeople and their madness as well. "Lord save the children," she intones. "The wind blows and they are cold, yet they abide and they endure."

None of the other American thrillers of this period quite attain the intensity of *Night of the Hunter*. These other late fifties thrillers include *Step Down to Terror* (made in 1958), an unacknowledged remake of Hitchcock's *Shadow of a Doubt* (both of which are based on the original story by Gordon McDonnell); *Cry Terror* (made in 1958), directed and written by Andrew L. Stone, in which the virtuous James Mason and Inger Stevens are terrorized by Rod Steiger and Neville Brand; *Cape Fear* (made in 1962), in which Robert Mitchum, again playing a sadistic villain, threatens the family of the

Archetypal scene of suspense in *Night of the Hunter:* in a dark basement, Robert Mitchum stalks the innocent children.

upstanding counselor Gregory Peck, with Peck victorious only after a long cat-and-mouse struggle and numerous sequences of shock and suspense; and *The Boy Cried Murder* (made in 1966), a British remake of *The Window* which changed the setting from a New York slum to an Adriatic resort community.

If a film like *Cape Fear* implicitly questions the ability of our government institutions to fight our moral battles for us, *The Singer Not the Song* (made in 1961) questions the ability of the church to do the same. Although as much a social drama as a suspense thriller, *The Singer Not the Song* nevertheless constructs itself around the antagonism of two men: an evil, atheist bandit who tyrannizes a Mexican town, and the Catholic priest who tries to stop the bandit's reign of terror. That their confrontation eventually proves fatal to both serves to emphasize the inextractable duality of good and evil and the necessity for good to continue the moral struggle at whatever personal cost. Although the bandit and the priest remain opposed, the bandit does develop a grudging respect for his adversary: as the bandit dies, he attests to the value in the singer (the priest) if not the song (the church).

Not all suspense thrillers need to be overt works of popular entertainment, as study of American thrillers might imply. Michelangelo Antonioni, for instance, has often taken the basic structure of the suspense thriller and then allowed the filmic elaboration of his own sensibility to elide, de-emphasize, disguise, or subvert these generic structures. *Blowup,* in particular, is similar to *Rear Window:* in both films, the photographer protagonist inadvertently uncovers a murder plot. While Alfred Hitchcock encourages identification with his protagonist and allows the spectator to continuously share his protagonist's point of view, Antonioni discourages complete identification and in part estranges his protagonist so the spectator can more objectively observe him as a symptom of his social milieu.

Blowup's thriller structure begins when Thomas, a high-fashion photographer (played by David Hemmings), follows a young woman (played by Vanessa Redgrave) and an older man in the park, at one point even removing a ridiculously close tree branch which covers his face and creates a traditional image of stealth. As Thomas hides behind trees and photographs the young woman and the older man talking and embracing, we sense the beginning of a recognizable and conventional narrative. When the young woman notices Thomas, she tries to grab the camera: "This is a public place, everyone deserves to be left in peace." Although Thomas responds that it's not his fault if there is no peace, there is nevertheless the sense that his camera is somehow raping the natural world. Our sympathy may be primarily with the woman and her desire for privacy, but our selfish curiosity commits us to Thomas.

The woman runs back, but her companion is gone. Later she comes to Thomas' studio; nervously moving about, she tries to steal the camera or buy back the film, willing even to sleep with Thomas if necessary. The "blowup" sequence after she is gone clearly represents the film's center. Thomas puts gigantic photographs of the woman and her companion on the wall: a shot of them in the park, a shot of them embracing, a shot of the woman running back toward her companion, a shot of the woman looking disturbingly at . . . what appears to be a man holding a gun in the bushes. A brilliant series of approximately fifteen photographs, which reconstruct in chronological order what must have happened, follows—climaxing with the final image of the woman's companion barely visible as a corpse in the bushes.

Thus, the still photographs, arranged according to a particular point of view into a properly narrative order, are transformed into the stuff of exciting melodrama, with Thomas at the center of a potential thriller of moral confrontation. Of course, since Antonioni tries to subvert the conventions whenever possible, Thomas is neither innocent nor good (indeed, closer to the opposite), and the ultimate confrontation never really takes place. Although Thomas catches a glimpse of the corpse in his photographs and then finds the actual corpse in the park, both the corpse as well as his photographs are mysteriously removed; with no images left and no personal confrontation in which to participate, Thomas must recognize that the suspense thriller remains only in his head (a situation analogous to the experience of the spectator after a suspense thriller is over).

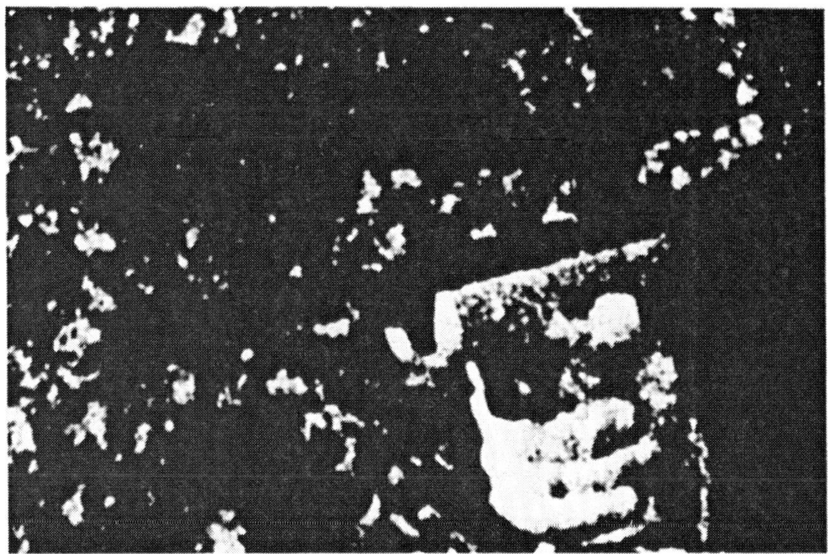

The close-up of the hand holding the gun in *Blowup*, semiological evidence of the thriller plot which ultimately disappears.

Even the passion or blood so conventional to the suspense thriller is primarily displaced onto the rubescent photography of Carlo Di Palma which dwells on pink walls and blood red bricks. Perhaps the best example of *Blowup*'s subversion of the genre is when—at the precise moment following the blowup sequence in which the spectator's anxiety and interest in the suspense narrative are at their greatest—Antonioni allows the only momentarily ominous visitors at the door to be simply two teenage girls, who engage Thomas in a mini-orgy which brings the film's thriller sensibilities to an abrupt abscission.

Except for the photography sequences, *Blowup* reveals Thomas' life much with the temperament of a documentary: the boring bits left in. Although Thomas has affairs, he reveals no real passion. At one point when Thomas comes home and finds his friend Patricia (with whom he has an ambiguous relationship) making love to her artist husband, he appears to respond with no emotion at all; *Blowup* is clearly no thriller of murderous passions. If *Blowup* can be seen as an antithriller of sorts, it is because, for Antonioni, the twentieth century does not provide the opportunity for heroic action; for there to be a meaningful struggle between good and evil, we must first be capable of articulating good and evil as distinct elements. But there are no clear distinctions in *Blowup*—only confusion, chaos, and the inevitable disappearance of absolutes and boundaries.[1]

The job of the artist who wishes to reflect the sensibilities of his age is, therefore, continually to question and destroy his own work. "It's like

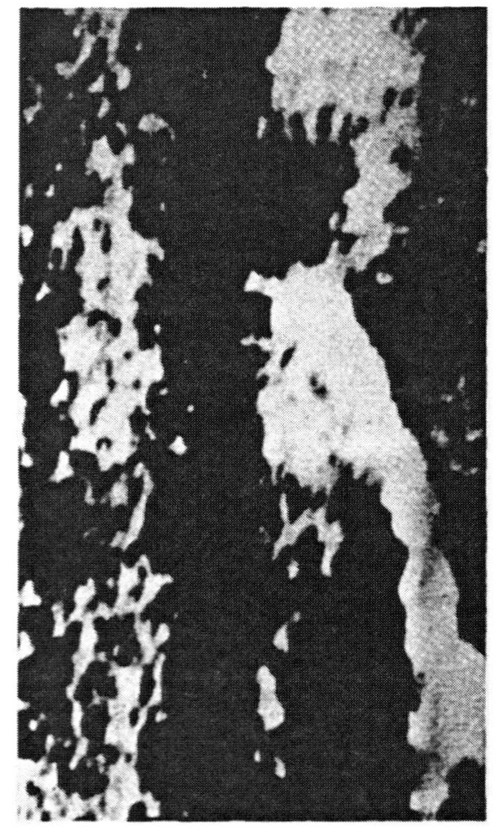

GO
AWAY

finding a clue in a detective story," says the visual artist who tries to understand and explain his own paintings, in which borders are indistinct and objects disappear into ambiguity. The same can be said of Thomas' photographs; as each one is blown up larger and larger, boundaries disappear and the world is reduced to a hazy and indistinct pattern of dots, floating atoms with no inherent significance. Even the musician (Yardbird Jeff Beck) at the Ricky Tick nightclub destroys his guitar when his amplifier continually creates static.

When Thomas points out to Patricia the corpse in one of his photographs, she remarks that it looks like one of her husband's paintings—inscrutable, hard to make out. It is with urgency that Thomas says to his friend: "There's a corpse. We've got to get a shot of it." Thomas' comment works as a metaphor for all of Antonioni's work—which attempts the impossibility of photographing contemporary society: its evaporation of values, its journeys without destinations, its subversion of passion, its celebration of leisure and its attendant ennui. After the corpse disappears and the whole suspense thriller plot evaporates before reaching a traditional conclusion, Thomas watches a group of mime players playing a mime tennis game. At one point, the camera follows the supposed trajectories of the "invisible" tennis ball, thus sharing the artistic endeavor of the players (who, by their art, celebrate "nothingness," and thus relate to the painter, the photographer, and the musician).

Earlier, during the blowup sequence, the spectator may have expected an ultimate explanation; now, he or she knows wisely that an explanation will not be forthcoming, and paradoxically, that therein rests the meaning. At one point, the camera follows outside the court to the spot where the tennis ball has supposedly landed. Thomas himself shares the experience by retrieving the ball and throwing it; as it bounces, its sound is quite audible. A long shot: Thomas stands immobile in the empty spaces of the grass, not knowing where to go or what to do. If the traditional suspense thriller leads often to a psychological claustrophobia in which the protagonist is inevitably forced into a specific action, *Blowup* leads to a psychological agoraphobia in which the protagonist is forced to realize that he cannot act at all. Although Thomas has unlimited choices, he has no values with which to direct them. In a uniquely modern *deus ex machina,* Antonioni himself rescues his protagonist by imitating the artists in his own film and reflexively allowing *Blowup* to self-destruct as well. Thus, quite literally, the image of Thomas disappears from the center of the frame, and the film ends.

As the photograph of the corpse (first picture) is enlarged more and more, it becomes increasingly indecipherable; clear boundaries disappear, almost as if following the instructions of the painted sign of the protagonist (second picture); ultimately, the photograph comes to resemble the modern art of the protagonist's artist friend (third picture).

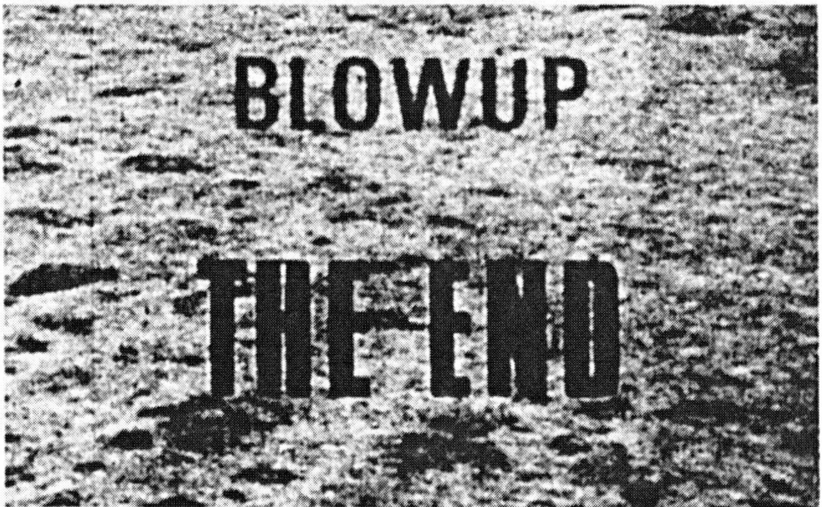

The primacy of nothingness: By the end of *Blowup*, the thriller plot has evaporated. In the film's last shot, even the protagonist evaporates from the screen, as the empty field itself comes to resemble the protagonist's hazy photographs and the artist's indecipherable paintings.

Two other thrillers of the period, if with fewer pretentions, are *Wait Until Dark* (directed in 1967 by Terence Young) and *The Bride Wore Black* (directed in 1968 by François Truffaut). Particularly interesting in *Wait Until Dark* (which has already been discussed in some detail) is the way the heroine's blindness works to invert the traditional black versus white color symbolism. Thus, darkness is associated with the heroine's struggles, and therefore goodness, whereas light is associated with her tormentor, and therefore evil. The plot even evolves to the point where the heroine's best chance to survive is predicated completely upon her ability to destroy all the light sources in her apartment.

The Bride Wore Black, Truffaut's conscious *hommage* to Hitchcock, imitates as well Hitchcock's predilection for making the moral confrontation as ambiguous as possible. Truffaut's protagonist is a melancholy murderer played by Jeanne Moreau; in the course of the film she manages to kill five different men, some of whom are presented to us with much sympathy. We finally learn that all five of the men were responsible for the accidental shooting of the protagonist's husband on the day of their marriage; thus, the bride of the title does not represent evil as much as she represents Nemesis.

I think it quite significant that the most stylish thrillers of moral confrontation in the sixties are European films such as *Blowup, The Bride Wore Black, Le Boucher,* and *La Rupture.* Because the French in general have always been perceptive to the thriller, it may be no surprise that directors like François Truffaut and Claude Chabrol work in the genre easily and honorably, with no condescension. Perhaps ironically, great American thriller writers like Patricia Highsmith and Cornell Woolrich are more critically esteemed abroad than in the United States. Thus, while one can imagine a Wim Wenders or a Claude Chabrol making a film from a Highsmith book, it becomes more difficult to imagine, say, a Francis Ford Coppola making a film from a Highsmith book—much less from a Simenon. Of the four European thrillers mentioned above, two are based on American sources: *The Bride Wore Black* on the novel by Cornell Woolrich, and *La Rupture* on the novel *The Balloon Man* by Charlotte Armstrong.

Le Boucher, written and directed by Claude Chabrol in 1969, has been internationally hailed as a great film, although its American reputation is significantly tempered by the usual American condescension toward and suspicion of a genre as entertaining as the suspense thriller. The two main characters in *Le Boucher* are Hélène (played by Stéphane Audran), an amiable but cool schoolteacher who tries to keep a formal distance between herself and those around her; and her butcher friend Popaul (played by Jean Yanne), who tries to court her and is gradually revealed as a homicidal maniac.

The title sequence over the primitive paintings in the caves near the town begins the film's contrast between the civilized and the primitive, between psychological control and uncontrollable impulse. Popaul inherently understands his need for people and reaches out to Hélène, who kindly rejects him. In one particularly expressive sequence, they go mushrooming in the woods with two of Hélène's students—the four of them comprising a virtual family. Popaul enjoys watching her with the children and asks why she doesn't have any lovers. "Because I don't want any," she responds simply, having withdrawn into herself after an unhappy love affair ten years ago caused her to come to the small town to teach. "That's not normal," says Popaul. "Of course it's normal," she answers.

"Not making love could make you mad," insists Popaul in a statement we later realize is from personal experience. "Making love could make you mad," retorts Hélène lightly. Although she does not want Popaul for a lover, she does want him as a friend and cements their friendship by the gift of a lighter. We have already been informed that a girl has been found brutally murdered and are therefore aware that the tranquility of the town is tenuous. Later, when Hélène takes her class on a field trip to the caves, which definitely represent the dark nature of man, she contends, in the tone of an objective academician, that the instincts of the Cro-Magnon were definitely human. The camera dollies in to the painted animals on the wall, which relate to the leg of lamb given her by Popaul in place of the traditional bouquet of flowers. "What if Cro-Magnon Man came back today?" asks one of her students. Without realizing the ironic appropriateness of her response, Hélène suggests that "He might adapt to our way of life or he might die."

Significantly, the initial scene of horror does not take place inside the cave, but outside in the fresh air and sunshine, for the primitive killer has indeed returned. A child says that it's raining; there is a shocking image of blood dripping on the white bread of a little girl's sandwich. Everyone looks up and sees a hand sticking out from over the cliff. When Hélène climbs up, she discovers that another woman has been brutally murdered. And then, most disturbingly, Hélène finds the lighter, presumably the one she gave Popaul. Her hands close on it; the picture goes black.

Hélène's immediate reaction now that she has become a silent witness to the murderous Popaul is to withdraw from the entire experience. In a sequence of three consecutive shots formally constructed, we see her doing yoga and trying to regain her objective control. Although the visiting police inspector tells her that "Somewhere in the town there is a madman," Hélène remains silent. In a suspenseful sequence later that night, Popaul suddenly calls out to Hélène from outside her home. An absolutely distraught Hélène allows him up to visit. When Popaul suddenly lights her cigarette with the apparent lighter that she gave him, her tension is released as she breaks down, crying, half-laughing.

In *Le Boucher,* as in most suspense thrillers, objects are crucially important: the lighter works as a symbol of Popaul's guilt, and Popaul's producing it frees Hélène from complicity and fear. But since most suspense thrillers reverse their expectations only temporarily in order to create more suspense, Hélène's freedom doesn't last; before long she discovers that the lighter produced by Popaul was merely an identical one he bought to cover up his loss of the original.

Again Hélène is alone at night, suddenly afraid that Popaul will return

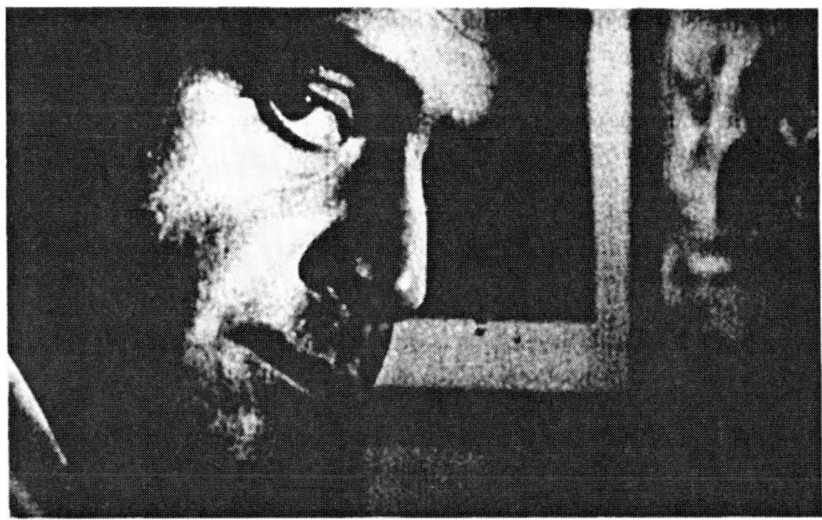

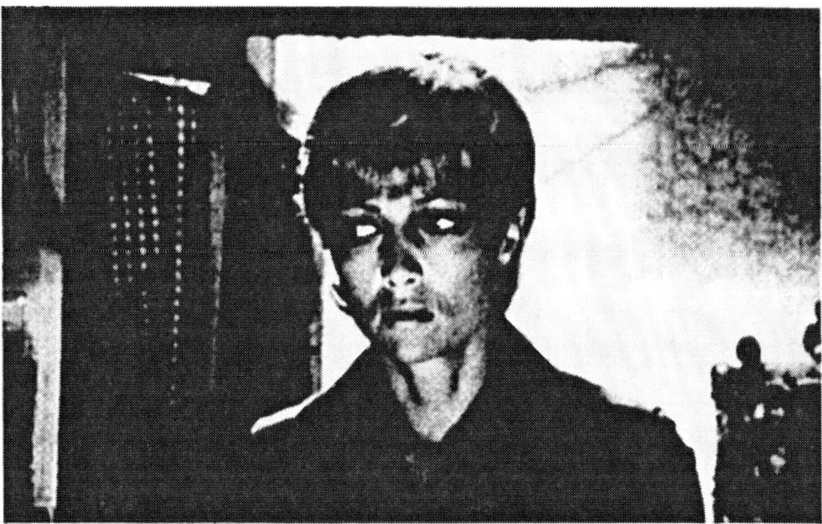

Portraits of evil and innocence in *Le Boucher:* Jean Yanne at the moment his guilt is unmistakably revealed (top), Stéphane Audran at her window as she looks into the darkness (bottom)

for her and that she will be helpless if forced to confront in Popaul the primitive urges she has all these years been trying desperately to repress in herself. She locks the door, turns off lights, then suddenly turns them back on so she can rush downstairs to lock another door and more windows. The suspense builds, as the inevitable generic confrontation between the protagonist and her adversary approaches.

From outside, Popaul calls out and asks to be let in; he presses his face against the window. Hélène adamantly tells him to come back in the morning. Upstairs, she looks out the window, but cannot see him; the camera zooms in to her face. Once again she suddenly races downstairs and turns on a light in order to lock another door she had forgotten. But Popaul is already inside. He turns off a light; in the darkness he walks toward her and confesses his murderous crimes. He holds a knife and claims that he can't help what he's doing. "I know I horrify you and I can't stand that." The confrontation is handled by Chabrol in a unique fashion: we see a close-up of the knife, a close-up of Hélène, a close-up of the knife, a close-up of Hélène, a close-up of Popaul; the last shots of montage fade almost imperceptibly to black. The ultimate moment of violence is not shown.

When, after a pause, the image fades up on Popaul, we see that he has turned his knife inward and stabbed himself, rather than Hélène. She helps him into the car and drives him to the hospital. Popaul sits in the corner of the front seat and confesses his love and passion for the cool Hélène. "What a long way," he says ambiguously—referring to the distance to the hospital, his love for Hélène, his manner of dying, the time ago when the Cro-Magnon flourished. "How long it takes." Popaul talks about blood: "They're all the same, the blood of men and the blood of animals." With only her eyes lit in the darkened frame, Hélène drives silently on the last leg of her journey into the darkness of the human soul. Popaul's confession is accompanied by expressive point-of-view shots: the trees speeding past, the road through the windshield stretching out and curving before them.

Hélène walks into the hospital as Popaul is wheeled in. As she stops, the camera leaves her slightly behind. Popaul asks her to embrace him; indeed, it was her inability to love him which had driven him to his crimes. She kisses him; he is taken up in the elevator. We see a close-up of Hélène as she watches the blinking of the red *"Occupé"* sign. It stops blinking, and we know that Popaul has died. Hélène is dressed in red, the color of meat, the color of blood, the color of passion; the hospital walls are white, as is her car, as was her temperament. She stands erect and still; the camera leaves her.

Like all thrillers of moral confrontation, *Le Boucher* ends with a coda of stasis. We see Hélène's car parked at the bank of the river at night. There is a medium long shot, then a medium close-up of Hélène standing by her car, its headlights on. In the morning, Hélène is standing there still. The same two shots are repeated, and then three more shots—each further away and from the other side of the river—of Hélène, who is isolated and forlorn as she tries to come to terms with the meaning of her experience.

Aside from its visual expressiveness, what makes *Le Boucher* particularly interesting is the way that Chabrol invests the evil adversary with so much sympathy, that the good versus evil confrontation becomes

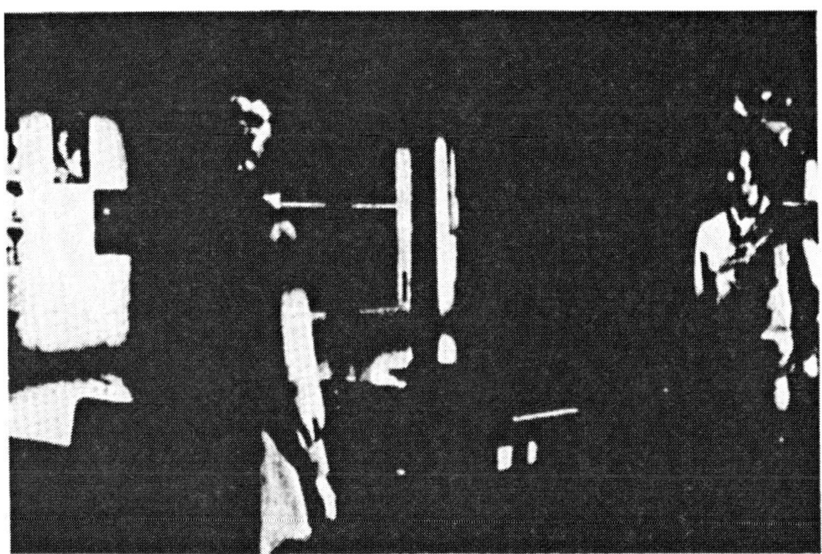

The climactic confrontation between innocence and evil, between Stéphane Audran and Jean Yanne in *Le Boucher*. Compare this composition, characteristic to the thriller of moral confrontation, with the composition of the frame enlargement on page 237.

subsidiary to Chabrol's examination of the ambiguity of moral values and the necessity for tempering civilization and technical goodness with empathy and human commitment.

Specifically underlying all of *Le Boucher* is the conflict between Hélène and Popaul, which can be generalized into a conflict between "control" and "passion"—between Hélène's statement that "Making love can make you mad" and Popaul's that "Not making love can make you mad." It is clear that both Popaul and Hélène are each in their own way mad, even if Hélène's madness would not be recognized as such by a society more disposed to recognizing aggression than withdrawal as antisocial. Also underlying the film is a consistent contrast between imagery relating to progress and light and imagery relating to the primeval and blood. Examples of the former include the very occupation of Hélène as a schoolteacher, which is to enlighten, Hélène's smoking in the street, the gift of the lighter, the blinking light on the elevator, and of course, the final images of her headlights, as Hélène awaits the dawn and the self-enlightenment that will accompany it. Examples of the latter include the very occupation of Popaul as a butcher, which is to spill the blood of beasts, the visit to the caves, the discussion of the animal instincts of the Cro-Magnon, the wall paintings of the cave dwellers which relate specifically to Hélène's walls, which are painted by Popaul, the gifts of lamb and blood-red cherries which Popaul

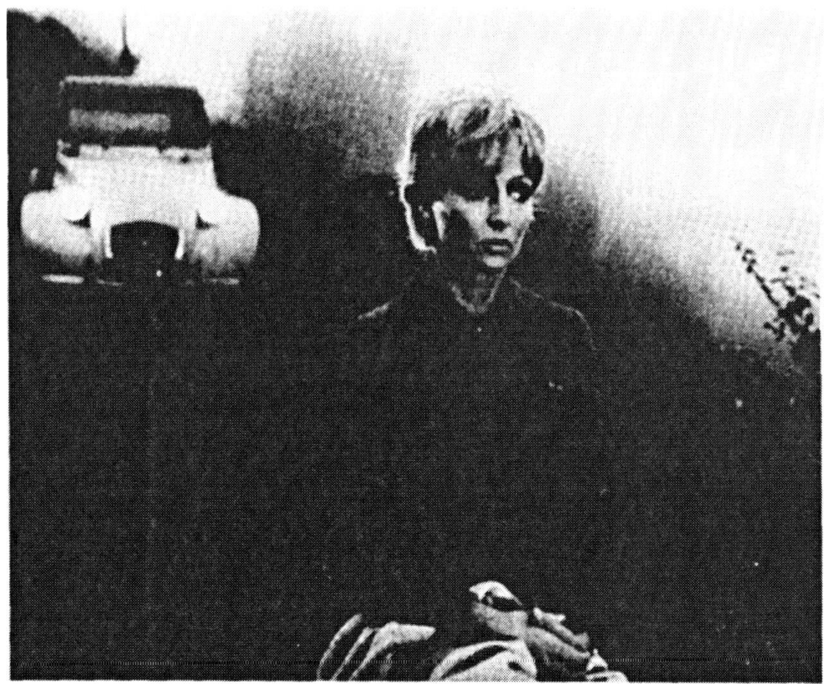

Stéphane Audran awaits the dawn at the river bank, as *Le Boucher* ends with a concluding scene of stasis so typical to the thriller of moral confrontation.

brings Hélène instead of the more traditional flowers, and of course, the final images as Popaul's own blood spills out.

Significantly, after the masterwork of *Le Boucher,* Chabrol returned to the same thriller genre in his very next film, *La Rupture,* again starring his wife, Stéphane Audran, as the good protagonist. Because I believe *La Rupture* to be one of the suspense thriller's most visually expressive masterpieces, if one virtually unknown in America, my analysis includes a detailed synopsis.

La Rupture begins with a quotation from Racine, "What an utter darkness suddenly surrounds me," which relates to the predicament of the virtuous heroine as she realizes the extent of the horrific plot against her. The first sequence shows the protagonist Hélène making breakfast for her four-year-old son Mike; when her husband Charles wanders into the kitchen in his pajama bottoms, he suddenly attacks his wife, picks up his son, and throws the boy across the room against the wall. Without a moment's hesitation, Hélène repeatedly beats her husband's head with a frying pan and then races outside to enlist the aid of her neighbors.

No longer able to put up with her husband's drug-taking and mental crises, Hélène decides she must divorce him even though they still love each other; she must think of her son. At the hospital, Regnier, her rich and aristocratic father-in-law, obsequiously offers his help, which Hélène refuses with a series of no's. She wants custody of her son; she wants his return to health; and although she is clearly the wronged party, she wants no settlement from the in-laws who have continuously disapproved of her background and her character. "I want what's legally mine," says Hélène, "and I'll get it." Regnier, however, determined to stop Hélène and get custody of Mike for his "wronged" son, hires Paul Thomas (played by Jean-Pierre Cassel) to undermine Hélène's reputation. Regnier claims Hélène is an unfit mother; his three major grounds are "immorality, vulgarity, [and] the incapability of raising Mike in comfort."

Hélène, absolutely exhausted at the hospital, is rescued by a young doctor who takes her across the street to a rooming house that she can stay in while her son remains in the hospital. A long tracking shot introduces the house. The room that Hélène is given is decorated in blue, the color of sky and release: blue walls, floor, bedspread. Hélène's orange hair and light brown suit contrast perfectly; she is photographed from above as she sinks down onto the bed. Later, Hélène tells her life story to her lawyer on a marvelously expressive streetcar ride, which recalls a similar ride in Murnau's *Sunrise.* When Hélène's mother died, her father became so ill that she had to drop out of school and become a nude dancer in order to support him. After she married, her husband became increasingly disturbed; under the influence of his oppressive family, he turned to the release provided by drugs. As Hélène speaks during the long streetcar journey, the camera reveals the ground moving by swiftly, the electric impulses crackling on the wires, the track extending infinitely away; on the soundtrack, the modern music of Pierre Jansen swells to an almost Messiaen-like expressiveness.

Paul begins his campaign to discredit Hélène. He insinuates himself into her life by pretending to be a friend of her husband and dying of cancer. He manages to estrange Hélène from those who might help her by subtly convincing others in the boarding house that Hélène has been a drunkard and perhaps even a molester of little girls. As Paul is defined simply in terms of his immorality, his girlfriend Sonia is defined simply in terms of her nymphomania. Hélène, on the other hand, is blameless; even Paul, who is trying so desperately to find something that Regnier can use against her, comes to the conclusion that "She's a saint, another Joan of Arc." Still, Paul continues his campaign. In one remarkably expressive scene in which Pierre Jansen's music is again prominent, Paul and Hélène walk in the park. The balloon man walks by; although Hélène has never talked to him, she has watched him before, always with a simple longing. The balloon man seems to be some symbol as of yet unconsummated. Still unaware of Paul's machinations against her, Hélène tells him that she can't understand why her friends are turning against her, why they will no longer talk to her.

We learn that Paul's master plan is to drug Hélène and Elise, the

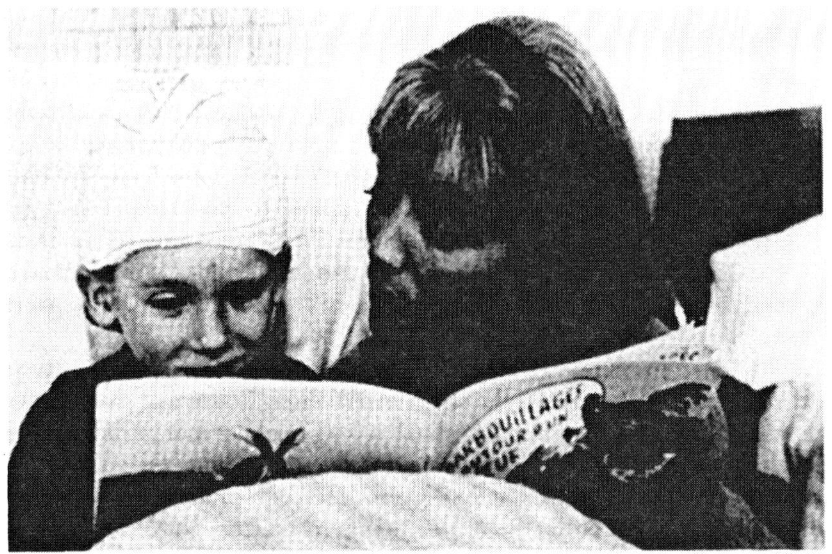

Innocence imperiled: Stéphane Audran as Hélène, with her son Laurent Brunschwick in *La Rupture*.

retarded daughter of the landlady, and arrange an automobile accident, so that the supposed child molester Hélène will be disgraced and lose custody of Mike. Throughout *La Rupture,* Chabrol is careful to follow Hitchcock's dictum to tell the spectator everything. Because we know about the continuing plot against Hélène, we feel inevitably helpless, anxious, and in continuous suspense as to whether Hélène will herself find out about it in time to save herself.

Finally, the series of estrangements and adversities is countered by a series of revelations. At the hospital, Hélène finds out that Paul was never really a cancer patient at all. When Hélène refuses to respond vengefully, the doctor proclaims her character flawless. Hélène then finds out from the actor tenant in the boarding house that Regnier asked him to lie about her reputation. "The world is horrifying," he says. "There aren't any kind people anymore." In the park, Hélène sees the balloon man, who speaks to her for the first time and tells her that a man has always been following her, where is he today? Even at that point when Hélène finally realizes the extent of the conspiracy against her, she is considerate to others. "Sorry I can't buy a balloon," she says to the balloon man, apologetic because she has no money. "You'll buy one when you can," he answers kindly.

Paul begins his master plan. He uses a piece of candy to drug Elise and then takes her to his apartment, where he shows her pornographic movies while his girlfriend, dressed as Hélène, molests her. Paul then steals Hélène's money and arranges for her to be falsely summoned to meet a friend at the airport. A tremendously suspenseful scene takes place as Paul offers to drive Hélène to the airport—but in reality, planning to consummate his scheme. Buoyed by the supposed arrival of her friend, Hélène tells Paul, "I'm not alone anymore, I'll win," and then, suddenly turning on him, "I know you're spying on me!" A desperate Paul confesses, pretends contrition, and asks forgiveness.

The suspense mounts as the strands of adversities and revelations finally come together in an overt confrontation with the spectator aware of all the possibilities: the horrible fate which will await Hélène if she falters for even a moment and goes off with Paul, the sticky dilemma which will face Paul if she doesn't. He begs her to prove her forgiveness: will she allow him to take her to the airport? She pauses, and then says no. At that moment, the street light goes on, bathing Paul in light as if revealing his true character. Hélène starts to walk off, but again she is stopped by Paul, who has one more gambit: he offers her a piece of the (drugged) candy as a peace offering. Will she take it? By this point of *La Rupture,* spectators often gasp at the thought that Hélène might still be taken in.

After being crushed by the realization that no friend was to arrive at the airport for her, Hélène races to her in-laws, who are having a party. She rushes up the stairway to talk to her partially-crazed husband. In the passionate and painful love scene that follows, the music comes in loudly and the camera moves continuously. Hélène and Charles embrace; the camera tracks in from a long shot to a tight two-shot, then gradually tracks out again to a medium long shot which reveals the mother-in-law standing limply against the doorway, entranced by the almost horrifyingly passionate expressions of love between Hélène and Charles. Hélène explains why she cannot stay in the marriage, and Charles breaks down tearfully. "Stay with me!" he repeats, and then, "Why am I alive!?" as the camera pans back to the two of them, still embracing, still crying. A new shot dollies in to the mother, who appears emotionally wounded. When the father-in-law enters, the mother beseeches him to leave the couple alone, but Regnier's presence pushes his wife out of the frame. Before Hélène leaves, she insists that Regnier pay her the 250 francs that was stolen from her purse, knowing implicitly that her father-in-law has been behind the entire plot. "I'm tired," she says simply, "But I still have my strength!"

But Hélène is not yet saved; one final confrontation remains. At the breakfast table the next day at the boarding house, Paul again asks Hélène for forgiveness. Everyone is eating; Hélène drinks from the orange juice which Paul has poured. When Paul purposely drops and breaks the pitcher, the moment is absolutely electrifying: the spectator knows, with a shock, that the orange juice has been drugged and that Hélène has been finally defiled. At this point, the film's style begins to rupture, to explode.

As Hélène finds herself in the grip of the LSD, the images become increasingly subjective, the colors wild, the camera moving, the compositions stylized, and the musical accompaniment frenetic. The three old women boarders, who so clearly represent the three fates, sit watching in unison. Hélène looks straight at the camera. The retarded girl, Elise, who has been safely returned to the boarding house, suddenly wakes up and claims that she wants more sex. But not with Hélène; no, with "the other Hélène." A distraught Paul begins laughing hysterically as he realizes that Elise has seen through the whole disguise after all. The three fates are smiling. "You're beautiful," says Hélène. Ironically, only after being drugged against her will by her evil adversary does Hélène achieve her long-sought release. Hélène goes skipping out the door, the three fates following her.

Back at the Regnier mansion, her husband senses that Hélène is in trouble; he pushes his mother down the steps and leaves in a frenzy. Hélène continues to wander as the screen is suffused with color. "Blue, blue," she repeats, "blue is very important"—thus relating the blue of the sky, her bedroom, and the drug trip to the release that she has been searching for. She begins to sing to herself, "Sadness of love lasts a whole life long" (the same song played at the wedding attended by the Hélène in *Le Boucher*). Wandering through the park, Hélène comes across the balloon man. "My friend," says Hélène, finally consummating what had been a mysterious symbol, "I know who you are. You are God. You do things to protect me. But your angels suffer. Release them."

Without a word, the balloon man lets the balloons go; it is Hélène, the good angel, who is now completely released—for the moment no longer forced to fight the constant battle against evil. The sky is filled with balloons of all colors floating freely against the blue emptiness. At the boarding house, Hélène's husband suddenly comes in and approaches Paul frenziedly. Paul panics, stricken with fear, and stabs Charles dead with a pair of scissors. Charles' falling out of the foreground of the frame reveals the frame's luminous and indistinct background; when the background comes slowly into focus, we see Hélène weakly leaning over, almost unconscious and uncomprehending, surrounded by the three fates who have protected her. "Self defense!" yells out Paul uselessly, realizing that everything has backfired and he is irrevocably lost.

Slowly regaining her control, Hélène says twice, simply: "I want to see my son." She leaves the boarding house, silently, steadily, almost monomaniacally keeping to her moral course. As she walks down the path to the hospital, she looks up: the last image is the sky, still filled with the balloons, the suffering angels that have finally been given their release.

La Rupture is built upon a very careful structure based upon the opposition between reality and transcendence. Hélène spends most of the narrative holding tightly onto reality, fearful that if she were to give up any control, she would lose custody of her child; Hélène's almost fanatical hold on reality is contrasted with the transcendence which is offered others. This antinomy of reality versus transcendence is reflected in at least three different spheres examined by the film: color, escape, and religion. In the sphere of color: reality is associated with red, brown, and pink, while transcendence is associated with blue. Thus, the villain Paul wears pink; his bedroom has red covers; Elise has a red coverlet when unconscious; the blood which comes out of Michel's head and Charlie's mouth is a dark red; Charles' room is dominated by a red mirror and red chair, and even his mother wears red as she attempts to comfort him; Paul's boarding house room has pink walls; red flowers fill Regnier's mansion; and so forth.

Although Hélène starts off wearing an earthy reddish-brown, she subsequently changes outfits and colors, to a magenta, then to a green, and finally to a transcendent blue at the very end of the film. Strikingly, the moment at which Hélène is revealed in blue (coming around a black divider in the boarding house dining room) is specifically punctuated by a striking chord of music. And of course, Hélène's bedroom is blue, as is the crucial image of the sky. The only other significant color seems to be black, which is associated with the horrific truth. The film's epigraph ("What an utter darkness suddenly surrounds me") suggests black and precedes the first image of the film — which is Hélène's home blotted out by the black trunk of a tree which obscures our view. As well, the actor who speaks the truth wears black; and at the film's depressing conclusion, the landlady and the three fates all wear black, a symbolic representation of the human condition.

In the sphere of escape: the film charts the struggle of a variety of characters who have such a horrific reality that transcendence is necessary. Ultimately, all the characters achieve transcendence of some kind (if only temporarily) except for Hélène's in-laws, who are melded to the repressive reality of their bourgeois existence. Hélène's husband Charles transcends through drugs; Elise, who has already transcended reality through her mental retardation, transcends further through drugs and sex; the landlord transcends through liquor; the landlady and the three fates attempt to transcend through their faith in finding a new house, which takes on a clear religious significance; the actor transcends through his profession, which allows him to discard his own identity and become other people on the stage; even Paul transcends, if briefly, through sex.

Ultimately, it is Hélène who is most in need of transcendence, yet most unwilling to give up her hold on reality. There is a certain irony in the fact that the few moments of release and transcendence that Hélène does achieve, through the LSD forced on her, is a result of the villain's plot. Images associated with the lack of escape, with entrapment in reality, include the ubiquitous bare trees, rooted to the ground; Michel immobile on the floor and then confined to his hospital bed; Charles knocked to the ground with a frying pan; Hélène on the bed and photographed from a high angle that makes her look both singular and trapped. In opposition to these images stands the supreme image of transcendence which ends the film: the balloons released to float up to the blue and expansive sky.

And finally, the opposition between reality and transcendence is reflected in the sphere of religion: On the side of mundane reality is the boarding house which is being torn down and which seems clearly to represent the destruction of a church, of belief, of hope. On the side of transcendence are the *Parcae* or Fates—the three women who live at the boarding house; the tarot cards that they play; the name of the street (Church) where the new house is located; the friend that Hélène hopes will come by airplane to help her—the hoped-for *deus ex machina* from the heavens; and of course, the balloon man, representing God, and who holds us prisoners in a world filled with horror. Thus, it should be clear that within the thriller structure of *La Rupture,* Chabrol has also fashioned a serious philosophical and theological message about human suffering and our relationship with God.

Less pretentious, certainly, and more typically American in its single-mindedness is *Duel,* made for television in 1971 by Steven Spielberg from a script by Richard Matheson. *Duel* can be seen as the apotheosis of the cat-and-mouse; indeed, there is so little narrative elaboration that the generic elements stand virtually naked. *Duel* takes place on a deserted stretch of highway and chronicles the adventures of a homeward-bound businessman as he attempts to escape the gigantic, flammable, gasoline tanker truck that for no apparent reason is intent on destroying him and his car. This simple idea seems tailor-made for a suspense thriller; Spielberg constructs his film almost exclusively in terms of montage, primarily using chains of point-of-view shots which enable the spectator to identify with the protagonist.

The symbolism of the truck versus the man is remarkable in its simplicity. Often in the film, the truck tailgates the protagonist; the way Spielberg photographs its front grill makes the truck a monster with two headlight eyes, crashing through barricades and wreaking havoc. The reappearance of the truck time and again after the protagonist had thought he had finally gotten rid of it is constantly horrifying. Because the truckdriver's face is never seen, the truck readily represents the threatening and evil unknown. Indeed, twice, the protagonist runs on foot after the truck, primarily to try to catch a glimpse of the truckdriver's face.

"How can he go so fast?" asks the protagonist near the end of *Duel* as the truck acts incomprehensibly untruck-like in its manageability and is transformed into pure symbol. Spielberg, thus, does not invite the spectator to identify at all with the truckdriver, but only with the protagonist (played by Dennis Weaver), who is a salesman trying to return to his home and his wife. Aside from that, we are given very little information about him except for that which we can pick up from miscellaneous metaphors; that is, he drives a Valiant and his name is David Manns (which suggests he is an Everyman), and his license plate is 149 PCE (which perhaps suggests he would prefer his existence to be peaceful). At one point in *Duel,* the spectator is allowed to share the protagonist's thoughts as he suddenly realizes how it is possible for one's whole life to change completely in twenty minutes.

At the film's crisis point, stylistically signified by four shots of the protagonist as he stands erect on the highway, all taken from the same angle, yet increasingly closer and ending with a close-up, the protagonist consciously accepts the challenge. He is now resigned that he can no longer just run, but must play the game by the truckdriver's rules. The suspenseful sequence at the end of *Duel* has the protagonist's success in gaining distance between him and the truck at an upgrade evaporating as his radiator hose (about which he had been warned earlier) goes faulty, the car overheats, the oil light goes on, and white smoke emerges from his exhaust. In an important sense, he must now rely on his own guile, his own person.

At the climax, he turns his car around and drives directly toward the oncoming truck—for the first time adopting the evil methods of the truckdriver for his own end: survival. At the last second he jumps out of his car; there is a crash, his car explodes, and the out-of-control truck dives off a cliff. From over the cliff, we hear two growl-like noises which suggest that a monster, indeed, is dying. Completely overjoyed, a very primitive looking protagonist literally jumps up and down for joy. *Duel* ends consistently to the genre with a scene of reflection as the protagonist sits quietly on the cliff overlooking the accident and watches the burning truck, like Hélène in *Le Boucher* or Charlie in *Shadow of a Doubt,* trying to come to terms with the meaning of the moral confrontation which has so tested his essence.

Directed by Sam Peckinpah in 1971, the same year as *Duel, Straw Dogs* seems to me one of the most skillful films of the decade, gradually and inexorably setting its antagonisms before unleashing them in an eruptive climax. Dustin Hoffman plays David, a mathematician who comes with his wife to a peaceful Cornish village because of his growing anxiety about the tensions in his marriage and the politics in America. The film's prophetic first image is of a gravestone, then of children playing in a cemetery. David's sports car is white, reflecting his good and decent nature.

His wife Amy (played by Susan George) is introduced by a camera movement panning up from her chest; she is thus defined as two breasts and a face. In the very first sequence as David buys a man-trap (a gigantic trap once used to catch poachers) to decorate his house, he sees another man making a pass at his wife. In a bar, violence disturbingly breaks out, started by an older villager. When this older man insists on paying for David's drink, David wants to be true to his own moral values and be left alone. "They're paid for," says the bartender. "They are now," responds David as he puts down his own money. The locals tell David that they hear it's awful in America—bombings, riotings, and shootings of blacks in the street. "Did you see any of that?" "Only on television," answers David.

The relationship between David and his wife is fraught with tensions. When in the car Amy puts on rock music, David switches to classical. Amy is constantly violating what David considers to be his own personal space; at one point she willfully alters an equation on his blackboard. Their conver-

sations are filled with double meanings and erotic undertones which add to the tension. At one point David says that the cat doesn't answer his call. "Do I?" asks his wife. "You better," responds David as he squirts soda water suggestively into a drink. They chew gum at each other—and even that is erotic and antagonistic. At one point David says, "I love you, Amy, but I want you to leave me alone." Amy's startlingly disturbing response is to carefully stick her gum on his blackboard.

Amy would like David to be more house-oriented—to be able to fix the toaster, to be more useful. She accuses him of leaving America because he couldn't take a stand. When the men from town are invited in, she serves them beer and humiliates David by providing him a bowl of milk. One striking image is that of a magnetic desk-top toy with two swinging pieces that consistently and alternately attract and repel: a clear metaphor for David and Amy. In Peckinpah's world, women are hostile and foreign, to be kept in their place, used sexually, and subjugated. And yet, at the same time, women ideally can be transformed into moral and physical helpmates.

Still, the primary antagonism comes from the men from town who have been hired to fix up David's house. The ratcatcher tells David that he feels close to the rats even though he kills them. "Rats is life," he says. Ironically, his statement is allegorical for the situation David will eventually find himself in at the film's climax, when he finally feels a closeness for the men from town only when he finds himself violently killing them all. In the course of the narrative, the men steal Amy's panties, watch her while she's nude, kill David and Amy's cat, and finally, rape Amy.

The rape is particularly gruesome and expressively filmed. It takes place while David is out hunting with the men in order to build up some kind of camaraderie; he shoots poorly and looks silly. One of the men, Charlie, visits Amy, drags her caveman-style by the hair, and rapes her. Peckinpah presents a montage of rhythmic shots; Amy holding her breasts, her hands trying to ward off the attack, her face streamed with tears, Charlie's shoulders, a bead of sweat running down her cheek, her eyes finally giving in to the passion. The rape images of brutality and tenderness are juxtaposed with images of the cuckold David killing a bird and being repulsed by the blood. "I'm sorry, Amy," says her attacker. "Hold me, hold me," she responds.

The ultimate crisis is precipitated when a young retarded man accidentally kills the teenage daughter of one of the villains, and David takes it upon himself to take care of the retarded man until he can be properly dealt with by the authorities. The *Walpurgisnacht* of violence begins in the dark at David's house when he explains to his wife that the retarded man is now his responsibility. Amy asks why; after a long pause, David answers: "This

Dennis Weaver as the Everyman protagonist in conflict with a monstrous truck in *Duel*.

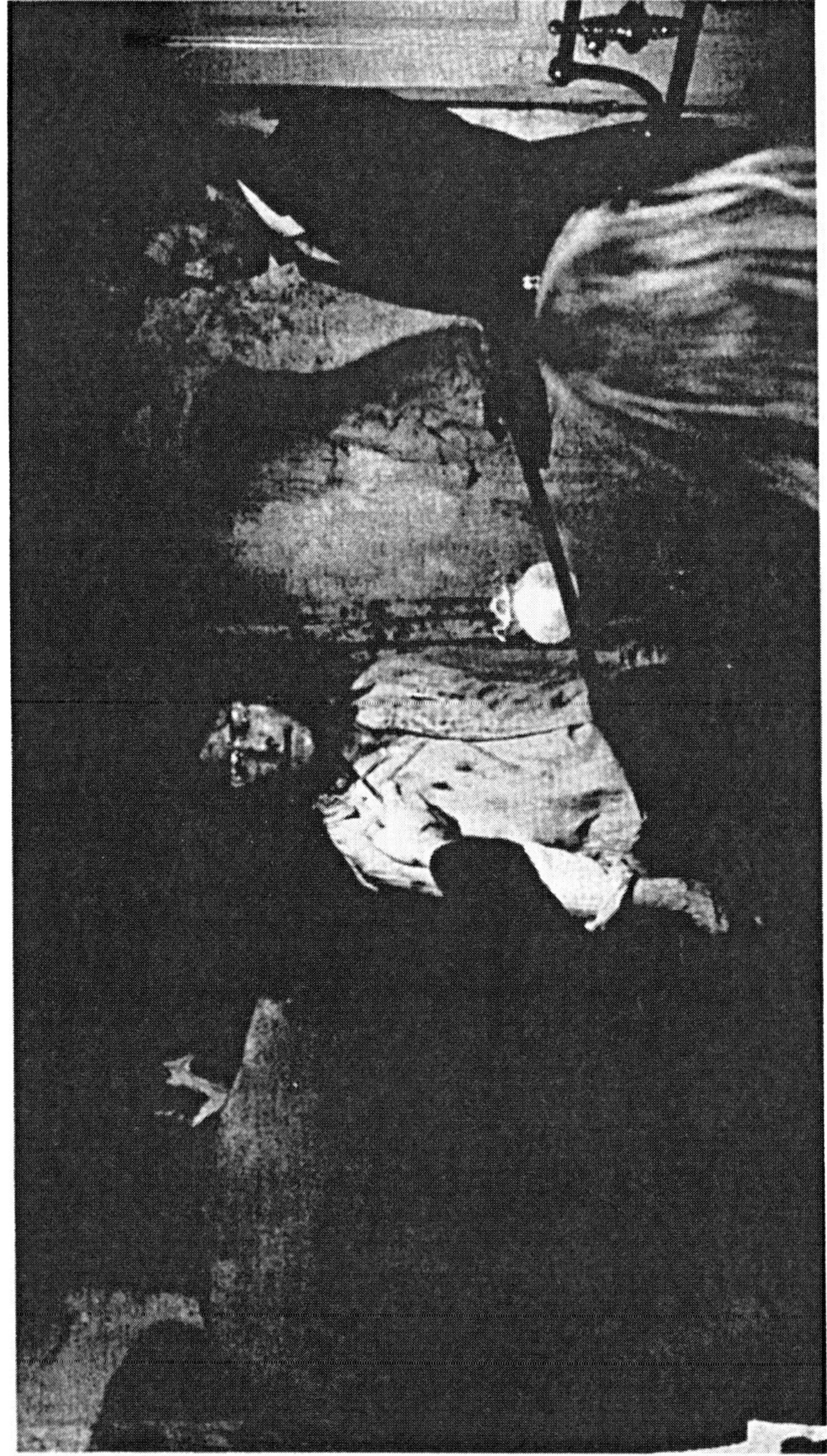

is my house." There is an immediate cut outside to the old man from the bar cocking his rifle. The men outside begin to attack, to break windows. David threatens to prosecute, giving them one more chance to go away, because he is still really afraid. By this time, Peckinpah has so carefully built up our expectations, that the typical audience finds itself urging David on to violence and murder; he has, after all, remained passive for so long. Amy (in Peckinpah's scheme of things, being only a woman) cannot understand why David is unwilling to allow the men outside to kill the retarded man. "I care," answers David. "This is where I live. This is me. I will not allow violence against this house." David then orders Amy to go upstairs and get out of the way.

When the major, the one potential law-keeping force, is killed outside by one of the men, David knows that there is no turning back. He is now completely alienated from those who could help him, a witness to murder, and about to engage in a battle for his very life. Finally absolutely committed to a stand and a specific course of action, David is willing to fight using any methods required of him. First, he physically abuses his wife, dragging her along in part by the hair (which suggests, for the first time, a bond between David and Charlie). Even as we may be horrified, we seem almost to approve of what David is doing—not only because Amy has been set up by Peckinpah as David's territorial imperative, but because we want the film to proceed to its conclusion so that all the tension Peckinpah has been so carefully building up can be released.

Sure enough, what follows is an all-out siege of violence, including shattering glass, gunshots, screams, Dutch angles, dark shadows, faces in pain, spurting blood, rapid montage. Although the violence is horrifying, we are willing to sanction it because we know that unless David manages to kill all of the villains, David himself will be killed. In his confrontation, David uses fire, wire, and boiling oil as a few of his weapons. An awful fight with one of the men takes place on the stairway. In slow motion, we see the contorted, struggling face of David as he eventually succeeds in putting the gigantic man-trap over the man's head. Finally, there is a respite to the violence; Amy is in tears, quivering. David, smiling and suddenly proud of himself, says wondrously: "Jesus, I got 'em all."

It is difficult to talk about *Straw Dogs* without talking about how skillfully Peckinpah builds upon what he knows will be the typical response; at this point, so cathartic has been the climax that the spectator (and here I posit that the spectator is male) often feels that he has done the same as David, that he shares responsibility for singlehandedly killing all the villains.[2] But the spectator is wrong, as is David: there is one more villain

Dustin Hoffman as the innocent Everyman who embraces violence when he defends the sanctity of his home in *Straw Dogs* (Ken Hutchison, left, Del Henney, right; Susan George, foreground).

left. The violence starts up once again, with another struggle on the stairs. A beset and incapable David orders Amy to shoot this last assailant. When she does, after excruciating hesitation, Amy finally becomes David's accomplice and ultimately, his moral and physical helpmate. There is a shot of David's car, the headlights cutting through the night fog as David drives the retarded man back into town. "I don't know my way home," says the man. "That's okay," says David, "I don't either."

There is a long pause while David contemplates the meaning of all that has happened. Silence. The last shot shows the white car driving off. Thus, Peckinpah has used the thriller of moral confrontation to work out his favorite theme: the innate violence that is part of every man's nature. Although David has won his confrontation with evil, David cannot be a whole person until he realizes that there is violence within him and embraces that violence as part of his identity.

Other thrillers of moral confrontation from this same period include *Sudden Terror,* directed by John Hough in 1970; *Outrage,* directed by Richard T. Heffron in 1973; and *Death Wish,* directed by Michael Winner in 1974. *Sudden Terror* stars Mark Lester as a boy who witnesses an assassination and is then pursued by the assassin when no one will believe the boy's story. Many critics noted the film's resemblance to the 1949 *The Window. Sudden Terror* ends with the boy triumphant and his story vindicated; in the film's coda, the boy announces at a party that he has just seen Hitler. *Sudden Terror* is thus a rather traditional, almost old-fashioned thriller.

Outrage and *Death Wish,* on the other hand, seem to be part of a new kind of thriller of moral confrontation exploring violent, almost fascist sensibilities. *Outrage,* a television movie starring Robert Culp, has many superficial resemblances to *The Desperate Hours* in that it presents a suburban family threatened by a group of juvenile delinquent thugs. As *Outrage* proceeds, however, it becomes increasingly clear that the film's focus is not so much on the balance between protagonist and antagonist as on the outrage of official law enforcement agencies unable to keep law and order. In *Outrage,* unlike in *The Desperate Hours,* the protagonist and his family are *not* isolated from the social agencies that could (or here, should) protect them. Thus, when the protagonist carries out his own vengeance, that vengeance is not just a personal rite of passage but also a scathing indictment of a society which is allowing its own destruction at the hands of criminals.

Because of the relative freedom allowed motion picture films as opposed to television films, *Death Wish* was able to take this same theme much further through the use of an incredibly graphic violence. *Death Wish* stars Charles Bronson as a civilized citizen who, after the brutal rape and murder of his wife, realizes that he cannot depend on the state to fight courageously in these moral confrontations with criminals. Bronson's protagonist then sets himself up as a one-man vigilante who seeks out evil and destroys it, adopting the very methods of his adversaries in order that good—that is, law and order—survive. With a film like *Death Wish* in which the protagonist is only marginally a victim, the genre shows its affinity to police films like *Dirty Harry*, which deal so centrally with issues of violence and the urban landscape.

Death Wish was a huge financial hit which tied in to the extant cultural sensibility; paradoxically, *Death Wish* exploits violence even as it apparently criticizes those criminals who perpetrate it; and of course the violent acts committed by the Bronson protagonist are glorified. *Death Wish* led to *Death Wish II* (directed by Michael Winner in 1982) and *Death Wish III* (directed by Michael Winner in 1986), both of which continued the saga by virtually remaking the initial film with the protagonist simply killing more and more criminals. *Death Wish III* particularly seems a thesis film, both exploiting and contributing to the widespread public support of Bernard Goetz, the New York resident who became a *cause célèbre* when on a subway train he shot several black youths that he feared would rob him. As these vigilante films became increasingly violent, they also became decreasingly thrillers, because their protagonists seemed to be not ordinary citizens but professional killers.

Victims, a television film directed by Jerrold Freedman in 1982, stars Kate Nelligan as a rape victim who organizes a group of other rape victims in order to exact revenge against the man who raped them, the system having failed to secure justice. *Red Dawn*, directed by John Milius in 1984, wrapped the vigilante theme in the virulent anti–Soviet ideology of the first seven years of the Reagan administration, and presented a story of "typical" American young men and women who join a resistance movement and fight when Russian-Cuban forces invade the United States—the Americans the good and innocent protagonists, the Russians and Cubans the evil adversaries. Ultimately related to these thrillers are other action-adventure films, like *The Exterminator* (directed by James Glickenhaus in 1980), which allowed a Vietnam veteran to exact his own justice and in the process become just as violent as any psychotic killer; and the great commercial success from Sylvester Stallone, *Rambo: First Blood, Part II* (directed by George Cosmatos in 1985), which glorifies violence within a stridently anti–Soviet context and which allows its protagonist to retroactively, if symbolically, win the Vietnam War.

Perhaps the one scene in all these vigilante films which best characterizes their sensibility is one from the very end of *10 to Midnight* (directed by J. Lee Thompson in 1983), again starring Charles Bronson. As the vigilante protagonist, Bronson has just chased down the psychotic killer, who has been frenziedly running naked down the street. "You sick son of a bitch," says Bronson disgustedly. The killer looks at Bronson and says, increasingly emotionally:

> I *am* sick. I *am* sick. I didn't know what I was doing. It's like something was happening and I couldn't control myself. Why else would I kill girls I don't even know? It's like I'm two different people. I hear voices telling me what to do. Once it begins I can't stop. Go ahead, arrest me, take me in. You can't punish me. I'm sick. You can't punish me for being sick. All you can do is lock me up. But not forever. One day I'll get out. One day I'll get out. That's the law. *That's the law. THAT'S THE LAW!* And I'll be back, I'll be back. You'll hear from me! You and the whole world!

"No we won't," says Bronson, and shoots him dead. In these reactionary thrillers, if indeed they can still be called thrillers of moral confrontation, there is no patience with the system and no compassion, only an urgent desire to rid society of anything which seems criminal or aberrant.

If we might consider these vigilante films a culturally "male-oriented" subset of the thriller of moral confrontation, we might also consider a different group of films a culturally "female-oriented" subset: those "women's thrillers" in which a heroine finds herself increasingly certain that her husband is either a killer or a homicidal maniac, such as *Rebecca* (1940), *Suspicion* (1941), *Gaslight* (1944), *Sorry, Wrong Number* (1948), *Midnight Lace* (1960), and *The Naked Edge* (1961). As the *Death Wish* films emerge from a chauvinist view of male potency and aggression, these women's thrillers emerge from a chauvinist view of female passivity and helplessness.

If the women's thrillers do not seem to set up the moral confrontation as strongly as the other thrillers discussed in this chapter, this may be because the guilt of the husband is never really clear from the beginning (either to the protagonist or to the spectator), and because the protagonist often finds herself as much in the position of detective trying to uncover the truth as in the position of innocent victim. Thus, these often gothic women's thrillers are predicated upon mystery structures as much as upon suspense structures. Occasionally, these films even include a detective figure who actually saves the hapless, helpless heroine. While psychotic killers appear often in thrillers of moral confrontation (as, for instance, in *Shadow of a Doubt*), the protagonists (like Teresa Wright's Charlie) are never as passive, hysterical or dependent as the heroines of the women's thrillers. A film like *Le Boucher* is related to these films, although Chabrol's emphasis on suspense rather than mystery, his presentation of his heroine as absolutely self-sufficient, and his refusal to allow the outcome of the ultimate confrontation to be decided by any third party work against any underlying traditional gothic structure; and unlike the women in the women's thriller, Hélène is never defined as a wife or sexual partner, her independence giving her equal status with the antagonist.

The dominant idea in these women's thrillers thus seems to be that of woman as archetypal victim by nature of her very sex. With the advent of the women's movement, it would have seemed unlikely that this subset of the thriller of moral confrontation would continue, except that, in the backlash against the women's movement in the Reagan years, which also marked the defeat of the Equal Rights Amendment, a film was released—*Jagged Edge*, directed by Richard Marquand in 1985—which was very much a throwback to this genre, as well as one of the most commercially successful thrillers of all time.

Jagged Edge tends to have it both ways: although it opposes male violence against women and thus takes the proper eighties political stance, it exploits violence against women in scenes in which we graphically watch a woman being tortured or hear a woman almost pornographically recounting her torture. Indeed, the film begins horrifically by showing us a woman being tied violently to her bed, gagged, and then brutally stabbed. To make the film more contemporary, the woman protagonist Teddy (played by Glenn Close) is not the wife of the potential killer Jack Forrester (played by Jeff Bridges), merely his lover, first entering Jack's life as the defense attorney whose job it is to save him. Although she quickly begins an affair with him, she wavers between her fear that he is a homicidal maniac and her conviction that he is not. Particularly notable is the skillful construction of the narrative which manipulates the spectator into constantly changing his or her mind as to the guilt of Forrester. Thankfully, when at the end of *Jagged Edge*, Jack is revealed definitively as a killer, Teddy (unlike the more traditional protagonist in the women's thriller) is able to dispatch him violently herself; although her friend Sam arrives just in the nick of time—it is not to save her, but to give her comfort after she has saved herself.

Three other recent thrillers of moral confrontation—*The Eyes of Laura Mars*, *The Fan*, and *Eye of the Needle*—also present women protagonists who must guard against male killers. What makes *The Eyes of Laura Mars* (directed by Irvin Kershner in 1978) unique is the film's gimmick, by which the psychic Laura finds herself actually seeing the murders from the point of view of the killer. Thus, while Laura gets closer and closer to the killer psychologically, she still is unable to identify him. Notable too is the way her high fashion photography, which features images of chic violence and sadomasochism, works as well to bring Laura psychologically closer to the sadistic killer. *The Fan* (directed by Edward Bianchi in 1981) is another story of a woman stalked by a psychotic killer: in this film, it is Lauren Bacall playing a stage and screen actress not unlike herself, who must embrace violence by the end of the film in order to vanquish her adversary.

Eye of the Needle, directed by Richard Marquand in 1981 from a script by Stanley Mann, seems to me one of the most interesting thrillers in recent years, with very memorable multidimensional characters. *Eye of the Needle* stars Kate Nelligan as Lucy, a strong-willed woman who lives with her weak, paralyzed husband David on the remote Storm Island off the English coast. Donald Sutherland plays Faber, who is the "needle," a ruthless killer and spy determined to secure for the Nazis information relating to the planned D-Day invasion. In the course of his mission, Faber makes his way to the household of Lucy and David. Lucy is incredibly lonely sexually; when Faber accidentally steps in the bathroom and sees her naked, she doesn't immediately cover herself. Faber, touched by Lucy's vulnerability and becoming human for the first time in his life, intuits her profound sadness. He and Lucy reveal themselves psychologically, and then make love. At one point Faber tells Lucy that he is writing a book with a heroine: "She lives, has an affair with the hero, she dies." How does she die? "He kills her. She broke his heart." Faber's story thus sets up strong expectations as to what will happen to Lucy. Before long, Faber kills Lucy's husband, who is stronger and more courageous than we might have guessed. One irony of the film is that while Faber is truly a villain, he does deliver Lucy from a dreadfully unhappy marriage which she otherwise would have been too loyal to have abandoned on her own.

Suspense crystallizes when Lucy realizes that Faber has been lying to her. There is a very striking scene when Lucy must sleep with Faber again so as not to alert his suspicions; this time Miklos Rozsa's music does not employ the romantic theme we heard before, but a theme which is tortured, as is Lucy. Certainly Lucy is strong and smart; and in the film's climax, when she and Faber must face off, she uses a rifle and even axes Faber's hand in order to protect her child. When Lucy calls for help on her radio, she is asked by authorities to destroy the radio so that Faber cannot send the information he has learned to the Nazis. Thus, Lucy's struggle becomes more than a personal rite of passage: it is a symbol of the global struggle, and Lucy represents the inherent goodness of the democracies which were forced to embrace violence in order to save the world from the fascists. The surprise at the film's end is that when Faber fails in his mission, he is content to try to leave the island without killing Lucy; but it is Lucy, a feminist fighter unwilling to cower gratefully like the standard movie heroine, who is unwilling to let Faber go without killing *him.* She shoots him first in the legs, virtually paralyzing him (which seems to be an irony relating to her husband's paralysis). In the film's final scene, Lucy is on the beach, and the wounded Faber is in a boat on the water, trying to row out to sea. They stare at each other, the love theme comes up, and then Faber dies. The film ends with a typical moment of reflection and stasis (which recalls the ending of *Le Boucher*), as on the beach Lucy attempts to make sense of the horrific encounter.

In comparison to *Eye of the Needle, The Mean Season,* directed by Philip Borsos in 1985, seems rather thin. Its protagonist is Malcolm Anderson, a reporter who finds himself "entering Pulitzer territory" when a serial killer, looking for attention, starts telephoning Anderson to give him the exclusive story of the killer's ongoing activities. Anderson's girlfriend is aware of the moral problem involved: "Are you reporting it or participating in it? It's turned into a collaboration." *The Mean Season* shows the influence of horror films like *Friday the 13th;* over and over, at times when characters are in no danger whatsoever, suspense music jangles the spectator's nerves in punctuation of all sorts of benign interruptions. By the film's end, Anderson shoots the villain, while his girlfriend (who had previously seemed among the more sensible and intelligent of all the characters) reverts to the role of the hysterical female, screaming and then clinging to Anderson's arm.

In contrast with the rather mechanical *The Mean Season* is the exceedingly interesting independent film *Perfect Strangers,* directed in 1984 by Larry Cohen. In some ways, *Perfect Strangers* is a very disquieting update of *The Window,* also set in Manhattan. As the film begins, two-and-a-half year old Matthew (played by Matthew Stockley in a strikingly natural performance manipulated by Cohen) witnesses a stabbing committed by Johnny (played by Brad Rijn). To find out whether Matthew might have some consciousness of what he has seen, Johnny becomes friendly with Matthew's mother Sally (played by Anne Carlisle). As *Perfect Strangers* progresses, it becomes clear, if subtly so, that Cohen is interested in that process by which we lose our innocence, that process by which we are conditioned to act violently. Early in the film, Johnny's crime superior tells Johnny that "up to now you were clean as a baby"—like Matthew?

Sally and her feminist friend talk often about pornography and violence against women. In fact, Sally and her friend are involved with the social action groups "Take Back the Night" and "Women Against Pornography." These feminist discussions put the thriller plot in a broader context: although Sally's friend is opposed to male violence, she nevertheless carries a gun and looks forward to the opportunity to perpetrate her own female violence against some male chauvinist pig. As the narrative develops, Johnny and Matthew—the evil and innocent forces involved in the moral confrontation—grow psychologically closer. Johnny increasingly gains our sympathy as he becomes much more nurturing and innocent himself. Matthew, on the other hand, in a subtle if realistic way, begins to slowly and insidiously show the effects of the violent society around him and certainly of having witnessed Johnny's crime. Although Matthew can barely speak, the two words he can say are "Kill . . . bug," referring to an action he himself takes pleasure in. When Cohen interposes a traditional pastoral love scene between Johnny and Sally, the scene is edited to the song "Mama, Look What the Big City Is Doing to Your Little Boy."

Before long, Matthew starts playing with knives, imitating the killer and coming in his truly inchoate way to an acceptance of violent behavior. Although Matthew is smart enough to pick out the picture of the killer from a group of photographs circulated by the gay detective, he is ignored because he is so young. Certainly there is a self-conscious irony associated with the fact that all three of the adult male characters in *Perfect Strangers*—the killer, the sexist if somewhat sensitive ex-husband, and the gay detective—all look pretty much the same, as they would in the eyes of Sally's most radical, feminist friends. As well, the spectator's sympathies tend to be manipulated in such a way that these sympathies are by no means "politically correct." There are several suspenseful scenes in which Matthew is threatened and in danger, and it seems increasingly certain that Johnny will kill Matthew after all.

In the film's stunning climax, it is the women—Sally and her friend—who commit the violent acts: most strikingly, when an hysterical Sally, in an attempt to find out where her son is, stabs Johnny in the heart, the dying Johnny falls out of the frame to reveal little Matthew standing behind him. Thus, while it is revealed that Johnny had ultimately been psychologically unable to murder Matthew, ironically Matthew has now witnessed his second violent murder. *Perfect Strangers* suggests that if women who are ideologically opposed to violence can commit violent acts, little Johnny doesn't have a chance: although he may be only two-and-a-half years old, his innocence is gone, his future path potentially charted.

And finally, if this chapter began with a discussion of Alfred Hitchcock's *Shadow of a Doubt*, it is appropriate that it end with a discussion of two recent films inspired by *Shadow of a Doubt: Blue Velvet*, directed by David Lynch in 1986, and *The Stepfather*, directed by Joseph Ruben in 1987. Both films express the same interest in small-town America, though with a particularly modern sensibility. Indeed, these two important films strikingly attest to the seminal position of *Shadow of a Doubt*, which has never seemed more important or more impressive than it does today, forty-five years after its initial release and still emotionally unforgettable, formally remarkable.

Whereas in *Shadow of a Doubt*, horror (as embodied by Uncle Charlie) *comes* to the small town, in *Blue Velvet*, the horror is already present in the small town, and it is the protagonist Jeffrey (played by Kyle MacLachlin) who returns to the town to discover it. To say that *Blue Velvet* is one of those rarities—a genuinely weird multimillion dollar film—is itself an understatement. Instructive too would be a comment on the peculiar response *Blue Velvet* elicited from its initial spectators, who, coming out of movie theatres afterwards—depressed, incredulous, angry, amused, superior, shocked—may have often appeared to be walking wounded. Many critics have called *Blue Velvet* a *film naïf*, in tacit recognition of the basic simple-mindedness underlying its rococo excesses.

The film begins by introducing us to the apparently quiet town of Lumberton: on this typical day we see bright red flowers, redder than red, and other images in dreamy slow-motion, dripping in nostalgia, a Technicolor throwback to some fifties wide-screen image of innocent America. We then see Jeffrey's father watering his lawn; suddenly, he is violently stricken and falls to the ground, the hose looking surreally phallic as a dog then jumps on the father irreverently. The camera dollies in to a close-up of the man inert on the ground and then continues beyond him to examine beneath the lawn, where grotesque insects are revealed scurrying back and forth in their own secret world. This one scene encapsulates the entire film; that beneath the surface prettiness, people in small-town America are like secretive, dirty insects and—as the film develops subsequently—overwhelmingly concerned with sex and the secrets of their dirty pleasures.

Jeffrey returns to Lumberton to help out during his father's illness, but the real drama begins when Jeffrey, while walking one day across a field in town, happens upon a severed human ear; as the camera dollies in to the ear, the soundtrack fills with a surreal and terrifying rumble. As the narrative develops and Jeffrey tries to explore the mystery of the ear, he comes in conflict with the evil Frank (played by Dennis Hopper), the drugged-out, sadistic sex maniac with a blue velvet fetish. As the innocent Jeffrey learns more about Frank, Jeffrey begins to lose that innocence, almost enjoying the worlds of voyeurism and sadomasochistic sex which are, horrifically, opening up to him. Jeffrey becomes witness to Frank's crimes, putting Jeffrey in danger and forcing him to fight in order to vanquish Frank. One of the most striking scenes in *Blue Velvet* is near the end when Jeffrey comes into an apartment and discovers a *tableau vivant* which resembles a modern sculpture: two dead men, one of them still standing erect, balancing precariously.

By the film's conclusion, the evil Frank has been destroyed; and as the film's thriller plot began with the dolly-in to the severed ear, so too does the thriller plot end with a dolly-out from Jeffrey's own ear while the singing of a robin is heard on the soundtrack. At that precise moment, a robin flies in through an open window and perches on the windowsill. The robin itself would appear to be a sign of hope and promise, but since the robin is obviously mechanical and carrying a bug in its beak, it rather unpleasantly recalls the insects we saw earlier, the sordid underbelly which the narrative is now turning away from. "It's a strange world," says the protagonist's innocent girlfriend in genuine wonder. The images which opened the film are then repeated in a way recalling the structure of *Citizen Kane*, as *Blue Velvet*—one of the most quirky and original thrillers of moral confrontation to be made in the last twenty years—comes to its rather incredible and memorable conclusion.

The Stepfather is certainly a less personal film than *Blue Velvet*, and it can be viewed almost as a remake or reconsideration of Hitchcock's *Shadow of a Doubt*. As *Shadow of a Doubt* was written by distinguished author Thornton Wilder, *The Stepfather* was written by distinguished author David Westlake. A formally stunning film, *The Stepfather* pits Stephanie (played by Jill Schoelen) against her murderous stepfather (played by Terry O'Quinn) in much the same way *Shadow of a Doubt* pitted Charlie against her murderous uncle. Both films have the same structure, beginning with a scene that establishes the antagonist's guilt and creates a disturbing and privileged audience identification with him. When Stephanie is introduced, she almost subconsciously understands (again, like Charlie) that something is "wrong" with her stepfather, that his charming demeanor disguises something murderous.

Like Charlie, Stephanie finds evidence against the killer in a newspaper; like Uncle Charlie, the stepfather tries to hide that evidence by destroying the newspaper in a benign game. Again like Charlie, Stephanie comes to doubt her initial suspicions, but by film's end she realizes her instincts were right after all and she must find the wherewithal to kill her adversary herself. And there are a great number of more playful resemblances to *Shadow of a Doubt:* Both films have key close-ups of their villainous protagonists accompanied by an expressive camera movement, as well as key scenes in which their young heroines express emotional vulnerability in the family garage. And as Uncle Charlie has a preference for pin-striped suits, the stepfather has a decided preference for striped shirts. For good measure, director Joseph Ruben includes references to Hitchcock's *Psycho* and *The Birds* as well as to Charles Laughton's *Night of the Hunter.*

Like *Shadow of a Doubt, The Stepfather* is filled with doubles: for instance, the unbalanced but competent stepfather physically resembles the psychologist (or "stress manager") who represents total psychological balance, if ultimately, incompetence. In one sense, Stephanie even has two boyfriends—her high school classmate, and the action-adventure hero whom the narrative apparently fatefully impels toward the inevitable rescue of Stephanie. Or is it inevitable? Whereas in *Shadow of a Doubt,* Charlie's detective boyfriend manages to stay around long enough for Hitchcock to imply a marriage for Charlie beyond the film's fade-out, Stephanie's would-be hero fails overwhelmingly—without even getting the chance to meet Stephanie—in one of the film's most shocking and surprising scenes.

What makes *The Stepfather* so fetching is the way it reworks the thematic considerations of *Shadow of a Doubt.* Whereas Uncle Charlie killed because he hated women as a result of a head accident when he was a little boy, the stepfather kills because he is so enamored of having a perfect family. Marrying one single mother after another, the stepfather tries to create the perfect nuclear family; and when that nuclear family fails to correspond to his (and society's) abnormally high expectations, he goes berserk, kills his family, and then tries again with a new identity and another family. At the climax of *The Stepfather,* there is an indelible moment when the antagonist, on the telephone, losing his mind and confused as to which life he is living, asks quietly, "Who am I here?" before perpetrating a shocking act of violence. A considerable component of the film's power derives from the authority which Terry O'Quinn brings to the role of the stepfather:

smiling and calm, he is half Pat Boone and half Robert Young of *Father Knows Best*—though covered with blood.

Although *Shadow of a Doubt* ended with the monster Uncle Charlie killed and the nuclear family intact, the ending had a melancholy undercurrent—for we knew that Charlie would marry her dull detective husband, and like her mother before her, would begin to lose her identity in the institution of the nuclear family, criticism of which Hitchcock only hinted at in the scene of Charlie's mother's emotional breakdown. *The Stepfather* ends as Stephanie and her mother realize that they cannot trust any men: for if men are worthy of being trusted, they are invariably too weak to be counted on (like the caring psychologist) or too hard-headed in their macho bravado (like the would-be hero) to be effective. The final scene has Stephanie cutting down the tall birdhouse which the stepfather had built in the exact image of their respectable middle-class home.

When *The Stepfather* is over, the men are all dead; the traditional values associated with home are shown to be good enough not even for the birds; and Stephanie and her mother, as two women alone, realize that they must fend for themselves without a man, in a more nontraditional, but healthier, family structure. If the Moral Majority in the eighties decries the decline of the nuclear family, *The Stepfather* rather celebrates that death as a good thing for women and children. If *Shadow of a Doubt* has sustained new generations of filmmakers, so too may *The Stepfather*, a film which was denied an extensive release or large commercial success, but which arguably represents the most successful and integrated reconsideration of Hitchcock's themes since Claude Chabrol's *Le Boucher*.

10
The Innocent-on-the-Run Thriller

Cary Grant, as Roger Thornhill in *North by Northwest*, has been arrested for drunken driving. In an attempt to clear his name and explain to the police a convoluted series of events, Thornhill goes to the United Nations to try to find the diplomat whose testimony can perhaps clear him. When he meets the diplomat, Thornhill is nonplussed, for the man is not the man Thornhill had anticipated, and the diplomat is oblivious to what has been going on in his own home. As Thornhill tries to think through the implications of what he has just learned, the diplomat suddenly opens his mouth wide and then collapses in Thornhill's arms. As he does so, the shocked Thornhill sees a knife in the man's back. Almost without realizing what he's doing, Thornhill reaches around behind the diplomat, grasps the knife, and pulls it out of the man's back. At that precise moment, onlookers begin to scream and a photographer in the room takes a picture of Thornhill—as if precisely in the act of stabbing the diplomat. Is it possible to explain? Can anyone believe the true story? Thornhill lets the body fall to the floor, drops the knife, and races out of the room, an innocent who must now run for his life until he can prove himself . . .

The innocent-on-the-run thriller is probably the genre most closely associated by the public with Alfred Hitchcock, who has made at least eight films of this variety. While Hitchcock and his collaborators undoubtedly pioneered in this genre, directors as distinguished and disparate as Fritz Lang, Stanley Donen, Alan J. Pakula, Arthur Hiller, and John Schlesinger have also worked in this genre.

The innocent-on-the-run thriller is organized around an innocent victim's coincidental entry into the midst of global intrigue; the victim often finds him or herself running from both the villains as well as the police. The protagonist proceeds to have an extensive series of adventures, meeting in the process a romantic interest whom he or she must learn to trust and who ultimately helps to provide a change in his or her moral outlook. In the course of the adventures, the innocent victim becomes, of necessity, the detective force. The antagonist or criminal element is generally divided into three (if not more) related adversaries.

Certain thematic ideas integrated into this generic structure again and

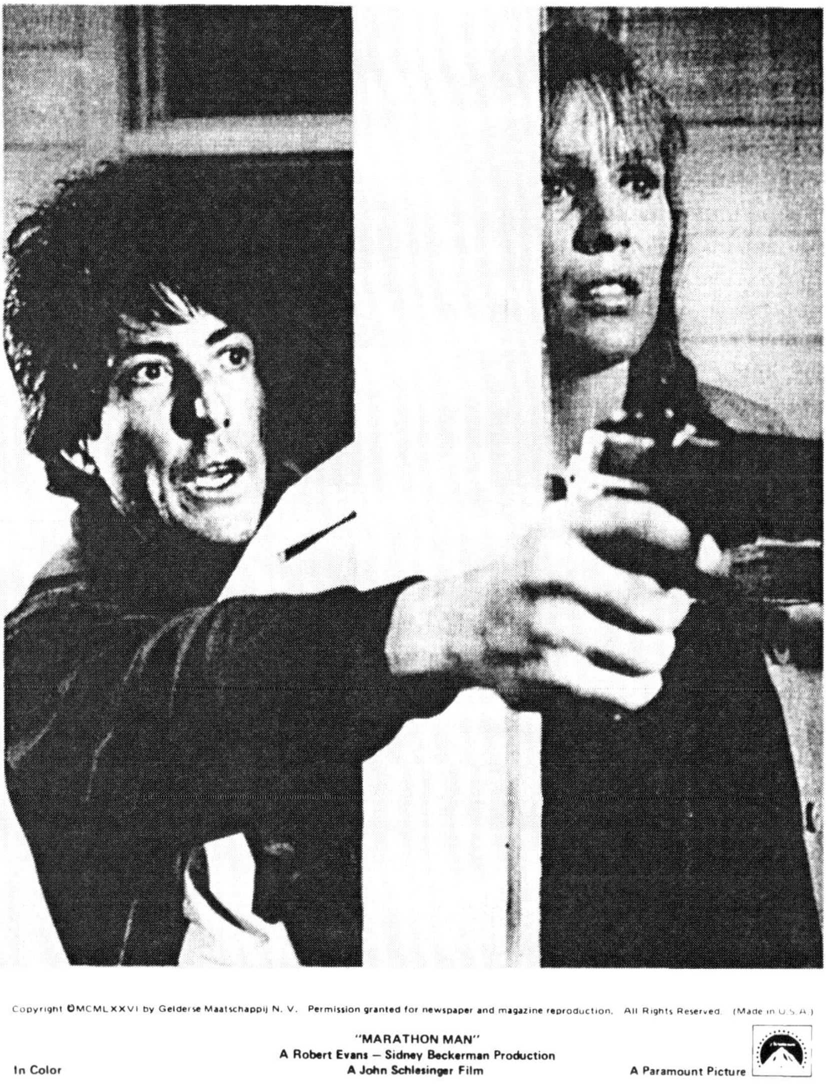

"MARATHON MAN"
A Robert Evans – Sidney Beckerman Production
A John Schlesinger Film

In Color

A Paramount Picture

The typical innocent-on-the-run protagonist often has a companion whose allegiance is only ambiguously given. Here, Dustin Hoffman uses Marthe Keller as a protective shield in *Marathon Man*.

again include the precariousness of the civilized world, the nearness of chaos and the possibility of the improbable, the significance of time and its relationship to fate, coincidence, suspense, and anxiety, the capacity of adventure to take on a "moral meaning," the pragmatic and often corrupt nature of political organizations and governments, and the absolute necessity for trust and commitment.

More specifically, these films tend to proceed along the following lines: the presentation of some "normal universe"; the introduction of the protagonist, who is generally irresponsible, or in a significant sense, morally uncommitted; an initial instance of coincidence which allows the protagonist to become involved in some murderous plot; the beginning of a series of confrontations between the protagonist and the villainous forces; the increased imposition of a chaotic world which challenges the protagonist to examine his or her lifestyle and to use intelligence and cunning in order to survive; the introduction of a love interest whose first response to the protagonist is either disdainful or ambiguous; the deflation of the protagonist's reputation and credibility in the eyes of the official authorities, often accompanied by the incrimination of the protagonist as a murderer as a result of various coincidental or circumstantial evidence contrived in part by the villains; and often a threatening of the protagonist with recognition and exposure in a public place as he or she tries to escape.

In addition, the innocent-on-the-run thriller tends to depict a generally antagonistic, erotic courtship between the protagonist and the love interest; a series of adventures characterized by constant reversals of expectations, generally including at least one instance in which the protagonist is enclosed in a space which requires creative escape; the eventual commitment of the love interest to the protagonist and vice-versa, indicating the need for trust; at least one separation of the protagonist and the love interest, followed by their subsequent reunion; the gradual uncovering of a conspiracy; the revelation of a MacGuffin, the pseudo-crucial and sought-after object around which the whole plot has (at least theoretically) revolved;[1] the complete eruption of chaos in one final set-piece; and the final resolution in which the villainy is vanquished, the protagonist and love interest are brought together once and for all, and the narrative is ended as some earlier threatening situation is humorously reprised as a fade-out joke.

A list of innocent-on-the-run thrillers would include the following:

The Man Who Knew Too Much (1934)
The 39 Steps (1935)
Young and Innocent (1937)
The Lady Vanishes (1938)
Foreign Correspondent (1940)
Saboteur (1942)
Ministry of Fear (1944)
The Man Who Knew Too Much (1955)
North by Northwest (1959)
The 39 Steps (1959)
The Prize (1963)
Charade (1963)
Arabesque (1966)
Torn Curtain (1966)
House of Cards (1969)
The Parallax View (1974)
Three Days of the Condor (1976)
Marathon Man (1976)
Silver Streak (1976)
The 39 Steps (1978)
Foul Play (1978)
Hanky Panky (1982)
Cloak and Dagger (1984)
Into the Night (1985)
After Hours (1985)
Jumpin' Jack Flash (1986)

In a psychoanalytic perspective, using Michael Balint's terminology, the typical innocent-on-the-run thriller presents a protagonist who is propelled by the plot to a philobatic adventure. In the course of the adventure, he or she must leave the safety zone of home and journey to both the physical and psychological philobatic outreaches before being able to return to the safety of home once again, although transformed by the adventure, altered by a more astute knowledge of both the nature of the world and his or her own psyche. While on the adventure, the protagonist confronts a variety of environments: an ocnophilic world in which there are countless objects to offer danger or threaten, a philobatic world in which there are few objects to offer security or provide equilibrium. Objects take on a life of their own, offering to the protagonist problems to be solved or alliances to be established; ultimately, the protagonist must evaluate a great number of significant objects, often finding the one ocnophilic object (or person) which can help the protagonist's navigation of the philobatic spaces.

These thrillers can also be recognized by the presence of various other elements, including an attempted or successful assassination, a MacGuffin (the microfilm, secret treaty clause, or other special object sought by the protagonist and villains alike), a constant intrusion of threatening objects, at least one antagonist who is sympathetic and charming, false identities, characters presumably killed or thought dead "coming back to life," friends of the protagonist turning out to be enemies; one or more kidnappings—sometimes of the protagonist by the villains, often of the love interest by the protagonist; a proof that disappears and therefore reduces the credibility of the protagonist, variations of the chase which include attendant apparatus of pursuit and escape, constant movement through the use of objects such as cars, trucks, boats, planes, and especially, trains; dialogue which consistently has double meanings, particularly that spoken between the protagonist and the love interest; a general construction by set-pieces, a blonde heroine, and occasionally, an ultimate *deus ex machina.*

Of course each of the thrillers listed on the previous page not contain all of the elements articulated above. The elements, rather, comprise a complex which is available to these films in a variety of configurations. Even when a film excludes an element or group of elements, the genre is generally modified or extended rather than subverted. For instance, the only innocent-on-the-run thriller on the list above that lacks a love interest to share the protagonist's adventures is *The Parallax View*. It is not surprising then, that because this film lacks a potential human object for the hero's trust and commitment, *The Parallax View* should also become the only film on this list in which the protagonist does not survive; after forty years of evolution, the genre thus may now sometimes express a tragic sensibility.

Undoubtedly, the genesis of this genre can be traced to the increased political tensions in Europe after World War I and the popular expression of these tensions in a variety of novels and in the cinema in Hitchcock's series of British thrillers, begun with *The Man Who Knew Too Much* (in 1934), continued with *The 39 Steps* (in 1935) and *Young and Innocent* (in 1937), and climaxed with *The Lady Vanishes* (in 1938).

If *The Man Who Knew Too Much* does not seem quite typical to the genre, it may be because the married status of its protagonist deprives the film of the precise brand of sexual tension which would become a hallmark of the genre. In its story of a married couple who accidentally stumbles upon an assassination plot, one can nevertheless recognize other of the genre's elements, including the initial coincidence which involves the protagonist in global intrigues, a series of adventures, and an eventual assassination attempt. Although the protagonist is never suspected of murder, he is nevertheless estranged from the police when the villains kidnap his child and forbid contact with the police. Other elements include the kidnapping itself, the MacGuffin (which in this case is knowledge of the time when a certain dignitary is to be assassinated), and the exotic and symbolic locations, which range from the Alps to Albert Hall.

Still, it is Hitchcock's 1935 film *The 39 Steps* (remade twice: by Ralph Nelson in 1959 and by Don Sharp in 1978) which must be considered the seminal innocent-on-the-run thriller. In this film, Robert Donat plays Richard Hannay, the protagonist who gets coincidentally involved in the international intrigue of a spy ring, runs from the police who think him responsible for the murder of a female spy, falls in love with the cool hesitant blonde played by Madeleine Carroll, exposes the conspiratorial plot, identifies the MacGuffin (which turns out to be secrets memorized by the music hall performer Mr. Memory), and wins the trust and love of the heroine only after both of them have undergone a series of adventures. One particularly engaging sequence has Hannay escaping from his pursuers by ducking into an enclosed hall, where, mistaken for a political candidate, he must make a speech in order to avoid being caught by the villains.

The 39 Steps is one of Hitchcock's most admired films; it has been extensively analyzed by others and probably needs very little additional exegesis. Its value rests not only in the way it manages to define the innocent-on-the-run thriller by incorporating virtually all the elements described at the beginning of this chapter, but also in the way it incorporates these elements in a consistent narrative tone which perfectly balances suspense, mystery, comedy, and romance.

If *The Lady Vanishes* seems a more gentle and charming film, it is because it is one of the few films in this genre with a woman as the protagonist. Like *The 39 Steps*, its construction is seminal to the genre. Particularly memorable is the disappearing evidence which makes everyone doubt the protagonist's story that Miss Froy has been kidnapped, including the scene (imitated in 1977's *Silver Streak*) in which a name, written on the window, disappears while the train is going through a tunnel. Notable too is the disguise of one of the villains as a nun, later given away by her tell-tale high heels; and perhaps, most charmingly, the MacGuffin's identity as the simple tune whistled by Miss Froy, which turns out to be a coded secret which must be communicated to the British authorities at all costs. *The Lady Vanishes* is probably most important for its use of the train: a romantic conveyance which has become conventional to the genre and which is reflected in films such as *North by Northwest* and *Silver Streak*.

The confusing politics of post–World War I Europe is reflected in all these Hitchcock films: spies, counterspies, government agencies, anarchists. Indeed, these films can be understood in direct relationship to the breakdown of political stability. A detective element is generally absent, because its presence would imply that some control could be restored as a matter of process. Although these films usually end with peace restored, the restoration is at best only temporary, and there is the implicit sense of a continuing struggle, an uneasy balance, another political chaos just around the corner. It is significant that although the innocent-on-the-run thrillers consistently have political underpinnings, their political content changes from era to era with little revision necessary to the basic generic elements.

In the films of the thirties, the villains are anarchists, spies, or agents from Central European countries; in the films of the forties, the villains become Nazis; in *North by Northwest* and the films of the Cold War era, the villains become Communists; in the 1969 *House of Cards*, the villains are right-wing Frenchmen; and in the thrillers of the seventies like *Three Days of the Condor*, the villains include even agencies of the United States government. Although up to the late seventies these films increasingly criticize the political structures which allow the protagonist to have adventures of this sort (such as in *North by Northwest*, for instance, in which Cary Grant's Roger Thornhill is presented clearly by the end of the film as morally superior to the pragmatic government agent played by Leo G. Carroll), the criticism is generally cursory, and the emphasis is on the excitement of the protagonist's adventures. Only the post–Watergate, pre–Reagan, innocent-on-the-run thrillers at all forcefully take exception to this pattern. In any case, the generic structure of the innocent-on-the-run thriller is not automatically connected to any particular politics, and as such, can be used quite easily to work for or against any political point.

It is not surprising that when Hitchcock came to America he should have chosen an innocent-on-the-run thriller as one of his first projects. *Foreign Correspondent*, directed in 1940, was specifically made as a propaganda film to alert Americans to the real danger of the Nazis; the choice of this genre as the vehicle for this message seems particularly appropriate, in that its basic structure compelling an uncommitted protagonist toward commitment can work on a concrete political level as well as a psychological level.

The first image of *Foreign Correspondent* is a spinning globe ultimately revealed as at the top of the newspaper building in which the protagonist works. The globe functions as a visual correlative so symptomatic of the thriller, in this case referring both to World War II, which would undoubtedly set the world spinning, and to the thriller itself, which requires chaotic intrigue and changing locations. The protagonist's identity as a conventional "uncommitted protagonist" is made clear by his average-sounding name, Johnny Jones, and by his characterization as a "fresh, unused mind."

By his editor, he is rechristened Huntley Haverstock, a new name which will eventually represent his new, committed life as well. The editor asks him to go to Europe and report on the story he finds. His first specific assignment is to talk to the diplomat Van Meer about a particular upcoming treaty, a specific clause of which develops into the film's MacGuffin. When Haverstock (played by one of America's most likeable, but not quite larger-than-life stars, Joel McCrea) gets to London, he coincidentally meets Van Meer in the street, and the two share a cab—the fortuity which allows the plot to go forward.

Two set-pieces follow. The first takes place in Amsterdam and marks the arrival of dignitaries at a press conference. It is a dirty, rainy day; the steps outside the convocation hall are lined with reporters and observers who wear trench coats and carry black umbrellas. Van Meer makes his way up the stairs; but when Haverstock approaches, the old man clearly doesn't recognize him. Suddenly, a photographer comes up to "Van Meer" and shoots him with a gun hidden by his camera. There is a shock cut of the man's bloody face; he then rolls down the stairs. The chase sequence of Haverstock pursuing the assassin is played against the bobbing black umbrellas, the panic in the crowd, the sudden pandemonium. This sequence presents the generic element of assassination, as well as of the imposter who takes on an assumed identity. Because of Haverstock's coincidental earlier meeting with Van Meer in the street, Haverstock alone knows that it was not Van Meer who was assassinated, but an imposter; Haverstock is thus put in the position of the only potential agent for good.

The second set-piece takes place after Haverstock follows the car of the assassin to a deserted expanse where sit three windmills. There is no trace of the car, which seems to have evaporated into thin air. When the wind blows Haverstock's hat from his head, he becomes conscious of the wind and realizes that one of the windmills has been turning the wrong direction temporarily: this as a signal for a plane to land in order to aid the assassin in his escape. As usual in the suspense thriller, objects (such as the camera, the windmill, the hat) are often the most important determinants of the plot. Investigating inside the windmill, Haverstock finds evil Nazis waiting for the plane as well as the real Van Meer, who is their prisoner. A suspense sequence follows as Haverstock's coat gets caught in the windmill gear and he barely escapes detection. When he returns to the windmill with the police, the Nazis have escaped and all the evidence which could verify Haverstock's story is, typical to the genre, completely gone.

The conventional sequence in which the protagonist must escape an enclosed location takes place later in the film when Haverstock is visited in his Amsterdam hotel room by two policemen who come to talk about his story. When Haverstock notices that his phone wire has been cut, he realizes that the two men are really villains. He goes into the bathroom on the pretense of taking a quick shower and then sneaks out the window. While crawling over the rooftop, Haverstock knocks into a portion of the neon hotel sign, thus altering it from "HOTEL EUROPE" to "HOT EUROPE," again a visual correlative. Haverstock's escape problem is compounded by the fact that he needs to get back into the room (which is undoubtedly still being guarded) in order to get his clothes. His clever solution is to send window washers, a tailor, a maid, room service, and others into his room so that his own messenger can retrieve his clothes undetected in the confusion.

The romantic interest in *Foreign Correspondent* is Carol Fisher (played by Laraine Day), the daughter of the peace party leader Stephen Fisher (played by Herbert Marshall). The romance between Carol and Haverstock is typical to the genre: it gets off to a shaky start when Haverstock unthinkingly criticizes the peace organization she is associated with. Later, Haverstock embarrasses Carol by escaping half-naked to her room in front of guests, humiliates her by an action she mistakes for a crude proposition, and finally attempts to get her father arrested and executed as a traitor. Typically, Carol's traitorous father is a very charming man whom we initially respect and sympathize with. Perhaps the most disturbing sequence of *Foreign Correspondent* is the one in which Fisher's true evil is made absolutely clear when he visits the hotel room where the real Van Meer is being held prisoner. Until this sequence, most of the film has been very funny; the mood now turns increasingly somber.

The Nazi villains shine a photoelectric floodlight on the old and weak Van Meer (played movingly by Albert Basserman), whose mind is wandering under the torture. But even a tortured Van Meer retains his integrity and eloquence: "You cry peace, Fisher, and there is no peace — only war and death." The speech overtly parallels the famous Patrick Henry speech ("Gentlemen may cry peace, peace, but there is no peace; the war is already begun!"), and undoubtedly works to connect with the patriotic sensibilities of American audiences. After expressing his moving sentiments that the Nazis will never conquer the little people everywhere who feed the birds, Van Meer is then tortured. The torture is offscreen, and because we cannot see exactly what is happening, it becomes all the more horrifying. We hear Van Meer's hideous screams, as the camera reveals the involuntary shudders of a female Nazi dressed in black, who, despite her evil, cannot bear

to watch. Fisher is a willing accomplice to the torture, and we can no longer regard the Nazis as mere adversaries in some comic adventure.

Hitchcock's device of the initially sympathetic villain works as an example of the package act described so well by Altan Löker. By our initial sympathy with Fisher and our desire to have his peace party succeed, we have implicated ourselves in the torture of Van Meer. Our only choice, therefore, is now to become anti-Nazi and renounce our pacifist sympathies (as Fisher himself does symbolically in the film's final sequence when he sacrifices himself so that the "good" characters can live).

Other sequences in *Foreign Correspondent* impress as unique even as they comply with generic conventions: one very long sequence handled almost completely for laughs in which a Mr. Rowley (played by Edmund Gwenn) tries to kill Haverstock, climaxing with Rowley's attempt—amazingly delayed and extended until the suspense is excruciating—to push Haverstock off the top of a cathedral; a sequence in which Carol is "kidnapped" for her own good by the protagonist; and a final, extraordinary air and water sequence in which the plane that is flying the main characters back to the United States is attacked by the Germans on the first day of the war and crashes into the torrential waters—all of which is handled with an expressive moving camera and rhythmic montage.

The film ends with Haverstock finally united with Carol and truly committed, giving a radio broadcast from London during the blitz. The lights go out, but Haverstock, at some danger to himself and his heroine, insists on trying to get the message through. "It's death coming to London," he intones dramatically in the dark over the transatlantic cable, "Keep those lights on, America. Cover them with steel, America!"

Because *Foreign Correspondent* was so successful, Hitchcock directed another innocent-on-the-run thriller very soon afterwards. Like *Foreign Correspondent, Saboteur* (directed in 1942) appealed to American patriotic instincts. While *Foreign Correspondent*'s propagandistic theme was American commitment in the struggle against the Nazis, *Saboteur*'s propagandistic theme was the necessity of continued vigilance against the subversion from within of the American war effort and way of life.

Saboteur begins with an image of a shadowed figure walking slowly across the steel gate of an airplane factory. Hitchcock then introduces the protagonist, Barry Kane (played by Robert Cummings), who almost immediately experiences the initial coincidence which propels the plot forward: he bumps into Fry (the saboteur) and glimpses an address on one of Fry's letters. A return to the image of the steel gate, this time gradually covered by billowing black smoke, is followed by the famous reaction shot of people rising in succession from the background to the foreground, ending with one single head suddenly filling the frame. As all the men race

The aftermath to the assassination of the Minister in *Foreign Correspondent*.

to help put out the fire, Fry hands a fire extinguisher to Barry Kane, who in turn hands it to his friend, who is instantly burned to death when he attempts to use it. Later, while visiting his friend's mother, Kane overhears the police saying that the fire extinguisher was filled with gasoline. Thus, the initial situation has been set: the protagonist, falsely accused of sabotage and the murder of his friend, becomes a fugitive from justice who will soon be both on the track of and on the run from the villains as well.

Barry Kane's normal world is thrown into chaos; and yet, there is value in a life of excitement. When the truck on which Kane is hitchhiking is stopped by the police, the truckdriver is gleeful, so tired is he of the monotony of his day-to-day existence. Later, the truckdriver will quite consciously help Kane elude the police, not only because the truckdriver implicitly believes Kane's innocence, but because he profoundly wishes to share in Kane's great moral adventure.

Characteristically, the criminal element is segmented into a number of villains: the initial saboteur Fry—a short, negligible, rather unpleasant man; the elegant and sophisticated Charles Tobin—a rather charming villain who presages incarnations such as Phillip Vandamm in *North by Northwest* or Devereau in *Silver Streak;* and Mr. Freeman—a rather pathetic villain who talks about his family, and like Leonard in *North by Northwest,* seems to be homosexual. During Kane's notable first meeting with Charles Tobin, Tobin is initially charming and benevolent; the two of them sit chatting around the swimming pool.

When Tobin no longer feels the need to keep up his pretense of respectability, he turns obviously evil. Kane makes an escape using Susie, Tobin's baby granddaughter, as a hostage, thus overtly countering Tobin's evil with symbolic innocence. In a later confrontation between Tobin and Kane, Tobin is photographed in a specially composed shot: he is dressed in black, sitting self-assuredly in the middle of a short couch slightly on the right side of the frame, flanked by two symmetrical pictures, and balanced by a lampshade on the left side of the frame. Tobin appears particularly secure and unassailable as he calls Kane a member of the "moron millions" who live "small, complacent lives" oblivious to and ignorant of the "competence of totalitarian nations." Kane is not impressed. "The world's choosing up sides," he counters in a speech of his own. "We're not soft, we're strong. And we'll win if we fight from now till the cows come home!"

Saboteur, like most suspense thrillers, constantly plays upon the spectator's expectations. At one point, a handcuffed Kane wanders into a cabin where a kindly old man helps him. Kane goes out of his way to try to conceal his handcuffs, for fear the man will realize he is a wanted criminal. The surprise reversal is that the man is blind and therefore can't see the handcuffs. But Kane is still not safe: for then Patricia, the man's niece (played by Priscilla Lane), returns to the cabin and herself sees the handcuffs. The situation reverses again as it turns out the blind man knew that Kane was

Priscilla Lane and Robert Cummings (in jacket) seek sanctuary in a circus train car in Alfred Hitchcock's *Saboteur;* others, left to right, Pedro de Cordoba, Billy Curtis, and Anita Bolster.

wearing handcuffs all along and even convinces Patricia not to turn Kane in. In fact, the blind man becomes an elegant, if obvious metaphor for the rightness of American society: "My duty as an American citizen is to believe a man is innocent until proven guilty. My duty is sometimes to disregard the law. I can see intangible things."

Still, Patricia refuses to trust Kane. When she tries to take him to the police, Kane virtually kidnaps her into helping him. Perhaps the central scene which works to establish their more trusting relationship is the famous one (scripted by Dorothy Parker) in which Kane tries to hitch a ride on a train car inhabited by circus freaks. The freaks in their car represent international factions in microcosm. The bizarre characters include Esmeralda, the bearded lady, whose mind is always on sex; Bones, the human skeleton, who is the great moral force for democracy; Titania, the human mountain; the Siamese twins who can't agree on anything ("I tossed and turned all night," complains one); and the Major, a fascist midget whose stature accurately reflects the fact that he cares only about himself.

The freaks must decide whether or not to turn in Kane and Patricia to the police who are searching the train. Bones becomes the legislative force and notes that the twins, as usual, are on opposite sides; Titania, as usual, is on both sides; Esmeralda, as usual, is undecided and will apathetically allow whatever will happen to happen; and the rest, as usual, are ignorant of the facts. The Major finds the whole thing subversive. Because this is a democracy, says Bones, we must vote. Knowing that the vote will come to a stalemate if Esmeralda abstains, Bones forces her to take a stand for once in her life. Esmeralda, who has been watching the couple and finding faith and trust (which are not really there) in Patricia's eyes, votes to protect them. Only then, when shamed by Esmeralda's faith, does Patricia finally commit herself to Kane.

A spiritually joined Kane and Patricia continue their adventures; at least twice they are separated and reunited. The generic sequence of enclosure requiring creative escape takes place when both Kane and Patricia find themselves virtual prisoners in a gigantic ballroom filled with dancers. The ball is being given by Mrs. Sutton, a matronly socialite whose reputation is beyond question, but who is actually an associate of Charles Tobin and a member of the spy ring herself. Of course none of the guests will believe the seemingly preposterous story of Kane, who is taken for an oaf. Still, the exits are blocked, and he and Patricia cannot escape. The two of them dance; someone cuts in—is it a diabolical plot? It is; and Patricia's new dancing partner dances her upstairs, and she is retaken prisoner. Kane starts to make a speech to warn everyone that the hostess is really a spy, but when he realizes a gun is trained on him, must give up his plan and instead achieve only a small victory by announcing that Mrs. Sutton will auction off a piece of the famous Sutton jewels and then forcing her to do so.

Saboteur builds to three sequences, each of which works as an enclosed set-piece. First is the suspense sequence in which Kane and Patricia separately try to make their way to the dock where the saboteurs plan to bomb a battleship as it is being christened: Kane's efforts to get through the line of the officials, Patricia's efforts to escape from her skyscraper prison, and the saboteurs' efforts to consummate their scheme are all juxtaposed as the seconds count down to the christening.

The second set-piece, one of Hitchcock's most interesting sequences, works as a self-reflective comment on the relationship between the suspense thriller and its audience. When the saboteur Fry escapes, he runs into a movie theatre where a thriller is being shown (although perhaps a comedy thriller, because the audience is laughing). The gunshots from the screen coincide with the gunshots from *Saboteur*'s own fictional reality. From the screen, we hear the dialogue, "Get out, get out; not that way," while in the "real" theatre, people begin rushing outside to safety when they realize that a real man in the theatre has inexplicably been killed. This sequence reflects our ironic response to suspense thrillers (if not to all movies): they entertain us while they are not real and represent only symbolic thrills, but they would disturb us, were they real and presented actual dangers. The sequence resembles a Chinese box: the fictional audience laughs at the murder on the movie screen until the murder impinges on its own reality; we in the theatre watching *Saboteur* cannot help but laugh and be entertained at the murderous juxtapositions in the fictional theatre, although we may half expect to hear real gunshots behind us as we watch the movie.

The third set-piece represents the final eruption of chaos so characteristic to the innocent-on-the-run thriller. Kane and Patricia's pursuit of Fry culminates on top of the Statue of Liberty; when Fry begins to fall from the torch, Kane rushes to his rescue. The montage images are all very formal; the consistent photographing of the Statue of Liberty at Dutch angles suggests the wartime vulnerability of the democracies. The sequence is prolonged, and both men dangle precariously. Only after the seams of Fry's coat finally give way after excruciating suspense (his life having literally hung by a thread) does Fry fall from the statue to his death. In a reversal of the similar rescue in *North by Northwest* seventeen years later, Patricia then helps Kane back up to safety.

Another significant film in this genre, *Ministry of Fear*, directed in 1944 by Fritz Lang and based on a novel by Graham Greene, reflects the generic interest in objects (and indeed, is often remembered and identified as "the film with the cake"). The film begins with the image of a pendulum of a clock, an image which underscores the theme of time and its relationship to suspense. As the narrative begins, the protagonist Stephen Neale (played by Ray Milland) is just being released from Lembridge Asylum and psychologically in need of an adventure to renew his psyche. One of Stephen's first actions is to attend a charity bazaar given by the Mothers of the Free Nations. A fortune teller tells him that she cannot tell the future, because it is against the law, but she can tell him his past and his present; Stephen expresses some ambiguous guilt to the fortune teller. The sequence ends with the protagonist winning the famous cake by most accurately estimating its weight.

Unbeknownst to Stephen, the cake is actually the film's MacGuffin, containing what the British authorities will later call "the new embarkation plans on our mine fields." The protagonist is then mistaken for the spy who was to have picked up the cake; thus, as a result of the initial coincidence associated with this genre, Stephen has become the innocent victim caught up in a plot of intrigue. Later, the spy who was supposed to have picked up the cake is killed during a séance. When Stephen is blamed for his murder, the genre's formula becomes complete as the protagonist finds himself on the run from the police as well. In this genre, things are rarely what they initially seem to be: blind men often can see, a cake is never just a cake, and those who are killed may sometimes remain alive. The "dead" spy continues his villainy when he makes another appearance later in the film.

The love interest in *Ministry of Fear* is provided by the blonde Carla (played by Marjorie Reynolds). The trusting relationship between Stephen and Carla is established in the London subway during a blitz, when Stephen confesses that he had bought lethal drugs with the intention of administering them to his dying wife. Although he had changed his mind about the mercy killing, his wife discovered the drugs and took them herself; as punishment, he was sent to the asylum. The organization that Carla and her brother run resembles the peace organization in *Foreign Correspondent;* we eventually find out that the organization is actually a front for Nazi activity, and that Carla's brother (like Carol's father) is a primary villain.

At the film's climax, in an apartment room illumined only by the hallway light which comes through the open door, an unbelieving Carla confronts her brother and discovers that he is a Nazi. The brother, positive that even though Carla has a gun, she will be psychologically unable to stop him, leaves the room and slams the door. For one instant, when the door slams, the screen goes completely black as the light source is cut off; and then, in a bravura effect, one dot of light appears through the door as the bullet goes through; Carla has shot her brother through the door.

The series of adventures has, as usual, a particular moral significance for the protagonist. Purged of his guilt for having allowed his wife to die, Stephen is able to begin a new life with Carla. The film ends with a fade-out joke so typical to the genre: Stephen and Carla are driving along the beach, discussing their imminent marriage. "I've always dreamed of a big wedding," says Carla, "with flowers . . . and a cake." "Cake!" responds Stephen, shocked at the possibility of the whole adventure beginning once again. Ending the film with a joke seems to be a way of disengaging the spectator from the thrills and of civilizing what was earlier represented as horrifying. Yet even this final joke relates to the suspense thriller's propensity for dualities: two killed relatives, two marriages for the protagonist, and potentially, two cakes.

Two major films in the genre were both released in 1959: a remake of *The 39 Steps*, directed by Ralph Thomas (very similar in plot to the Hitchcock version, but crucially different in style and tone), and Hitchcock's own *North by Northwest. North by Northwest* has been analyzed so many times (by Robin Wood, Raymond Bellour, Donald Spoto, Raymond Durgnat, and others) that a scene-by-scene analysis seems unnecessary here.

Actually, *North by Northwest,* a classic certainly, does not seem to adhere to the generic structure as much as to define it: the protagonist Roger Thornhill (played by Cary Grant) is a Madison Avenue man with two ex-wives who finds a new moral center as a result of his adventures. Thornhill is kidnapped by the villains when he is coincidentally mistaken for George Kaplan, a secret agent who turns out never to have existed in the first place; when he returns with the police to the scene to which he was kidnapped, the proof has disappeared and he is held up to ridicule; he is then framed for the assassination of a United Nations diplomat, which sets him running from the police as well as from the villains. In another coincidence, he meets Eve Kendall (played by Eva Marie Saint), with whom he falls in love and has an antagonistic, erotic courtship; and of course he eventually wins the heroine to his side, clears his name, vanquishes the villains, and lives happily ever after, a new man. The film moves from location to location and from set-piece to set-piece, including the famous crop-dusting sequence, as well as another striking sequence requiring creative escape in which Thornhill is a virtual prisoner in the midst of a crowded auction hall, and the famous, final climactic pursuit across the stone faces of Mount Rushmore.

I have previously noted how suspense thrillers in general construct themselves in terms of dualities, countering one scene with another, one antagonistic encounter with a second. This construction works to create in the spectator subconscious expectations that certain things will recur so that formal values will be upheld; waiting for these expectations to be fulfilled creates suspense. For instance, in the opening scene of *North by Northwest* in which Thornhill sits at the hotel table with his business acquaintances, he is photographed (without reason, it would seem) from a low angle which emphasizes the size of the drink in front of him. This shot has its double later, when Thornhill is force-fed the large drink by Vandamm's henchmen and is again photographed from below, the out-sized glass taking precedence in the frame. The stylistic duality establishes a connection between the two events: that is, coming to that hotel, and being pursued by the villains.

In *North by Northwest,* doublings such as this are constant. There are two police rescues of Thornhill: first, when the police stop him while he is driving drunkenly; second, when they rescue him from Vandamm's henchmen at the auction. Twice Thornhill visits the mansion supposedly inhabited by Vandamm, and twice Thornhill takes someone else's taxi. There are two visits to the Plaza Hotel in New York—once for lunch, once to trace Kaplan; and there are two coincidences which propel the plot—first, Thornhill's being mistaken for Kaplan; second, Thornhill's meeting of Eve at the railway station. Twice Thornhill finds himself in Eve's upper berth—once when he is hiding from the police and again during the film's final fade-out joke when they are about to consummate their marriage. There are two train stations, two different hotels (one in Chicago and one in New York), two different mansions (one in New York and one in Rapid City), and two different airplanes (one in Rapid City and one in Chicago, neither of which we see being boarded).

At different times both Thornhill and Eve are officially fugitives from justice: Thornhill when he has supposedly assassinated the United Nations diplomat, Eve when she has supposedly assassinated Thornhill in the Rapid City restaurant. Twice Thornhill waits for his clothes before he can

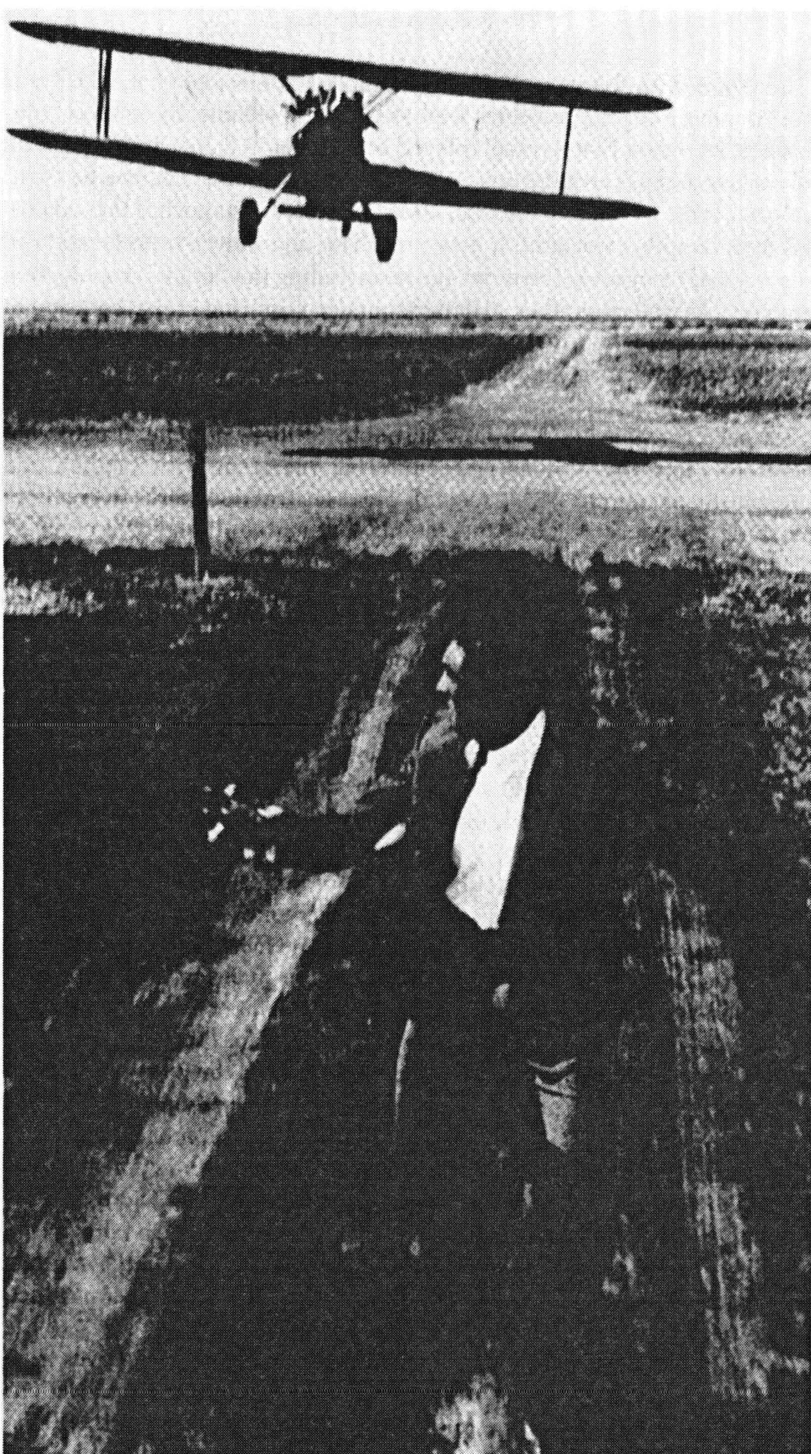

continue his adventures, and twice punches are thrown directly into the camera at a moment of realization—the first thrown at Thornhill as he realizes that Eve is planning to go with Vandamm and that the Professor (played by Leo G. Carroll) has actually double-crossed Thornhill, the second thrown at Leonard (played by Martin Landau) by Vandamm as Vandamm realizes that Eve has double-crossed him and did not really kill Thornhill.

Particularly expressive are the two instances in which the frame is composed in extreme long shot with Thornhill on the left side and someone else on the right side, both figures separated by space. This composition occurs first in the crop-dusting sequence, in which Thornhill faces the farmer standing silently on the other side of the road; Thornhill is unsure of their exact relationship—is the farmer his adversary? This image usually elicits laughter, in part because the formal structure so succinctly expresses its thematic idea.

This composition is repeated when Thornhill faces Eve after her pretend assassination of him in front of Vandamm. Can it truly be she is no longer an adversary? For the first time, Thornhill is aware of her identity and able to trust her; this is underscored by the fact that although there is space between them, the space is not empty (as in the former scene) but filled with trees, certainly a symbol of permanence and growth.

In a later sequence in which the housekeeper holds Thornhill prisoner in the Rapid City mansion, her arms are arranged exactly the same as the statue/lamp behind her; and she is no more effective as a terrorist than her alter-object, for when she shoots Thornhill, it marks the second time that he is shot with a gun loaded with blanks. This kind of doubling in *North by Northwest* is not merely imposed onto the structure, but emerges through it as an important component in the subconscious propagation of suspense.

The success of *North by Northwest* was enormous; indeed, one could argue that *North by Northwest* crystallized and influenced the film popularity of a type of story already popular in fifties literature: the extravagant super-spy. The popularity of the super-spy seems directly related to the presidency of John F. Kennedy, the Cold War, and the glamour associated with the CIA. Although the super-spy films reveal many resemblances to the innocent-on-the-run thrillers, their differences are ultimately quite significant.

This analysis of the suspense thriller has so far avoided extended discussion of the spy film primarily because the universe of the spy is a very ambiguous territory: can one, for instance, analyze the spy's position in relation to the crime triumvirate of detective/criminal/victim? The spy can

Cary Grant in one of the most famous images from *North by Northwest:* in Michael Balint's terms, a threatening object contributing to a dangerous, philobatic empty space.

sometimes be the protagonist-detective uncovering other spy criminals; the spy can sometimes be a double agent and would-be victim of some other spy ring's antagonistic force; or he or she can sometimes be the villainous secret agent who is actually a criminal undermining "our" side. More confusingly, the spy can be a combination of two or more of these identities or evolve within the course of one work from one of these identities to another.

Thus, one cannot easily chart the position of the spy film on the triangular crime grid, because the spy belongs nowhere, or more precisely, everywhere—perhaps in the very center of the triangle. The very concept of spying implies secrecy; and secrecy implies the impossibility of a clear distinction between the theoretically disparate elements of detective/criminal/victim. A thorough study of those spy films which cannot be subsumed under one of the typical genres of the suspense thriller requires a separate work beyond the scope of this volume.

If the professional spy is an ambiguous and problematic protagonist, James Bond is not. As Martin Maloney has pointed out, James Bond is not so much a spy as an assassin; his job is not to keep his identity secret, but to accomplish some preordained mission which consists in part of assassination.[2] Even though the James Bond and other super-spy films of the sixties and seventies avail themselves of many of the elements of the innocent-on-the-run thriller (such as thrills, pursuit and escape, an emphasis on things, secret identities, and so forth), their use of a professional protagonist irrevocably results in a very different attitude and tone. A film like *Dr. No* ultimately presents a kind of process; we watch James Bond do his job and admire his professionalism.

In *Dr. No,* the protagonist is no longer, like Roger Thornhill in *North by Northwest,* a character who could be one of us, a man who coincidentally gets involved; he is, rather, a character who we, perhaps, would like to be, a man who has consciously chosen his profession because of the glamour and excitement it affords him. Thus, the adventure is divested of its moral implications, love and commitment are replaced with sexual conquest, and the confrontation is altered from a personal one to a professional one. In films such as *In Like Flint,* the Bondian protagonist evolves into an almost comic-book super-hero, and the adventure becomes overtly fantastic.

Perhaps these super-spy films of the sixties and seventies can best be characterized (although in their most outrageous form) by an advertisement appearing in *Variety* in 1977 for a super-spy film then in preproduction entitled *An Orchid for No. 1,* No. 1 being the name of its Bondian protagonist. The ad pictures a handsome man in a tuxedo, about to shoot two phallic guns in the general direction of the four seminude women of different nationalities who surround him. According to the text of the ad, the film features "No. 1 and his two .357 combat magnums; beautiful Carlotta Muff; Lucifer Orchid, the villain who wants power and burns midgets with a lighter that throws thirty foot flames; Jensen Fury, the 'hyper agent' who carries two automatic .45's and wants No. 1's head; the Logotza, a car that has a six foot ejecting circular buzz saw that cuts other cars in half; giants, midgets, helicopters, beautiful women, assassins, a one-eyed surgeon, a drowning room, jet planes, a duplicate No. 1, exploding people, and exotic locations."[3] The hype is outrageous, perhaps—but certainly typical of these films' increasing interest in sensation.

If *North by Northwest* greatly influenced these super-spy films, it also specifically influenced 1963's *The Prize,* directed by Mark Robson from a script by Ernest Lehman, the screenwriter of *North by Northwest. The Prize* deals with the intrigue and chaos which breaks out behind the scenes of the Nobel prize ceremonies. Paul Newman plays Andrew Craig, a writer who is scheduled to receive the prize for literature; a noncommitted, sexually active man, Craig regards himself as somewhat of a fraud and intends to expose himself as such during the ceremonies. The initial coincidence that propels the adventurous plot and involves Craig is directly out of *Foreign Correspondent.* Craig accidentally meets Dr. Max Stratman (played by Edward G. Robinson), who is to receive the Nobel prize for physics; when Stratman later seems to have no memory of this brief encounter, Craig realizes the new "Stratman" is an imposter, leading to his involvement in a series of adventures while he tries to prove his story.

At one point, Craig comes across a dead body; when he returns to the supposed scene of the crime, the evidence has disappeared, and the police think him drunken and irresponsible. When, however, the lady occupying the room which housed the body takes a step back, the camera is careful to reveal the sinister shadow which crosses her face, as if to assure the spectator that Craig has not, after all, been seeing things. (The shot works the same as one in *North by Northwest* in which Hitchcock allows the spectator one quick and ominous view of a villainous conspirator, disguised as a gardener pretending to trim the shrubs.) At another point in Craig's adventures, a car tries to run him over as he hitchhikes; this scene of the protagonist being attacked by a black car on a dark night can almost be seen as the cliché which Lehman (and Hitchcock) inverted in the parallel crop-dusting scene in *North by Northwest.*

The scene of enclosure requiring creative escape takes place when, running from the villains, Craig takes refuge in a lecture hall filled with nudists listening to a speech. Craig tries to become "invisible" by leaving his clothes at the door. When he discovers that the villains are not about to leave, he follows Thornhill's gambit in the parallel auction scene in *North by Northwest* and creates a ruckus which climaxes with the police arriving to arrest him, incidentally saving him from the villains. "Easy does it," says Craig to the police, slyly adding the exact line Thornhill uses in *North by Northwest:* "Why do you think I sent for you?"

The love interest is provided by Elke Sommer, who plays Inger

Andersen, the Swedish hostess assigned to keep Craig comfortable. There is much dialogue between Inger and Craig relating to the conjoined ideas of nymphomania and frigidity; Inger is compared sexually to a smorgasbord, even though she constantly appears the cool, icy blonde. The relationship between Craig and Inger is, conventional to the genre, antagonistic and erotic. In fact, when Craig solves the mystery and finds both the real Stratman as well as Inger (from whom he had been separated), the first exchanged dialogue is a bit of sexual repartee, which is only then followed by the hasty plot explanation of a twin brother and a planned anti-American acceptance speech.

The climax of *The Prize*, like the climaxes of *North by Northwest* and *Saboteur*, has its protagonist and one of the villains struggling at a high elevation. Thankfully, the police intercede as *deus ex machina* and shoot the villain, who falls to his death. The protagonist Craig has just enough time to get back to the Nobel ceremony and graciously accept his award, no longer needing to expose himself as a fraud since his participation in this extraordinary adventure has worked to redeem and redefine his life, as well as to secure him Inger, to whom he can completely commit himself.

The commercial successes of these innocent-on-the-run thrillers led Stanley Donen to make two of them: *Charade* in 1963 and *Arabesque* in 1966. The tone of *Charade* is quite different from the other innocent-on-the-run thrillers; its tongue-in-cheek comedy seems occasionally to turn the film into outright parody. *Charade*'s refusal to take itself particularly seriously didn't upset its original extensive audience; its juxtaposition of grisly violence and funny quips did, however, upset quite a few critics who, during the film's general December release of 1963, a few weeks after the Kennedy assassination, were understandably concerned about the medium's potential to inure us to violence. In one scene, for instance, the three villains (the criminal element generically trichotomized as usual) attend the funeral of Reggie's husband and respectively sneeze on the corpse, hold a mirror to its mouth, and prick it with a needle—all of which are intended as comedy.

Perhaps *Charade*'s attitude toward its own material can best be expressed through a description of its first sequence: in a mountain resort, Reggie (played by Audrey Hepburn) is sitting outside, completely oblivious to what is about to happen. We suddenly see a black-gloved hand being extended from behind an umbrella; the hand holds a gun, which is pointed at Reggie's head. Suspenseful music comes up to tell us to be properly anxious. Finally, the trigger is squeezed . . . and Reggie is squirted in the face with water from a little boy's water pistol. The sequence thus goes beyond the tongue-in-cheek attitude of a *North by Northwest* (in which Hitchcock wanted Cary Grant's Thornhill to sneeze while standing in the nose of Mount Rushmore's Abraham Lincoln, because the filmmakers (in this case, through the music) invite us to laugh even at the way in which they can unabashedly manipulate our responses. *Charade* is also distinctive in that its protagonist is a woman, a situation which results in the romance being less problematic (it would be ungentlemanly for Cary Grant to actually disdain Audrey Hepburn) and allows the innocent protagonist to play the archetypal female victim as she is physically terrorized by the male villains.

There are no spies in *Charade; instead, the villains are all criminals after the hidden $50,000 that Reggie's murdered husband had stolen from the French resistance. Charade*'s MacGuffin turns out to be the valuable stamps into which the money has been cleverly converted. Although Peter Joshua (played by Cary Grant) becomes Reggie's partner in adventure, his identity and allegiance (like those of Eve in *North by Northwest* or Carla in *Ministry of Fear)* are continuously unclear. Yet, typical to the genre, there is a point at which Reggie turns to Peter and says: "Help me, you're the only one I can trust!" Almost immediately, the villain played by George Kennedy calls Reggie to tell her that she musn't trust Peter, thus compounding her predicament. At another point, Peter tells Reggie the story of the Whitefoots, a tribe which always tells the truth, and the Blackfoots, a tribe which always lies. The dilemma was that you could never be sure which was which: If, for instance, you came across one who said he was a Whitefoot, which would he be, a truth-telling Whitefoot or a lying Blackfoot? Reggie answers almost immediately: "A Whitefoot"—emphasizing the importance (in this genre) of giving trust and following it with commitment.

Although in the course of *Charade*, "Peter Joshua" lies to Reggie three different times as to his real identity (progressing from Peter Joshua to Alexander Dyle to Adam Cawfield to Adam Cruikshank), Reggie is still willing to believe in him. Only after each of the three major villains are killed—one found drowned in a bathtub, another killed in the elevator, a third strangled in a plastic bag—does Reggie's loyalty begin to flag. But in the final set-piece in which Reggie finds herself caught between Peter/Adam and Bartholomew (played by Walter Matthau) and forced to make a life-and-death choice of whose story to believe, she ultimately chooses to believe Peter/Adam; and he and she together manage to vanquish Bartholomew, the primary villain who had been working behind the scenes. As in the other innocent-on-the-run thrillers, *Charade* ends optimistically with the protagonist in the embrace of the love interest, a new life opening up to her.

In Donen's subsequent thriller, *Arabesque*, the chaotic and ambiguous nature of the imposed world of intrigue is emphasized in the way people and objects are constantly shown as photographed reflections: in dishes, in a television screen, in car windows, in train windows, in mirrored walls, in eyeglasses, in hubcaps, in microscope lenses, in mirrors, and in mirrors within mirrors. *Arabesque*'s credits are presented over spiral designs, many of them eye-like; the film's first image is that of a crystal ball. In the first sequence, an unknowing victim is administered eyedrops that cause pain, and ultimately, death. The world of *Arabesque* is thus a deceptive one: we cannot trust our eyes. Nothing is as it seems, and what we do catch is visible only in the reflection of some other polished surface. Even the film's MacGuffin, supposedly a secret message in ancient hieroglyphics, turns out to be a pictorial representation of the nursery rhyme "Goosey, Goosey, Gander."

Arabesque's protagonist is Professor David Pollock, played by Gregory Peck. An Egyptologist, Pollock is well aware of the outstanding lack which defines his character: his failure to commit himself. The initial serendipity occurs when Pollock is asked by a Mideast prime minister to try to decipher the film's crucial MacGuffin. For generations the Pollocks have been concerned with the past, says Pollock: Now it is time for a Pollock to deal with the future. Before long, Pollock comes into conflict with Negim Beshraavi; a wearer of dark glasses which conceal his expression, Beshraavi is revealed as a Vandamm-styled villain who speaks in soft, melodious tones and exhibits a constant sang-froid. His mistress is the beautiful Yasmin Azir (played by Sophia Loren), with whom Pollock immediately falls in love.

At one point, Pollock must hide in Yasmin's shower to escape Beshraavi. A naked Yasmin tries to convince Beshraavi, who is outside the shower, that she doesn't know where Pollock has gone: "If I were standing stark naked in front of Mr. Pollock, he'd probably yawn." It's interesting how often these innocent-on-the-run thrillers include a bathroom sequence which contributes to the intrigue or furthers the love relationship. In *Foreign Correspondent,* for instance, Huntley Haverstock pretends to take a shower and ends up in Carol's room; in *North by Northwest,* Roger Thornhill pretends to take a shower and eavesdrops on Eve; in *Charade,* a fully clothed Peter Joshua takes a shower in front of Reggie; and in *Marathon Man,* Dustin Hoffman's Babe is kidnapped while in the middle of his bath.

After Beshraavi is outsmarted, Pollock pretends to kidnap Yasmin in order to make his escape. Although Yasmin provides the romantic interest, the romance is ambiguous and fraught with difficulties, because Pollock cannot be sure of her allegiance. At one point, Yasmin and another of her lovers, Yussef, a supposed leader of guerrilla forces in her native country, use truth serum to find out what Pollock has done with the secret message. When they are unable to understand his answer, they push him out of their van in heavy traffic. A set-piece follows which is very similar to the sequence in *North by Northwest* in which the drunken Thornhill drives recklessly away from the villains. As Pollock wanders about in the midst of the traffic, point-of-view images of the approaching cars are intercut with his imaginings of charging animals. The animal imagery relates to an earlier chase sequence through the zoo as well as to the many animals on the hieroglyph. Despite the fact that Yasmin seems quite clearly to have betrayed Pollock, Pollock chooses consciously to trust her nevertheless, saying that "In this wicked, cynical world, you have to believe in something."

As they form their partnership in adventure, Pollock and Yasmin become spiritually closer. When the two of them go to the Ascot racetrack and one of the villains is murdered, Pollock is accused of the murder and now finds himself on the run from the police as well. In the course of their adventures, there are constant self-conscious references to the conventions of the genre and the expectations of the spectator. When Pollock jumps in a cab and instructs the driver to "follow that car," the driver responds with "All my life I've waited for someone to say that." In one set-piece in which Pollock and Yasmin are attacked by a demolition wrecking ball operated by Yussef, Pollock carefully maneuvers Yussef's electrocution, and then tells Yasmin: "I couldn't let you die until I've heard the end of your story." Familiar (if only subconsciously) with the genre's conventions, the spectator knows, like Pollock, that Yasmin will eventually tell a truthful story which will allow for a satisfactory union. In the central sequence in which the secret of the MacGuffin is finally understood, the dialogue reiterates the theme of trust. The MacGuffin's message turns out to contain a hidden microdot which reveals Beshraavi's plan to assassinate his own prime minister.

The sequence in which Pollock and Yasmin race to save the prime minister from assassination is typical not only to the conventions of the genre, but to the constructions of suspense. The sequence is constructed in a way that the spectator's expectations are constantly thwarted by a series of narrative reversals. This structure can best be expressed as a series of antinomies, thus:

A: Pollock and Yasmin must save the prime minister from assassination.

Anti-A: They fear they will not arrive in time to save him.

A: But they do arrive in time.

Anti-A: But they are refused entry.

A: But Pollock breaks in and saves the prime minister by jumping on top of him just as the assassin shoots.

Anti-A: But the prime minister is assassinated a few moments afterwards, anyway.

A: But Yasmin realizes that the man who has been assassinated is not the real prime minister, but an imposter who has been hired to officially condemn the important treaty.

Anti-A: But the real prime minister has been kidnapped and will be assassinated as well; will they arrive in time to save him?

A: They do, and in the nick of time.

Thus, two conflicting expectations—they *will* save the prime minister, they *won't* save the prime minister—are extended with the help of generic staples such as the imposter and the chase. The success-oriented expectation is ultimately fulfilled in the exciting climax in which Pollock and Yasmin, though attacked by a threshing machine and a helicopter, are able

to save the prime minister and triumph over their enemies. The film ends typically with a fade-out joke: when the rowboat of Pollock and Yasmin, who are out for a Sunday excursion, is accidentally rammed, both of them end up in the water. "Here we are taking a bath together," says Pollock, referring to the earlier shower they shared. The last lines of dialogue make fun even of the genre's crucial themes of trust and commitment. "David, you lied to me," says Yasmin. "Sure," responds Pollock. "It was my turn."

Torn Curtain, directed in 1966 by Alfred Hitchcock, although perhaps not strictly an innocent-on-the-run thriller, takes advantage of many of the genre's conventions. The primary anomaly here is that the protagonist does not get involved in the murderous intrigue because of any coincidence, but because of his own conscious choice. Paul Newman plays Michael Armstrong, a professor who pretends to defect to the Soviet Union in order to get information from a scientist behind the Iron Curtain. Julie Andrews plays Sarah Sherman, the romantic interest who follows Michael, unaware that his defection is a sham. Sarah is as disappointed with Michael's failure to trust her with his defection as she is with the defection itself. The central sequence in which Michael tricks the scientist out of the crucial information (the virtual MacGuffin) is disturbing, because the scientist is rather kindly and trusting; I daresay the spectator feels somewhat guilty at Michael's (arguably necessary) deception. The last half of *Torn Curtain* deals with the adventures of Michael and Sarah as they flee East Germany, fugitives from the Communist government now cognizant of Michael's real allegiance. The generic scene of enclosure requiring creative escape takes place when Michael and Sarah are in a theatre surrounded by their pursuers: Michael cries "Fire!" and causes a riot which enables them to escape.

Although *Torn Curtain* is ostensibly an anti-Communist film (we are clearly meant to sympathize with Michael and Sarah and all the characters who aid them), the Cold War politics as practiced by the West itself seem to be questioned. Perhaps *Torn Curtain*'s strongest scene is the one in which Michael and an accomplice brutally murder a Communist by stabbing him, beating him, and ultimately forcing his head into a gas oven. Without a doubt, it is Michael, the sympathetic protagonist, who does the nastiest things; still, this disturbing dimension doesn't prevent *Torn Curtain* from ending with the traditional fade-out joke as Michael and Sarah, victorious after all their adventures, are finally able to snuggle salaciously beneath a blanket.

House of Cards can be seen somewhat as a transitional film between the traditional innocent-on-the-run thrillers of the fifties and sixties and the

Gregory Peck and Sophia Loren narrowly miss being killed by the wildly swinging ocnophilic object in *Arabesque*.

Gregory Peck and Sophia Loren race to try to save the prime minister in *Arabesque.*

more cynical strain of the seventies. The villains in *House of Cards* (directed in 1969 by John Guillermin) are neither Communists nor petty criminals, but right-wing Frenchmen opposed to the liberal changes sweeping their country. The protagonist, Reno Davis (played by George Peppard), is an uncommitted American bumming around in Paris. The film's first and significant view of Reno shows him throwing in the towel in a boxing ring. Reno describes himself as a "vaccinated white Protestant American male with a slight sinus condition"—a characterization which accurately describes the genre's typical protagonist. Reno's friend, Louis, advises him to leave Paris, to go back to the United States and make something of his life. Shortly afterwards, the film presents the all-important initial coincidence: Reno's car is shot at; is he in danger? It would seem not, for his assailant is a little boy. A furious Reno goes to the boy's home and complains. So taken is Anne, the boy's mother, by Reno's style, that she hires him as her son's unorthodox tutor.

As the narrative progresses, Anne (played by Inger Stevens) provides the love interest. Her husband died in the Algerian War, and she now feels out of place in the old, aristocratic family into which she had married. In keeping with the genre's conventions, Anne's attitude toward Reno

Inger Stevens and George Peppard as the couple involved in intrigue in *House of Cards*.

vacillates between the provocatively loose and the coolly distant. Mysteriously, villains seem out to get Reno, and there are attempts on his life. When his friend Louis is killed, Reno is set up as his murderer and thus finds himself on the run from the police as well as from the villains. Later, in a train station while he is trying to escape, Reno (like Thornhill in *North by Northwest)* sees his picture in the newspaper and is almost recognized. On the train, Reno actually hides in Anne's bed. The dialogue is consistently provocative. "You keep your cool," says Reno. "Yes," answers Anne, "and I intend to see that you keep yours." Later in bed: "You're like an open manhole," says Reno, choosing a rather crude metaphor. "How many men have dropped in and never been heard from again?"

The villainy in *House of Cards* is provided by Anne's aristocratic in-laws who, with the help of right-wing sympathizers all over the country, have planned a careful campaign to overthrow the French government. The ubiquitous conspirators may number in the thousands and extend to the press, the military, the diplomatic corps, the police. The villainous element is also segmented (as usual), with the primary urbane villain, Leschenhaut, played by the very portly Orson Welles. When the villains kidnap Anne's little boy, the boy is transformed into the MacGuffin which Reno and Anne spend the rest of the film pursuing. Typical too to the genre is the revelation that Anne's husband is not dead after all, but underground, leading the conspiracy. Can anyone be trusted? One sequence in particular is constructed upon antinomies of expectations:

A: Someone enters Reno and Anne's train compartment; will he be a villain who will try to kill them?

Anti-A: No, because he's a priest.

A: But the priest has a perfect manicure; is he a villain nevertheless?

Anti-A: No, he really is a priest, but he is also a gardener who got a manicure for the first time in his life because he is delivering apples to the Pope.

A: But he is a villain anyway; and later, he pulls a gun on Reno and Anne.

A series of adventures at various picturesque spots (including the fountain of Trevi, from which Reno and Anne steal money) climaxes with the sequence at the Colosseum. Reno finally finds Anne's little boy, who, dressed exactly the same as Leschenhaut, is being groomed as a right-wing killer. In the suspenseful climax, Leschenhaut baits the boy to shoot Reno, but the boy, all innate innocence revolting against his programming, turns on Leschenhaut, who conveniently falls to his death. Since the film has consistently emphasized the extensiveness of the conspiracy, Leschenhaut's death would seem relatively unimportant in the overall scheme; there certainly seems no way to vanquish the tentacled network of the right-wingers. In the film's coda, Anne is reunited with Reno by the French Special Police, who make their entrance in the best *deus ex machina* style, announce that they "have been interested in this matter for some time," and depart, leaving Reno, Anne, and her son to begin their new life together—Reno no longer the uncommitted cynical profligate.

Because of its pervasive conspiracy, *House of Cards* can be seen as a reflection of the growing popular distrust of institutions and governments, although in this film the distrust is not yet manifested in a setting specifically American. While the various assassinations of the sixties suggested conspiracy, it was not until the Watergate investigations of the seventies that these conspiratorial theories evolved from left-wing hysteria to common belief. As political and social events made the popular audience cynical, the innocent-on-the-run thriller—amazingly stable in sensibility for forty years—began to express overt conspiratorial notions. A film such as

The Parallax View ends tragically precisely because the extensiveness of the villainous conspiracy makes a happy resolution untenable. If no one can be trusted—not the police, not the CIA, not the FBI—who remains to gallop in at the last moment to save the day? A cynical film like *Marathon Man* nevertheless almost paradoxically affirms the possibility of individual action triumphing over the pervasive conspiracies. *Three Days of the Condor,* on the other hand, is less sanguine about individual successful action and discovers a new *deus ex machina:* the press.

The Parallax View was directed by Alan J. Pakula in 1974 and can be seen as an attempt to deal with the rash of sixties American assassinations in a form accessible to mass audiences. The film begins at Seattle's Space Needle (like all suspense thrillers, using ostensibly real locations whenever possible), where reporter Lee Carter (played by Paula Prentiss) interviews independent senator Charles Carroll. When Carroll gives a speech, he's shot: red blood spurts against the window through which we see him. The ostensible assassin is then himself eliminated. Pakula cuts to a strikingly formal image: eight men sitting at a long judicial table. The chairman announces that the board has determined that there had been no conspiracy and that the assassin had acted alone. Throughout his speech, the camera slowly zooms in to the speaker—as if to emphasize that *The Parallax View* will examine the falsity of the findings he is announcing.

The narrative jumps three years ahead and continues with the adventures of the reporter protagonist Frady (played by Warren Beatty). We find out that Frady has had a drinking problem, has been suffering from a kind of creative irresponsibility, and is constantly hassled by the police who want him to reveal his sources. His editor (played by Hume Cronyn) advises him to "go to a movie and relax"—certainly a reflexive and ironic statement; is *The Parallax View* the kind of movie one goes to for relaxation? Frady gets involved in the murderous plot when an hysterical Lee Carter visits him and claims that someone's been trying to kill her. Already six witnesses to Carroll's assassination have been killed, and she is sure there is a conspiracy. Strikingly, Pakula cuts to Lee's dead body on a slab in the morgue; Frady is persuaded to investigate the assassinations for himself.

Although Frady has a series of adventures, he is unlike the typical innocent-on-the-run protagonist, in that he is an investigative reporter who has consciously taken on the task (in this regard resembling the character so common to the political thriller); the task thus provides him a supremely moral mission. One early scene between Frady and his ex.FBI agent contact takes place at an amusement park on a miniature train. The scene works as a subtle parody of the genre's traditional railway scene and as an indication that *The Parallax View* is up to something a little different. One early set-piece has Frady investigating a country area only to have the area suddenly flooded and Frady barely escaping with his life.

Much of the suspense in *The Parallax View* is communicated within

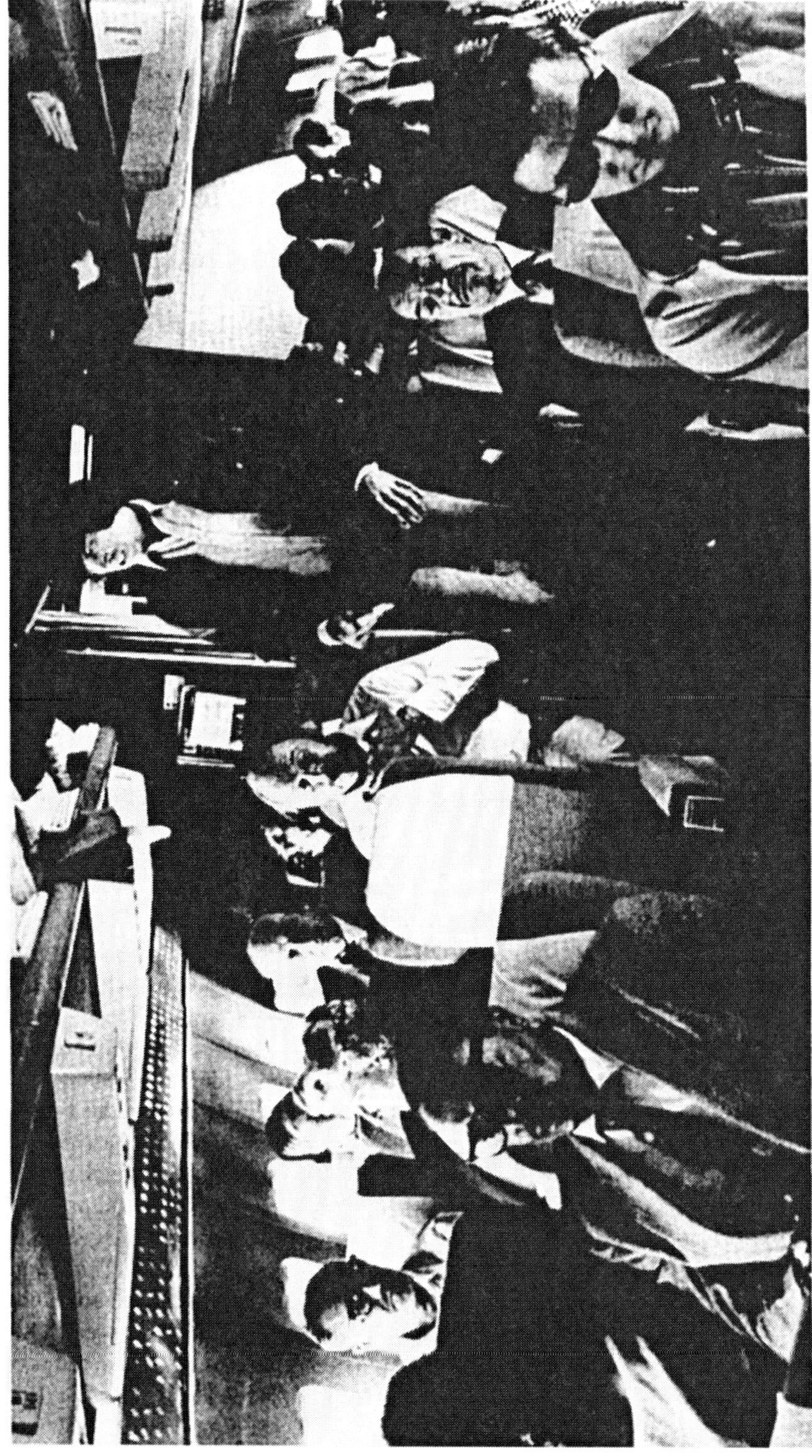

single widescreen images. When, for instance, Frady searches the sheriff's house and finds information on the mysterious Parallax Corporation, Frady is framed on the left of the widescreen image, while the right side remains most pregnantly empty. Sure enough, after what seems a long time, the deputy finally appears on the right side of the image when he walks into the house. Just as the deputy is about to discover Frady, the telephone rings, interrupts his discovery, and allows Frady the opportunity to escape. (This shot recalls the one in *Marnie* in which the protagonist tries to leave the office without being detected by the cleaning lady.)

The conventional escape from an enclosed location takes place when Frady gets on a plane and realizes that one of the villains has planted a bomb on the plane in an attempt to assassinate yet another senator. Frady's problem is that he must communicate the existence of the bomb without incriminating himself—a problem which he solves quite ingeniously.

In the course of his adventures, Frady manages to infiltrate the Parallax Corporation, the corporation which appears to be responsible for all the assassinations and terrorism in the country. When contacted by a Parallax official, Frady assumes the role of a psychopath in the hope he might be groomed as one of their assassins. The film's central scene takes place when the corporation scientifically tests Frady's physiological responses to a specifically constructed film. Frady sits by himself in the center of the frame, dwarfed by Pakula's huge widescreen image. The images of the film the Corporation shows him are increasingly violent and sexual, and alternate with the words: Love, Mother, Father, Me, Home, Country, God, Enemy, Happiness. Juxtaposed with the word "Me" are images of comic book heroes. Juxtaposed with the word "Country" are images of Mount Rushmore, the Lincoln Memorial, and the Statue of Liberty—the same images which appear so consistently in the innocent-on-the-run thrillers as recurring symbols of order and democracy. In a significant sense, because the spectator's point of view coincides during the film test with Frady's point of view, the spectator is being similarly tested (although, of course, the spectator's responses cannot be physically monitored).

The Parallax View climaxes with a stunningly photographed set-piece. In a huge amphitheatre with hundreds of geometrically arranged red, white, and blue tables, a high school band plays patriotic music in a rehearsal for a televised speech to be given later in the day by Mr. Hammond, who is running (presumably) for president. Frady, meanwhile, has come to this location and now watches the proceedings from a catwalk. The patriotic speech of Hammond is playing over the PA system so the students can practice clapping at appropriate points; while this is going on, Hammond

The generic scene where the protagonist must escape from an enclosed location: How can Warren Beatty in *The Parallax View* prevent a plane from taking off without arousing suspicion?

practices golf strokes. The sequence is partially disturbing, because up to now, we have assumed that Senator Carroll, as well as the senator who was to be assassinated on the airplane, were good, liberal men of integrity; Hammond's casual behavior implies that all politics may very well be just a game in which one learns how to manipulate the red, white and blue into a carefully planned campaign. If this is, indeed, the essence of politics, assassination is not so much an evil act that creates martyrs, but a pragmatic extension of an already corrupt system.

Finished with his part of the rehearsal, Hammond gets in a golf cart and begins driving from the huge amphitheatre's platform. A shot rings out—and he is assassinated. There is shock, disbelief; his golf cart travels in a circle, crashing into the red, white, and blue tables, destroying the symmetry, corrupting symbolically the democratic processes. On the catwalk, Frady sees a rifle that has been left there and suddenly realizes that he has not really infiltrated the organization, but been used by the organization which has now set him up as Hammond's assassin. A tremendously suspenseful sequence follows as Frady, determined to escape and live long enough to tell his own story, runs frantically for the little square of white light representing the open door at the end of the catwalk. Shots of Frady running alternate with point-of-view shots of the door as it and Frady's salvation loom closer, closer—when suddenly, a silhouetted figure appears in the square of light and shoots Frady dead.

Although he was an innocent on the run who found a moral meaning in his adventures, Frady underestimated his adversary and was thus undone by the omnipotent evil, its source and organization left mysterious even to the spectator. Instead of ending with the traditional joke, *The Parallax View* ends with a cynical, symmetrical coda as Pakula presents the perfectly framed shot of the board of investigation. This time the camera begins on a close-up of the chairman and slowly moves out to a long shot of the men sitting at the long table. "There is no evidence of a conspiracy," says the chairman in reference to Frady's "assassination" of Hammond. "This is an announcement; there will be no questions." The camera movement ends, the image remains stationary, and then the men disappear from the image. After the credits, there is a solemn fade to black.

The American Bicentennial inaugurated several more innocent-on-the-run thrillers, at least two of them, *Three Days of the Condor* and *Marathon Man*, overtly reflective of the Watergate mentality and increased American distrust in government institutions. Turner, the CIA researcher and protagonist of *Three Days of the Condor*, is not really an irresponsible man except in the sense that he is unaware of the moral bankruptcy of the government agency for which he works. The spectator is meant to like and empathize with Turner, if not because he is an enlightened liberal who rides his bike to work, then because he is played by Robert Redford.

When one day Turner returns to the CIA office and discovers that everyone there has been killed, his world is suddenly thrown into chaos. Everything takes on a sinister tone: a woman pushing a baby carriage, for instance, appears to be an assassin hiding a gun. Higgins, another CIA agent (played by Cliff Robertson), is supposed to bring Turner to safety; Turner gradually realizes that there is actually a secret organization within the CIA that has, for reasons mysterious and opaque, eliminated everyone in Turner's office. Turner himself has never participated in any CIA dirty work, but has merely read spy novels into a computer for potential, future CIA reference. As a shocked Turner himself says to operatives in Washington: "I'm not a field agent, I just read books!"

Although in the traditional innocent-on-the-run thriller the protagonist must run from the villains *and* the peace-keeping force, the peace-keeping force (be it police, FBI or CIA) generally becomes the protagonist's ally once the central misunderstanding is cleared up. In *Three Days of the Condor,* the peace-keeping force (the CIA) *is* the villain. Because, in an important sense, there is no higher police authority, a solution to Turner's dilemma seems unlikely. For good measure, the narrative also sets Turner up as the supposed murderer of his friend; thus, even the lower-level peace-keeping force, the police, is set against him.

As usual, the ideas of trust and commitment provide *Three Days of the Condor* with its primary theme. Even the advertisement for the film used the image of the eagle on a coin, with the words "In God We Trust" prominently displayed. Early in the film, Turner says he would like to be free to discuss his job with friends; as he puts it, "I actually trust a few people." Ultimately, *Three Days of the Condor* equates the whole survival of the American way of life with the concept of trust in some higher authority, although the precise nature of that authority is not revealed until virtually the film's final shot.

Like the typical innocent-on-the-run protagonist, Turner enters into a relationship with a beautiful woman who shares his adventures. Knowing that the CIA would be able to trace him were he to rely on any of his friends, Turner kidnaps Kathy (played by Faye Dunaway) completely at random. Blonde, cool, alternately terrified of Turner and sexually attracted to him, Kathy is a photographer whose favorite subject is bare trees. As Kathy warms to Turner, she discusses certain photographs she has taken which she has put away because they "aren't her." But then again, she muses, if she took them, they must be her. The metaphor is to those unpleasant things in current American society which, although hidden away, are inevitably there and must be dealt with. Will she show the photographs to Turner? "I don't know you well enough to show you." Kathy is attracted to Turner because she knows he may die soon. Their lovemaking is juxtaposed with her photographs: all evocative, lonely, bare.

It is significant that the relationship between Turner and Kathy is juxtaposed with photographs of bare trees; this metaphor compares with the

Although Faye Dunaway in *Three Days of the Condor* is originally treated by Robert Redford as an ocnophilic object, she enjoys her usefulness and aggressively helps him to defeat his adversaries.

sequence in *North by Northwest* in which the relationship between Thornhill and Eve is juxtaposed with a forest of green trees. In the post-Watergate era, trees are now bare and no longer symbols of life, but of potential death; American conspiracies and crimes of morality impede lasting commitment. (Interestingly, even the romance between Babe and Elsa in *Marathon Man* is juxtaposed with bare trees.) Only after making love to Kathy and killing in her presence a CIA assassin disguised as a mailman does Turner completely gain Kathy's trust and commitment. The theme of trust remains constant. Of Higgins, Kathy asks Turner, "Do you trust him?" "No. " "Does he trust you?"

The MacGuffin (of sorts) turns out to be Arab oil—certainly a relevant concern in an age of fuel shortages. Afraid that Turner has somehow

Objects are crucial in the suspense thriller, and particularly so in *Three Days of the Condor.* In the top frame enlargement, numerous clocks reinforce the film's suspense and emphasis on time; in the second frame enlargement, Faye Dunaway's photograph of bare trees represents her sadness and the bleak view of the film; and in the third, the *New York Times* building functions as a literal sign of the film's *deus ex machina.*

ST PAUL
SANTIAGO
NEWORLEANS MIAMI
CARACAS
HAVANA
DALLAS

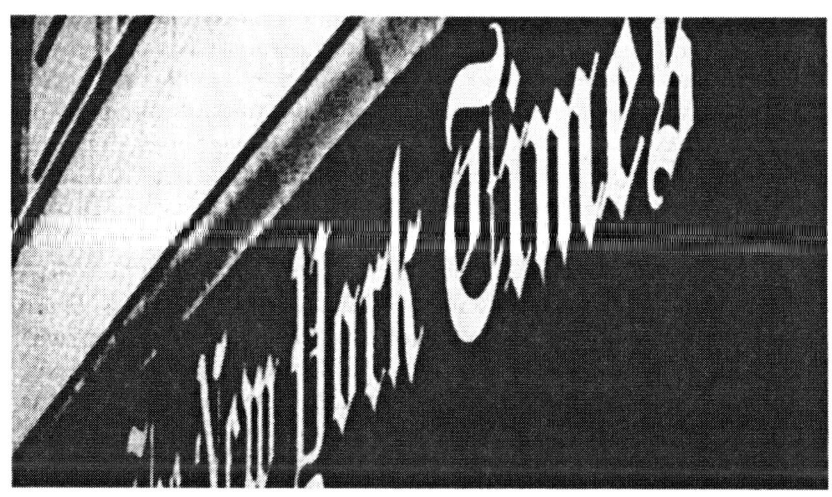
New York Times

managed to find out about his tentative and perhaps only theoretical plans to invade the Mideast, Atwood, the deputy director of Middle East Operations, had arranged to have Turner and all his colleagues killed to ensure their silence. Typical to the genre, the villainous element is segmented into a variety of characters: Mr. Wabash (played by John Houseman), a self-assured incarnation of bureaucratic evil; Higgins, the more sympathetic villain who, within the course of the film, finds out about the secret organization within the CIA and finally decides to support it; Atwood, the arranger of the assassinations; and perhaps the most interesting of all the villains, "Lucifer" (played by Max Von Sydow), a paid assassin who has no particular allegiance to the CIA.

At one point, Lucifer and Turner confront each other. Even though Lucifer has been trying to kill Turner for most of the film, Lucifer has gradually come to respect Turner's professionalism and his cunning. He is particularly fascinated by the manner in which Kathy was chosen as an accomplice—at random. Lucifer offers Turner both a ride and advice on how to stay alive. "No need to believe in either side," he says, "There is no cause. There's only yourself. The belief is in your own precision." Lucifer and Turner have each rejected the moral code of the CIA, and although they have arrived at different positions, they are both aware of their moral superiority.

Three Days of the Condor ends with a confrontation between Higgins and Turner, with Turner clearly in control. Knowing he would be killed, Turner refuses to come with Higgins to the "safety of the CIA." "You're about to be a very lonely man," says Higgins, "It didn't have to end this way." Self-reflectively for the film, Turner answers, "Of course it did." A shot of the *New York Times* building follows, as we realize that the press will provide *Three Days of the Condor* with its convenient *deus ex machina*. "How do you know they'll print it?" asks Higgins. "They'll print it," says Turner. "How do you know?" insists Higgins. The ending is ambiguous, suggesting that Turner will live only if the story is printed; the story will be printed only if there is a future for the United States. Although this ending was widely criticized as naive, it seems to me a forceful and relevant, if contrived, device, which works quite powerfully to reflect certain post–Watergate attitudes toward the press and its role in safeguarding liberties. As the film ends, the sound of a nearby Salvation Army band singing "to save us all from Satan's power" comes up loudly.

Marathon Man, directed by John Schlesinger in 1976, may be Schlesinger's most popularly-oriented film. Although many critics found *Marathon Man* fascinating, others faulted Schlesinger for his "too serious" treatment of a popular form. This criticism seems proscriptive and limiting. Suspense thrillers need not be unintellectual. It seems to me that auteurs *should* be encouraged to work in popular forms, for the collisions, or collaboration, between any strong director and an established genre is almost always fascinating. Imagine, for instance, an innocent-on-the-run thriller directed by a Buñuel or a Bergman. Certainly genre works can be self-conscious; could one imagine a Schlesinger work which would not be? In any case, *Marathon Man* uses the innocent-on-the-run genre in part to examine the related concept of personal responsibility.

From its very beginning, *Marathon Man* presents a chaotic world: we are presented with traffic, noise, juvenile delinquency, senior citizens living in fear, and general disorder. Almost immediately, while Jews come out of temple on Yom Kippur holiday, a squabble between two elderly drivers climaxes in a fiery automobile accident—a metaphorical representation of the Nazi holocaust. The film's protagonist, Babe (played by Dustin Hoffman), is a graduate student at Columbia University; his dissertation topic is the use of tyranny in American political life. Babe is attracted to the subject because of his own father's suicide after being accused during the McCarthy era of being a communist. The flashbacks to Babe's past—an image of Babe as a boy swinging on a swing; a dolly-in to an open window, its curtains blowing gently; a gun on the floor next to Babe's dead father—are all expressively composed with the kind of care usually associated with an art film.

The theme of commitment (constant in the genre as well as in the work of Schlesinger) is underscored throughout. One of our first views of Babe shows him spontaneously racing in the park against another, superior jogger. Babe's professor warns him that he must confront the McCarthy era in his dissertation clearly and objectively. When Babe writes a letter to his brother, he admits his failure in the past to confront things. Even when the curtains billow out around the near-naked and bloodied body of Babe's brother Doc (played by Roy Scheider) when he is attacked on his hotel balcony, Schlesinger juxtaposes the violence with images of a paralyzed man in a wheelchair watching helplessly from across the street; violence and horror will always result when commitment gives way to inaction.

The extremely complex plot of *Marathon Man* revolves around the return to New York of an old Nazi dentist, Szell (played by Laurence Olivier), in order to retrieve from a safety deposit box millions of dollars worth of diamonds purchased with money made from the sale of gold fillings extracted from the teeth of Jews in the concentration camps. Babe gets innocently involved in the horrendous intrigue, because his brother is a member of a CIA-like international agency, and because the villains think Babe may try to steal the diamonds and foil the plans of the war-criminal Szell.

Marathon Man's violence is horrifying, often indirect, and generally correlated with a particular object. For instance: (1) At a flea market in Paris, a baby carriage squeaks, and a mannish woman sits staring. After the camera dollies in to a close-up of the doll in the carriage, there is a close-up of the doll's eyes slowly opening, then a cut to a longer shot as the entire

Roy Scheider is killed by Laurence Olivier in a scene from *Marathon Man* which visually resembles the assassination of the United Nations diplomat from *North by Northwest*.

area is rocked by an explosion—but moments too late to kill Doc. (2) Doc is out walking in Paris with his friend Nicole. When she disappears into the darkness, there is the unpleasant sound of a bump (which presumably represents her murder). After a moment, a ball is thrown back to Doc and photographed in close-up as it comes to a stop. (3) In front of a fountain in New York, Doc confronts Szell. As Doc expresses his anger with Szell for

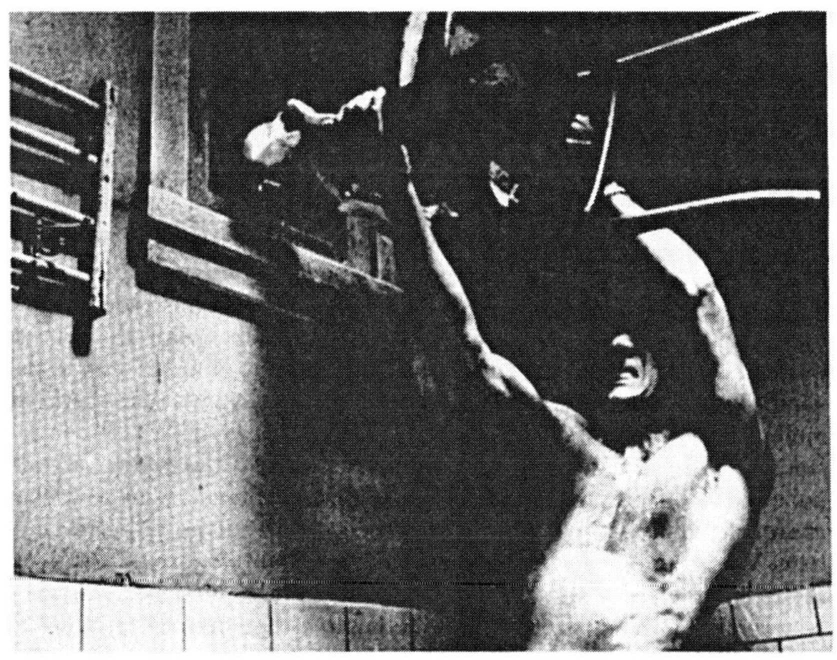

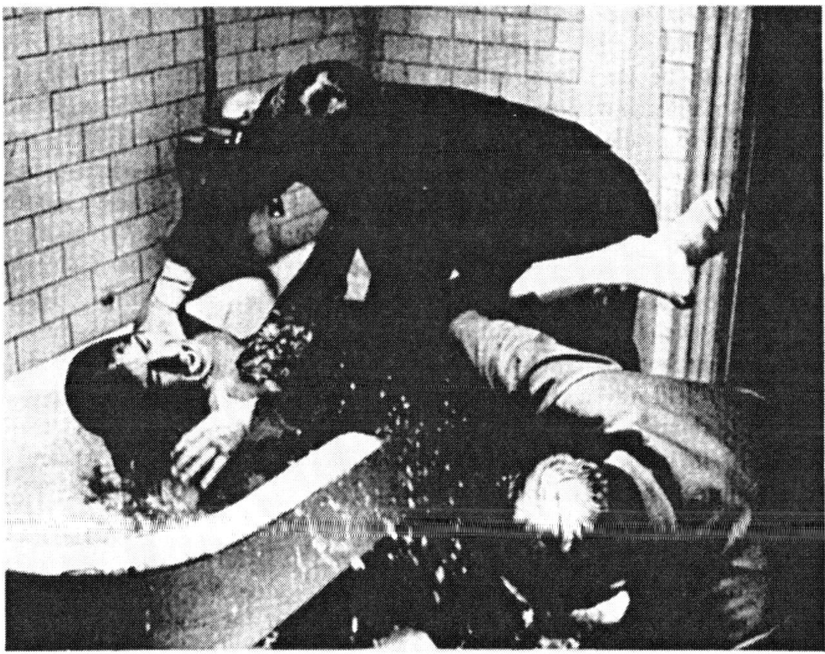

In *Marathon Man*, the confining space of the bathroom is a dangerous place: Dustin Hoffman attempts to use an ocnophilic object to accomplish an escape, but is brutally attacked.

involving the innocent Babe, Doc's eyes suddenly open in pain and shock. Although the knife is not shown, Szell evidently twists the blade with glee as the scene continues.

The preceding violence is just preliminary, for this moral adventure has been constructed for Babe. When Doc dies bleeding in Babe's apartment, Schlesinger emphasizes the dead body on the floor, the line being drawn around the body, the placing of the body in a zipped bag—the zipping noise surreally augmented. The entire process seems obscene: one can't help but think of the reality of the concentration camps, the process by which a human being is turned into an inanimate object. To try to unwind, Babe takes a bath. Schlesinger presents nightmarish flashbacks in muted colors of Babe's youth; a visual connection is made between his father's bloody corpse and his brother's. Suddenly while in the bathtub, Babe hears whispers, but is unable to see anyone. There is much suspense as a terrified Babe slams shut the bathroom door and puts on his pajama bottoms. We see the knife of the unseen intruders coming in through the wood of the bathroom door as they attempt to break in. Schlesinger cross-cuts between Babe yelling for help while trying to escape through the window and the door finally giving way as the men violently dunk Babe into the bathtub and then bring him to Szell.

The confrontations between Babe and Szell form the most suspenseful and disturbing sequences of *Marathon Man*. Szell is such an absolute force of evil that it becomes impossible for Babe not to commit himself in opposition. The first scene between the two of them takes place in a white, sterile room. There is silence, and Babe sits expectantly, tied to a chair. When Szell comes in, he takes a long time to quietly wash up. His mysterious and unanswerable question to Babe—"Is it safe?"—is repeated nine times, the actor Olivier ringing marvelous changes. Slowly Szell opens up a sheath of dental equipment. So effortlessly, to create suspense, does Schlesinger take advantage of the general fear of dentists, that the display of the dental equipment itself brings a gasp from the typical audience. Indeed, the anticipation of that moment when Szell will reach into Babe's mouth and cold-bloodedly drill into a nerve works occasionally to make some spectators leave the theatre (even though very little torture is actually shown). Szell holds up the dental equipment and the anaesthetic as he says, "Life can be that simple: relief, discomfort."

When Babe finally manages to escape, it is his long-distance running ability that provides him with the necessary skill. The conventional scene of creative escape from an enclosed location is acted out in reverse: Babe must somehow make his way into his own apartment to get some clothes without the villains, who are keeping guard, recapturing him. Babe's solution (not unlike Haverstock's in *Foreign Correspondent* thirty-six years earlier) is to hire the neighborhood delinquents to break in and steal everything, including some clothes. When Babe enlists the aid of the *femme fatale* figure Elsa (played by Marthe Keller), he realizes that even though she loves him, she is in on the plot and cannot be trusted. The romance, quite untypical to the genre, fails. Babe throws down the pain killer—the broken bottle symbolic of his resolve to face things squarely in a courageous and nonpassive manner.

In the final set-piece, Szell retrieves the diamonds and then prices others in the Jewish jewelry district of New York. Memories of the concentration camps are everywhere; for instance, Szell sees tattooed numbers on a jeweler's arm. One woman recognizes Szell in astonishment and begins shouting his name. When no one seems willing to help, she cries out, "I will stop him!"—herself willing to take on personal responsibility. When in her haste, the woman is struck by a car, she is still able to raise herself up with a moral force and continue to call out Szell's name. When the jeweler himself finally recognizes Szell and rushes after him, Szell cold-bloodedly slashes the jeweler's throat with his hidden wrist-knife.

Both incidents provide a kind of commitment model for Babe (and the spectator). Earlier, Szell had been worried that it would not be safe for him to carry the diamonds. Although at the time he was questioned, Babe knew nothing about Szell's mission, he is now committed to sabotaging it and stopping the evil. "Is it safe?" asks Babe as he suddenly comes up behind Szell. The suspense is great as Babe forces Szell into a waterworks: Will Babe inadvertently get close enough to Szell to allow him to use his wrist-knife? Babe resorts to Szell's tactics and tells Szell that he can keep as many of the diamonds as he can swallow. As Babe throws about the diamonds, Szell screams like a wounded animal and says (in a statement heavy with irony, certainly): "This is madness." Szell eats one diamond; but when Babe insists he eat another, Szell counters simply with, "No. I won't. You'll have to shoot me. You won't. You can't. You're too weak. Your father was weak in his way, your brother was weak in his way, and now you are weak in your way." In fact, Szell is correct: Babe will not, cannot use the gun—although it is more a moral choice than an act of cowardice.

In the struggle that follows, Szell accidentally impales himself on his own knife in an attempt to prevent the diamonds from being discarded by Babe. In one sense, there is no clear victor to the confrontation because Szell dies largely as a result of his own miscalculation and greed, rather than as a result of Babe's attack. In another sense, Babe achieves a moral victory because he was able to disavow the techniques of his enemy and yet emerge physically victorious himself. Certainly a physical victory would be more easily achieved through a compromised position. Outside the waterworks, Babe takes the gun (the symbol of his father's suicide as well as of the tyranny against which he has now committed himself) and throws it into the river; through the lattice-work of the fence, we see the water rippling out in concentric circles. Babe walks away. His tooth aches, but he has neither the pain killer nor the desire to use it. He nods, finally self-satisfied.

In the context of *The Parallax View, Three Days of the Condor,* and *Marathon Man, Silver Streak* (written by Colin Higgins and directed by Arthur Hiller) might impress as an anachronism. Although in 1977 it seemed more an *hommage* to *The Lady Vanishes* or *North by Northwest* than a contemporary variation, it is now clear that *Silver Streak* represented an innocent-on-the-run thriller less influenced by Watergate than suggestive of the Reagan era shortly to be ushered in.

The film begins at the Los Angeles train station where the Silver Streak is boarding and ends when the train crashes at its Chicago destination. Not only does *Silver Streak* eschew politics, but its villains are simple criminals rather than spies. The film follows the conventions of the genre precisely. The protagonist George Caldwell (played by Gene Wilder) is an average man, who, through an initial coincidence, meets and falls in love with a blonde woman, Hilly Burns (played by Jill Clayburgh), who involves him in murderous intrigue. Typical to the genre, Hilly speaks in double entendres and is alternately seductive and cool. Three times she is separated and reunited with George, who keeps getting knocked off the train.

The MacGuffin in *Silver Streak* is a packet of Rembrandt letters which could publicly expose one of the villains. As in *North by Northwest* and other thrillers, the villainy is segmented into three different characters: Devereau, the well-dressed sophisticate (played by Patrick McGoohan); Mr. Whiney, the sinister and slick gangster (played by Ray Walston); and Reace, the dumb heavy (played by Richard Kiel). As usual, in the course of his adventures, the protagonist is taken for a murderer and must flee from the police as well. At the Kansas City station, there is a sequence (very much like one in *North by Northwest)* in which George, with the help of Grover (played by Richard Pryor), disguises himself as a stereotyped black man with a radio and successfully gets back on the train unrecognized. (His wanted picture is, of course, on the front page of the newspaper.)

At least two aspects of *Silver Streak* seem particularly unique: the first is the way in which many of the protagonist's adventures are shared not with the love interest, but with his male friend, Grover. This relates to the backlash in the seventies against women's liberation and to the resulting male camaraderie films (also called "buddy films") such as *Butch Cassidy and the Sundance Kid, The Sting,* and *Freebie and the Bean.* In fact, during the confusion of the climactic shoot-out, one shot shows Grover on top of George on the ground—as if in a virtual embrace. During any other period, the character of the same sex friend would have been considered extraneous, and this particular sequence would have been translated into an erotic and dangerous moment for the protagonist and the love interest.

A second unique aspect is the way in which *Silver Streak* subtly subverts the genre's typical values of personal integrity and responsibility. According to *Silver Streak,* the ultimate value is simply having a good time. The protagonist's evolution is not from irresponsible to responsible man, but from a responsible man caught in the rat-race to a man open to liberating experiences. For *Silver Streak*, it is perfectly moral for Grover to steal a car in order to "stay loose." Indeed, the crimes of the villains were, rather, witlessness and hypocrisy than any particular legal or social transgression. Consistent to its morality, *Silver Streak* ends with the protagonist and the heroine going off to the park to make love.

The great popular success of *Silver Streak* allowed its writer, Colin Higgins, to direct his own screenplay, *Foul Play*, in 1978. Like *Silver Streak*, *Foul Play* totally eschewed the paranoid sensibility so symptomatic of the innocent-on-the-run thrillers only a few years earlier; and yet both *Foul Play* and *Silver Streak* are timely, post-sixties films in the way they both oppose conventional behavior and embrace sexual liberation. If *Silver Streak* seems largely an updating of *The Lady Vanishes* crossed with *North by Northwest*, *Foul Play* seems clearly an updating of Hitchcock's 1955 *The Man Who Knew Too Much*.

Foul Play begins with an archbishop being stabbed as he puts on a recording of *The Mikado*. Later, at the film's climax, an assassination attempt takes place during a live performance of *The Mikado;* thus, the music works—albeit less ingeniously—like the Bernard Herrmann theme with the cymbal crash in *The Man Who Knew Too Much*. The narrative then cuts to Goldie Hawn at a party, the innocent protagonist who will soon be involved in the intrigue. Hawn plays Gloria Mundy, a slightly repressed librarian who is urged by her friend to be more adventurous, to "show some cleavage." At the party, Gloria meets Tony Carlson, played by Chevy Chase, whom she almost immediately rebuffs because she is not yet, as the Barry Manilow theme song instructs her, "Ready to Take a Chance Again." Later, Gloria picks up an attractive hitchhiker in an attempt to get some adventure in her life; when he asks her for a date ("Come on, Gloria, take a chance"), she agrees. The hitchhiker gives her a pack of cigarettes to hold onto for him, because, he explains, he is trying to give up smoking. Unbeknownst to Gloria, the cigarette pack actually contains a roll of film—the movie's MacGuffin.

The hitchhiker meets her later at a movie theatre which is showing a thriller called *Killers Walk Among Us*—a reflexive title certainly. In the theatre, the hitchhiker says to Gloria urgently, "There is going to be a murder." We then see a huge close-up of her ear as he whispers to her, "Beware of the dwarf." This scene refers to the parallel scene in *The Man Who Knew Too Much* in which a close-up of Jimmy Stewart's ear filled the screen as he was warned in the same manner. When the hitchhiker is killed right in the theatre, Gloria screams, as does the theatre audience around her, but in relation to the film they are seeing on the movie screen—this, a reference to the parallel movie theatre scene in Hitchcock's *Saboteur*. Later, one of Gloria's friends will say to her, "People don't just drop dead in cinemas," although in thrillers, they actually do quite often.

What makes Gloria's story so hard to believe is that the body of the hitchhiker disappears, as does subsequently another body, so Gloria is constantly without any evidence to convince others that her life is in danger. Later, in a comic scene, another friend gives her an alarm, a can of mace, and some brass knuckles—ocnophilic objects which Gloria is able to use quite effectively to stave off a later attack.

The character of Tony Carlson does not effectively enter the narrative until about forty-five minutes into the film, functioning as the love interest who can ultimately take Gloria seriously. In the course of the adventures which bring her closer to Tony, Gloria is menaced by a variety of thriller adversaries: a dwarf, a snake, an albino in white, a man with a scar, and sundry thugs—the antagonist element being segmented as usual. If the tone of the film is ultimately less serious than that of the typical Hitchcock film, this lighter tone relates to the underlying theme of the film, which is that we should relax, take a chance, and not take life quite so seriously.

One explicit undercurrent, that of sexual liberation, is constant throughout the film. A minor character played by Dudley Moore is that of a swinging bachelor whose path constantly crosses with Gloria's. The swinging bachelor views porno movies, goes to massage parlors, has a home complete with disco lights, mirrored ceilings, a huge bed, and inflatable sex dolls, and is ultimately revealed as the conductor of a prestigious symphony. In conjunction with the pro-sex theme, the film is also subtly antireligion. In one scene, the apparent archbishop of San Francisco says, "At some point we have to draw the line on Christian charity." Although we discover that this archbishop and his secretary are actually imposters (another reference to *The Man Who Knew Too Much,* where the same thing happens), this does not lessen the rather negative treatment accorded them. We learn that these villains want to kill the Pope because they object to the wealth of the church and the way the church has managed to suppress true spirituality. It is interesting to note that while the film does not allow the villains to succeed, the film never questions or repudiates the validity of their position. And since the film begins, rather comically, with an archbishop being killed and ends with a set-piece in which the Pope is almost assassinated, it is hard to ignore the film's hostility toward the church.

Gloria and Tony work together, or try to. Tony, charming and bumbling, is rather chauvinist and says to Gloria at one point, "I play detective, you play damsel in distress." Although Gloria doesn't challenge his chauvinism, she remains the most active and intelligent agent of inquiry and the clear center of the narrative. In the climactic scene at the opera, a set-piece resembling the Albert Hall climax of *The Man Who Knew Too Much,* the two of them succeed in preventing the assassination of the Pope, who is oblivious to the plot against him. Tony says to Gloria, "You really took a chance." Gloria answers proudly, "I know." As the curtain rises for the first act curtain call, Gloria and Tony are revealed to the audience kissing. Even the Pope applauds their embrace, as, in the film's final joke, Colin Higgins is able to manipulate, from the Pope, an implicit endorsement of romance and sex. The film ends with a cuckoo clock as emblem, further evidence of the film's rather relaxed tone.

Similarly relaxed in tone is *Hanky Panky*, directed in 1982 by Sidney Poitier and a clear attempt to duplicate the success of the Higgins films. In the tradition of typical thrillers of this kind, the action in *Hanky Panky* spans the globe—from Maine and Manhattan to the Grand Canyon. The protagonist is Michael Horton (played by Gene Wilder), an Everyman who describes himself as "the only person you ever met who drives at 55 miles an hour." Michael gets involved in the intrigue when Janet Dunn (played by Kathleen Quinlan) jumps coincidentally into a cab with him in an attempt to get away from the men who are trying to kill her. When Janet is later killed in her hotel room, the innocent Michael—who wanted only to date her—picks up the gun used to kill her (as did Thornhill the knife in *North by Northwest*) and is immediately accused of the murder, thus initiating his life on the run. In the course of his adventure, Michael must learn to trust Kate Martin (played by Gilda Radnor), a woman who is not what she initially seems to be. Kate's lies, however, seem relatively unimportant, and we never seriously doubt her allegiance to Michael, which is given when she first hears and believes his rather improbable story. The MacGuffin in *Hanky Panky* is a computer tape which reveals a secret military base used to make an advanced weapons system. In one of the film's climactic scenes, Michael and Kate are forced to crash land an errant airplane in the Grand Canyon, where they discover, once and for all, the significance of the MacGuffin.

Like the Higgins films, *Hanky Panky* is fairly conservative politically. Although Michael says at one point that "for all I know, government people are trying to kill me," the government villains turn out to be spies: that is, anomalies to the system, rather than symptoms of pervasive conspiracy. If National Security Director Hiram Calder (played by Robert Prosky) is more interested in identifying the leak in the security system rather than in saving Michael, this only contributes to his strong resemblance to the "Professor" (played by Leo G. Carroll) in *North by Northwest:* the manipulator behind the scenes. Ultimately, the government is not criticized for its military impulse or its secretiveness; although in the film's final gag Michael tries to gain some measure of personal revenge by hitting Calder in the stomach, the punch itself is treated comically and the government's attitude toward Michael is shown to be rather benign.

Like *Foul Play* and *Hanky Panky, Cloak and Dagger* also shows Hitchcock's influence. Directed in 1984 by Richard Franklin, who also directed the first sequel to *Psycho, Cloak and Dagger* is a rather charming film (surprisingly overlooked by critics) which presents as its main character a little boy named Davey Osborne (played by Henry Thomas). Davey plays with a secret hero, an invisible friend named Jack Flack that no one else can see. Dabney Coleman plays Jack Flack as well as Davey's father, who has a less than perfect relationship with his son. Perhaps most interesting about *Cloak and Dagger* is the way it reworks the issue of trust so typical and critical to the genre, for it is Davey's father who must learn to trust Davey as much as Davey must learn to trust his father. When Davey witnesses a murder and the body disappears, no one is willing to believe him, and thus when Davey is chased by the villains, he has few resources other than his own wits. Because the film initially presents several fantasy sequences with Davey talking to Jack Flack, we may initially ourselves mistrust some of what we see.

The film takes advantage of the genre's typical elements. The MacGuffin in this film is a videogame given Davey by the assassinated man which reveals the schematics for an "invisible" bomber. At least twice Davey finds himself in an enclosed location requiring creative escape: a boat going down the San Antonio River and a bus which Davey escapes by pretending to have to throw up. On one level, the film is rather subversive, if not irresponsible: it implies (for a while) that children cannot trust their parents; it includes a scene in which Davey hides in a closed car trunk; it also suggests that grandparents can be evil. The warm grandparent-like characters of the MacCreadys, played by Jeanette Nolan and John McIntire, appear to help Davey, but are revealed to be evil, amoral, unfeeling spies. The revelation of their true nature takes place when the old woman removes her glove and reveals that she is missing two fingers—an incident paralleling a similar scene in *The 39 Steps.*

True to the genre, Davey has a blonde love interest: a little girl Kim (played by Christina Nigra) who helps him in his adventure. The climax of *Cloak and Dagger* is surprisingly moving: As Davey succeeds in killing one of the villains, Davey's own fantasies allow his super-hero and ally Jack Flack to die in the confrontation. At that moment, like the typical thriller protagonist, Davey has moved to a new moral position: he is now on his own, more realistic, less naive, no longer enamored of war games and violence, and without the support of his fantasy figure. In the final scene of the film, Davey jumps out of a moving airplane with the aid of his father. The last images reaffirm mutual trust and family values as Jack Flack and Davey's father become synthesized. "I don't need Jack Flack anymore," says Davey, "I've got you, Dad." Thus, the adventure has brought with it a moral meaning—allowing Davey to grow up and father to trust his son.

The moral meanings of two significant 1985 thrillers—*Into the Night* and *After Hours*—offer very interesting contrasts. Although both films clearly reflect the sensibilities of the Reagan era within a culture of narcissism, each takes a radically different position. *Into the Night,* directed by John Landis, refuses to explore the moral implications of the actions of its characters and instead seems to celebrate and support whatever yuppies do to get ahead, providing that those yuppies are intelligent and attractive. *After Hours,* directed by Martin Scorsese, however, finds narcissism and the Reaganization of America appalling, and by its end, rejects totally those values as bankrupt.

Into the Night begins by presenting its protagonist Ed (played by Jeff Goldblum), who is unhappily married to a career woman; in fact, her career (and thus women's liberation) is held to be a negative value, thus immediately positing the film as reactionary. Ed's Los Angeles life is comprised of backed-up freeways. He discovers that his wife is having an affair (which thus allows him to have an affair of his own), and he is conscious that his job is a dead end which does not give him pleasure. Into his torpor comes, one night, a screaming, hysterical woman who suddenly jumps into his car and demands that he help her to save her life—which he does, having nothing else better to do. These beginning sections are rather extraordinary: Ed's ennui with his wife, his inability to sleep, the suddenness with which he becomes involved with the blonde heroine played by Michelle Pfeiffer.

As the film proceeds, however, the narrative becomes less controlled, attenuated in part by the gimmick of a variety of cameo appearances by directors—including David Cronenberg, Roger Vadim, and John Landis himself, among others—a gimmick which suggests Hitchcock's typical stunt appearance, but compounded. The MacGuffin in this film is a cache of emeralds that the heroine had herself smuggled illegally into the country for her own gain. "I'm one of the bad guys," she says at one point, although we are expected to excuse her because of her beauty. The film never examines the moral implications of the heroine's actions, in that she is directly or indirectly responsible for all the deaths in the film. As well, *Into the Night* has little reverence for life or for people: we are invited to laugh at gay characters, at people's deaths, even at the killings of animals. The climax of the film, when the heroine returns to the protagonist as an act of love, is (if true to the genre) hard to take seriously as a moral impulse, given the number of deaths the two of them have been responsible for.

An archetypal Reagan-era film, *Into the Night* is yuppie in its orientation because everyone wants to get ahead, and the good guys are those whose ethics prevent them only from actively killing others. The violence of the film is extreme, in a comic book style, and the tone of the film is closer to *Charade* than to *North by Northwest*. The most effective set-piece of *Into the Night* which reflects its comic-violent sensibility is a scene in which the protagonist searches a millionaire's apartment which has television sets in every room. The action and violence in the apartment is then juxtaposed with that of the Abbott and Costello comic-horror film which is playing on every screen.

Martin Scorsese's film *After Hours,* on the other hand, is a subtle comedy, as interested in sly social commentary of its Soho milieu as in the typical generic conventions of the thriller. Like *Into the Night, After Hours* also presents a morally uncommited protagonist who, through a chance encounter, is gradually stripped of all the accepted civilized comforts he takes for granted. Whereas the protagonist in *Into the Night* is moved to ever more frantic action, the protagonist in *After Hours* is reduced, by film's end, to virtual catatonia—indeed, encased in a George Segal–like sculpture which allows him only to move his eyes. *After Hours,* though structured according to thriller conventions, lacks the sensibility or tone of the typical thriller. What emerges, therefore, is a comedy surprisingly out of step with the other comedies of its era (such as *Animal House* and its clones), a comedy filled with the auteurist resonances of its director, and one which surprises at every turn. Certainly surprising are the many references to *The Conversation:* a toilet which overflows—though not with red blood, but blue toilet bowl cleaner; Teri Garr, doing a comic turn on the unhappy character she played in *The Conversation* for Francis Ford Coppola; and even the character of the older woman (patterned after the Elizabeth MacRae role in *The Conversation)* who befriends the protagonist, dances with him, and then betrays him.

The characters in *After Hours* are remarkably interesting and vivid: the sculptress and her boyfriend, both interested in sadomasochism; the suicidal young woman who is psychologically inscrutable even to the audience; the lady who drives an ice cream truck and heads a neighborhood vigilante gang; and the variety of gay characters—who are presented with more variety and in greater proportion than in virtually any other Hollywood film without a so-called gay theme. The plotting and coincidences are ingenious—with everything tying together inexorably with a mathematical precision which is at once implausible and satisfying. Even set design is witty: the same lamp appears in a variety of Soho apartments, just as all the would-be Soho artists make the same George Segal–like sculptures—stultifyingly conformist in their attempts to be unique and creative. Even the marginal ambiences of the film—the hero's story of his treatment in a burn-ward; the mysterious burn cream of the suicidal woman; the ice cream lady's attempt to burn off papier-mâché from the hero's back; the fire-related lyric of Peggy Lee's "Is That All There Is?" which we hear on the soundtrack—suggest the tightness of the screenplay.

And through it all, mistaken for a thief if not quite a murderer, and running for his life, is the protagonist, who in the best tradition of the innocent-on-the-run thriller must find a way to get into a variety of locations (an apartment, a subway, an after-hours punk bar), as well as a way of escaping creatively from a variety of enclosed locations (a diner and several apartments). Unlike the typical innocent-on-the-run thriller where the protagonist trusts no one and must learn to trust someone by the end of the adventure, Paul in *After Hours* begins as an incredibly trusting person—only to have virtually every individual betray him. Paul's lesson, if one is learned, is indeed the opposite of that taught by the typical thriller: that is, that *no one* should be trusted—except, perhaps, one's word processor, the only entity greeting Paul with some warmth which is neither insincere nor a disguise for some future betrayal. Thus, *After Hours* in its own way can be seen as Scorsese's attempt to use the thriller format (as did Antonioni in *L'Avventura* and *Blowup)* to make a film which analyzes the values of contemporary culture even as it attacks them.

Jumpin' Jack Flash, on the other hand, directed in 1986 by Penny Marshall, is a much less ambitious film. Although it begins with a slam against Reagan (who is presented as an embarrassment who forgets that Hawaii is a state), the film presents values which are fairly conservative. In its combination of a thriller plot with wild humor appropriate for Whoopi Goldberg's comedic film debut, *Jumpin' Jack Flash* comes much closer in tone to the Colin Higgins films than to the paranoid thrillers of Schlesinger and Pakula or to the paranoid comedy of Scorsese. In 1986 it would seem that Vietnam and Watergate have in this subgenre lost their influence, eclipsed by the apotheosis of Ronald Reagan. Whoopi Goldberg plays Terry, who is zany, friendly, but hesitant to date, much like Gloria in *Foul Play*. She works in international banking at a computer terminal, much like Paul in *After Hours*. Terry gets involved in international intrigue when Jack Flash—a similar name, incidentally, as the super-hero in *Cloak and Dagger*—sends a message to her computer screen asking her to get involved and help him escape from behind the Iron Curtain, where he has been working as a spy. Thus, the Communists (and British communist spies) are presented as the villains.

There are a variety of scenes typical to the genre: Terry breaks into an enclosed space by dressing as Diana Ross; she escapes from an enclosed space by creating a disturbance so that the police will be called (recalling the auction scene in *North by Northwest)*; in the central scene she is held prisoner in a telephone booth which is dragged down a Manhattan street by a tow truck. One interesting aspect of *Jumpin' Jack Flash* is that Terry is never actually pursued by the police; although she is associated with the murder of a man whose body disappears, the police don't believe her, in part because she is black. Without the subplot of the protagonist running from the law, a certain component of tension and anxiety is removed from the narrative, allowing it more easily to emphasize comedy. In its place, somewhat, is pressure from her employer, who disapproves of what she is doing: the constant threat in *Jumpin' Jack Flash*, therefore, is not being put in jail, but the more yuppie punishment of being separated from one's income.

By the film's end, it is clear that a trusting and loving relationship has developed between Terry and the unseen Jack Flash. The film ends with their meeting, which implies that their romance will be fulfilling. Thus,

Jumpin' Jack Flash—although directed by a strong woman and starring a liberal black actress who has been active in many social causes—climaxes in a relatively conservative way: with love triumphant and Communists vanquished. It will be interesting to discover whether the paranoid antigovernment impulses so striking in the innocent-on-the-run thrillers of the seventies will continue to be repressed and regarded as anomaly or whether the relatively conservative impulses—in contemporary American society and in these thrillers—will diminish as we move into the nineties.

11
To Be Continued . . .

Each of the six previous chapters has articulated the conventions and discussed the development of a different kind of suspense thriller. Although perhaps the majority of thrillers may be subsumed under one of the six rubrics, these categories are by no means exhaustive. Indeed, it would be possible to pick out several other subgenres of the suspense thriller each elaborated primarily from an element that can be found in the general umbrella genre discussed in the fourth chapter of this book. Some of these other thriller subgenres which would profit from a similarly extended analysis include:

The Thriller of Time—composed of films organized around a limited period of time in which some particular action must be accomplished. Potential examples include *D.O.A.* (1949), *Fourteen Hours* (1951), *Split Second* (1953), *Time Lock* (1957), *City of Fear* (1959), *36 Hours* (1965), *The Slender Thread* (1965), *Pursuit* (1970), and *D.O.A.* (1988). In these films, suspense is often spectacularly central, as the protagonist races against time to achieve his or her goal. For instance, the 1949 *D.O.A.*, perhaps a seminal film here, presents a protagonist who has been given a slow-acting poison and has only a limited amount of time to find his own murderer. Recurring elements in these films include drugs, disease, and characters who slip increasingly out of control.

The Thriller of Place—composed of films organized around the navigation of a particular physical space by a protagonist or group of protagonists who must generally move, in the course of the film, from a starting point to a destination point. Potential examples include *The Wages of Fear* (1955), *Deliverance* (1972), *Sorcerer* (1976), *The Warriors* (1979), and *Runaway Train* (1985). In *The Wages of Fear*, for instance, the seminal film by Henri-Georges Clouzot, a group of prisoners undertake a treacherous truck journey transporting nitroglycerine in the hope of attaining pardons; in *The Warriors*, a street gang attempts to return home safely to Coney Island after a violent confrontation in the Bronx. In these films, the protagonists tend to be morally ambivalent, but worthy of our sympathies relative to the even more questionable moralities of those around them. As well, these films tend consistently to take advantage of profound existential themes and imagery: strikingly memorable is the explosion in *The Wages of Fear* which creates a huge crater and blows up its characters into nothingness; or the *Runaway Train*, which is last seen hurtling toward existential oblivion.

The Kidnapping Thriller—composed of films organized around the kidnapping of an innocent party by criminals. Potential examples include *Ransom* (1956), *High and Low* (1962), *Seance on a Wet Afternoon* (1964), *Night of the Following Day* (1969), and *Without a Trace* (1983). These films, with plots quite similar, tend to raise interesting social questions. The Japanese *High and Low*, directed by Akira Kurosawa (and adapted from an American novel by Ed McBain) shows a rich industrialist who is willing to pay any price to secure the return of his kidnapped son. But when it is discovered that the boy kidnapped was actually the son of a poor employee, the film raises the question: Is the life of someone who is poor worth the same as the life of someone who is rich? *Without a Trace*, one of the most recent kidnapping thrillers, reflects the whole eighties hysteria over missing and kidnapped children.

The Thriller of Cultural Anxiety—composed of films organized around some specific issue of grave importance to society's future which involves the protagonist in some murderous plot. Potential examples include *Coma* (1978), *The Terminator* (1978), *Brainstorm* (1983), *War Games* (1983), and *Dreamscape* (1984). Of all the thrillers, these films are the most closely connected to the science-fiction genre, because they address our profound fears of the future. *Coma* deals with organ transplants, *The Terminator* with our fears of automation and computers, and *War Games* and *Dreamscape* with the potential for nuclear destruction. These films freely borrow structural devices from other thriller subgenres: *Coma* seems in many ways to be a political thriller, suffused with a sense of conspiracy; *The Terminator* is almost a thriller of moral confrontation, balancing the evil machine adversary with the human protagonist who must turn himself into a machine in order to triumph. Perhaps the most theoretical of all these films is the science-fiction oriented *Brainstorm* (directed by Douglas Trumbull), which on one level is a simple thriller about a device which allows people to experience other people's thoughts, but which on another level is actually a cinematic examination of André Bazin's theoretical concept of total cinema, which imagines the evolution of the medium to a point at which reality and film will become indistinguishable, thus making the film creator a kind of god. *Dreamscape*, too, in the way it uses horrific dream imagery to express both personal and cultural fears, seems both fascinating and first-rate.

Undoubtedly, other subgenres of the suspense thriller could be articulated as well (perhaps a thriller of parallel narrative, as in *Family Plot*, or a thriller of the ocnophilic object, as in *The Gun*). Nevertheless, however many more subgenres can be identified, what remains common in all these films is their emphasis on suspense rather than mystery, and their concentration on the victim (or the criminal), rather than on the detective.

Aside from the thrillers which may belong to other potential subgenres, there are a significant number of suspense thrillers which may defy classification because their unique structures incorporate a variety of subgenres. Perhaps the best example of this is *The Conversation*, directed by Francis Ford Coppola in 1974, a film I believe to be one of the masterworks of the last twenty-five years.

A kind of aural equivalent to *Blowup*, *The Conversation* presents a three-dimensional psychological portrait of surveillance expert Harry Caul (played by Gene Hackman) who is hired to record one specific, meandering conversation that takes place between a young man and woman on Union Square in San Francisco. In the course of the film, this conversation is first recorded and then replayed in bits and pieces, each time differently, each time allowing us to hear and understand new things as we learn more about the horrific plot Caul finds himself increasingly involved in. Although *The Conversation* shares the sensibility of the Watergate-influenced political thrillers, it contains neither overt politics nor exploration of government conspiracy. However, in the way this film significantly *extends* the conspiratorial sensibility beyond government to *all* professional and personal relationships, *The Conversation* becomes, although not a political thriller *per se*, one of the single most influential thrillers of our time, influencing a great number of films, including *The China Syndrome*, *Dreamscape*, *Blow Out*, and so forth. In other ways, *The Conversation* resembles a thriller of moral confrontation: especially in how the protagonist ultimately comes to reject the evil he has been asked to participate in, and finds himself, for the first time in his life, involved in a moral conflict. And finally, and perhaps most fetching of all, is the way the somewhat secret structure of *The Conversation* (revealed in the conversation itself) suggests a thriller of murderous passions, with the romantic triangle at the film's core responsible for the climactic horror.

Aside from these suspense thrillers which are too uniquely expansive to conform to one subgenre, there is another larger group of films to be considered, which I call the *hybrids*. These hybrids are the films which do not fit snugly into any of the detective genres, but which nevertheless contain professional detectives of some kind. These films have the sensibility of a thriller because of their emphasis on the victim or the criminal, but they have retained many elements from the detective film, including a detective. Thus, these films become the hybrid between mystery on one hand and suspense on the other, between the "pure detective films" on the left side of the crime triangle and the "pure suspense thrillers" on the right side of the crime triangle.

No Way to Treat a Lady (directed by Jack Smight in 1968) is a good example of a hybrid. Although this film deals with the efforts of a police protagonist to catch a psychotic sex-killer, the emphasis is clearly on the thrills provided by the ongoing sex-killings of the rather outrageous antagonist played by Rod Steiger. As the film proceeds, it becomes clear that the narrative is not as interested in showing standard police procedure as in exploring the kind of relationship typical to that in the thriller of moral confrontation: two opposing values which come closer together psychologically as they confront each other. And in *No Way to Treat a Lady*, the protagonist (played by George Segal) has parallel sexual hang-ups, if not as extreme as those of his adversary. In these hybrids, the process of investigation is inevitably less important than the presentation of the crimes and their attendant sensations. Hybrid thrillers are numerous, and other notable examples include *Experiment in Terror* (directed by Blake Edwards in 1962) and Clint Eastwood's *Tightrope* (directed by Richard Tuggle in 1984).

Perhaps the most interesting recent example of a hybrid is the rather overlooked *The Naked Face*, directed by Bryan Forbes in 1984. This film stars Michael Caine as a psychiatrist who gets involved in a murderous plot. As a hybrid *par excellence*, *The Naked Face* synthesizes at least four different sensibilities: (1) that of the police procedural, with its important police lieutenant played by Rod Steiger; (2) that of the hard-boiled detective, with the performance of Art Carney; (3) that of the innocent-on-the-run thriller, with its protagonist himself pursued by both the murderer and the police; and (4) that of the psychotraumatic thriller, with the psychiatric sessions of the protagonists' patients containing clues to the film's murderous plot.

Certainly, on the most basic level, the spectator cannot help but wonder which of the forces of inquiry in *The Naked Face*—the protagonist, the policeman, or the detective—will be responsible for unmasking the murderer. Watching a hybrid like *The Naked Face* is thus suspenseful and fun; one's knowledge of genre adds to the experience, because the different genres compete for the narrative's attention, so to speak, just as our associated expectations for each genre lead us to conflicting anticipations which themselves create both mystery and suspense. While these hybrid films can usefully be called suspense thrillers, their employment of professional agents of inquiry would appear to situate them closer to the left of the crime triangle than the suspense thrillers discussed at length in this book. My own inclination is to call these films suspense thrillers only if we can do so without losing sight of their hybrid nature.

Inevitably, studying the suspense thriller leads to an examination of other related genres. Certain horror films, for instance, in which the "monster" is not a mystical or fantastic creature, but an insane individual who commits crimes, also warrant discussion in the context of suspense. Because their murderous protagonists are presented as objects of horror and virtual monsters, films such as *Psycho* (1960), *Repulsion* (1965) and *The Collector* (1965) might most accurately be perceived as belonging to both the suspense thriller and horror genres simultaneously. A more extended discussion of the conventions of these "horror of personality" films and their relationship to horror and suspense can be found in my own *Dark Dreams: A Psychological History of the Modern Horror Film* (A.S. Barnes, 1977).

Another major genre related to the suspense thriller is the disaster film. Films in this genre (such as *The Poseidon Adventure* in 1972 or *The Towering Inferno* in 1974) are organized around some gigantic disaster—generally caused by the natural elements, such as fire, flood, earthquake, or storm—which threatens a large group of victims who try to attain salvation. Although there may often be a criminal in the disaster film who is partially responsible for the plight of the victims, the primary criminal force so typical to the suspense thriller is replaced by the natural disaster itself, which inevitably must remain morally neutral. The emphasis in the disaster film is inexorably on the victims and specifically on the question, "Which ones will survive?" Other genres both fascinating and relevant to the thriller include the adventure film (such as *The Big Sky* in 1952 or *The Deep* in 1977)—which presents antagonisms, as in the disaster film, which do not necessarily derive from a criminal element; the prison film (such as *Riot* in 1969 or *Midnight Express* in 1978)—which, properly speaking, deals with the punishment which follows the commission of a crime; and the courtroom film (such as *Witness for the Prosecution* in 1957 or *Anatomy of a Murder* in 1959)—which deals with the task of socially defining crime and assigning culpabilities.

All that I have written in this study of the suspense thriller is, in an important sense, relative, as must be all generic analysis. We look, for instance, at a Vietnam-era western like *Little Big Man,* with its overt rejection of Manifest Destiny, differently than we would if we did not have in our consciousness hundreds of other westerns such as *The Searchers* or *Wagonmaster,* with their implicit acceptance of Manifest Destiny. And conversely, because of *Little Big Man,* we can no longer look at and respond to *The Searchers* and *Wagonmaster* as they were looked at and responded to in the fifties. And yet, all of these films belong to that evolving, complex genre most of us would have no trouble recognizing as "the western." Indeed, the study of genres is particularly fascinating precisely because genres are in a state of continual evolution.

The genre critic can perhaps be compared to the cartographer who attempts at any particular point in time to chart exactly the boundaries of the various countries, the relative proximities from one to another, the positions of their major cities. His or her attempts, of course, are only approximately useful, because the map is merely a guide and no substitute for travel in the countries themselves. And inevitably, boundaries change, revolutions take place, policies shift, and countries may divide or make allies with far-away lands.

The Suspense Thriller has been an attempt to map out previously uncharted lands. If I have drawn my boundaries a bit too strictly or omitted certain countryside too mysterious, exotic or unknown to me, it is in the secure knowledge that this initial map may allow other adventurous travelers to make more discriminating journeys of their own.[1]

Notes

Chapter 1: Perceptions and Dilemmas

1. John G. Cawelti, *Adventure, Mystery, and Romance: Formula Stories as Art and Popular Culture* (Chicago: University of Chicago Press, 1976), p. 16. Strictly speaking, Cawelti applies this definition to his term "formula." Although I have chosen to use the term "genre" throughout this book, I am referring to the same literary concept.
2. Gary Gerani with Paul H. Schulman, *Fantastic Television* (New York: Harmony, 1977), p. 49.
3. Gerani, p. 49.
4. Gerani, p. 52.
5. François Truffaut with Helen G. Scott, *Hitchcock* (New York: Simon and Schuster, 1967), p. 51.
6. Truffaut, p. 51.
7. Charles Derry, *Dark Dreams: A Psychological History of the Modern Horror Film* (Cranbury, N.J.: A.S. Barnes, 1977), p. 113.
8. Claude Chabrol, "The Evolution of the Detective Film," p. 3 [mimeographed article] n.d.
9. Brian Davis, *The Thriller: The Suspense Film from 1946* (London: Studio Vista; New York: Dutton, 1973), p. 1.
10. Davis, p. 8.
11. Davis, p. 74.
12. Davis, p. 55.
13. Gordon Gow, *Suspense in the Cinema* (New York: Castle, 1968), book jacket.
14. Gow, pp. 19–20.
15. Gow, p. 20.
16. Gow, p. 38.
17. Lawrence Hammond, *Thriller Movies: Classic Films of Suspense and Mystery* (London: Octopus, 1974), p. 8.
18. Hammond, p. 8.
19. Hammond, p. 17.
20. Ralph Harper, *The World of the Thriller* (Cleveland: The Press of Case Western Reserve University, 1969), pp. viii–ix.
21. Harper, p. 27.
22. Harper, p. ix.
23. Ayn Rand, *The Romantic Manifesto: A Philosophy of Literature* (New York: New American Library, 1971), p. 97.
24. Rand, p. 97.
25. C.A. Lejeune, *The Observer*, 11 November 1946, quoted by Gordon Gow in *Suspense in the Cinema*, p. 20.
26. Julian Symons, *Bloody Murder: From the Detective Story to the Crime Novel: A History* (London: Faber and Faber, 1972), p. 9.

27. Symons, p. 9.
28. Symons, p. 221.
29. Bill Hogarth, *Writing Thrillers for Profit: A Practical Guide* (London: A. and C. Black, 1936), p. v.
30. Hogarth, p. vi.
31. Hogarth, p. 135.
32. Hogarth, p. 140.
33. Hogarth, p. 140.
34. Patricia Highsmith, *Plotting and Writing Suspense Fiction* (Boston: The Writer, 1966), p. 1.
35. Boileau-Narcejac, *Le Roman Policier* (Vendôme: Presses Universitaires de France, 1975), p. 91.
36. H.L. Yelland, S.C. Jones, and K.S.W. Easton, *A Handbook of Literary Terms* (New York: Philosophical Library, 1950).
37. Stuart M. Kaminsky, "Crime: Introduction," in *Rediscovering the American Cinema*, ed. Douglas J. Lemza (Wilmette, Ill.: Films Incorporated, 1977), p. 82.
38. Davis, p. 55.
39. Gow, p. 20.
40. Highsmith, p. 144.

Chapter 2: Thrills; or How Objects and Empty Spaces Compete to Threaten Us

1. Michael Balint, *Thrills and Regressions*, the International Psycho-Analytical Library, No. 54 (London: The Hogarth Press and the Institute of Psycho-Analysis, 1959), p. 23.
2. Balint, p. 30.
3. Balint, p. 24.
4. Balint, p. 24.
5. Balint, p. 36.
6. Balint, p. 32.
7. Balint, p. 33.
8. Balint, p. 115.
9. Balint, pp. 29–30.
10. Balint, p. 34.

Chapter 3: Suspense That Makes the Spectator Take in a Breath

1. E.M. Forster, *Aspects of the Novel* (1927; rpt. New York: Harcourt, Brace, and World, n.d.), p. 27.
2. Boileau-Narcejac, pp. 89–90.
3. Hammond, p. 20.
4. Nora Sayre, "Notes on Being Scared—Properly—at the Movies," *New York Times*, 24 July 1977, section 2, p. 9.
5. Cawelti, p. 17.
6. Gow, p. 9.
7. Gow, p. 10.
8. Harper, p. 59.
9. Noël Carroll, "Toward a Theory of Film Suspense," *Persistence of Vision*, No. 1 (Summer 1984), pp. 65–89.
10. Carroll, p. 71.
11. Carroll, p. 66.
12. Altan Löker, *Film and Suspense* (Istanbul: Altan Löker, 1976), p. iii.

13. Löker, p. 11.
14. Sayre, section 2, p. 9.
15. Löker, p. 1.
16. Löker, pp. 1–2.
17. Löker, pp. 7–9.
18. Löker, p. 16.
19. Löker, p. 19.
20. Löker, p. 19.
21. Löker, p. 23.
22. Löker, p. 29.
23. Löker, p. 30.
24. Löker, p. 32.
25. Löker, p. 34.
26. Löker, pp. 41–47.
27. Löker, p. 98.
28. Löker, p. 87.
29. Löker, p. 116.
30. Löker, p. 124.
31. Löker, p. 125.
32. Löker, p. 159.
33. In the short history so far of gay and lesbian film festivals in major American cities, typical patterns have developed in which the audiences for the films tend to be polarized. Despite their political bond and common interests, gay men tend to comprise the vast majority of the audience for films with gay male protagonists, and lesbians tend to comprise the vast majority of the audience for films with lesbians. As well, neither gay nor lesbian filmmakers (except for those working in documentary forms) have so far shown much interest in including both gay men and lesbian protagonists within the same film.

Chapter 4: A Definition

1. Cawelti, p. 91.
2. For a detailed analysis of *Two Are Guilty* in relation to the specific concept of film narrative, see Charles Derry, "Toward a Categorization of Film Narrative," *Film Reader* (Evanston: Northwestern University Film Department, Vol. 2, 1977), pp. 111–122.
3. Not very dissimilar from John Cawelti's genre of the "social melodrama," Cawelti, p. 260.
4. Tzvetan Todorov, "The Typology of Detective Fiction," in *The Poetics of Prose*, trans. Richard Howard (Ithaca, N.Y.: Cornell University Press, 1977), pp. 42–52.
5. Chabrol, p. 7.
6. Except—in all the years the show was on the air—in one episode, which as a gimmick held the murderer's identity secret until the end.
7. It is interesting to note that as the conservative Reagan years definitively supplanted the more liberal sixties, the characteristic detective presented by the genre allowed less deviation and required considerably more conformity. Thus, the detective protagonists of the sixties (*Cannon*, who was fat; *Barnaby Jones*, who was old; *Ironside*, who was physically challenged; *Longstreet*, who was blind) were replaced by detectives who were handsome "hunks" almost indistinguishable in terms of their perfect looks and athletic bodies (*Magnum*, both *Simon and Simon*, *Remington Steele*, *Matt Houston*, and so forth). I would argue, however, that of the three detective genres, the police procedurals—from TV works such as *Police Story*, *Cagney and Lacey*, *Hill Street Blues*, and *Baretta*, to film works such as *Fort Apache, the Bronx*

and screen adaptions of the novels of Joseph Wambaugh or Ed McBain—have provided the most interesting and significant work in the last two decades.

Chapter 6: The Political Thriller

1. *Two aspects of Drury's novels are especially interesting: one, that each novel takes a different institution or specific political situation as its base; and two, that each novel begins where the previous novel ends. The second book in the series, A Shade of Difference,* published in 1962, deals primarily with the United Nations and the issue of civil rights. It also contains material on the emerging third world phenomenon, as well as on the war in Gorotoland, which is Drury's Vietnam allegory. The third book, *Capable of Honor,* published in 1966, deals primarily with a party convention to nominate a president and the horrible violence outside the convention halls (a situation which parallels in many ways the 1968 Chicago Democratic convention). This book also contains material on the outbreak of war with Panama, as well as a sustained attack on the increasingly liberal-biased and manipulative press. *Capable of Honor* ends suspensefully with the serial-like suggestion that harm may come to the re-nominated president.

The fourth book, *Preserve and Protect,* published in 1968, deals primarily with the crisis that results when the President is assassinated only a short time before the presidential election and the subsequent efforts of his party to come up with a new candidate acceptable to the polarized and collapsing country. *Preserve and Protect* contains Drury's most fascinating and tantalizing ending: in what appears to be the book's relaxed denouement, the conservative and heroic presidential candidate and the liberal and cowardly vice-presidential candidate are standing side by side on a dais when one of them is suddenly assassinated. A careful use of pronouns by Drury conceals which of the two has been killed.

Drury kept the outcome secret for five years, until he published *Come Ninevah, Come Tyre* in 1973. This novel deals with the political crisis which develops after the conservative presidential candidate is assassinated and the liberal vice-presidential candidate becomes president. Through the new president's cowardice and inaction, the government comes to a complete standstill and is ultimately taken over by the Soviet Union. (Ironically, although Drury writes about a liberal president incapable of governing, the novel significantly presages the final Watergate days in which Nixon became incapable of governing.)

The final book in the series, *The Promise of Joy,* published in 1975, was indeed an occasion for Drury's fans to celebrate, in that it provided an alternate conclusion to the series of novels. Like *Come Ninevah, Come Tyre, The Promise of Joy* begins where *Preserve and Protect* ends—only in this version, it is the cowardly vice-presidential candidate who is assassinated, and the courageous, conservative presidential candidate who survives. Drury is not, however, "easier" on his conservative hero: *The Promise of Joy* deals primarily with the nuclear war which breaks out between the Soviet Union and China and the dilemma the President finds himself in when both countries request American intervention.

2. David Bartholomew, "De Palma of the Paradise," *Cinefantastique,* Vol. 4, No. 2 (Summer 1975), p. 14.

3. Harold Kalishman and Gary Crowdus, "'A Film Is Like a Match: You Can Make a Big Fire or Nothing at All': An Interview with Costa-Gavras," *Cinéaste,* Vol. VI, No. 1 (1973), p. 1.

4. Joan Mellen, "*Executive Action:* The Politics of Distortion," *Cinéaste,* Vol. VI, No. 2 (1974), pp. 9–11.

5. For an excellent analysis of the political implications of *Special Bulletin,* see Steve Bognar, "The Omnipresent Eye: Television News and *Special Bulletin,*" *Filament,* No. 4. (Wright State University, 1984), pp. 28–45.

6. Kalishman, pp. 5–6.

7. Jean-Luc Comolli and Jean Narboni, "Cinema/Ideology/Criticism," trans. Susan Bennett, in *Movies and Methods: An Anthology*, ed. Bill Nichols (Berkeley: University of California Press, 1976), p. 24.

8. Comolli, pp. 26–27.

9. Jean Fièschi and Emile Breton, "La Série Z," *La Nouvelle Critique*, No. 49, quoted by Guy Hennebelle, "Z Movies or What Hath Costa-Gavras Wrought?" *Cinéaste*, Vol. VI, No. 2 (1974), p. 29.

10. Kalishman, p. 6.

11. Truffaut, p. 240.

Chapter 7: The Thriller of Acquired Identity

1. Sayre, section 2, p. 1.

Chapter 8: The Psychotraumatic Thriller

1. Charles Derry, *Dark Dreams: A Psychological History of the Modern Horror Film* (Cranbury, N.J.: A.S. Barnes, 1977), pp. 16–47.

Chapter 9: The Thriller of Moral Confrontation

1. Even Antonioni's spelling of his film's title ("BLOWUP") omits the distinct boundary represented by the hyphen present in most commentators' spelling of this film ("Blow-Up").

2. *Straw Dogs* is certainly sexist and appeals to men's socially conditioned sense of *machismo*. Whether the most typical male response is congruent to the most typical female response—given the film's exclusion of women as full and equal human beings—is unlikely. Certainly, one would welcome more scientific and statistical ways of evaluating audience response in order more accurately to make perceptive generalizations.

Chapter 10: The Innocent-on-the-Run Thriller

1. Truffaut, pp. 98–99. According to Hitchcock: "You may be wondering where the term originated. It might be a Scottish name, taken from a story about two men in a train. One man says, 'What's that package up there in the baggage rack?' And the other one answers, 'Oh, that's a MacGuffin.' The first one asks, 'What's a MacGuffin?' 'Well,' the other man says, 'it's an apparatus for trapping lions in the Scottish Highlands.' The first man says, 'But there are no lions in the Scottish Highlands,' and the other one answers, 'Well then, that's no MacGuffin!' So you see that a MacGuffin is actually nothing at all." And indeed, as anyone who examines these films quickly discovers, the MacGuffins in these films—apparently what the films "are about"—are actually rather irrelevant and interchangeable. The films are actually about the moral meanings of the adventures; their respective MacGuffins merely provide the devices which set the plots in motion.

2. Conversation with Martin Maloney (Evanston, Ill.), 24 August 1977.

3. *Variety*, 28 September 1977, p. 27. [advertisement]

Chapter 11: To Be Continued . . .

1. As one who has journeyed extensively into the lands of the suspense thriller, I would like to offer the reader my own evaluations of those special sights which ab-

solutely should not be missed. Herewith are a variety of lists: five great suspense thriller directors, eleven great suspense thrillers, eleven great performances in suspense thrillers along with secondary listings. Lists of this kind are, of course, personal and subjective, but useful in making explicit the biases which may be only implicit elsewhere in this book.

Five Great Suspense Thriller Directors

Claude Chabrol
Alfred Hitchcock
John Frankenheimer
Costa-Gavras
Michelangelo Antonioni

Eleven Great Suspense Thrillers

Shadow of a Doubt (1942)
The Wages of Fear (1955)
North by Northwest (1959)
Marnie (1964)
Seconds (1966)
Blowup (1966)
Le Boucher (1969)
State of Siege (1973)
The Conversation (1974)
Black Sunday (1977)
The Stepfather (1987)

Also Notable Suspense Thrillers

Night of the Hunter (1955)
Vertigo (1958)
La Femme Infidèle (1968)
La Rupture (1970)
Capricorn One (1978)
The China Syndrome (1979)
Body Heat (1981)
Missing (1982)
Under Fire (1983)
The Year of Living Dangerously (1983)
Dreamscape (1984)
Runaway Train (1985)
Blue Velvet (1986)

Eleven Great Suspense Thriller Performances

Teresa Wright in *Shadow of a Doubt* (1942)
Robert Mitchum in *Night of the Hunter* (1955)
Tippi Hedren in *Marnie* (1964)
John Randolph in *Seconds* (1966)
Stéphane Audran in *La Femme Infidèle* (1968)
Stéphane Audran in *Le Boucher* (1969)
Gene Hackman in *The Conversation* (1974)
Kathleen Turner in *Body Heat* (1981)
Jill Clayburgh in *Hanna K* (1983)
Linda Hunt in *The Year of Living Dangerously* (1983)
Terry O'Quinn in *The Stepfather* (1987)

Also Notable Performances

Albert Basserman in *Saboteur* (1942)

Joseph Cotten in *Shadow of a Doubt* (1942)
Cary Grant in *North by Northwest* (1959)
Audrey Hepburn in *Wait Until Dark* (1967)
Jean Yanne in *Le Boucher* (1969)
Irene Papas in *Z* (1969)
Stéphane Audran in *La Rupture* (1970)
Yves Montand in *The Confession* (1970)
Cindy Williams in *The Conversation* (1974)
Laurence Olivier in *Marathon Man* (1976)
Brenda Vaccaro in *Capricorn One* (1978)
Jane Fonda and Jack Lemmon in *The China Syndrome* (1979)
Joanna Cassidy in *Under Fire* (1983)

Bibliography

Balint, Michael. *Thrills and Regressions.* The International Psycho-Analytical Library, No. 54. London: The Hogarth Press and the Institute of Psycho-Analysis, 1959.

Bartholomew, David. "De Palma of the Paradise." *Cinefantastique,* Vol. 4, No. 2 (Summer 1975), pp. 8–14.

Bognar, Steve. "The Omnipresent Eye: Television News and *Special Bulletin.*" *Filament.* Dayton: Wright State University, No. 4 (1984), pp. 28–45.

Boileau [Pierre]-Narcejac [Thomas]. *Le Roman Policier.* Vendôme: Presses Universitaires de France, 1975.

Carroll, Noël. "Toward a Theory of Film Suspense." *Persistence of Vision,* No. 1 (Summer 1984), pp. 65–89.

Cawelti, John G. *Adventure, Mystery, and Romance: Formula Stories as Art and Popular Culture.* Chicago: University of Chicago Press, 1976.

Chabrol, Claude. "The Evolution of the Detective Film." [Mimeographed article] n.d.

Comolli, Jean-Luc and Narboni, Jean. "Cinema/Ideology/Criticism." Trans. Susan Bennett. *Movies and Methods: An Anthology.* Ed. Bill Nichols. Berkeley: University of California Press, 1976, pp. 23–30.

Davis, Brian. *The Thriller: The Suspense Film from 1946.* London: Studio Vista; New York: Dutton, 1973.

Derry, Charles. *Dark Dreams: A Psychological History of the Modern Horror Film.* Cranbury, N.J.: Dutton, 1973.

________. "Towards a Categorization of Film Narrative." *Film Reader.* Evanston: Northwestern University Film Department, Vol. 2 (1977), pp. 111–122.

Forshey, Gerald. "Disaster Films: Judgement and Salvation." *Christian Century,* 5 March 1975, pp. 231–233.

Forster, E.M. *Aspects of the Novel.* 1927; rpt. New York: Harcourt, Brace, and World, n.d.

Georgakas, Dan and Rubenstein, Lenny (eds.). *Art Politics Cinema: The Cinéaste Interviews.* London: Pluto Press, 1984.

Gerani, Gary, with Schulman, Paul H. *Fantastic Television.* New York: Harmony, 1977.

Gow, Gordon. *Suspense in the Cinema.* New York: Castle, 1968.

Hammond, Lawrence. *Thriller Movies: Classic Films of Suspense and Mystery.* London: Octopus, 1974.

Harper, Ralph. *The World of the Thriller.* Cleveland: Case Western Reserve University Press, 1969.

Hennebelle, Guy. "Z Movies or What Hath Costa-Gavras Wrought?" *Cinéaste,* Vol. VI, No. 2 (1974), pp. 28–31.

Highsmith, Patricia. *Plotting and Writing Suspense Fiction.* Boston: The Writer, 1966.

Hogarth, Basil. *Writing Thrillers for Profit: A Practical Guide.* London: A. and C. Black, 1936.

Kalishman, Harold, and Crowdus, Gary. "'A Film Is Like a Match: You Can Make a Big Fire or Nothing at All': An Interview with Costa-Gavras." *Cinéaste,* Vol. VI, No. 1 (1973), pp. 2–7.

Kaminsky, Stuart M. *American Film Genres: Approaches to a Critical Theory of Popular Film.* Dayton, Ohio: Pflaum, 1974.

———. "Crime: Introduction." *Rediscovering the American Cinema.* Ed. Douglas J. Lemza. Wilmette, Illinois: Films Incorporated, 1977, p. 82.

———, with Mahan, Jeffrey H. (eds.). *American Television Genres.* Chicago: Nelson Hall, 1985, pp. 53–85.

Löker, Altan. *Film and Suspense.* Istanbul: Altan Löker, 1976. [Printed by Istanbul Matbaasi, Manifaturacilar Carsisi, 2. Blok, No. 2274 Unkapani]

Maltin, Leonard, ed. *TV Movies: 1985–86 Edition.* New York: New American Library, 1984.

Mellen, Joan. "*Executive Action:* The Politics of Distortion." *Cinéaste,* Vol. VI, No. 2, 1974, pp. 8–12.

Rand, Ayn. *The Romantic Manifesto: A Philosophy of Literature.* New York: New American Library, 1971.

Russo, Vito. *The Celluloid Closet: Homosexuality in the Movies* (revised edition). New York: Harper and Row, 1987.

Sarris, Andrew. *The American Cinema: Directors and Directions 1929–1968.* New York: Dutton, 1968.

Sayre, Nora. "Notes on Being Scared—Properly—at the Movies." *New York Times,* 24 July 1977, section 2, p. 1 and p. 9.

Scheuer, Steven H., and Pardi, Robert J. *Movies on TV: 1988–89 Edition.* New York: Bantam, 1977.

Symons, Julian. *Bloody Murder: From the Detective Story to the Crime Novel: A History.* London: Faber and Faber, 1972.

Taylor, John Russell. *Hitch: The Life and Times of Alfred Hitchcock.* New York: Pantheon, 1978.

Todorov, Tzvetan. "The Typology of Detective Fiction." *The Poetics of Prose.* Trans. Richard Howard. Ithaca, N.Y.: Cornell University Press, 1977, pp. 42–52.

Truffaut, François, with Scott, Helen G. *Hitchcock.* New York: Simon and Schuster, 1967. Revised 1983.

Variety, 28 September 1977, p. 27. [advertisement]

Warshow, Robert. *The Immediate Experience: Movies, Comics, Theatre and Other Aspects of Popular Culture.* Garden City, N.Y.: Doubleday, 1962; rpt. New York: Atheneum, 1970.

Yelland, H.L.; Jones, S.C.; and Easton, K.S.W. *A Handbook of Literary Terms.* New York: Philosophical Library, 1950.

Index

Entry numbers in **boldface** indicate a photograph.

A

B

C

D

E

F

I

J

K

L

P

Q

R

S

T

U

V

W